Hermann Balck,
Hitler's Forgotten General

After graduating in European history from the University of East Anglia, Philip Kay-Bujak spent ten years in the Royal Anglian Regiment as a TA officer and twenty-three years teaching history and classics in the independent sector. He was a housemaster at Langley School, in Norfolk and Headmaster of Stover School, in Devon. An Associate of the Royal Historical Society, he is now retired and is a full-time writer. His previous works include *Undefeated* (2008), *The Bravest Man in The British Army* (2018), *The Life of Cicero* (2023) and *Gallia Narbonensis*, which details the Roman invasion and occupation of what is now southern France. He lives in East Sussex.

Other books by Philip Kay-Bujak

Norfolk & Suffolk in the Great War

Attleborough: the evolution of a town

Undefeated

Around the World in 100 Years

The Bravest Man in the British Army: The Extraordinary Life and Death of John Sherwood Kelly VC

My Heart is in the Highlands: The Life and Work of Archibald Kay

The Life of Cicero: Lessons for Today from the Greatest Orator of the Roman Republic

Empire Javelin, D-Day Assault Ship: The British vessel that landed the US 116th Infantry on Omaha Beach

The Roman Province of Gallia Narbonensis

Hermann Balck, Hitler's Forgotten General

Philip Kay-Bujak

Pen & Sword
MILITARY

First published in Great Britain in 2025 by
Pen & Sword Military
An imprint of Pen & Sword Books Limited
Yorkshire – Philadelphia

Copyright © Philip Kay-Bujak 2025

ISBN 978 1 03611 848 8

The right of Philip Kay-Bujak to be identified as
Author of this Work has been asserted by him in accordance
with the Copyright, Designs and Patents Act 1988.

A CIP catalogue record for this book is
available from the British Library.

All rights reserved. No part of this book may be reproduced, transmitted, downloaded, decompiled or reverse engineered in any form or by any means, electronic or mechanical including photocopying, recording or by any information storage and retrieval system, without permission from the Publisher in writing. NO AI TRAINING: Without in any way limiting the Author's and Publisher's exclusive rights under copyright, any use of this publication to "train" generative artificial intelligence (AI) technologies to generate text is expressly prohibited. The Author and Publisher reserve all rights to license uses of this work for generative AI training and development of machine learning language models.

Typeset by Mac Style
Printed in the UK by CPI Group (UK) Ltd, Croydon, CR0 4YY.

The Publisher's authorised representative in the EU for product
safety is Authorised Rep Compliance Ltd., Ground Floor,
71 Lower Baggot Street, Dublin D02 P593, Ireland.
www.arccompliance.com

For a complete list of Pen & Sword titles please contact

PEN & SWORD BOOKS LIMITED
47 Church Street, Barnsley, South Yorkshire, S70 2AS, England
E-mail: enquiries@pen-and-sword.co.uk
Website: www.pen-and-sword.co.uk
or
PEN AND SWORD BOOKS
1950 Lawrence Road, Havertown, PA 19083, USA
E-mail: uspen-and-sword@casematepublishers.com
Website: www.penandswordbooks.com

To my Father, Jan Felix Bujak (1919–1982)

*3rd Heavy Machine Gun Battalion, 3rd Carpathian Division,
II Polish Corps, British Eighth Army, 1943–1947*

Contents

Acknowledgements		ix
List of Maps		xi
Part I: Hermann Balck, The Making of a General, 1900–1939		1
Chapter I	Serving the Emperor, 1900–1914	3
Chapter II	The Impact of the Great War on the German Military – Sacrifice and Treason, 1914–1919	10
Chapter III	Years of Uncertainty – The Reichswehr, 1919–1930	23
Chapter IV	The Great Paradox – the New Panzerwaffe, 1930–1938	32
Part II: Fighting for Hitler, 1939–1941		43
Chapter V	The Battle for France and Sedan, May–June 1940	45
Chapter VI	Greece and The Balkans, October 1940–April 1941	53
Chapter VII	The Prophecies of Doom, 1941–1942	72
Part III: The Russian Front, 1941–1943		79
Chapter VIII	General of Mobile Forces at the OKH, November 1941–May 1942	81
Chapter IX	Command of 11. Panzer-Division, May 1942–March 1943	93
Chapter X	The Planet Suite and the Chir River Battles, November–December 1942	115
Chapter XI	11. Panzer-Division, December 1942–February 1943	135
Chapter XII	Remodelling Panzergrenadier-Division 'Grossdeutschland', April–September 1943	152

Part IV: Fighting for Germany 1943–1945 — 159

Chapter XIII	Italy – Acting Commander XIV. Panzerkorps, September–October 1943	161
Chapter XIV	Hidden from View – Atrocities in Campania, September–October 1943	175
Chapter XV	Commanding XLVIII. Panzerkorps in Russia, November 1943–August 1944	181
Chapter XVI	Commanding 4. Panzerarmee in Poland, August–September 1944	204
Chapter XVII	Commanding Heeresgruppe G – the Western Front, September–December 1944	212
Chapter XVIII	6. Armee, Hungary, December 1944–May 1945	240
Chapter XIX	The Final Offensive, April 1945	259
Chapter XX	Surrender and the Post-war Period, 1945–1982	288

Appendix I: Balck's Letters to His Wife as Russian Troops Swarmed into Austria — 296

Appendix II: Teletype Reports from Army Group Balck and Balck's 1st Staff Officer (1a) Colonel Marcks — 300

Appendix III: Original Surrender Transcript between McBride and Balck — 301

Appendix IV: Hermann Balck's Decorations — 304

Notes — 305

Bibliography — 318

Index — 321

Acknowledgements

By its very nature, any biography is incomplete. The responsibility of charting and then commenting on another person's life is immense and requires the net of research to be cast as far and wide as possible, and that is what I hope I have done in this book – provided a fair coverage based on all the information I have been able to gather. There is still more to do, but that will be for another author in the future.

Any omissions in evidence are entirely my responsibility, but I do want to thank those who have given their time to help me paint the most accurate picture I can of General der Panzertruppe Hermann Balck. Mr Ali Khan and his wide range of research into all aspects of the Wehrmacht was an invaluable resource for which I am very grateful, as I am also to the staff of the US Army War College in Virginia for their assistance in tracking down certain research papers from the immediate post-war period. My gratitude also to Mr Michael Autengruber of Fritz Künker GmbH & Co in Konstanz, who provided unique and authentic images of the personal awards and decorations presented to Hermann Balck, and to numerous others who in their own ways contributed both large and small amounts of information which enabled me to capture so much. Thank you to Janice Cape, Rolfe Weber, Peter Sinzendorf, Geoffrey Kay for his support and to Brian Elliot whose editing skills so skilfully avoided those elusive errors that can occur in any book. I am especially grateful to Professor David Stahel of the University of New South Wales in Sydney for his guidance on where to locate new archival material for this book.

For information on Balck's 'forgotten' *Rochade* manoeuvre and the dramatic impact that this had on the German southern front in March 1945, I am indebted to Colonel Douglas E. Nash Jr (United States Army Rtd). This was a military disaster that had almost been omitted from this book, as I momentarily fell into the trap of believing that memoirs are honest and complete. Thanks to Colonel Nash and his excellent book on the Dirlewanger Brigade, I was able to see through the smokescreen of deliberate omissions to understand a great deal more about how the war on the southern front came to a close and the role that General Balck played in these closing weeks.

I am very grateful to Michael Herden in Freiburg for his friendly and professional skills working through the enormous German Army archives, also to Janina Jedamzik for her very helpful and positive support in translating some of the radio signals to and from Sixth Army in the front lines and OKW and some letters between Hermann Balck and his wife, Marianne. I am indebted to my copy editor, Tony Walton, who, through a combination of his expertise and dedication, guided my way through the often complex maze of troop movements and changing unit designations on the Eastern Front and in other theatres.

Thank you also to Philip Sidnell and Pen & Sword Books for supporting the concept and creation of this biography, and to my family – Helena, Skye and Cameron – for, yet again, their gracious and patient understanding while I missed numerous family dinners and TV shows as I became AWOL once more on this journey.

Philip Kay-Bujak
East Sussex, March 2025

List of Maps

1. After breaking through the Metaxas Line and Salonica, Kampfgruppe Balck fought through 21st NZ Battalion at Tempe Gorge while the rest of the 2. Panzer-Division outflanked Mount Olympus, April 1941. (*Map by Donald S. Frazier © 2015 The University Press of Kentucky. Used by permission*) 62
2. Case Blue was the result of Hitler's pivotal decision to effectively halt his forces and create a sustained thrust south to seize the oilfields of the Caucasus Mountains. Hermann Balck commanded 11. Panzer-Division of XLVIII. Panzerkorps within 4. Panzerarmee in the attack on Voronezh between June and November 1942. 105
3. Operation Uranus was part of the trilogy of Russian offensives aimed at sealing off Stalingrad and pushing the German front line back as far as possible before the winter of 1942–1943 halted the fighting. Hermann Balck proved himself a genius panzer division commander in the defensive battles along the Chir River in December 1942. 116
4. As commander of 11. Panzer-Division, Hermann Balck participated in one of the key moments of the Chir River battles – the breakthrough by 1st Soviet Tank Corps to State Farm 79 on 7 and 8 December 1942 – which was repulsed by brilliant close working collaboration between 11. Panzer- and 336. Infanterie-Divisions. *(From Robinson, p.212)* 122
5. The Soviet armoured penetration deep into the German rear led by 24th Tank Corps under Major General Vasily Badanov on 24 December 1942 represented a serious threat not only to the stability of the German front but also any hopes of resupplying Stalingrad with the destruction of Tatsinskaya airfield. 140
6. This 1950s map from US officer training at West Point shows the impact of Hermann Balck, as temporary commander of XIV. Panzerkorps, and his counter-attack at Salerno between 12 and 14 September 1943 south-east along the valley of the River Sele. The 16. Panzer-division attacked McCreery and the British 56th Infantry

Division, while 26. Panzer-Division and arriving elements of 29. Panzergrenadier-Division fell on the US 45th Infantry Division. (*West Point Academy*) 171

7. Appointed Oberbefehlshaber (OB) Heeresgruppe G on 20 September 1944, the situation that faced Hermann Balck was very challenging – as were the orders he was given by Adolf Hitler. Balck originally commanded three armies: 19. Armee to the south was a shadow of its former self as a result of the retreat from the south of France; 5. Panzerarmee was critically short of tanks; and 1. Armee was spread far too thinly and depended on new Volksgrenadier divisions to hold the front. (*Map by Donald S. Frazier © 2015 The University Press of Kentucky. Used by permission*) 214

8. The attacks by US XII Corps resumed after 8 November 1944 and Balck was unable to prevent the loss of territory due to overwhelming US firepower in the air and on the ground. Only the courageous but undermanned 11. Panzer-Division was able to once again hold the US 4th Armored Division's advance. (*Map by Donald S. Frazier © 2015 The University Press of Kentucky. Used by permission*) 225

9. Demoted to commander of 6. Armee, Balck was tasked with leading Operation Konrad II – the attempt to relieve Budapest from 18–26 January 1945. The IV. SS-Panzerkorps had been secretly redeployed to the Lake Balaton area and their attack penetrated 60km through to the River Danube within twenty-four hours. Turning north, although 3. SS-Panzer-Division 'Totenkopf' reached to within 30km of Budapest, ultimately, Balck, as commander of 6. Armee, would order corps commander Herbert Gille to fall back, leaving Budapest to its fate. (*Map by Donald S. Frazier © 2015 The University Press of Kentucky. Used by permission*) 253

Part I

Hermann Balck, The Making of a General, 1900–1939

Chapter I

Serving the Emperor, 1900–1914

'One day the great European war will come out of some damned foolish thing in the Balkans'

Otto von Bismarck

A family steeped in military service

The genealogy of the Balck family suggests that they came originally from Scandinavia and, like numerous other ethnic groups, settled in northern Germany – apparently along the banks of the River Elbe. Hermann Balck's great-grandfather had, at some point around 1800, lived in England and, with the Napoleonic threat, had joined and served in the Des Königs Deutsche Legion (the King's German Legion) – a British Army unit of expatriate Germans who were largely living in London between 1803 and 1816. Balck's grandfather had continued this association with the British; Georg Philipp Balck was born and brought up largely in England, and decided to follow his father and pursue a career in the British Army. He served with the Sutherland Highlanders, 93rd Regiment of Foot, throughout the 1840s and 1850s – he almost certainly served in the Crimea and India, eventually reaching the rank of lieutenant colonel of the 93rd Regiment before retirement.[1]

The association of the Balck family with military service was therefore a well-established norm by the time Hermann's father, Wilhelm, continued the family tradition of soldiering. After Colonel Balck had lost his sight serving with the 93rd overseas, perhaps in India, he returned to the independent state of Saxony and married Charlotte Lutgen. Hermann's father, Wilhelm Balck, had been born in October 1858 but not in Gdansk; instead, the family seems to have moved to Osnabrück in Lower Saxony, in the west of what was to shortly become the new German nation.[2] Konrad Friedrich August Henry William Balck (Wilhelm) would spend his life in uniform, just like his father and grandfather, but this time it would be a German – or Prussian – uniform, and he would ultimately rise to the rank of lieutenant general in the Prussian Army.

The 'Balck' independent spirit

The notion of a national armed force, a Wehrmacht, was but a distant dream in 1871, when Germany was created. By the time Adolf Hitler entered service as a 25-year-old Soldat (private) and later Gefreiter (lance corporal) in the First World War, it was as a member of a Bavarian, not a German, regiment that he would fight. His uniform, officers, language, expectations and even tactics were those of the Bavarian Army, not a national one – Bavaria was a 'nation' at that time. The same would be true of the 21-year-old Hermann Balck, who as a young lieutenant in 1914 would serve in a Prussian regiment, not a German one. The independent nature of the state armies was very real, and the divisions and rivalries at the top of the command structure were equally serious, even prejudiced, in terms of which states were considered the best – this continued to frame the military character of the German Army until well after the Great War.

From the army barracks at Onsnabruck, the ambitious Wilhelm Balck moved to Danzig on the north coast at some point before 1893, and this is where his son, Georg Otto Hermann Balck, was born on 7 December 1893.

What we now regard as northern Poland, the area around the great port of Gdansk, was and is a melting pot of cultures and ethnicities. Family names reflected and still reflect the history of a typical port area, where the interchange of trade also brought with it the exchange of genetic DNA; the pre-war port of Danzig was no exception. Prussians knew the region as Pomerania, while the Poles referred to it as Pomorskie – a large, low-lying area of rolling woodland and inland mountains that contain over 1,500 lakes known as the Kashubian Lakeland – or 'Polish Switzerland'. Mild winters and cool summers characterized the climate that the young Hermann Balck would recall. Over 70 per cent of the pre-1900 population lived in the urban centres, largely along the northern coastline, such as Danzig, Gdynia and Sopot.

The Balck family became settled in one of the finer parts of Gdansk, the suburb of Langfuhr or Wrzeszcz in Kashubian. Before the expansion of Gdansk inland to the south, this area was a flatland of forests, wolves, wild boar and heather. Gradually, the draw of urban living saw the area developed into homes for wealthy city dwellers. Classical style residences with architect designed gardens and tree lined driveways sprung up, and Langfuhr become the most desirable of suburbs. This was where Hermann Balck, together with his sister, Matilde, grew up, was schooled and was taught by his father about the military heritage of their family.[3]

Hermann Balck would be unable to escape his earthy, meritocratic background in what was an officer class primarily centred upon a core of class and heritage rather than talent and skill – but having a lieutenant general as a father definitely opened doors. During the Second World War, there were numerous opportunities for Hermann Balck to become part of the elite, the largely Prussian-dominated General Staff. Balck would be offered this chance at least twice, and both times he would reject the invitation – was this because he preferred to be with his troops in the front lines, as Stephen Robinson, author of *Panzer Commander Hermann Balck* suggests, or could it be part of his character, a reluctance to be part of a club, preferring his independence of both thought and action?

> 'Balck [also] distinguished himself with his forward presence on the battlefield, trusting his subordinates [such as von Mellenthin] to keep everything under control at his headquarters.'[4]

From the very start of his military life, Balck demonstrated two strong characteristics which marked him our as part of a much smaller 'club' – that of the battlefield commander – and it was this that prevented him from joining the General Staff. His predisposition towards making independent tactical decisions was one such trait, while the other was a desire to be at the front with his troops. Both of these qualities had their roots in the new Prussian officer education system that Balck experienced as a young man. His wartime experiences – both from 1914–1918 and 1939–1945 – would be those of a font-line commander, immersed in the smoke and speed of battle, not writing memoirs each evening from the luxury of a rear-echelon headquarters in a requisitioned castle or Loire Valley château. He would not be alone in this group of 'hands-on' commanders, but it was destined to be a lonely existence.

Paternal influences and the education of the Imperial officer corps c. 1890–1914 – a focus on the tactical, not the strategic

> 'Tactics reigned supreme in Prussia. The system concentrated on the nuts and bolts of the military profession.'
>
> Holger H. Herwig

By the 1880s – when Hermann's father, Wilhelm, trained as an officer – a War Academy (or Kriegsakademie) was well established, having been founded during the wars of unification that ended in 1871, and still retained Scharnhorst's vision of the educated army officer: the able, not the titled one. The liberal curriculum was based on a three-year course that included a wide range of topics, such as mathematics, history and geography but also justice, physics, French, Russian and literature – wider than a university programme and also including military studies. This made Hermann's father widely conversant across a range of intellectual pursuits, and Hermann Balck credited his father with helping him gain an appreciation of classical civilization and history:

> 'In the subjects of history, geography and German, I was always far above average. On modern languages, mathematics, and natural science I was average. But when it came to the ancient languages, I had no interest. It was only through my deep and thorough knowledge on antiquity, where my father had been my teacher and motivator, that I was able to barely maintain the necessary grades.'[5]

Balck was growing up in the age of the earliest stages of *Truppenführung* – the modern study of how to lead men, creating officers who could use their initiative and mission command. Europe was awash with books and pamphlets dedicated to the new age of the Imperial officer class and their responsibilities of modern leadership, as opposed to the previous age of total military subordination to the commands of one person.

Hermann Balck would have sat in lessons on field intelligence, fortification theory, siege warfare, international law, surveying and numerous tactics courses. The focus was increasingly on defeating an enemy as defined by a higher authority, and less on ruminating on whether a war was right or wrong or where the armed forces sat within the state. This narrowing of vision is at odds with the concept of the enlightened officer, but was part of the move away from armies based on state lines and towards a German army for a nation as opposed to a nation state. On the one hand, the army wanted its officers to be paragons of virtuous learning, of high moral quality and intelligence, but on the other they were not to involve themselves in strategic concerns and whether or not a war was legitimate. In thirty years' time, when junior officers of the imperial army had moved through the rank system and had become generals, it was their earlier training that remained in their memory, alongside unquestioning obedience to commands. General Wilhelm Groener, Chief of the War Office from 1916–1917, stated that in his own reading, he was 'more occupied with books of the practical service, than with books on high strategy'. In his 2005 article 'The German Way of War', Samuel J. Newland wrote that von Moltke the Younger (commander of the German Army at the outbreak of the First World War) advised his son, who was just about to enter the War Academy himself, not to worry about books on strategy, such as those of von Clausewitz, but instead to focus on winning battles – such as Hannibal's victory at Cannae.[5]

In his biography of Hermann Balck, Stephen Robinson refers to the postwar literature of Wilhelm Balck – in relation to Germany's defeat in 1918. But it was the impact of his pre-1914 publications that we need to focus upon, as it was these that made their mark on the early development of his son. For some years prior to publication in 1903, Wilhelm Balck, by now a colonel in the Prussian Army, had been researching and writing his own academic papers, which were published in a combined six-volume work entitled *Introduction and Formal Tactics of Infantry* and *Cavalry, Field and Heavy Artillery in Field Warfare*.

Interestingly, it was to be a young American army officer named Walter Krueger who would shine international attention upon these detailed and prescient works on how to wage war on land. Krueger had been born in Flatow in West Prussia in 1881 – his father having served in the Franco-Prussian War as an officer in the Prussian Army.[6] Krueger, who was now an instructor in Spanish, French and German at the US Army base at Fort Leavenworth, Kansas, had obtained copies of both the major works of Wilhelm Balck and translated them fully for interpretation and use by the United Sates Army. Catching the attention of the then Chief of the General Staff, Major General Leonard Wood, these books became widely read and adopted in US Army infantry training.

So how might these and other works have influenced Hermann Balck? We know that Balck revered his father, whom he described as 'the last great tactical theoretician of the Kaiser's army'.[7] It is logical to conclude that Hermann read his father's books and no doubt experienced his theories in his classes in officer school as a result, and these mantras would inform his core beliefs.

Many years later, as a Wehrmacht general in Russia, Balck would become renowned for his battles with the Russians on the Chir River Front in 1942 and 1943. The rapid movement of troops and bringing in equipment, mostly at night, and surprising the Russians by how quickly Balck transferred his forces became the hallmark of the 11. Panzer-Division – nicknamed the Gespenster (or Ghost) Division because of the rapidity with which Balck could move his troops. One conclusion is that Balck was not only heavily influenced by what he learnt as a young officer but also by the teachings of his father. In terms of what was to be Hermann Balck's preference for leading from the front, his father had written: 'Leader and organisation should keep each other constantly in view.'[8]

On the Eastern Front during 1943 and 1944, Hermann Balck was one of the main proponents of the Kampfgruppe (fighting group) – an independent formation within a larger force that could be put together quickly and contained combined arms units. The concept of quickly assembling a combined arms force to meet sudden changes of circumstances was a key feature of the German Army at a tactical level, especially when on the defensive in Russia. This concept was not new, as his father had written in 1914:

'On the battlefield, the formation of the division depends on the situation and the terrain. The formation in groups enhances readiness for combat and, under certain circumstances, reduces losses.'[9]

Substitute tanks for cavalry and panzer divisions could also be broken up into combat units, which made the formation battle-ready quicker and more mobile, and thus had the benefit of the potential for lower casualties. For Wilhelm Balck, it was not the fighting power or durability of cavalry that was their main weapon – it was their sudden appearance on the battlefield and their rapid movement around and through the terrain that was where their true power lay:

'The unfavourable proportion of cavalry to the other arms, the improvement of rifles and guns, the greater independence of the infantry, and the everywhere increasing cultivation of the soil, materially restrict the employment of cavalry. But these factors never restrict its employment to such an extent that its fight against the other arms would offer no chance of success. Cavalry acts above all else by the moral effect that the sudden appearance of its swiftly moving mass produces. Men have not changed, and are now, as of old, susceptible to the impression produced by danger that threatens them unexpectedly.'[10]

Mobility was one of the the cornerstones of the Blitzkrieg (lightning war), the founding principle behind Guderian's *Achtung Panzer*, the philosophy of tank warfare that Hermann Balck would so expertly demonstrate. The influence of Wilhelm Balck's treatise on the main use of cavalry may have been forgotten by 1939, but it was influential enough to affect both European and American cavalry doctrines. However, it would be the German commanders – with their insistence on the importance of tanks being mobile, punching together and acting like ghosts – that showed this tactical approach at its best. Unfortunately, Blitzkrieg would succumb to the *Festung* (fortress) doctrine of Adolf Hitler, which was diametrically opposed to the concept of free-flowing movement on the battlefield.[11]

Expectations and indoctrination to 1914

Alongside the heavy focus on tactical control of the battlefield, young officers across the new German nation were also immersed in the culture of the military traditions of service, loyalty and honour. There was no escaping, regardless of social background, the powerful and suffocating impact of expectation across all ranks of the new German Army, and this affected enlisted men, experienced non-commissioned officers and officers alike. Linked to these high expectations, suicide rates across all European armies were disturbingly high, and it was perhaps not surprising that the highest rates of all were in the German Army, within which the Prussian armed forces suffered the greatest annual number of suicides. It is also now well known that Hitler exploited military loyalty to the full.

In his 2014 article 'Explaining Suicide in the Imperial German Army', published in *German Studies Review*, Andrew Bonnell provides a detailed analysis of some of the statistics and possible causes, and despite the obstacles to truth he opens a comparatively new window into military service in the German Army prior to 1914.[12]

The government and military were quite prepared to besmirch the character of individuals after their death:

> 'Official sources sought to minimise evidence of the mistreatment of soldiers in their presentation of suicide data, while critics of militarism, especially in the Social Democratic Party, used suicide in the military to expose what they regarded as systemic abuse.'[13]

Uncompromising obedience

In his training in Jäger-Regiment 10, Hermann Balck would have not only been subject to harsh and uncompromising discipline, but also an unforgiving level of expectation. The prospect of a failure to live up to the expectations within the regiment was one of the key drivers behind enlisted men and officers turning towards suicide as the only logical response to totally illogical situations. One could suggest that it was in fact the most rational of minds that saw suicide as the only way out, as opposed to the 'sick' or confused mind which the authorities preferred to blame.

How and why Prussian military influence came to characterize so completely the personality of the new German state up to 1914 is a book in itself. It was not inevitable that Germany developed into a militaristic nation, but this notion was fostered by Hitler, who was able to seize upon and manipulate militarism combined with the unfinished business of 1918.

To join the German military in the period between 1900 and 1914 was therefore to join an expanding, vibrant, confident and transitioning national army, with regional recruiting affiliations and a leadership basking in the sun of imperial and later Nazi favouritism. It was a high point for German militaristic pride, and this was when Hermann Balck began his life journey dedicated to the German Army.

Chapter II

The Impact of the Great War on the German Military – Sacrifice and Treason, 1914–1919

Lessons in leadership – *Truppenführung*

The year 1913 found Fähnrich – Officer Cadet – Hermann Balck serving in the light infantry with the Royal Prussian Hanoverian Jäger-Bataillon 10. Jäger units saw themselves as elite light infantry, sharpshooters and a fast reaction force, which complimented Balck's love for fast-paced combat on the battlefield. This would show itself especially well when he commanded the 11. Panzer-Division during 1943, Balck's philosophy being centred upon well-led, elite troops moving quickly and decisively over the battlefield. Interestingly, only a few weeks earlier, Heinz Guderian had graduated and served with the 10th Jäger, and had been transferred to the War Academy in Berlin – perhaps helped by the fact that his father was at that time his battalion commander. In his memoirs, Balck recalled how Guderian's father was a consummate officer:

> 'The battalion was still under the influence of its second to last commander, the father of Colonel General Heinz Guderian, who had inculcated a sense of respect for even the lowest-ranking Jäger, freedom of all to express his opinion, toughness and justice while on duty, and the sense of achievement in one's accomplishments.'[14]

Heinz Guderian and Balck were both to follow and exhibit the same attitude to operational tactics on the battlefield – dash and speed, concentrating on weak points in the enemy front and not dispersing their forces. Both men were inculcated with a philosophy that was alien to the average infantry regiment. Almost certainly, Hitler appreciated the loyalty within the panzer force and admired his panzer generals in a way that he could not with his infantry commanders – they were more likely to be given a second chance and even be able to speak bluntly to Hitler in ways that other generals could not.[15]

Graduating as a leutnant from the Hanoverian Military College in the early spring of 1914, Balck was to be thrown into war almost immediately as the dominoes tumbled across Europe in the August of that year. Jäger regiments began the war in their green tunics and black shakos, rather than the dark blue tunics and spiked helmets of their more numerous comrades in the line regiments.[16] Looking more like parade ground soldiers, the Jäger were battalion-sized units of around 600 men attached to division-sized formations. At the start of the war, there were only sixteen Jäger units, hence the elite nature of their role in the order of battle.

Before the onset of trench warfare, the Jäger maintained their reconnaissance and skirmishing roles, far ahead of the main formations. They sought out the enemy and probed for weaknesses, appearing where and when least expected and being involved in the opening engagements with the enemy. With the onset of static war, these elite troops were simply folded into the main regimental and divisional structures, even though they tried to maintain their light infantry *esprit de corps*. In every unit that he commanded, Balck tried to instil that same sense of being special and even unique; again, the best example came in his leadership of 11. Panzer on the Eastern Front. In *Order in Chaos*, Balck is clear that his distinctive approach in those very early years was formed not just by his own father and Guderian's father, but also by his mentor, a young Leutnant Hans Kreysing who, during the Second World War, would become general officer commanding the German 8. Armee.[17]

The shadows of war could be seen for many months before August 1914, and when it did come, Hermann Balck happened to be with his father, who was now a brigade commander and was in Göttingen on a communications exercise. The upswell of patriotic fervour and support for the war was vividly portrayed: 'All social classes were swept away. Germany was a sea of black, white and red flags.'[18]

It was approaching Liège in early August 1914 that Balck first came under fire. As he led his troops towards the Belgian city, hundreds of wounded stragglers were returning back down the lines. Gossip spread of night attacks that had gone horribly wrong, street fighting with ambushes around every corner and confusing orders. The German Army was not experienced in fighting at night, and urban warfare was a very specialized concept that was beyond their training, so it is unsurprising that Hermann Balck never forgot either of these lessons and always avoided both. Another result was that Balck quickly realized that higher commands were not infallible in war and that troops of all kinds could be brutal. The German advance into Belgium was swift and marked by a shocking savagery – including the execution of civilians and even priests who were marked out as spies. This was the action of ordinary German infantrymen, not some hardened cult like the later SS.

Leutnant Hermann Balck would have been leading his reconnaissance platoons at the very front of the huge Army of the Meuse, with its massive siege guns and thirty-five divisions. From Liège, Jäger-Bataillon 10 pressed on deeper into Belgium. Balck experienced the exciting freedom of action and manoeuvre behind enemy lines that would characterize his later roles – moving quickly, making operational decisions on the spot and reporting back to his superiors much later. Unfortunately for Balck, this flexibility in fighting and movement was to be short lived, the September rains and the sacrifices by French, Belgian and British forces blunting and then halting the German advance. The great plans orchestrated by von Schlieffen ultimately failed.

By 18 August, heavy losses amongst the Jäger battalions and the need for larger forces saw four partial battalions merged into one large regiment. Balck, though only very young and inexperienced, was selected as adjutant. The next day, Balck was exposed to new orders which required the rounding up of hostages and the collection of a large tax as punishment for the manner in which the Belgians had resisted – they had been using any means to defend themselves with guerilla warfare, shooting out of churches and employing other methods the German forces regarded as dishonourable. Balck was not required to shoot the hostages he rounded up, but this was nonetheless a precursor to Balck's later challenges dealing with the French resistance in 1944.[19]

By the time his Jäger force had reached Tournai, north-west of Mons, Balck was fighting French cavalry. Still dressed in their shining brass and silver Napoleonic era breastplates, they fell in their hundreds against disciplined rifle fire and were brushed aside in what was now a mission to reach the sea and cut off the British Expeditionary Force from the Channel ports. Marching up to and even over 50km a day, Balck knew what mobile infantry were capable of. He related how at Fontaine-au-Pire, a single engagement 'remained a lesson for me throughout my entire career – successful attack is less costly than a failed defence'.[20] Fighting the tough, brave and stubborn English regiments, now in defensive positions as ordered by Field Marshal Sir John French on 26 August, Balck was forced to develop his concepts on focussed attacks rather than defensive lines.

The slow, heroic drift to static warfare

Along the length of the benign River Marne, the flower of both the British and German armies were destroyed in a series of murderous advances from the German perspective – or fighting retreats from the vantage point of the British Expeditionary Force (BEF). With no known front line as yet, September 1914 was a month of face-to-face fighting in fields, dykes, farmyards and along roads. In daylight or at the darkest hours of night, moving troops unexpectedly bumped into each other. Sometimes it was a Scottish regiment in kilts, at others a French regiment of Chasseurs Alpins or an English cavalry screen. Occasionally, Balck saw white flags as some French or British troops decided to surrender, while at other times he saw ambushes as they had changed their minds. Once again, this heralded what he would experience fighting the Americans in 1944 and would inform his mistrusting attitude, resulting in orders never to accept a flag of truce.[21]

For Hermann Balck, the rapid deterioration and consequent failure of the German attack into Belgium and France was due to a lack of political will to fight to the finish, which, when so many had already sacrificed their lives, was unforgivable. Ultimate failure would also reinforce his suspicions of senior officers promoted beyond their abilities, and this would play a leading part in his career in 1944 and 1945.[22]

The views Balck developed of both the military and political leadership during the Great War would remain with him as totemic reminders against which to judge future events. He would view politicians with suspicion and generals with scepticism, both until proven otherwise. This would not endear him to his colleagues and contributed to his reputation as a loner and difficult personality to work with.[23]

By 30 October 1914, Balck and his battalion were near Ypres. In a frontal attack, his men, including his old 2. Kompanie, charged forward and over successive English lines. Balck watched helplessly as his company commander, Hauptmann (Captain) Radtke, fell dead, shot through the heart, and then felt the searing pain of a British bullet tear into his own left hip – Balck was fortunate to survive from such close range and soon found himself evacuated through the rear lines, in great pain and on a troop train to Leipzig.

In a poignant paragraph, Balck relates how he recuperated at home with his mother, his father then being on active service at the front with the rank of generalmajor. Balck recalled the Germany of 1914 as being one of patriotism, enthusiasm for the war and a willingness to sacrifice all, which may have been true in his family circle but was not necessarily an accurate portrayal of the entire nation. Not was it necessarily widespread practice to be able to pull strings to ensure the postings that one wanted – this was the preserve of people with good connections and influence. With his father also having been severely wounded fighting in Poland against the Russians, Hermann Balck was able to avoid the stalemate on the Western Front and use his father's contacts to get a posting to the Eastern Front; his choice and a prophetic one, as twenty-six years later he would be back in Russia, fighting this time as a general himself.

Balck's formative views on Russia

Balck describes the Russia of 1915 in very disparaging terms:

'Clearly, the Russian generals and soldiers were not equal to the German art of leadership and the independent thinking of German soldiers. But the true reasons [for the complete collapse of Russia in 1917] lay deeper.'[24]

By the 1970s, Balck had reflected on the events within Russia between 1915 and 1917 and had very nearly come to the same conclusions that Hitler had in 1941 – that the ineffectiveness of the Russian armed forces centred upon poor leadership, poverty of equipment and ineffective state leadership. In Hermann Balck's mind, little had changed since 1941 in terms of his and many others' perceptions about Russia. We might reflect on these judgments as we view the current war in Ukraine. Balck remained of the opinion that poor communications, poor leadership, low morale and the widespread corruption of the Tsarist regime inevitably meant than an efficient fighting force such as the German Army would easily triumph in any conflict with Russia:

'Hitler had recognised the threat that Russia and Bolshevism posed much more clearly than his western adversaries. The conclusions he drew were influenced by his experiences as an infantryman on the western front in World War I. His experience in that war formed him. He was not able to let go of that experience, but he was also not able to move beyond it.'[25]

In February 1915, the now fully recovered Leutnant Hermann Balck once again left his home barracks in Goslar in a troop train, but this time headed eastwards. On his uniform, Balck now wore the Iron Cross 1st Class for his actions and bravery near Ypres, the first of many such awards that would ultimately see him as a member of one of the most elite group of German medal holders by 1945. He was one of the first 100 recipients of the Iron Cross 1st Class following its reintroduction by Kaiser Wilhelm II on 5 August 1914. Worn on the left breast of the tunic, as opposed to hanging from a ribbon or denoted by a ribbon through a button-hole, the Iron Cross 1st Class was always a distinctive and revered symbol of courage.

Balck was often at a loss to explain why the Russian Front attracted him so much, although he did recall with clarity just how far it was even to reach the front lines. Stuck on troop trains for days on end, with dwindling supplies and rations, Balck was already experiencing the problems that the extended supply lines caused for any army taking on Russia by way of a land invasion. Napoleon had seen it at first hand, Balck was seeing it in 1915 and Hitler was to see it to its deadliest extent from the winter of 1941 onwards. The inexorable tide of new horizons beyond which the enemy could retreat was as effective a weapon as any good general. Add to that a Russian winter and no supply line in the world could cope, a situation with which Balck would continue his fascination when he wrote academic papers in the 1920s as an officer in the new Reichswehr.

Serving now with Reserve Jäger-Bataillon 22, his old 10. Jäger still being on the Western Front in the area of Verdun, Balck lamented that the XXV. Reservekorps to which he was attached was 'one of the so-called Kindercorps' due to the very large proportion of young and poorly trained recruits who had rushed to join the army in the summer of 1914. Much like the flower of English youth, they too would be harvested by death and destruction in the early phases of the war.

Balck may have not had the Prussian preposition of 'von' in his title, but in all other respects the Balck name carried considerable weight in military circles and he was always well known by his father's reputation. A glimpse of this atmosphere of privilege and patronage can be gained in the following extract from *Order in Chaos*:

> 'The corps commander, General of Infantry Reinhard von Scheffer-Boyadel, ordered me to report to him and invited me to dinner. I sat across from him, to my left was his Chief of Staff, Colonel von Massow, to my right the Duke of Coburg. His Excellency von Scheffer toasted me, and when I got up, he also rose and said, "One must rise in honour of a Knight of the Iron Cross 1st Class."'[26]

The early summer of 1915 saw Leutnant Balck posted southwards towards Poznan and current-day Slovenia – part of the melting pot of nationalism and political intrigue as the decaying Austro-Hungarian Empire slowly recoiled from increasing opposition to its rule. Fighting the Russians in and around Breslau meant that, before long, Balck and his regiment would encounter the River Danube to the east and pockets of German-speaking communities ready to welcome their troops with open arms. Some measure of the level of German nationalism that Hermann Balck felt at the time is expressed in the following passage from his memoirs:

> 'Our first camp was in Antafalva, a large clean friendly Slovenian village. Then we reached the first German settlements and we crossed the Temes River. We would have done anything for our German brethren.'

In 1944, Balck would rediscover these emotions as he fought to repel Russian attacks seeking to conquer once and for all these rural areas where so many German families resided. Memories of 1914 would fuel his hatred of the Russian soldiers raping and pillaging their way through what he saw as German territories.

Turning north, Leutnant –Balck and his regiment trudged through the mud and trench lines of Galicia and into southern Ukraine, ending up positioned along the upper reaches of the Bug River. It was here that Balck experienced almost daily clashes with Russian cavalry and infantry, an invaluable experience for later senior command positions, and where he received a second wound – this time from a bullet ricochet which hit him in the back. Surviving a bout of appalling dysentery that accompanied his wound, Balck returned to the front lines only ten days later and caught up with his unit in the Rokitno Marshes, where the strategic plan was to try to cut the major Russian advance at the neck. Balck was able to spend weeks leading his company on their own initiative, often behind enemy lines, allowing him to create opportunities while preserving the integrity of his small force.

News reached Balck in June 1916 that his old unit, the 10. Jäger, had been embroiled in the dreadful fighting in Verdun. A pang of guilt encouraged him to push to obtain a transfer back to his unit, but although he achieved this, all was not as he expected. No longer in Verdun, the remnants of the 10th were licking their wounds in the vicinity of Caineni, due east of Belgrade and in the centre of huge wild forests – one of the forgotten battlefields of the Great War. The toll of the new key weapon in infantry fighting – the machine gun – showed itself graphically, Balck recalling that he hardly recognized anyone from the original company he had loved so much and left behind the previous year.

In many respects, destroying Russian forces in the early 1940s must have felt like a retribution for Hermann Balck – he had 'history' with them. On into the Transylvanian Alps and onwards to Wallachia, Balck and the 10. Jäger experienced the demands of fighting through heavy snow and cold, at the same time witnessing first-hand the physical manifestations of the collapsing Austro-Hungarian Empire. Abuses handed out by over-fed officers to their starving men sat very badly with Balck.

The philosophy of *Truppenführung* may not yet have condensed into Fedor von Bock's future 1930s exposition and manual for the German Army, but the roots of it were everywhere.[27] In contrast to large field armies reacting to the commands of a single general or field marshal, the realization that modern warfare rested on increased movement and that new weapons were able to destroy large concentrations of forces meant that independent action by more junior commanders in smaller forces was encouraged. By the 1930s, the German Army would be the most advanced proponent of *Truppenführung* and *Auftragstaktik*.

Central to *Truppenführung* was the concept of the officer being a leader and a teacher to his troops, sharing their privations, while core to *Auftragstaktik* was the increased amount of independent action, within the larger mission, that was delegated to all levels in the chain of command. In his later career, when

Balck was praised (or criticized) for his totally independent tactical decisions during the Second World War, he was acting in homage to his training in the First World War. The contrast with other European armies in the Great War could not be more stark:

> 'We were horrified as well by the things we saw ... Every night their [the Austrian] soldiers sat around the fires and got drunk until they just passed out. The officers, on the other hand, established a mess, where they were fed cooked meat twice a day. They had pastries, candy, cigarettes, and every night plenty of women ...
>
> 'Does a state like the Austrian monarchy still have the right to exist?'[29]

If the decadence of their allies and their foes showed itself so plainly, it is no surprise that these views on the enemies of Germany would remain in Balck's consciousness and feed into his opinions as a combat general.

Balck's army commander was Erich Ludendorff, whose experience of the huge distances involved in fighting in the East gave rise to the German General Staff's awareness that a war of movement and independent action was both necessary but also a practical solution for the strategic training of the whole German Army fighting in Russia.

Military catastrophe and the seeds of destruction

By 1917, much had changed in Hermann Balck's life and experience of war. Demands for an end to the war grew in every combatant nation, and hard on the heels of a desire for peace came an equally powerful impulse for the losers to blame someone or something for the catastrophic losses suffered for so little gain. But it was in Germany that the real crisis was brewing, fundamentally affecting both how the war would end and the psychology and political future of the military class across the nation. This would include how Balck viewed the causes of Germany's defeat and affect how the German military caste would behave in the coming two decades.

While such heady thoughts occupied the minds of politicians and ambitious pacifist philosophers, the men in uniform continued to fight, and the German General Staff were well aware that the war could now easily be lost. For Hermann Balck, the war continued against the Russians, and in August 1917 he was wounded again, this time in the left side of his upper chest, just above the heart, the rifle bullet lodged in the top of his left arm. Another inch and this book would never have been written and Hitler would never have been able to reward one of his generals so highly. Balck treated his wounds as if they were scratches – such was and is the tenacity and arrogance of youth. With his arm in a sling, he returned to the front lines, although not yet wearing his *Verwundetenabzeichen* (Wound Badge) in gold, as this would not be introduced until March 1918.[29]

The concept of an enemy matched in tactical abilities with the German Army is totally absent from Balck's recollections. In his mind, the only way Germany could be defeated was by subterfuge and crookedness. Alexander Kerensky rose to power as chairman of the Russian Provisional Government in the political vacuum left by the early phase of the Bolshevik Revolution, between the arrest of the Tsar and his family in March 1917 and the successful uprising in October of the same year. In June 1917, Kerensky ordered a disastrous campaign in Galicia, which Balck felt was part of a secret deal with the British and Allied powers. The subsequent 400,000 Russian casualties saw Russia incapable of continuing the war, and in the train of events that followed Kerensky fled Russia just before his arrest. What is notable is how Balck viewed Kerensky's actions:

> 'The result was a victory for radicalism in Russia. At the decisive point Kerensky had thrown the wrong switch in world history. The English gave him a good pension after the war. He had delivered for them right on time.'[30]

The bitterness that German soldiers felt, believing they were up against a gang of hostile nations, was important in their future psychology.

Young dogs, new tricks

Now aged 25, Hermann Balck continued to fight bravely on the Eastern Front at the same time as Aldolf Hitler, now a Gefreiter (Lance Corporal), aged 29, was recovering from being gassed on the Western Front. By March 1918, Balck's 30-year-old comrade from the 10. Jäger, Hauptmann Heinz Guderian, had avoided front-line command, having been a signals staff officer for the 4. Armee. According to historian David Harding, it was Guderian's experience of the staff, providing communications to fast-moving cavalry units in the 5. Kavellerie-Division on the Western Front, that began to focus his mind on the need for wireless communications, later insisting that every single tank should be able to communicate with all the others in a unit:

> 'The experience of providing signals support to a highly mobile formation such as a cavalry division built upon the basic principles of mobility Guderian absorbed as a young Jäger officer. His technical training as a

signals officer and the opportunity to put it into practice in a wartime situation brought home to him the potential of wireless communications.'[31]

While men like Hitler and Balck experienced the futility of static warfare, Guderian could see a solution if massed attacks met by concentrated artillery fire no longer worked, then smaller, swifter and harder-hitting mechanized infantry and tanks were the answer. A 'lightning war' stood a far better chance of disrupting the enemy's battlefield control, probing for weaknesses, and lightweight mobile thrusts would ensure that the battlefield of the future would be fluid, ever-changing, and the key would be communications.

There was evidence to support Guderian's thinking. The *Stosstrupp* (Stormtroop) tactics of the Eastern Front, where Balck and others like him were having success, showed that Russian, French, Italian and Romanian lines could be broken by smaller, independent units, where the officers on the ground could make tactical localized decisions without constantly referring to a higher authority. This meant that forces able to operate autonomously and with all the arms and equipment they might require needed to be considered, and thus the concept of the Kampfgruppe (combat group) was born.[32]

The three principles of localized leadership by gifted officers, state-of-the-art communications and independent units formed the core concepts of Blitzkreig, one of the few positive outcomes of the First World War for the German armed forces in what was otherwise an unmitigated disaster. Guderian's vision of modern warfare, even in defence, would be a hard, if not impossible thing to sell to the later leader of Germany, Adolf Hitler. During the Second World War, Hitler often wielded his ultimate control and reverted to what he knew best – trench lines, such as the Atlantic Wall, Siegfried Line and Gothic Line, and fortresses (*Festungen*) such as Cherbourg, Budapest and Stalingrad, along with orders to 'fight to the last man'.

Unequivocally, 1918 was a year of catastrophic failure – militarily and politically – for Germany. Balck is often critical of the wartime leadership of the German armed forces by the OHL (Oberst Heeresleitung, the Supreme Army Command). Pointing out missed opportunities, mistakes and miscalculations in wars of the past are what historians do; hopefully from a position of observational independence. The memories and recollections of participants are crucial sources of evidence, but they are inevitably coloured by their limited access to the wider picture. In the case of Hermann Balck, the almost constant and often sardonic tendency to criticize the war effort of his Austro-Hungarian allies, through the prism of his own high regard for the perfection of the German Army, leaves much doubt as to his objectivity. For example, it seems both ironic and hypocritical to criticize the largesse of the dining habits of an Austrian general when Balck attended similar events himself – while his own troops gallantly and willingly, according to Balck, suffered their own privations on the nearby front lines:

> 'Rain, mud, and a thick layer of sludge [in Italy] covered everything. Not a button or a rank insignia could be recognised. Desperate, on the edge of mutiny, the column pressed ahead, eyes glazed over, breathing heavily, muttering hard and angry words. As we were marching past the billets of an Austrian general officer's headquarters, a cook dressed in white, wearing his chef's hat and carrying a tray of baked pastries, tried to shove his way through the column. I thought to myself "This is not going to go well." At just that moment the cook was picked up and dumped on his head, and the tray of pastries was passed down the column. While the mud-covered cook sat on the side of the road, faces brightened, bodies straightened up, and marching along they sang, "Hurrah, I am a hunter of the 10th Jäger Battalion".'[33]

In reality, the Austo-Hungarian Army fought bravely and suffered huge losses, in spite of poor equipment and a lack of investment in the armed forces before 1914 – unlike Germany, the Austrians had not been preparing for war. Furthermore, the almost twenty different languages used across the Austro-Hungarian forces caused huge communication and leadership problems to which Balck seems deliberately oblivious:

> 'But our Austrian allies had shown such weakness that we had to be grateful that they were even able to hold the Italian front.'[34]

There was a far bigger picture to consider than a tray of pastries to illustrate the indolence of a single officer and therefore the contributions of an entire army. However, in the search for scapegoats to explain Germany's defeat, there would be lots of finger pointing but little self-assessment.

Internal German politics were badly fracturing into extremes. On the right were supporters who were wedded to Germany still winning the war and annexing territories that they believed belonged to Germany – such as Alsace. They were naturally supported by the German OHL and the officer corps. Opposing them were men from the parties of the centre and left, led by Matthias Erzberger, a Jewish former teacher and writer. Erzberger had seen a rapid rise in his political influence. Equally swiftly, he had changed his political views from being a right-wing annexationist supporting Germany's claims to lands to the west and the east, to having an ardent belief that the war could not be won and that the declaration of unrestricted submarine warfare was a sign of imminent defeat.

After 6 July 1917, Balck, along with the entire German Army, would have heard that Erzberger had given a speech declaring Germany should give up its territorial claims and seek an end to the war. As if this was not shocking enough, pressure within the Reichstag from the socialist and Marxist left-wing parties forced Chancellor Bethmann Hollweg to cave in to demands for equal manhood suffrage after the war. The Kaiser had no option but to accept this advance of democracy, and watched in humiliation as the Reichstag gradually increased its confidence to take over the running of the country.

Sensing a critical moment, Erzberger gambled that he could force the political right to accept his 'peace resolution', which was announced on 19 July. A further dangerous fracture opened in the Reichstag; even though the peace resolution passed a vote in the Reichstag, it merely created a new and ultra-conservative Fatherland Party, dedicated to keeping the conflict going and sticking to Germany's war aims. Wolfgang Kapp was a leading figure in this new right-wing party and Ludendorff was persuaded to give his public support – ending the avowed non-political alignment of the German Army. Interestingly, another member was a certain Anton Drexler, future founder of the German Workers' Party, which would later become the Nazi Party.[35]

Although the myth of the *Dolchstosslegende* (stab in the back) of the German Army is mostly associated with the eventual terms of the 1919 Treaty of Versailles, it was in fact the Erzberger speeches of July 1917 that began the whole concept of a weak, treacherous and duplicitous democracy acting to undermine German sacrifices in blood. To make things worse, many of these perceived traitors were Jewish, and the notion of the international Jewish conspiracy gained greater acceptance and currency. Already violently antisemitic, this later fitted perfectly with Hitler's conclusion that all Jews were evil.

It was not just Balck, Hitler and Guderian who watched the progress of the war and heard of the defeatism from home during 1918. In that year, Günther von Kluge was a Hauptmann on the General Staff, Erwin Rommel was a young leutnant on the Italian Front, Ewald von Kleist was a Hauptmann of a cavalry squadron, Friedrich Fromm was a leutnant in an infantry regiment, Ludwig Beck was a Hauptmann in the General Staff and Erich von Manstein was a Hauptmann on the Russian Front. Another future Generalfeldmarschall under Hitler was the Breslau-born Erwin von Witzleben, who fought in Flanders and at Verdun and ended the war as a young General Staff officer of the 121. Division.

These young officers on all fronts watched with anger and concern as their political bosses agitated for an armistice in order to prevent a total collapse on the front lines. Both Ludendorff and Paul von Hindenburg – who had established a *de facto* military dictatorship in the latter part of the war – openly blamed the parliamentary forces for letting the army down, and the officer corps accepted and believed in this myth. Socialist agitators were everywhere, undermining the confidence of the soldiers, sowing discontent with the monarchy and the militarist upper class that, in their warped view of history, had led Germany into this catastrophe.

In his memoirs and testament of political aims, *Mein Kampf*, Adolf Hitler referred to this period by saying:

> 'My personal attitude was established from the very start. I hated the whole gang of miserable party scoundrels and betrayers of the people in the extreme. It had long been clear to me that this whole gang was not really concerned with the welfare of the nation, but with filling empty pockets. For this they were ready to sacrifice the whole nation, and if necessary to let Germany be destroyed; and in my eyes this made them ripe for hanging.'[36]

The slow, inexorable slide into defeat was exacerbated by what the troops witnessed. As Balck and his men tried to make their way back to Germany, they travelled through a Serbia descending into revolutionary chaos and a Hungary riddled with riots, workers' soviets and armed civilians taunting and intimidating the uniformed soldiers – who, in their eyes, had failed. The collapse of social order and what Hitler and others saw as the disease of socialism and communism, impacted on the emotional memory of Balck and his men. The Allies were not the enemy; the enemy was at home, worming its way through their own people. Like tens of thousands of officers and men in the German Army, Balck and his fellow officers discussed the same causes of defeat, experienced the same socialist efforts to undermine the loyalty of their soldiers and built an image in their psychology of a fatherland falling sick and becoming prey to the pacifist and Marxist forces of revolution:

> 'So this was the grand finale. There was revolution in Munich, and workers' and soldiers' councils everywhere. Typically enough, the troops who had not done any fighting for four and a half years were the ones now making revolution. If a good portion of the army resisted the storm, everything would not yet be lost. The present poison had to be eradicated. The core of the German people was healthy enough to overcome the disease.'[37]

Even half a century after these events took place, Hermann Balck was still wedded to the myth of good and bad soldiers, loyal and disloyal soldiers, that all politicians were rotten and Germany had been victimized.

Chapter III

Years of Uncertainty – The Reichswehr, 1919–1930

The Kaiser abdicated on 10 November 1918, the German fleet mutinied and armed troops were on the streets in every city, with even Munich in disarray. For Balck and his unit, there was a hard and eventful march to get back to Germany from the southern front. They crossed the border on 23 November near Salzburg, from where trains took them back to their barracks – their war was over.

In his retrospective on the causes of defeat, Balck provides a trenchant narrative, blaming Germany's implosion on the decadence of the ruling monarchy, a failure to read the signs of modernization and social change, and the inevitability of a war-weary population, yet he saved his most vitriolic criticism for the far left in German politics. For Balck, it was the German officer corps that was the main pillar of the state, and the German Army was the back into which the Marxists, communists and democrats drove their knives. But there were two sides to the 'stab in the back' legend: those that held the knife and the body that allowed itself to be stabbed.

By the end of November 1918, a soldier's council controlled the 10. Jäger, not their officers. Orders came that the troops were to be demobilized and dispersed; within weeks, weapons had been handed into the armoury or handed out to members of the councils, and the regiment had ceased to exist. Across Germany, the same thing was happening. Officers similar to Balck decided to stay and command any troops who did not wish to return home, while others disappeared back to their homes, never to be seen again. All eyes were on Berlin, each day bringing with it new uncertainties.

Poland – round one

After the Congress of Vienna in 1815, concluding the Napoleonic Wars in Europe, the Kingdom of Warsaw and the rest of what were historically Polish lands were divided between the Russians, Prussians and the Austro-Hungarian Empire. Polish nationalists struggled against varying degrees of brutal administration for the next century, but with the disintegration of Russian forces in the eastern regions of what was about to become the new nation of Poland (at Versailles in the summer of 1919), and the withdrawal of Austro-Hungarian troops during early 1918, Polish nationalism resurfaced.

Dmowski in Paris, Paderewski in Washington and the imprisoned Pilsudski were just three of the key leaders of the new movement for Polish independence.[38] In June 1918, Britain, France and Italy declared the creation of a free Poland as one of their war aims; it would be the added provision of access to the sea that provided Hitler with his pretext for war in 1939. When the Armistice was declared on 11 November 1918, Poles swelled out onto the streets of Warsaw and the disorientated German troops based there gave up their arms, surrendering to the new Polish state.

Declaring what happened to their troops there as 'the most shameful episode in German history', the Reichstag had to find as many loyal and able units as possible to send eastwards to hold onto what was deemed to be German lands. Balck, with his composite company of hastily thrown together Jäger, received orders to head from Goslar for train depots, further feeding Balck's philosophy of needing to defend German lands in the east from Slavic nations. In January 1919, Balck arrived in the province of Posen. During that year's early spring, he and his small but loyal unit fought and killed hundreds of Polish troops in an effort to maintain control of towns and farms that were considered German. This was in response to the arrival of Paderewski in Poznan the previous month, after which Poles had immediately begun expelling Germans from their homes in the city.[39] Poles and Germans had co-existed in these disputed areas for hundreds of years, but on 18 February 1919, the Entente Powers – the victors meeting in Paris – declared a truce and the fighting officially ended. Nevertheless, the expulsions continued, and many Germans were ethnically purged from Polish towns and vice versa.

Uncertainty about where people were now going to live was matched by concerns over the future of the German Army. The vast majority of enlisted men had been disbanded and were now either on the streets as members of 'Red' or Spartacist units, or were unofficially armed as members of the SPD, the Social Democratic Party. Thousands had thrown away their uniforms and wanted nothing more to do with the army, while a minority – including Hermann Balck and his company of Jäger – stood firm, armed and in uniform, acting as a full-time military unit and waiting for news. The troops felt 'deceived and abused', and politicians in Berlin talked about the *Diktat* – the dictated peace – signed at Versailles on 28 June.[40] No words could capture the venom and disgust that millions of Germans felt about the terms of the Treaty of Versailles or how much the army felt unfairly blamed and criticised. As far as the army was concerned, they had never surrendered.

A reunion with Hauptmann Heinz Guderian, also now back in Goslar, gave Balck a chance to discuss the future with someone who at least saw events from the position of the General Staff. During December 1919, all trust in Chancellor Friedrich Ebert and the head of the army, General Wilhelm Groener, had gone. Their 'pact' to protect the army if it in turn supported the socialist government merely tarred them both with the slur of collaborators – even though the reality was they did the only thing that could have been done to stop Germany sliding into revolutionary chaos. Remaining centralist politicians began to move to more extreme positions on both the left – joining the Spartacist or Red brigades – and the right, now festering for a return to power of the monarchy under Wolfgang Kapp. The polarisation of German politics created a revolutionary fervour.

By 1920, the German Army was officially composed of just 100,000 officers and men. However, there were at least double that number still under arms, sat in the middle of a seething, boiling pot of blame and counter-blame. Any thoughts of resuming the war were just fanciful thinking. The terms of Versailles now had to be implemented, with the central question of who would stay and who would have to leave the officer corps. Balck described the mood of the times:

> 'A bad winter was behind us. Morale had been horrible. Ever since the signing of the peace treaty the trust in the government and the leadership had gone to hell. Everybody, officers and men alike, felt the insecurity of an unknown future. Who was going to be able to stay in uniform? Everybody was looking for an alternative civilian career. Whenever someone thought he had found something, he grabbed it. This festered and affected the cohesion of the troops.'[41]

As political power struggles dragged Germany into chaos, Balck tried to preserve what he could by way of order amongst his ever-dwindling unit, still quartered in the dilapidated old barracks in Goslar. The right-wing Kapp Putsch of March 1920 saw a confused situation made even worse. 'Red brigades' – loose-knit units of workers attracted to the Bolshevik cause and incited by agitators from Russia – fought against government forces and armed militias of former soldiers for the control of cities all across Germany. Balck was ordered to move his men to Hildesheim, where the workers had taken over the armoury and the streets of the town. Balck responded to an order from his battalion commander, Major Pflugradt, telling his men to fire on a large group of German workers, whom he saw as infected by the disease of Bolshevism. The workers' machine guns and other weapons were then seized. Germany was on the verge of social, economic and political collapse.

Meanwhile in Munich …

As young, vibrant and committed junior officers such as Guderian, Balck, Rommel, von Manstein, Paulus, von Kleist, von Witzleben and many others remained in uniform and led their small composite units, they naturally wondered about their future in the new slimmed down Reichswehr. In July 1919, just as the Treaty of Versailles was being signed, Adolf Hitler had volunteered as a Verbindungsmann (intelligence agent) in the Reichswehr. With no qualifications to speak of and no career ahead of him, Hitler also hoped to wear his Iron Cross 2nd Class for as long as he could. As part of an *Aufklärungskommando* (reconnaissance unit), Hitler was tasked with trying positively to influence other soldiers and to collect intelligence on some of the smaller political parties that were springing up in Munich, where he had returned after the war. It was while attending one such gathering in a beer hall in the centre of the city on 12 September 1919 that Hitler was moved to speak and take issue with a visitor named Professor Baumann over the possible independence of Bavaria. This embryonic group of twenty or so individuals of varying backgrounds and ambitions was Anton Drexler's German Workers' Party (DAP). Hitler had so impressed the small gathering that he joined the tiny DAP, with the aim of nurturing himself as its leader as member number fifty-five.

By the spring of 1920, Hitler was established as a member of the committee of the DAP in Munich, while Hermann Balck and the majority of the remaining German Army were being assembled in the nation's industrial heartland – the Ruhr. Hitler was fighting for control over the party and Balck was fighting for the future economic and therefore political future of the nation. Both were successful. The DAP expanded quickly, Hitler's vibrant and passionate speaking style bringing in many new members. A programme of antisemitic, anti-Marxist and nationalistic policies soon followed, Hitler surrounding himself with his now often forgotten but crucial ideological influencers – men such as Drexler, Dietrich Eckart, Hans Franck, Karl Harrer and Gottfried Feder.

In the Ruhr, Balck once again met up with Guderian as they took part in assaults on Red 'army' units – which included men who had once been part of the German Army – and inflicted serious casualties while freeing towns from revolutionary control.

Another future field marshal also fought alongside Balck and Guderian in the Ruhr, the outspoken and terse Walter Model. During the Great War, Model had fought across the Western Front at Mons, the Marne and Verdun. Like Balck, he received the Iron Cross 1st Class, and like Guderian and Balck, he had twice been wounded by shell fragments, in the shoulder and right thigh.[42] The shared experience of these young officers was remarkable, with a generation of army officers welded together in common bonds. They had been commissioned just before 1914, had fought and been wounded fighting for Germany and what they were told was a just war, had learnt much about how warfare needed to change in the face of new technology and had the bitter experience of feeling betrayed by social democracy.

The impact of Versailles – the Reichswehr

It took a little over eighteen months to reduce the Imperial German Army from two million men down to the 100,000 allowed by Versailles, the new Reichswehr, which came into being on 1 January 1921. Amongst the scepticism and jumble of conflicting orders, there were small signs of revival amongst the armed forces. A large number of former soldiers retained their uniforms and added their 'unofficial' status to the available numbers of armed men. Many had been and were members of the Red army units still hoping for a further revolution to overturn the new Weimar Republic, while others had joined the Freikorps (Free Units), which included Der Stahlhelm (The Steel Helmet), unsanctioned but tolerated militias supporting law and order and, by implication, democracy.

It was largely left to the German Army to decide who was demobilized and who was retained. Many general officers were offered a role in the new state force – one that now owed its obedience to a president rather than the Kaiser – while the junior officer cohort was selected largely on their background and connections in order to retain the class-based nature of the system. As importantly, the key Reichswehr commanders – General Hans von Seeckt and later General Werner von Fritsch – targeted recruitment on the rural areas of Germany, where they felt more reliable and loyal troops could be found who were not tempted by municipal social democracy and who tended to be physically stronger.[43] The Imperial Army would survive into the post-war period, which was important as it preserved the old imperial notions of independence from politics (although this was increasingly difficult) and maintained the key elements of autocracy and nobility; in 1926, 96 per cent of officer candidates still came from the upper classes in Germany. This meant that the social groupings amongst the officer corps were retained and not broken up by a more democratically minded recruitment process. In the Nazi period, this was a double-edged sword for Hitler. One the one hand, he had a loyal military force, but on the other, it was an ultra-conservative one, averse to risks and which wanted to operate in the way it had always done. This would cause Hitler to feel he could rely on the loyalty of the army (at least up until 1943 and the military reverses of that traumatic year), but it could also frustrate him. For Balck, von Kluge, Model, Rommel, Guderian and many others, the Reichswehr thus felt like an elite army of the best of the old, where their careers mirrored each other through the ranks, ultimately to the position of general. With only seven infantry divisions (now renumbered) and three cavalry divisions, competition for combat roles was fierce.

Developments to 1933

By January 1920, Hermann Balck was frustrated with a lack of challenge. Having always harboured a desire to become part of a cavalry unit, he requested a transfer to Kavallerie-Regiment 18. Posted to Stuttgart, Balck was now able to experience the thrills of horsemanship and camaraderie that came with the small and elite mobile forces. Indeed, his memoirs display a high regard for the men with whom he now served. A capable horseman, Balck was able to practise and enjoy training to move quickly and over long distances. He boasted how he had once ridden with his fellow officers and NCOs 60km a day for fourteen days before returning to barracks.

As the 1920s progressed, so did the ability of the Reichswehr to bend and break the rules. Inspectors from the allied commissions were deceived, with extra weapons hidden from their visits and additional men added to the army but hidden on paper declarations. Von Bock played a key role in the creation of the 'Black Reichswehr', labour units that were in fact nomadic former German troops who were now disguised as labour battalions.[44] Like the rest of the army, Balck also continued to venerate Feldmarschall von Hindenburg, whom he saw as untouchable in reputation and courage, the epitome of the victory that they felt they had deserved from the Great War:

> 'The entire cavalry division, six mounted regiments, dashed with thundering hooves at full gallop past the field marshal, in an unbelievable cloud of dust. And there at the place of honour, in a haze but clearly distinguishable like in a halo, stood old Hindenburg, unreal, iron-like, as if he were a stone monument.'[45]

Perhaps one other thing had also changed. The question of just how independent the new army of the Weimar Republic was remains an open one. All of the commanders in chief of the army, and indeed the tiny naval forces, professed to be neutral in terms of political activity, but of course they had their natural conservative inclinations. Numerous officers remained monarchists and hoped that one day, the Kaiser or his descendants could return to rule Germany. Indeed, inactivity regarding political events was a political act in itself. A prime example was the decision not to protect the Republic from the dramatic Kapp Putsch in 1920, despite a request from the government for the army to intervene. There is no question that the Reichswehr divisions would have acted had they been so ordered, Balck himself saying that 'it was unthinkable that orders [from von Seeckt] would not be followed'.[46]

Claims that the Reichswehr was politically neutral are simply untrue. Although officially prohibited from being involved in politics, in the new democratic world the commanders of the army had to be politically active in order to protect and extend the position of the Reichswehr, and indeed their own jobs. In a post-war world of recrimination and vengeance, some commanders went a lot further and took deliberate decisions not just to ignore events during the right-wing Kapp Putsch, but to go out of their way to create relationships with right-wing political groups. The Stahlhelm political movement of ex-soldiers and comrades could expect nothing but support from the regular army, but so too could uprisings or even revolts – such as that in Munich in October 1923. While Balck had been training in the use of cavalry, Adolf Hitler had recruited nearly 55,000 dissolute members and, in the crisis of hyper-inflation in late 1923, his new party felt strong enough to attempt to take power. Although the Munich Putsch failed and Hitler ended up with a five-year prison sentence, an emphatically benign Reichswehr had attempted to allow him the time and space to succeed. It was left to the local police force to contain the attempted revolt. In this case, inaction was indeed a sign of political activity.

Publishing a philosophy of change

While Hitler spent his prison time writing and dictating his thoughts to his deputy, Rudolf Hess, from 1923–1924, Hermann Balck also turned his notes of his wartime experiences into a series of articles on 'Russian operational concepts'. In a fascinating parallel period of reflection, while the future leader of the Third Reich was detailing his strategic war aims – including the acquisition of *Lebensraum* (living space) by taking land from a successful war in the East – one of his future senior generals was also writing how such a war in the East could be won. For Balck, little had changed since the Polish-Russian War:

> 'I believe I analysed correctly the Russian operational concepts, which were based on exhausting the enemy's reserves by cleverly committing Russia's sheer human masses. By World War II the Russians were still trying to do much the same thing.'[47]

At the same time, Balck was invested with the responsibility of providing men for psychological assessment studies to be used in the future selection of officer candidates. He was convinced that psychological testing was a vital tool in keeping the officer corps clear of undesirable influences and nepotism. It was whilst Balck was writing up some of his research results in 1924 that his father, Wilhelm Balck, died aged 65 on 15 July in Aurich, Hanover. Wilhelm Balck had busied himself writing several books after 1918, and the relationship between father and son had remained strong and respectful.

But it was not just Balck, his father and Adolf Hitler who used the 1920s to reflect on the disasters of the 1914–1918 war. Guderian too became a recognized expert on the development of new tactics, and his ability to communicate saw his ideas read across Europe and in the USA. Later, in 1937, his book *Achtung! Panzer!* would form the manifesto for German tank tactics in the Second World War. While Hitler wrote about the need to overturn the Treaty of Versailles in a series of short and fast wars, Guderian was trying to persuade his fellow Reichswehr officers of the need to create a new, modern armoured force. Guderian's views found both opposition – he named General Ludwig Beck as one of the most stubborn – and supporters, with men such as Major (later General) Oswald Lutz encouraging him to pursue his passion for new armoured mobile warfare.[48] Guderian, in his forthright way, declared that Germany needed to find a new hero, a leader who could take the country forward, right the injustices of Versailles and retore the rightful place of the army in German society. According to historian David Harding:

'Guderian was profoundly affected by the revolution [of 1918–1919] and the turmoil of his homeland and longed, like most Germans, for the restoration of order and for Germany once again to regain her rightful place as a great power. During his service in the Baltics in 1919, Guderian, like many of his colleagues and countrymen, began to voice the opinion that a saviour must be found for Germany who would lead her out of the chaos of the postwar years. These feelings were reinforced by what he saw in Munich upon his return to Germany in the fall of 1919. Hitler promised deliverance and more. Guderian and Hitler had found each other.'[49]

It is less obvious how Hermann Balck viewed Adolf Hitler in these early years up to 1930. Obviously a deliberate omission, Balck's memoirs jump from 1921 and resume in 1933. In the meantime, the collective German psychology was tested again and again by what H.G. Baynes has called 'the daemonic possession and primitive medicine-man who gained a magical ascendancy by playing the role of medium to the German unconscious'.[50] Just how far members of the army were entranced differed from individual to individual. There was certainly something about Hitler that was unique, and his past service was an asset in terms of admittance to the military psyche, but there was no collective intoxication throughout the army, whereas there was in society generally. Balck wanted a Messiah and Hitler seemed to be exactly that.

What we do know is that Hitler appealed to the Reichswehr to support him, and Balck was in no doubt about how tremendously hard the officers of the Reichswehr had worked to create the foundation of a small, modern army:

> 'No other army has managed to achieve what the thirty-six-hundred-strong officer corps of the one hundred-thousand-man army accomplished during World War Two in terms of training, organising, and developing tactical and operational leadership. This was largely the product of the Reichswehr's personnel selection process.'[51]

Chapter IV

The Great Paradox – the New Panzerwaffe, 1930–1938

'The Military must learn to follow the civilian authority blindly.'

So spoke Philip Scheidemann, Chancellor of Germany in 1919, in what must have seemed in retrospect one of the most prophetic pronouncements in German history – laying out as he did one of the principal foundations of Hitler's future relationship with the German armed forces.

By the close of 1928, Hermann Balck had been given command of his first mobile unit – the newly established bicycle battalion of the 3. Infanterie-Division based at Tilsit in East Prussia. A precursor to the new motorized divisions that would be created during the 1930s, Balck was committed to mobile warfare, which must have meant that he maintained a close correspondence with Heinz Guderian. This is borne out by later promotions that kept their careers in parallel,– although it was always to be Guderian who was remembered and Balck who would become largely forgotten.

It was in 1934 that Balck first met Adolf Hitler, the new chancellor and hopefully, for officers like Balck, the Messiah that the nation needed and the army wanted. Hitler was due to visit Frankfurt in the late summer of 1934 for a political meeting with local Nazi Party officials, but part of the trip was allocated to a review of the emerging 3. Panzer-Division which was quartered around the city. The wise and cultured divisional commander, Curt Haase, had a good rapport with Balck, so much so that he delegated organization of the entire programme for Hitler's visit to Balck.[52].

The 'Night of the Long Knives', where the entire leadership of the Sturmabteilung (SA) had been murdered on Hitler's orders, had occurred only weeks before in late June 1934. Hitler now wanted to tour key parts of Germany to oversee and install new party functionaries who were totally loyal to him. The speed and brutality of the purge showed the power that Hitler now wielded in the state, and this dictatorial element appealed to some parts of the army but alarmed and repulsed others. Balck seems to have been in the former camp. The window he opens very slightly in his writing gives the impression of Hitler as a man of action – ensuring complaints from the 3. Panzer-Division were dealt with within twenty-four hours – as well as someone immersed in detail, revealing a micro-manager by nature:

> 'Then he [Hitler] visited the newly constructed barracks, in which he was very interested, particularly the reinforced concrete roofs that provided protection from incendiary bombs. He had not known about this particular feature, and it was remarkable how quickly he grasped everything.'[53]

Hitler had arrived on his newly constructed special train, and Balck further relates how he shared a coffee with Hitler. When they met again, Hitler would recall this positive and happy meeting.

Das Fug, *Auftragstaktik* and the new *Truppenführung*

It is hard to underestimate the tactical changes that evolved during the early 1930s and fundamentally changed the Reichswehr. Most of the tactical changes in what we can refer to as the new German Army (or Wehrmacht) of the 1930s relied on what von Seecket, Guderian and others had hoped for in the 1920s – Hitler's takeover of power acting as a catalyst to allow these dreams to become reality, although there was also much alarm about Nazi ambitions and the power of the SA.[54]

While Balck was writing about fighting the Russians and their tactical approaches to warfare, and Guderian was declaring his new theories on mobile warfare and the use of mechanized forces, von Seeckt was publishing a brand-new manual for the Reichswehr in *H. Dv.487*, also called *Fuhrung und Gefecht der Verbundenen* (Command and Battle of the Combined Arms). Known as *Das Fug*, it was here that any aspiring general officer of the future began his understanding of how the new army would fight, and Balck would draw on one of the key precepts ('Section 15') for the rest of his military life:

> 'The first criterion in war remains decisive action. Everyone from the highest commander down to the youngest soldier, must be constantly aware that inaction and neglect incriminate him more severely than any error in the choice of means.'

For any future commander in the German Army of the 1930s, it would be decisive local action that marked out the best commanders in the field. While field marshals communicated their overall objective, it was now left to the local commander to act as he saw fit, so long as it was directed in the furtherance of the overall mission. However, this would take time to build, and even by the start of the Second World War, there were still senior army commanders who were apprehensive that armies could actually be led from the front. In a rare interview in 1979, Hermann Balck repeated a story that Guderian had related to him regarding a conversation he had with Generaloberst Werner von Fritsch, a member of the German High Command and Commander-in-Chief of the German Army from 1934–1938. An arch anti-democrat and antisemite, von Fritsch was as right wing and reactionary a German general officer as one could imagine. Guderian recalled that he was trying to explain the concept and organization of the new Panzerwaffe (Germany's armoured force) and how it fitted with the new doctrines of *Auftragstaktik* and modernized *Truppenführung*. The conversation went something like this:

> General von Fritsch: 'And how do you intend to control this division?'
> Guderian: 'From the front using radio.'
> General von Fritsch: 'Nonsense! The only way to command a division is from a desk at the rear, using a telephone.'[55]

The fifth man

One of the more penetrating questions put to Hermann Balck during his audio interview of 12 January 1979 was regarding what the most fertile grounds were for change and the introduction of Blitzkrieg within the German military. Balck answered thus:

> 'Prussia was a small country surrounded by superior forces. Therefore, we had to be more skilful and more swift than our enemies …
>
> 'With the mass armies it was thought to be no longer possible for a commander to lead from the front or from the point of action. Telephony had to be used to control the mass army, and therefore the commander had to attempt to influence the battle from a desk at the rear connected with his troops by telephone.
>
> 'The decisive breakthrough into modern military thinking came with Guderian, and it consisted not only of a breakthrough in armour weapons but also a breakthrough in the communications weapon.
>
> 'In any case, Guderian made two very important contributions in the area of panzer warfare communications. The first contribution was to add a fifth man [to each tank crew of four], a radio operator, and a radio in each tank in the tank division. This allowed both small and large tank units to be commanded and manoeuvred with a swiftness and flexibility that no other army was able to match.

'Guderian's second contribution was to give the Panzer division a signal organisation that allowed the division commander to command from any point in the division.'[56]

These new concepts liberated men like Hermann Balck and Heinz Guderian, men who believed that Germany should lead the field in what was now also referred to as *Auftragstaktik*, or 'mission command'. With the objective in mind and a timeframe within which to operate, the best commanders and all of their subordinates could now make fast decisions on the spot, using state-of-the-art close battlefield communications developed in the 1930s, without having to waste time waiting for higher authority to act and risk losing the initiative to the enemy. This marked the Wehrmacht out as the most modern fighting force in the world at that time.

By 1930, another future Wehrmacht general, Ludwig Beck, was creating an extension to these principles and studying formation command in battle.[57] It was Beck who collated the new military doctrines for the German land forces (the Heer) into his *On the German Art of War – Truppenführung* manual in 1933, which was adopted and then taught throughout officer schools across Germany. Beck was not an ardent Nazi, but he captured the mood of many fellow officers when he said: 'I have wished for years for the political revolution, and now my wishes have come true.'[58]

Although Beck would later be executed as a leading member of the July Bomb Plot in 1944, he was a talented and committed officer in the formation of the German fighting forces that both Guderian and Balck would later take into battle.

At the divisional level, with forces of around 8,000–15,000 men, all the necessary support was allocated – signals, medical, logistics, artillery, reconnaissance and so on. The division commander was at liberty to act and move independently of higher command, as he already had with him all the necessary support units. Right down the chain of command, reaching to the private soldier, *das Fug* and *Auftragstaktik* preached the necessity of positive action within the overall mission. This freedom of action, coupled with a self-sustaining force, created German infantry and later Panzer divisions able to move much faster, operate more unpredictably and seize upon opportunities far faster than all their counterparts.

The combination of *Truppenführung* and *Auftragstaktik* fed into the new guidance for the Heer in the 1930s and released a whole range of junior officers into careers within the new cavalry – or tank – arm. With their film star-like status, men such as 'Fast Heinz' Guderian, Erwin Rommel, Hans Hube, Leo Geyr von Schweppenburg, Walter Model, Gerhard von Schwerin, Heinrich

Eberbach, Sigfrid Henrici and Joachim Lemelsen learned their skills as mobile commanders influenced by these new ideas.

> 'On the question of tactics, the *Truppenführung* was a brilliant exposition of modern principles and drew sound lessons from Germany's terrible experience in the 1914–18 war. Initiative, decisive manoeuvre and envelopment were the keynotes of the German tactical doctrine. Its success in the war years was to prove immeasurably superior to the methods of its enemies.'[59]

The end of the Reichswehr and the creation of the Wehrmacht

Like the second coming of Christ, Hitler made a great deal of his self-sacrifice between 1914 and 1918, his Iron Cross and his time in prison – a sacrificial lamb for the future of Germany. The militaristic and uniformed nature of the Nazi movement chimed well with the Reichswehr, with its emphasis on good order and self-discipline. The Nazis would play on these ideals as they merged National Socialism into militarism.

Between 1931 and 1932, the Reichswehr played a key role in helping to create conditions where Adolf Hitler and his SA and Nazi Party were able to depend on the support of the German Army. By the time that Hitler had finally achieved his goal of becoming Chancellor of Germany, it was clear that the support of the Reichswehr would be compensated by a grateful Führer. Between 1933 and 1936, Guderian worked feverishly in planning the expansion of the mechanization of the German Army. Working for General Oswald Lutz and his staff in the Motorization Department, Guderian was as active as he could be in promoting a change of gear throughout all sections of the army and industrial centres of production.

Renaming the Reichswehr as the Wehrmacht to encompass all three services, Hitler sponsored a new shipbuilding programme, developments in the air force and of course the expansion of Germany's ground forces. Hermann Balck was intrinsically linked to these developments, as evidenced by his promotion to major in 1936. However, it was clear from a very early stage that aspirations regarding production could not be matched by reality. It would take time to persuade German industry to stop making unnecessary items and instead to focus on war production, and it would take even longer for them to abandon precision manufacture in preference for mass production of basic models.

It was Generaloberst Friedrich Fromm of the Army General Office who perhaps best captured the problem in a memorandum of 1 August 1936. Hitler's political ambitions and hubris had accentuated the problems that the departments

The Great Paradox – the New Panzerwaffe, 1930–1938   37

in both the OKH (Army High Command) and OKW (Armed Forces High Command) could plainly see ahead. Every few months, a new calculation was announced regarding exactly how many infantry and tank divisions would be needed to move from a defensive posture to an offensive one. The numbers always climbed, as did the realization that the German economy and industrial production would always be behind the curve. It would remain that way until the arrival of Albert Speer as Minister for Armament and War Production in February 1942. Fromm spoke for many in August 1936 when he wrote that it:

'would lead to serious difficulties ... in the areas of tanks and munitions deliveries, fulfilling truck requirements, and ... with regard to raw materials, machines and skilled workers.'[60]

In response to these shortfalls, Hitler positioned Luftwaffe chief Hermann Göring to lead his 'Four Year Plan', which was launched in 1936 to ensure that the German Army and the economy were ready for war by 1940. When war actually broke out in 1939, this Four-Year Plan would need to be an eight-year one and was well behind schedule, so equipment would need to be pilfered from the armaments industry in Czechoslovakia and many divisions went to war with a bare minimum of supplies and logistical support. Furthermore, the total number of divisions ready for war in 1939 was woefully below target.

Guderian must have exerted considerable influence in order to keep Balck at a desk job in the ministry. Balck, along with Lutz, played a leading role in the creation of the Panzerwaffe. Not everything ran smoothly, but Guderian was definitely encouraged by the support of Lutz, who had always seen the potential for armoured warfare. It would be Lutz who appointed Guderian as his chief of staff in the Inspectorate of Motorized Troops. He never gave up in his determination to create a series of new Panzer divisions and to employ all the lessons of 1914–1918, such as speed, self-supporting units, different types of tanks for different tasks, supply, transportation and tank-to-tank communications on the battlefield. According to Russell Hart, Guderian and Lutz had a symbiotic relationship, both men working tirelessly in their shared objective of creating an independent and self-sustaining Panzer force.

But there was intransigent opposition to overcome, including within the OKW, where, for example, General Otto von Stülpnagel – later a key subordinate of Rommel in France in 1944 and who was one of the earlier holders of the office of Inspector of Motorized Troops – rejected the notion of an independent Panzer command. Balck refers in his memoirs to his immediate superior, Colonel von Schell, being specifically tasked by the General Staff to 'constrain Guderian'.[62] No doubt these internal rivalries held back the development of many improvements in the Wehrmacht, as personal views, history, career experience and personalities clashed while the Panzer arm grew in size.

When the first three Panzer divisions were created in 1935 – 1. Panzer based in Weimar, 2. Panzer in Würzburg and 3. Panzer in Berlin – Guderian was given command of the 2. Panzer-Division, leaving the ageing Lutz and his new chief of staff, Friedrich Paulus, who was a less than vigorous officer. Sensing the decline in the abilities of Lutz, Hitler retired him and it was to Hermann Balck that Guderian turned in 1938 to give his precious role of Inspector of Motorized Troops in what was now called the Panzerwaffe. Promoted to Oberstleutnant, Balck had to reinvigorate the impetus behind the Panzerwaffe. Worthy of note at this point is Guderian's assessment of Paulus. He described him as a brilliant and skilful officer, but doubted his decisiveness and toughness as a battlefield commander. Years later, it would be Paulus whom Hitler would appoint to lead the assault in Stalingrad, with the disastrous consequences that befell 6. Armee. But as Balck would later state, Guderian had his faults too:

> 'As an aside, Guderian was constantly involved in battles with everybody else. He was very hard to get along with, and it's a tribute to the German Army, as well as to Guderian's own remarkable abilities, that he was able to rise as high as he did within the German Army.'[63]

Guderian was confrontational primarily because he wanted things done well and at speed. Balck tells us very little about his own personal relationship with the father of the Panzerwaffe, but from the roles and promotions conferred on him, it can be safely inferred that Balck and Guderian shared a similar vision.

The most flagrant disregard so far for the Versailles Treaty came in March 1935, when Hitler issued the *Gesetz für den Aufbau der Wehrmacht*, the 'Edict for the Buildup of the Wehrmacht'. Paradoxically, the new 'Wehrmacht' title for the combined German armed forces, coined from 21 May 1935, was etymologically derived from the German words *wehren* ('to defend') and *Macht* (with 'power or force'). The inference from Hitler's propaganda point of view was that the combined armed forces of the Heer, Kriegsmarine and Luftwaffe, were designed to defend German interests. Hitler initially proclaimed that, via a mixture of volunteers and conscription, the Heer would be composed of thirty-six divisions and a further forty-eight tank battalions; this was prior to the concept of entirely self-supporting Panzer divisions. Once he was in post, Balck played a key role in the creation of two more Panzer divisions – the 4. and 5. – as part of this build-up of 'defensive' forces. Impressively, both these additional armoured divisions were also combat-ready when Germany went to war in September 1939.

The new Panzer divisions

No doubt Hermann Balck harboured a desire to return one day to front-line command with one of the Panzer divisions that he had helped to create. This day would eventually arrive, but in the meantime, 1938–1939 was a frantically busy period that witnessed the build-up of the logistical support required for the new formations.

In parallel with creating the new tank formations, Balck and Guderian had to indoctrinate the new ideas which lay behind them. The key principle was that tank formations were no longer there to support operations by other arms, as in the First World War, but would now lead the way, with all other arms acting in support of them. This did not initially sit well with the traditionalist infantry and artillery officers, but Guderian, with Hitler's support, managed to push ahead with this change. As importantly, they needed tanks and trained crews, and everything was being done at great speed, the tempo being set by Hitler's political designs, especially regarding Czechoslovakia.

The original Panzer divisions (the 1.–5.) were new 'combined arms' units composed of two tank regiments, one motorized infantry regiment of two battalions and the organic supporting arms of artillery, anti-tank, signals and associated logistics. They were a miniature mobile army. The motorized infantry were able to follow the tanks at speed, either in new armoured vehicles or troop lorries. They should not be confused with the new Panzergrenadier divisions, dedicated armoured infantry formations that had tanks, but a far smaller number than a Panzer division, and a higher proportion of infantry, assault guns and troop vehicles.

This is how the first five Panzerwaffe divisions entered the war against Poland in September 1939. Neither the Anschluss with Austria or the occupation of the Rhineland had required the Panzer arm to fight, so they were still largely untested. Their capabilities were indeed tested in Poland, and Balck and Guderian worked on an adjusted structure for the next five Panzer divisions (6. through to 10.). These were adjusted to one tank regiment instead of two – which dealt with the supply problem of not having enough tanks – and doubling the motorised infantry to two regiments. Tank supply would be a key until 1943, but nevertheless there would be twenty-one Panzer divisions available by the time Operation Barbarossa began in June 1941. To this number could be added the impressive new Waffen-SS Panzer divisions which were available from the summer of 1943 and the single elite Fallschirm-Panzer-Division 'Hermann Göring'.

The first tank designs had been approved as far back as 1934 with the Panzer I and Panzer II. Both these tanks were very lightly armed and designed mostly for training purposes until the main battle tanks, the Panzer III and IV, were into production – this would not start until 1938.[64] German arms manufacturers had to start from scratch. Versailles had robbed German industry of the need for factories to create tanks or any other heavy weapons, and there would be a time lag between the recruitment and training of the many new divisions formed under Hitler's rearmament policies and the arrival of heavy weapons.

The small three-man Panzer Mk I looked impressive at rallies and on parades through the cities of Germany, row upon row of them rolling by in perfect formation. However, with only thin armour and armed with just two machine guns, they were significantly weaker than most tank designs of the other European powers. But it was these tanks that were supplied, along with early-model armoured cars and trucks, to the five new Panzer divisions.

It was slow going for the Nazi Party to exert its control over private industry and there was no movement towards full war production until well into the Second World War. In his memoirs, Balck refers to these challenges:

> 'Listening to a presentation by Colonel von Schell [Balck's immediate superior], it became clear to me that our tank production was completely fragmented and without any significant output. We had built a tank army, without establishing the necessary tank production lines. Our tank force was hollow.'[65]

German industry also adopted a craftsman approach, where tanks were technically superior to those of their adversaries but consequently took far longer to build and their lists of spares and support required was formidable. They were thus also far more expensive. It would not be until 1942–1943 that Albert Speer was able to redress some of these major structural problems, by which time the war at the strategic level had already been lost. The Panzer III and IV became the main battle tanks of the armoured divisions, but these were only available in large numbers well into the war. For example, there were only 157 Panzer Mk IIIs manufactured in 1939, compared to 3,379 in 1943. The same was true for the Mk IV, with only forty-five available in 1939 compare to 3,822 in 1943 and 6,625 in 1944.[66] Consequently, we must think of the first five Panzer divisions to be fast, with the new mission-led tactics of *Auftragstaktik*, but lightly equipped and somewhat experimental in nature when Germany invaded Poland in 1939, and indeed France and the Low Countries in 1940. They were also composed of a mixture of tanks to create the establishment numbers required on paper. Balck worked well with the Army General Office, led at that time by Generaloberst Fromm, whom he described as 'a generous and clear organiser'.[67]

The smash and grab nature of the early Panzer divisions

By the time the plans for Fall Gelb – 'Case Yellow', the codename for the invasion of France – were ready, the Panzerwaffe had doubled in size to ten divisions. Structurally, it had developed enormously from that of only seven months previously during the invasion of Poland.

In the plans for Fall Weiss – 'Case White', the attack on Poland in September 1939 – it was the speed of breakthrough by the tanks, combined with close air support and supporting artillery, followed by envelopment in the rear of Polish units, that was the essence of the strategy. This all matched with Guderian's Blitzkrieg and Panzerwaffe tactics and would be carried through using the mission command approach to allow free movement and speed on the battlefields. Thus, during the invasion of Poland, one of the key roles for Balck and his Inspectorate Number 6 (In 6) – the Inspectorate of Mobile Troops – was to monitor how units such as the 3. Leichte-Division (Light Division) performed, how effectively they moved and how the supply problems of fuel and repairs could be dealt with.

The 3. Leichte-Division is a good example of the botched-together nature of the early divisions. It became one of the first five Panzer divisions but was still composed of many horses, and what tanks it was provided with were the distinctive Czech Panzer 38 (T). With the annexation of Czechoslovakia in 1938, Hitler was able to take over the Skoda and CKD factories, a tremendously valuable resource to add to Germany's tank and vehicle programmes. Part of what came to the Germans were ten brand new Mk 38 Czech tanks, and within months this had been expanded to thirty on the Czech production lines, allocated to what was now called the 3. (T) Panzer-Division by Balck's department in January 1939. The 'T' stood for *Tschechische* – or Czechoslovak – and these tanks were referred to as the Panzer Mk III (T). During the Polish campaign, the 3. Leichte-Division fought against the Poles in the south under von Rundstedt and pressed on towards Warsaw. Although lightly armoured, the Mk 38 (T) performed well enough against Polish anti-tank weapons, and some were still in service right up until the end of the war. Balck later wrote: 'After the conclusion of the [Polish] campaign, I was sent to inspect the lesser quality Panzer divisions, to accelerate their reconstitution.'[68]

Balck confessed in his memoirs that Germany should have started mass tank production far earlier in the 1930s, but the lack of steel, the privatization of production and the endless arguments between Guderian and those resistant to the new tactics all combined to allow Hitler to put the cart before the horse.

The month after Poland surrendered, Balck was finally posted to a front-line unit, taking command of Infanterie-Regiment (mot) 1 (1st Motorized Infantry Regiment) of the 1. Panzer-Division, which came under the command of Guderian, now a corps commander.

Part II

Fighting for Hitler, 1939–1941

Chapter V

The Battle for France and Sedan, May–June 1940

'On s'engage partout et en voit'
('One jumps into the fray, then figures out what to do next')
(Napoleon Bonaparte)

By the time the French campaign opened in May 1940, the 3. Lichte-Division had been broken up to help form the 7. and 8. Panzer-Divisions. There were now a larger number of Mk 38 (T) tanks available from the Skoda plants, with ninety-one given to the 7. Panzer-Division and 116 to the 8. Panzer-Division. Hermann Balck would have been instrumental in starting this process of reconstructing the Panzerwaffe before he left the Ministry of Mobile Troops in Berlin, which had recently been formed under the Department of Army Motorization, but as Erich von Manstein reiterated in his memoirs, this process was far from complete prior to the spring of 1940:

> 'The other reason [for delaying the attack on France in the winter of 1939–1940] was the still inadequate standard of training of all the new formations set up on the outbreak of war. The only troops really fit to go into action in autumn 1939 were the active divisions. None of the others had had enough experience of handling weapons or of operating as integral parts of a larger formation: nor did they as yet possess the requisite degree of inner stability.'[69]

Von Manstein's closing comments are a reminder that numbers of men and divisions were one thing, but that unit cohesion and *esprit de corps* only came with time spent training and fighting together. Balck had done what he could to accelerate expansion, but creating a welded unit took time, and time was not on Hitler's side.

For Oberstleutnant Hermann Balck, military life now took on a whole new perspective. Not only was he back on active duty, but he was also preparing to invade France once more. Balck is clear in his memoirs that the original notion of a winter attack on France in 1939–1940 was out of the question, with Hitler having to be restrained by his closest advisors. The seeds of mistrust between Hitler and the German General Staff had been sown years before, the natural conservatism of the senior generals not sitting well with an impetuous dictator with a world view. One by-product of the unexpected success over Poland was that it created the myth of invincibility amongst sections of the army and German society. Many of course hated Hitler, hundreds of thousands were already languishing in concentration and labour camps, and prophecies of doom were abundant from those prepared to defy the regime or who had been lucky enough to escape overseas. For the German Army, however, the fact was that they had been successful and there was no such luxury of complaint. Balck is an example of a senior officer, about to become one of the key figures in the Heer, for whom loyalty came at the cost of logic.

Describing his first combat command since 1918 as 'the most modern regiment in the army', Balck also admitted that it was he who had outfitted the Infanterie-Regiment (mot) 2 of the 1. Panzer-Division with 'the most modern equipment', which suggests that Guderian had earmarked this unit for one of his most able officers. Composed of three fully mobile motorized battalions, Balck was able to train and mould his new command for his style of warfare between October 1939 and May 1940.

Early attempts at managing Hitler

General (later Generalfeldmarschall) Erich von Manstein, like Hermann Balck, had risen through the ranks of the Reichswehr, and at the age of 53 (to Balck's 47) was now chief of staff to Generaloberst Gerd von Rundstedt, commander of Heeresgruppe A.[70] From this position, he was able to keep himself appraised of OKH plans for Fall Gelb, the invasion of France.

Similar to Balck and any other former Imperial German Army officer who had served in 1914 as part of the attack on Belgium and the Schlieffen Plan, von Manstein was filled with horror by the thought of a straight-forward repetition of the strong right hook through Belgium to overwhelm the French, Belgians, Dutch and British. To the talented and intelligent von Manstein – whose original surname was von Lewinski – the initial plans formulated by the Commander-in-Chief of the Army, Generaloberst Walther von Brauchitsch, were unimaginative and risked becoming blunted and stagnating, just as in 1914. Crucially, Hitler was not happy either, and the discussions, as far as they went, between Hitler and the Army High Command were difficult and tense. The surprisingly easy victory over Poland had perhaps confirmed in Hitler's mind that it was his instincts that mattered most in high-level military matters, rather than any logic that the OKH and von Brauchitsch may try to apply. The problems that flowed in conversations over when or whether to attack France laid out much of the future relationship between Hitler and his army commanders.

There were many issues to be worked through, but three key ones stood out. Firstly, the OKH was having to accept Hitler as supreme commander, but was still finding that concept difficult. Secondly, Hitler was well aware that, after the invasion of Poland, he was effectively at war both on the Western Front and in the East; it was only a matter of time before matters with Russia came to a head. Finally, the acceleration of the Nazi rearmament programme was still in its infancy, giving Germany a narrow window in which to act before Britain and its allies began to catch up.

During October and November 1939, von Manstein and Guderian worked on an alternative scheme, which called for the Schlieffen Plan right-wing movement in the north to be a faint to lure the Allies advancing their forces into Belgium, just as they had in 1914. To the south, in Alsace, another advance would be made to confuse the French manning the Maginot Line and tie down their concentrated forces there. Meanwhile, the main thrust would come in the centre, through the apparently impenetrable Ardennes, cross the River Meuse and smash the defences at Sedan, driving due west and then north to the English Channel, cutting off any British, French and Belgian forces then in Belgium. It was a brilliant and daring plan, but, although Balck does not mention this in his memoirs, von Manstein's plan was opposed – especially by von Brauchitsch and General Franz Halder, the OKH chief of staff – and the net result of von Manstein's efforts was to see him removed by Halder and sent to cool his heels in Stettin, northern Poland, commanding the yet-to-form XXXVIII. Korps.[71] However, Hitler's acute sense of strategy, both political and military, played on his mind and he asked for a secret meeting to be held with von Manstein and five other newly appointed corps commanders, one of whom was Erwin Rommel. At this breakfast get-together on 17 February 1940, the Führer asked von Manstein to once more explain his Unternehmen Sichelschnitt ('Operation Sickle Cut'). The premise of concentrated forces of armour aimed at the *Schwerpunkt* (centre of gravity), where defensive lines could be pivoted and breached, followed by intensive drives inland to the coast, saw the majority of what became known as the 'Manstein Plan' adopted. Von Manstein pointed out with some irony how the OKW and OKH vied to claim the revised operational plan was their own.[72].

For Hermann Balck, this meant that he and his unit were relocated southwards from the Dutch border and now faced southern Belgium and Luxembourg to become part of the very powerful Panzergruppe Kleist in Heeresgruppe A, commanded by von Rundstedt. Panzergruppe Kleist was composed of XIX. Panzerkorps under Guderian (1., 2. and 10. Panzer-Divisions) and XLI. Panzerkorps under Generalleutnant Georg-Hans Reinhardt (6. and 8. Panzer-

Divisions). Von Manstein was uncertain how and why Hitler had decided to aim for a crossing at Sedan as he had advised him, but it was possible that he had investigated the terrain on his many maps and agreed with von Manstein's appreciation that a decisive breakthrough could be made here:

> 'It is also possible that Hitler reached the decision on his own. He had a keen eye for tactical openings and spent much time brooding over maps. He may have realised that the easiest place to cross the Meuse was at Sedan.'[73]

At this stage of his career, Balck knew very little, other than hints dropped in personal conversations, about the challenges of working with Hitler at the highest levels. Thanks to the evidence that came out at the Nuremburg trials and other memoirs, such as those of General Walter Warlimont – Deputy Chief of Operations at the OKW between 1939 and 1944 – we can see the power struggle that broke out between a fanatical, determined and instinctive Führer and the largely Prussian career professionals of the Heer:

> 'Hitler's complete lack of balance is well illustrated by Jodl's diary of the next few days [this was in the early stages of the attack on France in May 1940]; he was determined to retain the power he had abrogated to himself but, having no depth of knowledge or experience, his moods and emotions swayed from one extreme to the other and the diary registers them like a thermometer.'[74]

Gaulier, Sedan and the River Meuse

Guderian's XIX. Panzerkorps had a pivotal role as part of Panzergruppe Kleist, commanded by General der Kavallerie Ewald von Kleist. In the centre of the German lines facing west, Guderian, the man who had revolutionized the German Army's approach to warfare – based on modern tactics, communications and timetables – now had the opportunity to show that it could work. Just prior to the opening of the campaign, Guderian and von Kleist vehemently disagreed as to where the *Schwerpunkt* should fall, Guderian having to fight hard to get von Kleist to agree that this should be Sedan.

There was another, often forgotten, aspect which also now aided Hitler and his attacking forces: intelligence gathering. The German High Command was fortunate to have an outstanding military intelligence analyst and officer in Oberstleutnant Ulrich Liss. It was Liss and his small department, Fremde Heere West ('Foreign Armies West'), that assessed every aspect of the French capability and predicted their responses during war games in 1939. Such was the success of Liss and his team that leading international relations historian Dr Ernest R. May has commented: 'As far as I know, no intelligence analyst has ever, in all of human history, had comparable influence on a great event.'[75]

It was from the intense and detailed work of Liss that the Germans were briefed that the French Army would be slow to react, dogged by obsolescent bureaucratic processes in communication and unable to respond to the cuts in their defensive lines, coupled with forward thrusts that would disorientate their headquarters staff. Nevertheless, to make the maximum use of Liss' findings, the Wehrmacht needed quick-thinking and decisive field commanders such as Rommel, Guderian and Hermann Balck.

As part of 1. Panzer-Division in his XIX Panzerkorps, Guderian needed speed and power concentrated in the right hands. Balck crossed the border into Luxembourg during the early morning of 10 May 1940, leading the advanced force of Kradschützen-Bataillon 1 (1st Motorcycle Battalion) and the 3. Bataillon of his own Infanterie-Regiment (mot) 1, together with other detachments. He describes how the speed of the advance was aided by close air support provided by Stuka dive-bomber aircraft. German artillery units were often unable to keep up with the tanks' advances, so the Stukas of Luftflotte (Air Fleet) 3 took their place. The Stukas' devastating accuracy clearing French artillery so quickly that Balck was able to maintain the speed of the advance ahead of schedule, with little time to rest for the first three days of the advance. The near-perfect communication links between the Panzerwaffe and the Sturzkampfgeschwader (Close Support Air Corps) was remarkable. Following the precepts of *Auftragstaktik*, Balck was at the front of his columns and in direct contact with French opposition, and he was proving himself to be a decisive, popular and effective Panzer commander.

Having trained and prepared perfectly, and with accurate intelligence on the defences facing them, Guderian and Balck agreed that Balck should lead his men across the Meuse near Gaulier on 13 May, using rubber dinghies that his men had been trained to use. After a concentrated series of 'rolling raids' by II Fliegerkorps, they would continue to force the rate of advance to the point of exhaustion and the destruction of the French 55th and 71st Infantry Divisions.[76] On either flank, the 2. and 10. Panzer-Divisions did the same, as did elements of the small but elite Infanterie-Regiment 'Grossdeustchland'. The advance was rapid – partly due to surprise, devastating close air support and a commitment to speed, but also the inspirational leadership of dashing and cavalier commanders such as Balck and Rommel. Balck displayed his bravery as a calculated risk as part of the matrix of what was needed to win in battle. His enduring faith in and praise for the ordinary German soldier was predicated by his belief that he would fight better if led by his officer.

At times the advance was threatened, for example when, having left their Panzers behind, Balck's troops came under a counter-attack from a large French tank force. Had it not been for a nearby anti-tank unit of the 'Grossdeustchland', they could have been overwhelmed before their own Panzers caught up.[77] Once across the Meuse, Balck displayed an inherent characteristic of his military personality – being prepared to ignore orders. Instead of consolidating and widening the bridgehead near Sedan, as he had been ordered, Balck forced his men to continue their advance:

> 'At Sedan, my combat leaders told me that they were finished – that they just simply couldn't advance anymore, and I said "Fine. Whoever wants to stay here can stay here. I'm leading the attack on the next village," and of course, the entire regiment sprang up as one man to follow me.'

With the help of highly trained combat engineers who had caught up with the advance, under the command of Leutnant Günther Korthals of the 43. Sturm-Pionier-Bataillon (43rd Assault Engineer Battalion), Balck and his men were able to force passages through the lines of French bunkers. The defenders were left in total shock by the size, speed and ferocity of the German attack. By the morning of 14 May, Balck and his dirty, exhausted but still advancing troops had travelled through the dense Ardennes forest, crossed the Meuse under heavy fire, bypassed Sedan, fought their way out of a tiny bridgehead and were now in the rear of the bunkers. But instead of pausing their advance to clear his rear areas, Balck continued to drive his men on into open country, through Donchery and on to Bouvellmont.

In his biography of Balck, Stephen Robinson expands on just how totemic the appearance of Hermann Balck was to maintaining the advance of his men by using an extract from Balck's then adjutant, Leutnant Andreas Braune-Krickau:

> 'Lieutenant Colonel Balck, accustomed to satisfying himself personally about any situation, hurried forward. Suddenly he appeared right at the entrance to the village and in the middle of the front line. Inspired by the presence of their commanding officer, the companies renewed the attack.'[78]

It was this very success by mobile infantry, however, that also exposed the weakness in Guderian's tactics. While wedded to the notion of concentrated armour in a Panzer division format, Guderian had recognized very quickly that fast-advancing infantry would often be without close tank support. Indeed, the Panzers did not cross the Meuse until 14 May. They arrived to force through the gains made by the infantry, but it was hard and bloody fighting, and the idea of the Kampfgruppe then became a reality. In the post-Sedan phase, Balck would become one of the first Heer commanders to lead this new formation, composed of one armoured regiment and all the other arms required for a miniature mobile armoured division. According to Balck's future talented chief of staff, Generalmajor F.W. von Mellenthin, it was to Hermann Balck's credit that this new unit became a standard throughout the Heer:

> 'From Sedan onwards armour and infantry were used in mixed battle groups. These Kampfgruppen embodied a principle as old as war itself – the concentration of all arms at the same time in the same area.'[79]

It was at the storming of Bouvellemont on 16 May that Guderian caught up with Balck, congratulating his key Panzer commander on the speed of his advances. It would be Guderian who ensured that Balck was awarded the Knight's Cross of the Iron Cross on 3 June 1940. In October, the OKH distributed thousands of badges to the invasion troops, and Balck also received the Panzer Combat Badge in Silver on 14 October, alongside clasps to both his Iron Cross 2nd Class and 1st Class.

Tired, dirty from the summer dust, with petrol fumes leaching from his dusty tunic and the smoke of battle woven into his shirt, Hermann Balck spurred his men forward, on to the Oise River, which they crossed on 18 May. His Panzergrenadiers could at last stop to rest, their job now almost done. Next, they had to turn northwards and try to reach the sea as quickly as possible, holding their flanks all the way. As other units such as the 2. Panzer-Division and Rommel's 3. Panzer-Division pressed on into the open country of central France, Balck was able to rest and refit his regiment.

With the race to the coast underway, we can take stock of the role that Balck had so far played in the campaign. What we can judge about his character, and where does he sit in the pantheon of German generalship? Perhaps the most important facet of all was his physical and emotional capacity to fight. Not all senior commanders either wanted to or could face being at the spearhead of the front line, and certainly not all the time. Stamina and the ability to stand up to emotional stress are essential prerequisites for any combat commander. Balck's small but strong frame was ideally suited to an active lifestyle. He kept fit by training with his men and was a keen athlete. All of this plays into what he was able to achieve. Often, a promising career could come to a surprise halt because of illness or the inability to cope. Evidence of physical or emotional collapse is rare, but was in fact commonplace. For instance, Balck's immediate superior, Colonel Johannes Netwig, collapsed with physical and mental exhaustion in early May 1941, and on 13 May Balck was asked to take temporary command of the 1. Panzer-Brigade.[80]

Balck was always full of praise for his motorcycle troops. Asked how important he felt they were, he responded:

> 'The motorcycles were very valuable as a pure means of rapid movement and, as a result, motorcycle units were often far out in the front of the tanks ... in order to grab a bridge before it could be blown up. This happened time after time in the advance through France.'[81]

It was not just the mobility and firepower of the BMW-designed and built motorcycles and side cars that characterized the opening of a new phase in modern warfare, but the use of massed tanks concentrated in tight formations, able to communicate with each other as they outmanoeuvred the often faster and better-armed French tank forces.

> 'The fact that makes the German victory almost inconceivable to this day is that the Allied tank force outnumbered the Germans and in many ways was superior .... Guderian felt that his greatest enemy at this time was not the Allies but the German General Staff which, even in 1940, had doubts about the ability of Panzer divisions to conduct long-range operations.'[82]

The reality was that once Hitler launched his wars, mass production techniques amongst his enemies – both in the East and the West – would always leave the Panzerwaffe in the minority. To his credit, Hitler also saw the sense in a combined arms unit of brigade level size. According to Robinson, the Führer allowed this to feed into the further expansion of the Panzerwaffe to twenty-one divisions. However, by the time of the invasion of Russia in the summer of 1941, each division had been reduced from 300 to around 150 tanks in its Panzer regiments. Their better-quality new Mk III and IV tanks, plus their able and determined commanders, meant that that the fighting quality of each division was not significantly tested by this reduction. Indeed, the greater number of condensed and faster mobile units on the battlefield gave the Germans a distinct advantage. However, the German Army could only last so long with smaller overall numbers, so Hitler was spurred on to maintain the pace of the war in order to end it before Germany ran out of either raw materials or quality men. This inevitably meant a war with Russia had to be fought earlier rather than later. But before then, other countries would fall to the Panzerwaffe, and Hermann Balck would continue to see his star rise in the eyes of the Führer.

Chapter VI

Greece and The Balkans, October 1940–April 1941

The successful Polish and French campaigns, taking almost a year to complete, confirmed in Hitler's mind that time was against him, and that the war, if it was to be won, had to be completed quickly with the crushing of Russia. The Treaty of Versailles had now been avenged and Hitler stood as the Messiah that much of Germany had hoped for, but he was also an old man in a hurry. Even with these two incredible victories in his hands and a reputation as a successful wartime leader, Hitler knew that most of his generals were sceptical that such fortune could last. At the OKW, its chief, Generaloberst Wilhelm Keitel, responded to the numerous doubters in the General Staff by stating: 'The Führer himself has recognised that we cannot last out a war of long duration. The war must be finished rapidly.'[83]

Additionally, many senior officers were aware – more than Hitler was willing to accept – that the campaigns against Poland and France had crippled what minimal reserve stockpiles of war materiel had been built up since 1935. With German industry unable to contemplate mass production techniques for fear of destabilizing the monopolies of the great German engineering companies, the long-term defeat of Germany was already a reality. Historian Stephen Fritz has suggested:

> 'In truth, the Polish campaign had largely exhausted the German Army. Critical ammunition shortages loomed, while the panzer forces urgently needed repair and replacement vehicles.'[84]

With frantic efforts at restocking the infantry and panzer divisions underway, Hermann Balck was promoted to colonel on 14 August 1940. Still in command of his beloved Infanterie-Regiment (mot) 1, as he and his men rested, repaired and refitted in what was a glorious summer, and while the Luftwaffe and Royal Air Force battled for dominance in the skies above southern England and the Channel, Hitler was deep in meetings regarding the future strategy of the war.

It is this period that undermines attempts at credible claims that the Wehrmacht was in any way non-political. Try as they might to distance themselves from blame for later events and to shift responsibility to Hitler and his Nazi cronies, the fact is that the high command of all three armed services were well aware of the sensitive interplay between political and economic necessity, military capability and war aims. Hitler, who had a genius for sensing the state of the geopolitical weather map, spent many meetings trying to educate, or if necessary evangelize, bully or hypnotize his politically naïve generals and field marshals to see that not only was war in the East inevitable, but also that time was not on Germany's side. The fact that Unternehmen Seelöwe (Operation Sealion) – the amphibious and airborne invasion of the United Kingdom – was merely a ruse to throw attention away from the planning which was already well advanced for the invasion of Russia, demonstrates quite clearly that the Wehrmacht, and specifically the Heer, were well aware of what Hitler had decided.

The myth of the 'Clean Wehrmacht' begins

Two significant insights into the character development of Hermann Balck come at the end of his chapter on the fall of France, where he illuminates his feelings and actions in detail in two areas. The first relates to a disciplinary matter, where what seems like an example of high-spirited behaviour coupled with alcohol led a junior clerk to celebrate wearing the uniform of a deceased French admiral around the bars of a French town. His playing of the accordion, plus his newly acquired uniform, no doubt caused great hilarity amongst the weary but jubilant troops. But not to Oberst Balck. Discipline is essential, but so is camaraderie, and *Truppenführung* – if it was not just to be window dressing – preached the notion of understanding the men under one's command, and indeed leading them. However, in a display of strict Prussian reality, Balck had the man apprehended and 'beaten' – perhaps some part is lost in translation, but Balck commented that: 'the beating he received was one of the best things I have done in my life'.[85]

Hitherto, the elegance of Balck's language, rhetoric and appreciation of culture and learning reflects very positively to create the impression of the articulate and civilized officer; the very sort of officer that the *faux* display of gentlemanly honour and virtue idolized as part of the mythical image that the Prussian elite superimposed upon their caste. Yet not very far under the surface was also a ruthless and unemotional response to acts that offended this unwritten code of honour. It was only in response to the tearful pleas of the deceased French admiral's sister that Balck 'got very mad' and ordered the sustained beating of one of his men, thereby revealing another brutal side of his character.

The second window that Hermann Balck allows himself to open, with a certain air of pride, concerns his reaction to the opening of the partisan campaign after the surrender of France:

> 'When we left France, the relations with the population were good. There was no talk about resistance and partisan warfare. How did that situation change? A small group of Frenchmen, a handful of people, thought that the good relations were detrimental to the honour of France, and they wanted to do something about it. They decided to do something that would force the Germans to react, and consequently make their own people take a stand for or against. A harmless German soldier was thrown in front of a train in Paris. As expected, retaliatory measures were taken and the vicious cycle of partisan warfare started.'[86]

This paragraph was described as 'naïve and simplistic' by Major General David Zabecki, the editor and translator of Balck's memoirs. However, it is possible, perhaps even essential, to call this view out for what it tells us not only about Balck as a German commander, and what motivated him, but also to see it as representative of views more widely held.[87] It is difficult to know quite where to begin to deconstruct the statement on why 'a handful of people' thought it was right to throw out an invading army. No German soldier was 'harmless', and by killing one soldier, the French resistance knew full well that there would be retaliation – but that is war, and this was a war begun by Germany. The suggestion that the French people should just acquiesce under the Nazi jackboot was a misguided assertion. In *Panzer Battles*, first published in 1958, von Mellenthin refers more honestly to the true causes of growing French resistance:

> 'It is a matter of regret that Gestapo officers and party officials soon raised a barrier between the occupation troops and the civil population; their complete lack of consideration and ruthless conduct alienated many potential friends [and swelled the ranks of the resistance].'[88]

Taking Nazism to the Balkans and Greece – the home of democracy

With Oberst Hermann Balck's appointment to command Panzer-Regiment 3 of the 2. Panzer-Division in December 1940, his future as a front-line tank commander was assured, as was a clear route to becoming a general. Together with Panzer-Regiment 4, these two units formed the Panzerwaffe element of the 2. Panzer-Division, which, although only formed in 1935 as one of the first five armoured divisions, was already full of experienced troops who had fought in both Poland and France.

By the middle of winter 1940, plans for the wider escalation of the war were well advanced. The elite 2. Panzer-Division, which was garrisoned in Mödling in Austria, was able to repair, rest and train for the operations it would fight in 1941.

As Balck familiarized himself with his new unit and began working with subordinate commanders such as his regimental adjutant, Leutnant Ramsch, events on the geopolitical level were developing fast. (Ramsch would later return to Panzer-Regiment 3 as its commander.)[89] Among the many things that Hitler's actions in 1939 and 1940 had set in motion were the imperial ambitions of Benito Mussolini in Italy, and it was to be Il Duce's decisions in the autumn of 1940 that significantly impacted on Hitler's strategy concerning Russia.

Not wanting to be outdone by Germany, Mussolini calculated that he could get away with an invasion of Albania and his forces attacked in April 1939, a campaign that was still being fought when Hitler invaded Poland. This move was of concern to Hitler as it began to affect his strategy in the Balkans. With his eyes firmly fixed on an attack on Russia in the spring of 1941, Hitler needed to ensure that the huge oil fields that spread across Slovakia, Hungary and Romania were at the very least secure from Russian attack, and at best in German hands. Furthermore, Britain's encouragement to these states to fight back was a real concern – ergo, the support of Mussolini did not come without its own problems.

For Balck and his Panzer regiment, opportunities to refine the all-arms drills of *Aufragstaktik* were essential. Balck could see that the further development of the self-contained Panzer division should extend to breaking down the formation into smaller, self-contained elements – the Kampfgruppe (KG). This 'fighting group' made the Panzer division even more mobile. These sub-units were able to move faster than a whole division, and given that they would also contain tanks, infantry and supporting artillery – anti-tank and flak – they could stand and fight alone whilst reporting to their divisional headquarters. These formations, which could vary from company to brigade in size, were named after their commander. Some very famous Kampfgruppen would make history during the Second World War, such as Kampfgruppe von Luck in Normandy, Kampfgruppe Piper in the Ardennes and Kampfgruppe Das Reich in the Kamenets-Podolsky Pocket in Russia. However, in the spring of 1941, this untested formation would get its first real exposure in the new age of warfare with Kampfgruppe Balck in Greece.

By the spring of 1941, despite the delicacy and hard work of Foreign Minister Joachim von Ribbentrop, Hitler saw too many loose ends in the Balkans, which he wanted dealt with before re-focussing on Russia that summer. This meant a radical movement southwards of forces designated for Barbarossa to conquer Yugoslavia and invade Greece in support of the flagging Italian Army.

Some of the young officers of the German Imperial Army who had fought together in the Great War were now generals or of even higher rank. Generalfeldmarschall Wilhelm List had at one time been a young officer in the same regiment as Hitler, and had recently proven himself as an able commander leading 14. Armee in the invasion of Poland and 12. Armee in France. Promoted at the famous 'Field Marshal Ceremony' in 1940, he was now ordered to take 12. Armee into Greece and Yugoslavia.[90] With four armoured divisions and eleven motorized infantry divisions, the attack was launched on 6 April, proving to be another example of Blitzkrieg in action. Belgrade would be occupied by 13 April and Athens just a fortnight later on 27 April.

The role of 2. Panzer-Division in the invasion of Greece

Given that Hermann Balck is generous with praise for individual officers throughout his memoirs, it comes as a surprise that he fails to even mention his divisional commander in the Greek operation. Guderian passed the leadership of his cherished 2. Panzer to Generalleutnant Rudolf Veiel. Clearly Guderian thought highly enough of Veiel to make this recommendation, but equally obvious is that Hermann Balck did not feel him worthy of a mention in his memoirs. There could be any number of reasons for this on Balck's part, but it is worth noting that Veiel would be implicated in the July 1944 plot to assassinate Hitler – although, fortunately for him, he would survive the war.

'OCHI!'

In his biography of Hermann Balck, Robinson devotes the largest portion of his book to the Greek campaign. Mussolini had long had eyes on the conquest of Greece, and Hitler struggled to contain Il Duce's irrepressible imperial ambitions. Relations between Italy and Greece had a very long history of friction and strife. Ioannis Metaxas, the Greek Prime Minister, lived in a world of paranoia as Greece was used by other European powers as a foil to Mussolini. During October 1940, matters further deteriorated and Metaxas became a national hero by, according to his wife, shouting at Grazzi, the Italian ambassador, '*OCHI!*' ('NO!') upon the presentation of an Italian ultimatum. Mussolini gave the order to invade Greece from a still unconquered Albania on 28 October 1940, but by December the Italians were already in trouble against a fierce counter-offensive by Greek forces. Matters were further complicated by the British agreement of

1939 to send aid to Greece in the event of the country being attacked. Hitler watched with fury as squadrons of British aircraft arrived in Crete and mainland Greece during November, with an advance guard of troops landing in the same month from Britain's Mediterranean base of Malta.

Hitler responded by issuing Führer Directives Number 18 and 20. The first directive (issued on 12 November) ordered the Wehrmacht to be ready to invade northern Greece from Bulgaria (as his Foreign Ministry prepared the way for the transit of forces through Romania and Bulgaria), while the second (on 13 December) ordered the occupation of the whole of Greece. The invasion of Greece would be codenamed Operation Marita, which required the redirection of twenty-four divisions southwards, which had a massive impact on plans for the invasion of Russia. Hitler hoped that the Greek campaign could be wrapped up quickly, with the majority of men and tanks returned to their original start lines in Poland in time for the proposed June launch of the eastern offensive.[91]

Under the command List, lead elements of 12. Armee moved into a bitterly cold and snow-covered Romania during December 1940. The 2. Panzer-Division was ready by February 1941, and began its move south from Mödling in north-east Austria on 5 March – just about the same time that three British and Commonwealth divisions were landing in southern Greece. The route to the Greek border, where a successful invasion was intended to aid the failing Italian armies in Albania and Greece, took Balck and his Panzer-Regiment 3 through Hungary and into Romania – both of whom had agreed to their *fait accompli* to allow the transit of German forces – and then on into Bulgaria. Hitler launched his attack on Yugoslavia at 0520hrs on 6 April, a route through the country quickly being opened up so that an anti-Nazi coup in Belgrade could be crushed. Hitler added pressure on the British forces in Greece by committing Rommel and further German troops to fight in North Africa.

Rommel and Balck – a shared sense of duty or devotion to the Führer?

Hitler had a special reverence for officers who had proven themselves with accomplishments on the battlefield; he merely tolerated the rest. Both the OKW and OKH wished Rommel to be cautious in North Africa, pursuing a prudent posture rather than expanding the conflict further. In fact, they did not wish him to be there at all, believing his presence only diluted the German forces available for Barbarossa. However, Rommel, in his devotion to Hitler, used 'subterfuge and insubordination' to take the offensive to the British.[92] Privately, the Führer urged Rommel forward; the greater the aggression and achievement, the greater the rewards for Rommel. Some observers have reported how Hitler and Rommel were able to converse together in great animation.

Within three years, Hermann Balck would also be in the presence of Hitler and also be seen speaking animatedly with the Führer, who was in the process of elevating Balck to the same level of honours as Rommel – the award of the Knight's Cross with Oakleaves, Swords and the ultimate award of all, Diamonds. If we are looking for conclusive evidence as to the commitment of Balck to Hitler and what he stood for, then we have to accept that Balck was as supportive of the Führer as was Rommel. Equally like Rommel, Balck was a breaker of rules, a renegade and was to become almost untouchable under the protection of the Führer's admiration. Rommel was often seen as an outsider by the Army High Command and by his peers given his devotion to Hitler and Hitler's admiration in return. The jealousy of his fellow officers saw Rommel isolated, and the same would happen to Balck. Both Rommel and Balck mimicked Hitler's riding rough-shod over the wishes of the OKH and OKW, and they got away with it. General Warlimont at the OKH recorded how Hitler behaved in relation to unfolding events in the Balkans:

'I myself [Warlimont] was detailed to carry on negotiations with the Bulgarian General Staff and the directions given me by Hitler are a good illustration of his method of working with allies. They ran:

"I propose to keep the overall direction of this campaign in my own hands, including the allotment of objectives for the Italian and Hungarian forces within the framework of the operation as a whole."'[93]

It was this type of approach to involvement in operational matters that enraged numerous high-ranking figures in both the OKH and the OKW, officers such as OKH chief of staff General Franz Halder, as Warlimont further explained:

'Even before the short campaign in the Balkans opened on 6th April and while it was in progress, Hitler and his immediate entourage still could not keep themselves from interfering in army operations. Their reasons were always the same. The following extracts from Halder's diary of 1941 are illustrative:

"11 April. I told them [speaking to Luftwaffe chief of staff Hans Jeschonnek, who reported that Göring was unhappy and had complained to the Führer about the progress of XVIII. Gebirgskorps, or Mountain Corps] forcibly how disgusted I was with this continual interference in operations. Their timidity, their desire to avoid all risks but to gather in victories nevertheless, may be a good idea politically but militarily it is intolerable."'[94]

But Balck and Rommel were not, however, immune from criticism. When, during the Greek invasion, Göring was unhappy with the performance of XVIII. Gebirgskorps, which included Balck's troops, he went direct to Hitler and the inner circle were able to infect the Führer's appreciation through misinformation. Göring knew nothing about military matters, and all his intervention did was further erode Halder's position as commander of the Army. Perhaps it should come as no surprise that Halder was later a key collaborator with the Army resistance movement against Hitler, and was dismissed before the end of the war – miraculously, he survived Hitler's retribution against other plotters.

Thus, the light and benefaction that Hitler shone on both Rommel and Balck was always tinged with poison. With Hitler's grace, officers such as these would rise through the ranks and achieve the highest honours, but they would also attract jealousy and isolation on their journey. For Rommel, this process was now well underway in North Africa, whereas for Balck it was about to begin. For now, Rommel was tasked with sweeping the British out of North Africa to pre-empt further criticism of his methods, while Balck, two ranks lower in the Army hierarchy, needed to get to Athens before Göring complained any further.

Breaking through 'W' Force

Facing Balck and his Kampfgruppe of Panzer-Regiment 3 was 'W' Force, with elements of the British 1 Armoured Brigade, 6th Australian Division and 2nd New Zealand Division, broadly spread across two defensive lines – the Metaxas Line, along the border with Bulgaria, and the Aliakmon Line, between the Gulf of Salonika and the Yugoslav border.

List positioned Generalleutnant Franz Böhme's XVIII. Gebirgskorps on the eastern flank of 12. Armee, and Böhme ordered 2. Panzer-Division and Generalleutnant Veiel to force their way southwards as fast as possible.[95] Within 2. Panzer, Oberst Balck and his Panzer-Regiment 3 was to break through what was known as the Metaxas Line on the Bulgarian border. Once clear of the defences, Boehme, a 'calm, deliberate and thorough' corps commander, would order 2. Panzer-Division to head for Salonika on the east coast of Greece, the route of march taking German forces south along the coast via Mount Olympus, which they would bypass to the west and east. The route to Strumica, due west into Serbia before turning south to capture Salonika, was marked by mass surrenders of both Yugoslav and Greek forces. Stunned by the speed of the German advance, again using motorcycle outriders as reconnaissance, and the ability of the Germans to move tanks through what were locally considered to be impassable areas for armour, German casualties were very light. The mountainous terrain tested both men and equipment used to the open landscape of Central Europe, but close communications with artillery, close support from pioneer units to repair bridges and close support from the Luftwaffe squadrons combined to show that *Auftragstaktik* was working supremely well. As in France, decisions could be made quickly on the spot. With Balck always in the lead echelon, he was able to judge exactly what was needed on the spur of the moment to maintain the attack's momentum and not allow the enemy any pause to recover. At one point, Balck was so far forward that he and five men from his headquarters unit found themselves surrounded by some sixty enemy soldiers; his career could have come to an abrupt halt by just one bullet finding its target.[96] In the event, Balck's strong personality and some confident bluff saw him march towards the Greeks, pistol in hand, and order them to stand to attention, which they promptly did as they were captured.

Keeping moving at all times, Veiel and his commanders – including Balck – drove the 2. Panzer-Division hard and ever southwards, reaching Lake Dorian and crossing the Greek border. Fighting and destroying the Greek 19th Motorised Division, by 8 April – only two days into the battle for Greece – the tanks were in open country and on their way south to Salonika. Mud was a problem, and so was the terrain, but Balck was helped by the general collapse of Greek forces, whose intelligence units were unable to guess either the size or the direction of the German invaders. General Bakopoulos of the Greek Army made contact with Veiel to request a ceasefire, Balck commenting in his memoirs:

> 'The Greek commander did not really know what was moving against Salonika. In fact, it was only elements of a division whose main body was still far behind at the border, stuck in the mud.'[97]

By 9 April, Generals Bakopoulos and Veiel had met face-to-face and the Greek forces on the Metaxas Line capitulated. Their namesake had passed away from a throat condition the previous January, not living to see either the invasion or the collapse of his much vaunted defensive line with the consequent imprisonment of 60,000 Greek troops.

With German formations experiencing similar success in Yugoslavia, it was clear that the Greek and Allied forces would soon feel the full impact of the Wehrmacht. Not only would they have to try to hold back 2. Panzer-Division on the east coast, south of Salonika, but soon they would be fighting against the XL. Armeekorps (mot), which included 9. Panzer-Division, 73. Infanterie-Division and a motorized regiment of the Leibstandarte-SS 'Adolf Hitler', commanded by Hitler's former chauffeur, Josef 'Sepp' Dietrich. Generaloberst Maximilian von Weichs' 2. Armee that was left the task of tidying up around Belgrade and the rest of Yugoslavia.

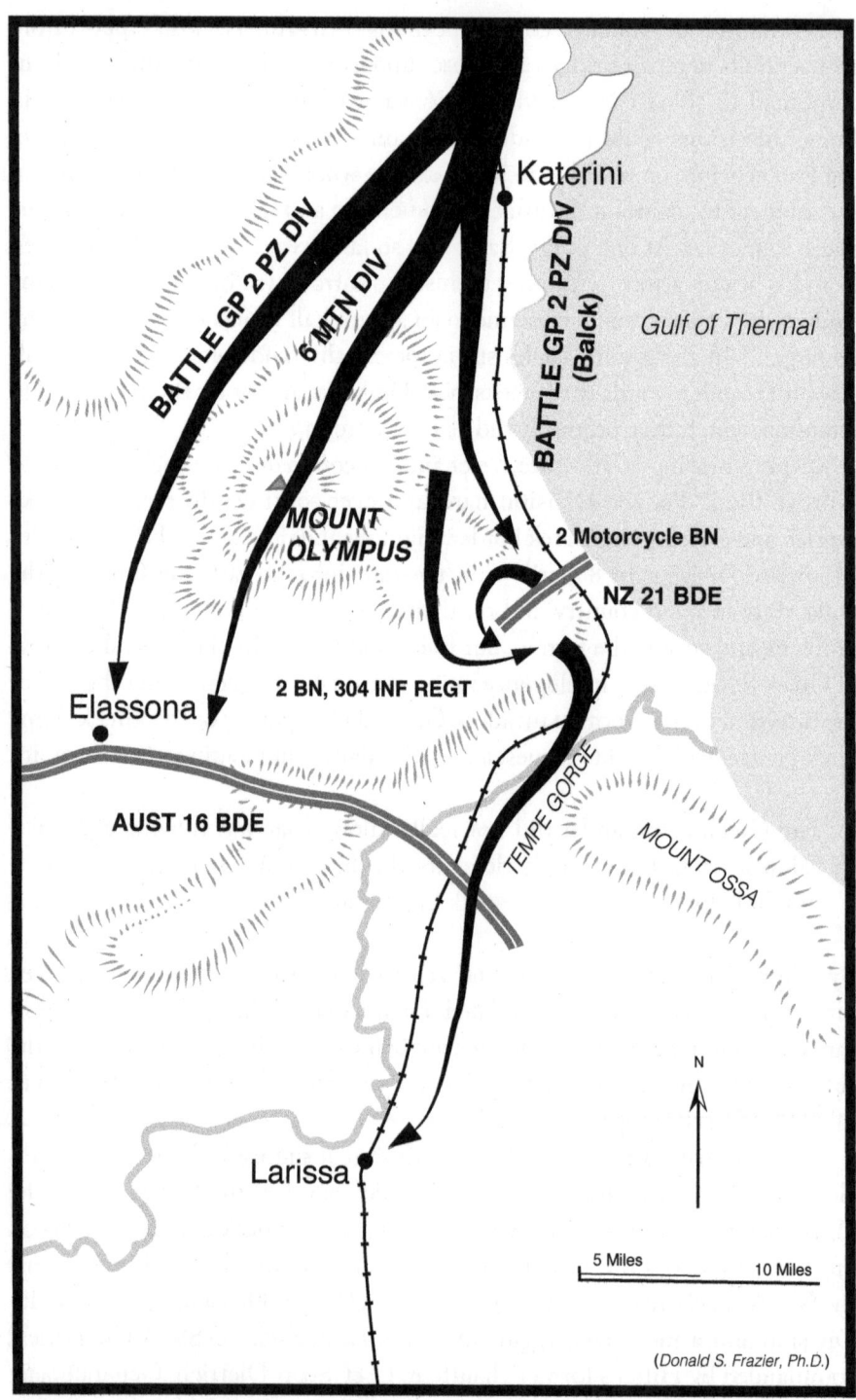

Map 1. Kampfgruppe Balck from 2. Panzer-Division in its assault on Mount Olympus and Tempe Gorge, April 1941. (© 2015 The University Press of Kentucky. Used by permission)

'W' Force – named after their commander, Lieutenant General Henry Maitland Wilson, withdrew southwards, abandoning well-prepared positions in order to get to higher ground from which to delay the fast-moving German forces. The Germans had planned for this, and within 12. Armee, Boehme's corps contained not only the 2. Panzer-Division but also the 5. and 6. Gebirgs-Divisions (trained to fight in mountainous country), as well as the 72. Infanterie-Division. Wilson discussed the fast-deteriorating strategic situation with Major General Bernard Freyberg, who commanded the 2nd New Zealand Division, and agreed to position the New Zealand 21st Battalion in defence of the narrow pass at Platamon. This was directly in front of the coastal route south that Kampfgruppe Balck would take as it pushed to the east of Mount Olympus, whilst a second Kampfgruppe advanced to the west of the mountain and the 6. Gebirgs-Division would move straight over the top. As his forces approached the dug-in New Zealanders, Balck recalled:

'North of Salonika my regiment and staff were quartered in Nicopolis. When I opened my window [in what would have been a forcibly requisitioned home] in the morning I could see snow-covered Mount Olympus against the blue sky, hovering over the dense fog of the Warda Plains. It was overwhelming. I had seen a lot of the world. Nothing compared to Mount Olympus. So there I sat, pensively in awe, holding a copy of Homer that I had brought along. I never put him away while I was in Greece.'[98]

Balck would have been well aware of the classic phrase from Homer's *The Iliad*:

'Let me not then die ingloriously and without a struggle, but let me first do some great thing that shall be told among men hereafter.'[99]

He would almost certainly have also been affected by further lines from *The Iliad*, those concerning Achilles, who wept along with Priam, sharing the expression of grief, a reminder that in war there are rarely winners: 'And overpowered by memory both men gave way to grief.'[100]

Platamon Ridge

Balck was anxious not to slow the momentum, and his Kampfgruppe approached the four companies of the 21st New Zealand Battalion commanded by Lieutenant Colonel Neil Macky and their four 25-pounder field guns. The New Zealanders had been digging in all around Platamon Ridge, the coastal paths and a tunnel through the hillside since 10 April, with instructions from Freyberg to hold Platamon 'at all costs'.[101] The scrub and dusty flatlands that led south towards the old Frankish castle were going to be an easy killing ground for the artillery and machine guns that the New Zealanders could fire from the walls and the eastern slopes that led inland to Mount Olympus.

The advanced reconnaissance of Balck's Kradschützen-Bataillon 2 of 2. Panzer-Division, commanded by Oberstleutnant Karl Stollbrock, was the first to experience the fire power of the New Zealanders, suffering a number of casualties, mostly from accurate artillery fire, during their advance on the morning of 15 April. Despite counter-battery fire from the two batteries that were attached to Kampfgruppe Balck, Stollbrock halted his attack. Stollbrock had been a young leutnant during the First World War, and his career to date had mirrored that of Balck (he would reach the rank of Oberst/colonel on 1 February 1942, but advance no further). Stollbrock later commented about his advance: '[the artillery] plagued us, front and rear, right and left.'[102]

During this action and towards midday, Balck caught up with his reconnaissance unit. Receiving a report from Stollbrock, Balck immediately took command and saw that his only option was to try to outflank the enemy position, showing he had the ability to see a problem and craft a quick solution. He decided to order up his 1. Panzer-Abteilung of his Panzer-Regiment 3 to make a frontal assault, while dismounting his motorcycle infantry and sending them – with a recently arrived infantry battalion – in two long arcs around the ridge to fight their way back eastwards into the flank of the New Zealanders. Balck's tank battalion commander was the highly experienced Oberstleutnant Karl von Decker – yet another Great War survivor and product of the Reichswehr – a former Jäger who thought and acted as Balck would have done himself.[103]

Equipped with the lightly armoured Panzer Mk II and some Mk III tanks, all was ready for the attack from the north and flank positions by 1900hrs on 15 April. As the attack went forward and the New Zealanders fought tenaciously, von Decker's Panzers halted some 1,200 metres away and began firing on the ridge and castle, while the infantry pressed on up the hillsides, which in places were several hundred metres high. This was no easy battle, and they were facing a stubborn enemy. Many among the motorcycle infantry would no doubt have cursed their commander – they were used to riding on a comfortable seat, not climbing up hills under fire – but Balck had no sympathy, having been an Alpine officer himself.

Time was not on Balck's side. With a number of tanks abandoned through losing their tracks on the rocky and shell-marked ground, Balck took stock and decided to inform Veiel of the delay – hopefully this news would not reach Berlin and enable Göring to make another pointed jibe to Hitler about the fighting bravery of the Wehrmacht. But the pressure was clearly on Balck and he was already right at the front, the epitome of *Auftragstaktik*, with fast decision-making and the delegation of orders to get his officers thinking on the spot. Higher in the chain of command, though, it appears that concern may have been growing, to the extent that, according to *The Official History of New Zealand in the Second World War*, orders had been issued for men from '8/800 Brandenburg Regiment' to outflank the 21st Battalion by motor boats and land behind their positions; only a heavy sea swell on the night of 16 April prevented this. Balck makes no mention of this in his memoirs, but he must have been made aware that if he could not force a passage, then others would.[104]

By early morning, after a night of constant fighting patrols, star-shells and machine-gun fire, Balck had received further reinforcements as units flooded south along the Aegean coast. It was now vital that he broke the stubborn New Zealand defensive line and pressed on down through the Tempe Gorge. The third attack began on the morning of the 16th with a thunderous bombardment, heavy machine-gun fire, destroyed and broken-down tanks and mounting casualties on both sides. By around 1100hrs, the New Zealanders began to withdraw south, abandoning all their equipment and leaving Balck to rue the delay:

> 'That was done, but there was still hell to pay. The mule path that we had been moving forward on had to be reinforced to handle tanks [step forward his engineer and pioneer units] and wheeled vehicles. That took time, a lot of time ... It took twenty-four hours until 11.00hrs on 17 April, before we managed to get anything across that damned mountainside.'[105]

The withdrawing New Zealand battalion made one final communication: 'WT station 21 Bn closing down. Getting out.'[106]

Despite his reputation for leading from the front, Balck would have breathed a sigh of relief that a breakthrough had been achieved. Behind 2. Panzer-Division were the heavier formations of 12. Armee that were needed in the advance on Athens. Fortunately for his reputation, Veiel, his divisional commander, had reported that Kampfgruppe Balck had been involved in 'bitter fighting against the troops of 2 NZ Div'.

There was no to be no let-up in pushing the advance forward, and on the morning of 17 April, a signal from Boehme at XVIII. Gebirgskorps informed Balck of the necessity of getting what tanks were still serviceable moving over the mountainous ridge, through the minefields and over the Pinios River: 'Please push on with all possible speed to Elason and Larissa. Very important to reach Larissa.'[107]

With the SS units under Sepp Dietrich in their own Kampfgruppen cascading from the north and led by officers such as Fritz Witt – who would, in 1944, be the commander of the 12. SS-Panzer-Division 'Hitlerjugend' in Normandy – Lieutenant Colonel Macky's tired, dusty and exhausted men in Tempe Gorge were sent another order: 'essential to deny the gorge to the enemy till 19th April even if it means extinction'.[108]

A new battle now loomed between 2. Panzer-Division and the New Zealand battalion for Tempe Gorge and what Robinson refers to as 'the race to Larissa'.[109] The fate of 'W' Force now rested on events at Larissa, as General Wilson was convinced Greece could not be held and a fighting withdrawal had been ordered. This meant all his units would have to pull back through the vital crossroads at Larissa. The Royal Navy was preparing for a mass evacuation from southern Greece to save what they could, and 12. Armee's Generalfeldmarschall List could see that it was now a race to the south. Yet again, the tanks, motorcycles and vehicles of 2. Panzer-Division would be thrashed onwards, with repairs made as they went and already overstretched supply lines extended even further.

The defence of Olympus Pass, the Tempe Gorge, to the east and south of Mount Olympus, was now a brigade action. It was here that the Greeks had tried to stop the Persian hordes under Xerxes in 480 BCE, retreating to Thermopylae to the south to make their famous last stand. For the New Zealanders, however, retreat was not an option – not for at least three days – and the entire gorge became a prime example of defence in depth, with anti-tank guns, machine-gun pits, mortars and artillery spread the entire length of the valley. For Balck, this battle would be the most challenging of his life so far. His natural predisposition for momentum was frustrated by the rocky terrain, with tracks coming off many of the light tanks and the engineers battling to make the paths into roads. Meanwhile, the tunnel had been blown and would take at least five days to clear. Following the course of the river, the very capable Decker was ordered to press on with all speed, using motorcycle and cycle infantry, while his tanks found any route they could and even drove along a nearby railway line. By 17 April, Balck's troops linked up with the 6. Gebirgs-Division of General der Gebirgstruppe Ferdinand Schörner, which had successfully climbed, cleared and descended from Mount Olympus – but not before Schörner was photographed hoisting the swastika on the summit of the mountain.

The battles for Tempe Gorge and Larissa

As the Germans crossed the Bulgarian border on 6 April, elements of 'W' Force had begun hastily working on the defences of the Olympus Pass. By 17 April, the best part of a brigade formed of Australian and New Zealand troops now defended what was already a naturally difficult route to attack, now protected by barbed wire, mines, explosive charges and extensive killing grounds. The defending forces, it should be noted, were not full-time professional soldiers. Many of the officers had served in the First World War and then gone on to civilian careers – Major B.I. Basset was a barrister (he was killed in action in 1942), Colonel S.J. Kelly was a school teacher, Captain L.J. Bell was a grocer's assistant (he would be killed in action the following month), Captain J.H. Ensor was a farm manager before the war and Major S. Hanton was a printer. All these men had volunteered for service and were now facing Kampfgruppe Balck, which was in no mood to take many prisoners. Again making a command decision on the spot and from the very front of his column, Balck saw a chance to outflank some of the forces arrayed against him by asking Decker and his tanks to ford the River Pinios.

In the vanguard, Decker watched as his Panzer Mk I tanks crossed with water right up to their turrets – and in one case over their turret. Within hours, six tanks had crossed, and more were to follow – the notion that tanks could not operate in this mountainous region was put to the sword by the German crews' determination to keep advancing. Balck made sure he was everywhere he could be seen, either shouting operations from his command tank while wearing his trademark forage cap or on foot – the epitome of *Truppenführung* and *Auftragstaktik* in one officer. On the morning of 18 April, from the totally unexpected direction of the Pinios River, troops of Kampfgruppe Balck then fell upon the defenders, which included their adversaries from the previous day's fighting of Lieutenant Colonel Macky's 21st New Zealand Battalion. The Panzergrenadiers destroyed vehicles and trucks, capturing and killing a great number as the defending forces withdrew and blew up what they could. Balck was now able to move fast towards his objective of Larissa: 'The enemy was caught completely by surprise, wondering where we had come from.'[110]

The town of Larissa had been partially destroyed by a recent earthquake and artillery bombardments. Little was left except masses of fallen homes, along with abandoned equipment and supplies, which the German forces eagerly picked up as the speed of their advance had once again outstripped their ability to maintain adequate supply lines. Forward elements of the 2. Panzer-Division once again linked up with 6. Gebirgs-Division – for Balck, the war in Greece was over and he and his exhausted men collapsed.

Private Pervitin

Within all the historical analysis, scholarly research and anecdotal evidence regarding the ability of the German Heer to perform almost superhuman feats between 1939 and 1941, the role of Pervitin often has been overlooked. Hermann Balck, and indeed all Wehrmacht field commanders in both the Luftwaffe and Heer, remained tight-lipped about the use of methamphetamine in aiding the performance of their troops, specifically in the ability to maintain long hours of endurance and fighting energy without the need for sleep.

In the advances in Poland and France, there were plenty of examples where German troops never paused in their assaults on enemy positions, in fording rivers, building bridges or moving onto the next lines of enemy defences. However, in Greece, German forces also had to deal with periods of intense heat as well as energy-sapping hill climbs, building roads, clearing destroyed tunnels and maintaining a constant pace of advance that saw the country overrun in less than three weeks. Numerous attempts to hold back the Germans in Greece's gorges, valleys and defensive lines seemed unable to prevent a constant, rolling, moving and attritional German force performing far beyond the expected physical ability of the average soldier. This was down to 'Private Pervitin'.

As a young man, the Nobel laureate Heinrich Boll joined the German Army and then fought in Poland, France and Russia. While serving in Poland, he wrote to his family:

> 'It's tough out here, and I hope you understand if I'm only able to write to you once every two to four days soon. Today I'm writing you mainly to ask for some Pervitin.'[111]

The prevalence of drug use in the German armed forces had a long history, with chemical companies such as Merck and Bayer developing powerful painkilling drugs to treat the many severe wounds and offer pain relief to the millions of German troops injured during the First World War. The Weimar Republic took a tolerant view of drug use and subsequent drug abuse as a means of dealing with chronic pain and the consequent opioid dependence. In 1938, Pervitin was released into the domestic market by Temmler Pharma and was quickly popular throughout Germany, offering increased alertness, confidence and risk-taking behaviour as well as having the side effects of reducing sensitivity to pain and hunger. Otto Ranke tested the drug on students in 1938 and announced that he believed it could help German troops win any war.[112] Methamphetamine, our modern-day 'meth', is believed to have been issued in large doses to troops in the Polish and French campaigns – hence the often-reported post-drug-taking collapse and images of masses of German troops completely unconscious when the fighting ended. Vice Admiral Helmuth Eye also requested a stronger medication, one that 'would keep soldiers ready for battle when they are asked to continue fighting beyond a period considered normal'.[113]

In 2015, Norman Ohler published *Der Totale Rausch*, which was published translated into English as *Blitzed: Drugs in Nazi Germany*.[114] By accessing military archives and the Nuremberg files of Hitler's doctor, Theodor Morell, Ohler established that Pervitin had been marketed to rival the USA's Coco Cola and was in widespread use across Germany well before 1939. It was often mixed with chocolate, and it was not until much later that it was seen as a drug with habit-forming properties. Consequently, there was no attempt to prevent its sale, no legislation to prevent its use, and the entire German Army was riddled with Pervitin. Ohler wrote:

> 'Introduced in the daily rations and consumed up to twice a day, the drug gave the soldiers supernatural capabilities. Fearless and cheerful, they could spend more than three days without sleeping and walk up to 60km without interruption. This allowed for the fast invasion of Poland in 1939, the Blitzkrieg through the French Ardennes in 1940, and the Balkan Campaign of 1941, fought without rest for 11 days.'[114]

According to Fabiana Natale, writing in 2020, manufacture of Pervitin exceeded 35 million doses of 3 milligrams each during April and May 1940. However shocking this statistic is, for ordinary German soldiers there was a further dimension. With tank troops, for example, there were orders to use Pervitin, often in the shape of Panzerschokolade. However, the Luftwaffe was the most interested branch of the armed forces in the increased attention span it gave servicemen, particularly pilots, naming it 'pilot's salt'.

The OKW knew and encouraged the continued use of Pervitin in the Wehrmacht to help facilitate the monumental achievements of their troops in the lightning quick campaigns of 1939–1941. Hermann Balck would have known full well that virtually all, if not all, of his troops – especially his tank crews – were taking Pervitin. It was just another component in their preparations for combat and the tactics that Blitzkrieg demanded of them. The fact that Balck fails to mention the use of Pervitin, or indeed any drugs, in his memoirs can only be because in the drug-riddled world of 1970s America, such an admission would have ruined the reputation of the German Army that he was so devoted to preserving. The question of whether Balck enlisted the aid of drugs to maintain his outstandingly energetic efforts remains unanswered. However, given the prevalence of the drug throughout the Wehrmacht and that there is documented proof that the Führer himself was prescribed Pervitin by his physician, Dr Morell, it seems most likely that he would have done so.

As Balck's men collapsed in their post-Pervitin relapse, with some experiencing the chest pains and heart problems that were a side effect of the prolonged and intensive use of methamphetamine, and others being hospitalized and even dying, Balck and his senior officers toured the sites of classical antiquity that surrounded them.

After Greece

As the 2. Panzer-Division and Panzer-Regiment 3 took stock of the past few weeks and another successfully concluded operation, one of the duties of a wartime commander in the field was to record events in the unit war diary and then complete the follow-up recommendations for citations for awards and promotions. Balck was efficient in both respects, making certain that Oberstleutnant von Decker would receive the Knight's Cross and that numerous of his non-commissioned soldiers were recognized, with wound badges and awards distributed.

The 12. Armee lost just under 1,200 men killed and nearly 4,000 wounded in the campaign, and Panzer-Regiment 3 lost nineteen tanks to enemy fire, mines or being submerged in rivers. For Balck himself, there was little time to reflect and no lingering as there had been in the French countryside. The Wehrmacht was focussed on the coming Armageddon in Russia and needed the 12. Armee, minus a few crucial divisions to hold what had been gained in Greece and Yugoslavia, back in Germany to refit and then move into Poland. On 13 May, Balck received the news that he had been appointed to command the 2. Panzer-Brigade; by 17 May, he was sailing out of Patras and into the Adriatic, heading for Taranto in southern Italy, where trains were waiting. Balck recorded the tragedy of a few days later, when the same ships – the *Marburg* and the *Kybfels* – that had taken him and his headquarters staff to Italy, encountered a minefield laid by HMS *Abdiel* and sank, with heavy losses to personnel of the 2. Panzer-Division aboard. At around 1400hrs on 21 May, just off the island of Lekada, both ships struck mines, and tanks and equipment essential for the invasion of Russia were lost, along with 226 brave men who had survived the fighting in central Poland, been the first to force their way through to the Channel coast in France and had now conquered Greece. The Italians had already lost two ships in this area but failed to inform the Germans; by this time, relations had become very strained between the two Axis allies, the Italian and German high commands hardly communicating.[115]

2. Panzer-Brigade

Robinson devotes more space and time to the Greek campaign than any other part of Balck's life. This disproportionate focus obscures the fact that the only reference to Balck receiving command of 2. Panzer-Brigade comes in one sentence on page 186. However, the importance of that brief posting deserves far greater emphasis, as it illustrates an often forgotten but vital aspect of the ability to successfully command in war – physical, psychological and emotional stamina.

Balck's immediate superior, Oberst Johannes Netwig, had collapsed with physical and mental exhaustion, which is why Balck was asked to take temporary command of the 2. Panzer-Brigade just as he left Greece. Interestingly, Netwig had arrived at this point in his life along the same route as Balck: he had been a young officer in the Prussian Pomorskie Artillery during the First World War, then served in the Reichswehr, was promoted to Hauptmann and met Guderian at the Tank Troops School before leading Panzer-Regiment 1 in the invasion of Poland. In collapsing, Netwig was far from alone; during the course of the war, hundreds of officers would see their careers either interrupted or terminated through either failure in battle or nervous and physical exhaustion. Even Hermann Balck found himself on the reserve list at one point. Naturally, this aspect of war tends not to make headlines and is rarely referred to in diaries and memoirs.

Sadly for Balck, this new appointment was brief and only a paper exercise. He arrived at the brigade headquarters in early June, began the process of sorting out his command and received formal notification of his appointment on 6 June, but on 7 June he received fresh orders to report immediately to Berlin, to the office of Generalmajor Adolf von Schell at the Organizational Directorate. Still with the rank of Oberst, Balck had been selected to oversee the 'cleaning-up of the wheeled vehicle fleet with full directive authority'.[116] Balck relates in his memoirs how he 'resisted vigorously all efforts to get me to come back to Berlin to work on the issue of organizing the motorisation of the whole army, but my luck eventually ran out'.[117] Balck found himself posted to the Führerreserve on 19 July and was about to begin an entirely new phase of his military career – one which would see him play a seismic role in the war against Russia which had begun a few weeks earlier on 22 June.

Chapter VII

The Prophecies of Doom, 1941–1942

A series of meetings in Berlin from 7 June onwards merely confirmed in Hermann Balck's mind what he already knew – that an attack on Russia was imminent. What he perhaps did not know was the reasoning that lay behind this decision. To put events into context, Balck was still recovering his energy from the Greek campaign, sorting out in his mind how he had left 2. Panzer-Division and his beloved Panzer-Regiment 3, and trying to formulate how he would now command 2. Panzer-Brigade. It seemed that promotion to general could not now be far away; it was only a matter of time. However, all was about to change.

Present at these meetings were Generalmajor Adolf von Schell, Generalleutnant Walther Buhle and Generaloberst Friedrich Fromm.[118] Athough Balck records in some detail the comments made in the various meetings he attended, he is specifically vague about attribution. So although we gain a valuable insight into views on the strategic situation vis-à-vis the invasion of Russia, we are unable to match the comments to any one individual.

Sparkommissar in the OKH – the 'Agent of Frugality'

Von Schell was another survivor of the First World War who had gone on to serve in the Freikorps rather than the Reichswehr. In 1938, von Schell had held a key appointment as Undersecretary of State in the Reich Ministry of Transport and designed the Schell Plan, which tried to convert production in the civilian vehicle industry into a few basic types to release capacity for wartime production.[119] Between 1939 and 1941, von Schell worked within the OKW in the department to motorize the army, with the rank of Generalmajor from 1 March 1940, by which time he had also published a number of academic works. As a young Hauptmann, von Schell had been on an exchange in the USA and gave a lecture on battle leadership, including the psychological reaction of troops in a campaign, which is now a small book that is today still part of the US Marine Corps' professional reading programme.

In his memoirs, Guderian speaks very highly of von Schell, calling him a 'clever, resolute and eloquent man' who came into contact with Hitler numerous times in meetings regarding the Reich's motor vehicle system and trying to simplify production.[120] Von Schell spoke his mind bluntly, but friction with vehicle management executives led to him suffering poisonous treatment. Hitler responded by removing him from his circle of influence, also transferring him to the Eastern Front in October 1943. There, von Schell commanded the woefully underequipped 25. Panzer-Division, which was wiped out within two months. Such was the ease in Nazi Germany with which a life could be changed by gossip, revealing how receptive Hitler was to accusations of treasonous behaviour and to being undermined.

The second key individual whom Balck met, Walther Buhle, was at that time a highly thought of Generalleutnant leading the OKW Organizational Directorate.[121] Balck reported to Generaloberst Fromm. At this stage in the summer of 1941, Friedrich Fromm had been promoted from head of the General Army Office and was now Commander-in-Chief of the Reserve Army and head of the Army Rearmaments Office. Fromm is one of those key Nazi officers who kept the Wehrmacht moving but never receives the credit he deserved.[122]

While Oberst Hermann Balck was still proving himself as a regimental commander fighting in France and Greece, huge preparations had been going on along the entire border between German-held territory and Russia, which was set to become the front line for the forces of totalitarianism and those of communism. When Balck met with Fromm, Buhle and von Schell, he quickly became aware that the notion of a war in the East was widely supported, as indeed was the Führer's grasp of strategy. As Stephen Fritz underlined in his book *The First Soldier*, many of Germany's successful campaigns could not have been won without a significant and positive input from Hitler. What was now new was the degree to which Hitler's ideas on Lebensraum ('living space') were supported by the OKH and OKW. The famous meeting of 5 November 1937 (known as the 'Hossbach Memorandum') at which Hitler explained his future strategy to his key leaders may have shocked his military audience at the time, but now – four years on and several successful campaigns later – not only could they see the logic of the Führer's views, but they saw him as the prophet or Messiah whom they had longed for during the years of the Weimar Republic. For Hitler, risks were necessary and matters had to be resolved quickly, even if the armed forces and industrial production were still not ready. The Hossbach Memorandum summarized:

> 'The necessary space [would] have to be found in Europe [since] areas containing lots of raw materials were better located in direct proximity to the Reich …. expansion could only be carried out by breaking down resistance and taking risks; setbacks were inevitable. There had never in

former times been spaces without a master, and there were none today; the attacker always comes up against a possessor.'[123]

There was also the key question of what to do with the expanding Wehrmacht, as by 1942, conscription and the Four-Year Plan had created armed forces that the German economy could not afford to let stand idle – they had to be used. This and other matters now had ready solutions that had somehow diffused down the chain of command and made perfect sense as they were explained to Balck – although as already mentioned, we do not know who said what in the following notes taken from meetings between Balck, Fromm, Buhle and von Schell in early June 1941:

> 'We are at a decision point in the war. England has been driven out of Europe, but is still sitting in the Mediterranean. Our follow-on mission will have to be their complete removal from there in order to control the oil of Asia Minor, the cotton of Egypt, and the considerable treasures of Africa.'
>
> 'What do we do with the rest of the overwhelming mass of the Wehrmacht? England will not return to the continent, even with American assistance. That would be suicide for them. To keep Europe subdued, we only need minimal forces, since almost everyone has accepted the New Order, some of them most agreeably.'
>
> 'The remaining problem is Russia. Its existence forces us to maintain a strong army in the East. At the present time we are so superior to the Russians that they cannot seriously compete with us.'

Prophetic though these statements are, they are also indicative of views widely supported throughout the high command echelons of both the OKH and OKW prior to the invasion of Russia in 1941. As Stephen Fritz wrote:

> 'Frontline commanders such as Reinhardt, Hoth, Hoepner, Kuchler, von Kluge, Henrici and others in the weeks and months before the attack on the USSR expressed support for the necessity of a showdown with Bolshevism and the conquest of Lebensraum.'[124]

The meetings between Balck and his three superiors were not the isolated ramblings of hypnotized senior officers, but commonly held beliefs throughout the OKH and OKW. What reservations or even embryonic rumblings of resistance existed, were spoken of in the shadows and in drawing rooms, not in the offices of the main ministries in Berlin. It was now Balck's turn either to be indoctrinated himself or perhaps give into what might have been self-delusional wishful thinking – that war in the East was going to happen anyway, Hitler had willed it, the army was invincible and war could not be stopped, so one needed a moral and intellectual foundation on which to base one's efforts. If Balck wished to see himself promoted and wear the red and gold oak leaves of a general, then he could not sit on the fence. This does, in one sense, make him a Nazi.

There is plenty of anecdotal and documentary evidence that Hitler received and welcomed the reassurance that, compared to the Aryan race (i.e., the Germanic peoples), the Russian state was corrupt, their armed forces poorly equipped and their leadership deficient in inspired generalship. These were views that were disseminated widely throughout the Wehrmacht, and Balck had already made up his mind on the capacity of the Russian military.

The question of whether or to what extent Hermann Balck was a committed Nazi was first raised in this book in Chapter I, and it is important that we maintain a watchful eye on events and responses in order to be able to come to a balanced and evidence-based conclusion. Balck's willingness to cover the tracks of pro-Nazi colleagues hints at either an officer who was respectful of the anonymity of his peers or a man who shared these convictions and his memoirs act as a vehicle for such ideas. For now, there is no doubt that Balck was an enthusiastic supporter of the war, and by implication the war aims as far as the OKH and his peer group were aware. Officers like Balck, who gave above and beyond what was necessary to fight the war and indeed shared the strategic views of the Führer, were therefore complicit in sustaining and enabling the Nazi regime to carry out and achieve its wider political and world aims. Further examination is required into the extent to which we can label Balck, and other committed officers in the Heer, as an 'ardent Nazi', which was how Hugh Cole, author of *The Lorraine Campaign*, saw him.

For Hitler, the wars in the Balkans and against Greece had been a necessary diversion, not the main act. Mussolini's incompetence and impetuosity had provided Hitler with an opportunity to secure his southern flank in Europe against any British resurgence or attacks on the Ploesti oilfields in Romania. Securing Greece also provided better supply lines to Rommel, who was providing German newsreels with stunning victories in North Africa. But Hitler was not prepared to further dilute his forces allocated for the attack on Russia, and Rommel was asked to fight and win on what Fritz calls a 'shoestring budget'.[125]

Within the OKH and OKW, prolonged wrangling persisted throughout the spring of 1941 over what the precise strategy should be to defeat Russia. The eventual plan mirrored what Hitler envisaged: a three-pronged invasion in the north, south and centre, with the immediate objective of eliminating Russian forces within four months using Bliztkrieg tactics, modern weapons, better leadership and shock. The second objective was Moscow. It was in this second strategic aim that there was most disagreement. Underscoring all the arguments were the issues of supply, logistical capabilities and replacements. Estimates of what was possible meant that many of Hitler's wishes could not be fulfilled, and certainly not within four months. Russia was an enemy that had distinct advantages over Poland, France, Belgium, Norway, Holland and Greece – the major one being scale. Apart from the enormous areas involved, the railway system in Russia did not match German rolling stock, leaving road supply as the major artery, with all that entailed – there were simply not enough trucks for both a fully motorized infantry army as well as feeding the supply lines, nor were there enough men available to the German Army. Even the three million troops that the OKW aimed to put in the field could not match Russia's almost endless supply of manpower. If Russia did not succumb to Blitzkrieg in a fast knockout blow, then it spelt disaster; Hitler knew this, as did all of his generals. Fritz comments:

> 'Much of the later wrangling over operational strategy was thus conducted in a surrealistic atmosphere, since logistical difficulties rendered many of these disputes meaningless.'[126]

If the Red Army did not collapse like a pack of cards as Reich Minister of Propoganda Joseph Goebbels predicted, then the slowing of momentum would derail Germany's ability to sustain its attack. The longer the invasion went on, the stronger Russia would become, with the entire notion of Blitzkrieg running the risk of degenerating into the hell of trench warfare. The senior generals at the head of the German Army, Halder and von Brauchitsch, resisted as far as they could, but both were overpowered by the messianic power of Hitler, who was revered by many as a leader with the power of prophecy.

By the time that Hermann Balck arrived at the OKH south of Berlin, the pressure was on him to achieve results. The attack on Russia was but a few weeks old, but already demands for new equipment were coming in fast. However, before Balck could respond in any meaningful way, he received some terrible personal news. Friedrich-Wilhelm Balck, his eldest son, was killed in action in the first week of the war against Russia. Apart from noting his son's bravery, Balck says no more, and currently he is lost to anonymity.

The office of Sparkommissar to which Balck was appointed was a key role within the OKH. He was invested with sweeping powers to make what decisions he felt best. Both Fromm and von Brauchitsch trusted Balck implicitly, aware of his administrative efficiency as well as his ruthless approach to accuracy and performance. As what he describes as the 'Agent of Frugality', Balck was charged with eliminating waste, creating silk purses out of sows' ears and finding as much equipment for the Russian campaign as he could.[127] He was far more than just a good combat officer; he was a devoted soldier of the old Prussian school, and the formative influences discussed in Part I of this work all now came into play. There was no place for favouritism or cliques; everything in Balck's life had been governed by a strict self-imposed discipline that made him part of a small club of independent-minded senior officers. His disregard for elitism and army politics was no doubt refreshing, and probably saved his life after the events of the July 1944 Bomb Plot.

Dividing his time between his offices in Berlin and Hitler's 'Wolf's Lair' headquarters in Rastenburg, Balck travelled by light aircraft at night and car by day, his eyes firmly fixed on how he could quickly create a reserve pool of vehicles for new divisions in the process of being formed. Balck had his two recent adjutants from Panzer-Regiment 3 called to Berlin to assist him, and together, within four months, they had 'conserved' 100,000 vehicles together with their personnel.[128] This was an incredible feat in terms of revealing inefficiency, no doubt partly created by the speed of rearmament, but also of imagination, as redundant units were discovered doing nothing and were added to the reserve list of vehicles and troops. This huge mechanized pool would be vital for the remainder of the year and into 1942. Those red and gold oak leaves soon followed for Balck, promotion to Generalmajor coming early in November 1941, as did the role of General of Mobile Forces. One of his notable predecessors in the latter position had been Guderian, and in mid-November 1941 it was to Generaloberst Guderian in Orel (modern Oryol) that Generalmajor Hermann Balck flew, where his old acquaintance was now commanding the 2. Panzerarmee.

Part III

The Russian Front, 1941–1943

Chapter VIII

General of Mobile Forces at the OKH, November 1941–May 1942

The initial news from Operation Barbarossa was very positive. Even counting for the often misleading propaganda emanating from Goebbels and his aptly named Ministry of Propaganda, the reports were still good. Blitzkrieg appeared to be working, and the forces of the three great Army Groups – Nord (North), Mitte (Centre) and Süd (South) – were all making wonderful progress. Russian forces had been cut to shreds, their communications had failed and upwards of 500,000 prisoners had been encircled in vast pockets created by the fast-moving panzer forces. In his memoir *Five Years, Four Fronts*, Georg Grossjohan of the 198. Infanterie-Division recalled:

> 'When I was moved to the East, I was actually convinced I would be too late to see action. Reichspresschef Dr. Dietrich declared on the radio that all that was needed in Russia from the late summer would be "police actions".'[129]

Within Generalfeldmarschall Fedor von Bock's Heeresgruppe Mitte, Generaloberst Guderian's Panzergruppe 2 was one of two such armoured formations – the other being Panzergruppe 3, under the command of Generaloberst Hermann Hoth. There were also two infantry armies – the 4. Armee under Generalfeldmarschall Günther von Kluge and 9. Armee, commanded by Generaloberst Adolf Strauss. Panzergruppe 2 was in turn divided into four Panzer corps. Balck's old 2. Panzer-Division, containing his former command of Panzer-Regiment 3, had missed the opening of Operation Barbarossa in June as it was still recovering from the Greek campaign and being refitted after the losses in the sinkings in the Adriatic. However, it did arrive in October to reinforce Heeresgruppe Mitte during the Battle of Moscow.

Raputitsa and the disaster before Moscow

After the successes of June, July and August 1941, all eyes were directed towards Moscow. For the German generals, Moscow meant little by way of a strategic necessity, and by making it a predictable key target, they knew the Russians would certainly fight harder than ever and concentrate their forces on defending the capital. Yet for Hitler, Moscow was a politically vital objective. In his mind, it was a simple way of drawing the Russians into oblivion. Operation Typhoon was the codename given to the capture of Moscow and Heeresgruppe Mitte was allocated this task, with supporting thrusts from the north and south. Telegraphing the central strategy to Stalin and his Russian generals was borne of arrogance and certainly helped the Russians to plan and prepare for the destruction of the German forces. If the Germans could be held up by huge sacrifices of men and materials during October and November, then Stalin would have enough time to transfer significant unused formations – including tank divisions – from the Far East, where they had been expecting a Japanese attack in support of their Axis German allies.

When Balck arrived to meet Guderian in November 1941, it was soon clear that Guderian's troops, now renamed the 2. Panzerarmee, were in trouble. The initial overwhelming successes of summer had slowed. Overextended supply lines, the need for repairs and shortages of fuel were already creating significant challenges, as Guderian had complained to OKH during September.

Successes at the Battles of Bryansk and Vyazma from 2–21 October saw Guderian's 2. Panzerarmee surround two further huge Russian formations, the Third and Thirteenth Armies, but they had not surrendered. Furthermore, the arrival of General Georgy Zhukov from Leningrad – where he had frustrated the advance of Heeresgruppe Nord – meant that that twenty-eight German divisions would be further exhausted over a two-week period in reducing resistance in the pockets. Worse still, Heeresgruppe Süd had stalled in trying to take Kiev in Ukraine. Hitler now made his pivotal decision. The Führer was so focussed on taking Moscow that no other strategic options would be considered. Hitler wanted to secure the flanks of Heeresgruppe Mitte before advancing further, and to do this he ordered the still-powerful 4. and 9. Armees to dig in and stop the advance, while the two Panzer Armies were detached – 3. Panzerarmee was diverted north to support the attack of Heeresgruppe Nord, while 2. Panzerarmee under Guderian moved south to help Heeresgruppe Süd in the advance through Ukraine. A convincing argument can be made that this decision decided the outcome of the Second World War. It had three main consequences. Firstly, it gave unexpected breathing space for Stalin to regroup and transport 1,500 factories and 10 million workers away from Moscow and further to the east, where they could be rebuilt and continue war production unmolested. Secondly, it also gave Stalin time to bring reinforcements from Siberia to fight the German invaders. Lastly, it pushed the German advance ever closer to the arrival of snow and the *raputitsa* – the muddy season, when roads became impassable. This was a fatal decision for an army predicated on movement and up against the clock.

This was the strategic situation when Hermann Balck arrived in Orel, 230 miles south of Moscow, in early November. Neither Balck nor Guderian would have known that just a couple of months before, in September, just outside Oryol in the Medvedev Forest, some 160 political prisoners had been executed by the NKVD (the Soviet secret police) on the direct orders of Stalin. Those executed were a fraction of the 5,000 held in Oryol's prison, but they were well-known opponents of Stalin and hoped for the Germans to arrive and liberate them. They included Fritz Noether, a German-Jewish mathematician and friend of Albert Einstein who had fled to Russia in the hope of protection. There was also Maria Spiridonova, one of the original Russian revolutionaries from 1906, and Dmitry Pletnyov, a famous cardiac doctor. Rather than let them fall into German hands, Stalin had them shot.[130]

The conversations between Balck and Guderian concerned new problems that they had not faced before. There were overextended supply lines, terrible roads (only 5 per cent of Russian roads were paved or concreted), rear actions to deal with involving growing numbers of partisans, nearly a million Russian prisoners to guard and feed, and exhausted troops (even with the availability of Pervitin). They also faced a huge consumption of oil and fuel for the trucks required for supplies and, more recently, a Russian Army seemingly revitalized and fighting back to save Moscow.

The Mozhaysk defences

In retrospect, it was only in a nation led by a man like Joseph Stalin that the October 1941 defence of Moscow could have been so robust. The Mozhaysk defence line was created by Georgy Zhukov by reconstructing what was available of Russian forces and producing an entirely new front. Zhukov installed new leadership and inspired the will to resist amongst the 90,000 or so available troops. On their own, the 5th, 16th, 43rd and 49th Armies were nowhere near enough to hold back Heeresgruppe Mitte, so the people of Moscow were mobilized. At least 250,000 men, women and children moved 3 million cubic metres of soil by hand, building huge anti-tank ditches in the form of concentric rings to the west of Moscow. Massive numbers of militia battalions were armed and sent to man defences all around the outskirts of the Moscow Oblast. Guderian and the reconnaissance units of 2. Panzerarmee pushed to within sight of Moscow, but by November the mud, lack of supplies, exhaustion and counter-attacks brought them to a halt. Generalmajor Balck's mood dropped considerably, as his memoirs illustrate:

'A Russian battlegroup had been encircled east of Stalinogorsk (now Novomoskovsk). The following night that unit, a Siberian Division, broke out of the encirclement. With their leaders up front in tanks, the unorganised mass of troops followed like a herd. In the process, two battalions of our 25th Motorised Infantry Division, which still had nine and seven rifle squads respectively, were overrun. There were so many Russians that even the machine guns could not finish them all off.'[131]

There are a number of interesting parts to this statement. Balck reveals himself to be a man repulsed if not nauseated by the way he saw the Russian armies – 'leaders' not officers led the breakout, the Russians were 'unorganised', a 'herd' – as if they were cattle – and most of all, even the Germans' lethal MG34 and MG42 machine guns were unable to kill them all off – as if a slaughter of 'rats' would have been the ideal solution but was unfortunately not possible. This statement does not make Balck a Nazi. He was just another soldier, but it does shed light on the ruthless aspect of his character that, up to now, had remained hidden.

During November, as General of Motorized Troops, Balck made sure he toured as much of the front as he could. He met with General der Panzertruppe Leo Geyr von Schweppenburg, who was commanding XXIV. Armeekorps within Guderian's 2. Panzerarmee.[132] The XXIV. Armeekorps was composed of 1. Kavallerie-Division, 3. Panzer-Division, 4. Panzer-Division, 10. Infanterie-Division (mot) and 267. Infanterie-Division. On paper it was a powerful formation, but in reality it had been worn down by weeks of attritional fighting. Von Schweppenburg was a talented commander and now sat a full two ranks above Balck. In conversation, von Schweppenburg appealed to Balck, whom he knew would be reporting directly to Berlin, to ensure that the grave condition of his corps was understood. Even the renowned Infanterie-Regiment 'Grossdeutschland' had been almost destroyed. Balck himself witnessed what impact the fighting since June had on the XXIV. Armeekorps:

'The corps formed up that day [26 November] with three divisions in three columns near Tula. With the three divisions equal in size to only three reinforced battalions, the movement naturally ground to a halt.'[133]

If XXIV. Armeekorps was anything to judge by, then the whole of Heeresgruppe Mitte had been ravaged by the fighting over the past five months. By late November, it was still short of its objective of Moscow and had been eaten away by enormous casualties, losing the majority of its experienced fighting men and seeing its officer cadre almost extinguished. The 'Grossdeutschland' had very nearly been eliminated by its own bravery, while at the same time establishing its notoriety for atrocities. Similarly, the formidable 2. SS-Panzer-Division 'Das Reich', which had been chosen to spearhead Operation Typhoon, had already sacrificed 60 per cent of its battle strength once the assault was launched, losing vast numbers of talented, courageous and ruthless troops. In his excellent book on the sacrifices of the Red Army, David Glantz recorded how many German infantry regiments were now down to just 150–200 men from a starting compliment of 3,000.[134] According to T.H. Flaherty, the 'Das Reich' had been 'mauled' as badly as if they had been fighting against tigers – hardly the cattle-like herd that Balck described.[135]

Prophetically, the massive size of the Russian battlefield, length and vulnerability of the supply lines and the onset of mud and then snow had all been predicted before the invasion. However, the constant egotistical and philosophical rivalries amongst officers of the Wehrmacht for Hitler's favour persisted, as did the reluctance of German industry to appreciate the damage they were doing by refusing either to move to mass production or design more basic models. The stubbornness of the industrial giants created a log jam in production that only the appointment in 1942 of Albert Speer as Minister of Armaments and War Production would unlock – by which time it was too late. In his 1979 interview, Hermann Balck reveals what research has subsequently proven:

> '[T]he crisis of the German Army in front of Moscow at the end of the first autumn was really a production crisis. Because of General von Schell, we were still at peacetime production rates for tanks during the entire autumn. And, as combat attrition accumulated, we wound up with valuable tank crews fighting in black [the uniform colour of the Panzerwaffe] uniforms in the snow as infantrymen – and being totally wasted.'[136]

Later in the same interview, Balck expands on this production crisis:

> '[Von Schell] was never able to control the very powerful automobile industry – because of their political connections. Their interests, of course, were always primarily directed at being in a good position for peacetime automobile production at the end of the war.'[137]

But it would not be the industrialists who paid the price. These men had been part of the 'enablers' in the 1920s and 1930s that provided funds for Hitler to come to power. In return for their investment in him, they expected Hitler to maintain their profits, and the Führer would rather blame his generals than his bankers.

Just before he left to make his report to Berlin, Hermann Balck made sure that he also saw the commander of Heeresgruppe Mitte, Generalfeldmarschall von Bock. This was a pivotal moment with a central character at this stage of the war against Russia, yet the only comment that Balck makes in his memoirs is that 'It was an interesting evening'. Brevity and clarity are to be admired in a soldier, but this inscrutable phrase eludes any sort of interpretation that can be relied upon as evidence of what was discussed.

Reporting to the Führer, 30 December 1941

Balck arrived back in Berlin in the late November 1941. The task of reporting to the Führer in good times as well as bad about the performance and status of the Heer was the role of Generalfeldmarschall Walther von Brauchitsch, as head of the German Army, and his deputy, Generaloberst Franz Halder. Both men had been in post since 1938, and both had seen all the various chimeras of Hitler's personality. But in December 1941, they witnessed something new. Balck records how he first briefed von Brauchitsch on 30 November.[138] Describing von Brauchitsch as a 'sick, broken man' – such was how fast the commander of the German Army had declined since the start of the Russian campaign the previous June – he seemed fatalistically to accept that the entire war was already lost. The atmosphere worsened with the start of the Russian counter-offensive on 5 December, and Hitler was forced to sign Directive 39, which ordered the Wehrmacht to assume the defensive along the entire length of the Eastern Front.

Barbarossa had failed, as had the Panzerwaffe and *Auftragstaktik*, and, on 19 December, von Brauchitsch was sacked by Hitler, who now took over command of the German Army himself. Despite the atrocious losses of men to the winter cold, with minus 40-degree temperatures, Hitler refused to endorse a partial withdrawal that had been prudently ordered by von Kluge and Guderian. By the time Balck arrived, Hitler had also decided that Guderian was no longer reliable as an ideologically committed commander – consequently, Guderian was also sacked on Christmas Day.

Balck's accounts of relationships within the military hierarchy in Berlin and his impressions of the most senior figures – and indeed Hitler himself – open windows that allow us to gain further insight into how the German command structures functioned at the very highest levels. Balck was sent back to Russia soon after the sacking of von Brauchitsch, arriving in Smolensk at the headquarters of Heeresgruppe Mitte on 23 December. The Red Army was destroying large sections of the Heer; the entire XXXV. Armeekorps, was nearly lost in the defence of Guderian's southern flank while its commander tried to hold back the Soviet 3rd Army, commanded by Vasily Kuznetsov.[139] The situation was so dire that Hitler ordered OKH staff officers to travel to the Eastern Front to bolster morale and encourage combat commands to maintain their defensive actions, acting in a similar role Stalin's own commissars.

Hermann Balck was sent to the 3. and 4. Panzerarmees near Moscow. He knew the forces and many of the commanders. Hitler had sacked von Brauchitsch on 19 December, but the previous day he had also sacked von Bock as commander of Heeresgruppe Mitte and promoted von Kluge from 4. Armee to command the entire Heeresgruppe. In total, Hitler sacked forty senior German officers for the failure to take Moscow in 1941.

Von Kluge impressed Balck, as did Erich Hoepner – the commander of 4. Panzerarmee – who had been part of that earlier move of being detached from Heeresgruppe Nord (Generalfeldmarschall Wilhelm Ritter von Leeb) to try to encircle Moscow from the north. Hoepner advocated 'ruthless and complete destruction of the enemy' and oversaw the carrying out of Hitler's Commissar Order (under which all Soviet political commissars captured were to be summarily executed).[140] In total, over 100 captured commissars were shot by Hoepner's forces and his advance on Leningrad was followed by the activities of Einsatzgruppe A – the SS killing squad – the movement of which was noted by the commander of Einsatzgruppen A, Franz Stahlecker, as being 'effected in agreement with Panzer Group 4 and at their express wish'.[141]

Hoepner, in what would shortly contribute to his removal from command, told Balck bluntly that Moscow could not be taken. One unit, 11. Panzer-Division, had, for example, come to a complete stop through a lack of fuel and only just survived fighting from a static position when attacked by the Soviet 316th and 78th Rifle Divisions. Another unit, 160. Infanterie-Division, had only eighty men left.

It was now Balck's turn to brief Hitler back at Rastenburg on 30 December. It is easy to imagine how he must have contemplated what he should and should not say, the tone he should use and the advice he should give, if asked by the Führer. The energized meeting is described in his memoirs as 'taking two hours', during which time Hitler 'hardly spoke'. One wonders if Hitler recalled taking coffee with Balck on his train in his visit to the new 3. Panzer-Division back in 1934.[142]

The overall impression of this meeting was that Hitler and Balck were in agreement that there should be no withdrawal on any part of the Eastern Front. Hitler reasoned through dogged stubbornness and instinct rather strategy, but Balck suggested that the current crisis would not be solved by an operational solution. Conditions were so dreadful that the men would need just to hold; it would be a Napoleonic-size disaster to try to retreat from Moscow at the present. Balck tells us he used his time with the Führer to labour the need for increased tank production. Hitler seems to have been misled by Keitel at the OKW, who was also present at the meeting, in terms of tanks delivered to the front. An embarrassing dose of reality was needed in the otherwise suffocatingly sterile bubble in which Hitler operated at the Wolf's Lair – dependent on others for absolutely all information and drip-fed controlled data, and yet omnipotent in all military matters. Hitler was still what General Warlimont described as 'at the height of his power and authority' and was 'supported almost unanimously by the German people; he was firmly obsessed by a crusading ideal'.[143] Thus, Warlimont states, the only way an officer could divert or subvert Hitler was 'by working undercover' – for which we can read, feeding him false data. This terrible state of affairs seems to have been exposed by Balck. Hitler demanded to see his Minister for Armaments and Munitions, Fritz Todt, straight away, and the Führer and Balck developed what Balck liked to think was a 'good rapport'.[144] To what extent Hitler, a psychopath and paranoid schizophrenic, had a good rapport with anybody is impossible to tell, but perhaps what Balck meant was that Hitler, at this moment in time, was receptive, acknowledging and grateful. To feel special in the company of an enigmatic figure is part of the mystique of power of charismatic leadership, something with which Hitler was abundantly blessed. As the war entered 1942, Hitler seemed to have confidence in Balck – as future events and awards were to show – ultimately making the currently comparatively humble Generalmajor one of only twenty-seven holders of the Knight's Cross (already awarded at this point) with Oakleaves, Swords and Diamonds.

The impact of the defeat before Moscow – the example of Erich Hoepner

In his memoirs, Balck described Hoepner as a 'powerful leader', but even he was relieved of his command when he ignored both von Kluge and Hitler's 'no retreat' order to pull his battered forces back and avoid the threat of encirclement.[145] Up to this point, Hoepner seems to have been a loyal, experienced and committed commander, but he could not survive the temper of the Führer as the reality of the first Eastern Front winter was driven home.[146]

Hitler's assumption of total control over the Wehrmacht was one of the most important results of defeat before the gates of Moscow. He may have hated Bolshevism and loathed Stalin, but he mistrusted his generals, seeing duplicity, weakness and efforts to direct his actions – manifestations of paranoia. The anger that overcame Hitler by failing to take Moscow showed itself not only by sacking his generals but in his new-found sense of total power and an open display of ruthlessness. Hoepner was badly let down by von Kluge, who had led him to believe that he would be able to make a limited withdrawal of his troops once his superior officer had cleared this with the OKW. However, 'OKW' now effectively meant Adolf Hitler. Hoepner made the mistake of thinking that Hitler would see things as a soldier and began the withdrawal on 8 January 1942. *Auftragstaktik* had taught him to make decisions on the spot, within the framework of the mission. Von Kluge, fearing Hitler would find out, reported Hoepner – and the Führer exploded. Hoepner received a message the same day that he was relieved of command and recalled to Berlin. If Hitler's intention was to strike fear into his generals, then he succeeded. This would make his weaker disciples even more compliant and drive more sceptical officers into the embryonic resistance movement, fearing a madman was now in charge of Germany. Hitler demanded unconditional obedience as the ultimate elixir of leadership.

Strategically, the failure to take Moscow was not terminal, and the coming of spring would bring not only optimism but a realization that the Wehrmacht was able to resupply the front-line officer vacancies with new rising stars who would step into the shoes left by so many recent departures. Balck, feeling that he had the ear of the Führer, set about creating 'tanks, tanks and more tanks'.[147] Moreover, Balck states that Hitler was right to have sacked so many generals, though he does not comment on the fate of the respected Hoepner. Balck also felt Hitler was correct to take over direct command of the Wehrmacht on a temporary basis as a pragmatic response to the current strategic situation, possibly because Hermann Balck was himself in awe of his messianic leader.[148]

An opportunity to clarify his support for Nazism

In one section of his memoir, Balck tells of the moment one of his trusted aides, Oberst Krahmer, suddenly and formally announced that he was not a National Socialist. Balck records that he responded by saying they were all soldiers and such things did not matter. He did not, however, tell Krahmer that he too was not a true Nazi. In the confines of a private conversation with a loyal and trusted aide, this was a moment that Balck could have used to clarify his own position, but he did not.[149] In his defence, Balck does point out in his diary entry for 15 January 1942 that Hitler was militarily inexperienced and that he was not overly influenced by Hitler's thinking at the time. This in itself was a somewhat strange thing to record, almost as if he was trying to gauge and self-assess whether he too had been sucked into the hypnotic atmosphere that surrounded close contact with supreme power.[150]

Meeting with von Stauffenberg

As the thaw began in the new year of 1942, Balck writes of the quality of his hand-picked staff and reveals that he met with Oberst Claus von Stauffenberg, who became one of the leaders of the plot to kill Hitler. On his personal staff, apart from Oberst Krahmer, were Major Hans-Georg Lueder and the courageous Oberstleutnant Helmuth von Pannwitz, the later self-appointed leader and guardian of the Russian Cossack forces who fought for Germany. Balck often takes time to credit his forgotten staff officers, the engine room of any mobile and efficient unit.

Balck was quite easily able to get information to Hitler and ask for meetings, which he says he could achieve within ten days. Through his connections, von Pannwitz also often went back to the Führer and always pushed through whatever Balck needed. We can therefore see that Hitler ensured his staff officers opened up clear routes for those individuals he was happy to meet, and no doubt closed such routes to almost everyone else. Balck worked through Hitler's adjutant, General Rudolf Schmundt, to gain this access to the Führer.

The meeting with von Stauffenberg is interesting. At this stage, von Stauffenberg was working in the OKH's organization department in Berlin, so it was in this capacity that Balck had 'many evenings' discussing military matters with him. At one such dinner, Balck relates the following in his memoirs:

'In the course of one conversation he [von Stauffenberg] suddenly said to me

"Colonel, we have a peculiar solution [presumably to Hitler's assumption of command of the Army]. Himmler should be made commander in chief of the army. Then he could not put all of his efforts into the SS, but would have to take care of the army as well."

'That conversation shows how little we were able to look really deep inside the characters and the issues of that time. Although our discussion at the time was little more than a dinner table conversation, von Stauffenberg typically loved to throw such thoughts unexpectedly into a conversation in order to clarify his own thoughts in the process of the discussion that would instantly follow.'[151]

There could be another interpretation that Balck had perhaps missed entirely. Given that he called Balck 'Colonel' when by the spring of 1942 Balck was a Generalmajor, this discussion must have been during 1940, by which stage von Stauffenberg was already well advanced in his membership of the secret military resistance which was slowly gaining members amongst army officers. It is possible that von Stauffenberg's best way of testing potential members

General of Mobile Forces at the OKH, November 1941–May 1942   91

of the resistance was to throw out intimidatory comments to gauge what sort of reaction came back and thus determine whether his dinner guest could be attracted into the circle of resistance. Balck seems to have interpreted such comments in an entirely innocent and naïve way, which is exactly how they were intended to be seen – unless the recipient was receptive. Balck was not receptive and the plotters carried on without him through to July 1944, when they finally struck.

Hermann Balck spent the following months of spring 1942 deep in efforts to re-equip and create two new panzer divisions in Germany on the orders of Hitler. The 22. and 23. Panzer-Divisions were quickly formed through some imaginative adjustments.[152] Balck notes, with some vehemence, how the one thing he was not able to provide was experienced and strong leadership, from commanding generals down to the regimental and even battalion levels, with the result that both divisions would suffer almost complete and premature annihilation on the Eastern Front.

The losses of the 22. Panzer-Division, under the command of Generalleutnant Wilhelm von Apell, hurt Balck more than any other, as he had been a prime mover in its creation with new men and equipment. Attached to 11. Armee, commanded now by a newly promoted Generalfeldmarschall Erich von Manstein – the architect of the invasion of France in 1940 – 22. Panzer became part of the efforts to take the remaining parts of the Crimea. Von Manstein had been selected personally by Hitler after the former commander of 11. Armee, Generaloberst Eugen Ritter von Schobert, was killed when his plane landed in a Soviet minefield. Balck describes how the division was arriving piecemeal by train and vehicle transport at its forming-up area in the Crimea as part of XLII Armeekorps when it was immediately ordered to mount an attack at 0600hrs on 20 March.[153]

Warfare on the Eastern Front was often characterized by 'fire fighting' against Soviet breakthroughs. The Soviet 51st Army had begun an offensive on 13 March, and von Manstein ordered the 22. Panzer-Division into combat despite only being partially formed. Panzer-Regiment 204 attacked, and its I. Bataillon became disorientated in marshes and deep fog, arunning into a minefield where it was ambushed by Red Army anti-tank units and counter-attacked by the Soviet 55th Tank Brigade. Within three hours, by 0900hrs, the I/204 had lost 40 per cent of its men and equipment. Overall, the division lost thirty-two of its 142 tanks, including nine Panzer IIs, seventeen Panzer 38 (T)s (the Czech tanks once used in Poland and France) and six Panzer IVs. In his book on the fighting in the Crimea, Robert Forczyk describes this episode as 'one of the most badly bungled German armoured attacks of the entire war on the Eastern Front'.[154]

Hermann Balck wanted to see the damage for himself, and it was no doubt a difficult meeting for the commander of the I/204, Oberstleutnant Wilhelm Koppenburg, but there was nothing that could be done. Balck notes that he was 'moved' by what he saw and heard from the tank troops and field commanders, and ruminated that a more experienced divisional commander would have found a way to avoid making an attack until all his division was assembled – wonderful in hindsight and perhaps wishful thinking, as Balck would find out later when he too had to order partially formed units into the line.[155]

Chapter IX

Command of 11. Panzer-Division, May 1942–March 1943

By May 1942, Hermann Balck seems to have had enough of the OKH, the internal politics, egotistical rivalries and diminution of its role in the face of Hitler's leadership. Balck says that he asked for a combat command – he may have even specified the only partly reconstructed 11. Panzer-Division – and almost immediately his offer was snapped up.

Within the context of what was developing at a strategic level on the Eastern Front, such a command was perfect for him. Earlier in January, Hitler had continued to rant about the changes needed in the leadership of his front-line units.[156] To Luftwaffe General Wolfram von Richthofen, Hitler raved that his generals were too old and not physically capable of fighting the sort of war that was now needed. He wanted men who had proven themselves, 'have strong nerves and do not topple over at the first crisis'. The Führer stated in March 1942:

> 'This winter has allowed us to find a group of truly tough generals. The longer the war lasts, the more valuable will be such personalities ... Unknown men move to the foreground.'

In May 1942, 11. Panzer-Division was part of Generalleutnant Willibald von Langermann und Erlencamp's XXIV. Armeekorps and was positioned near Orel in the Voronezh Oblast, 570 miles north-west of Stalingrad. The unit that Balck took over on 16 May had been through a hard time. Raised as one of the new Panzer divisions in August 1940 after the Battle of France, it was originally composed of mostly units of Silesian troops welded together from parts of the 5. Panzer-Division and 209. and 311. Infanterie-Divisions. Commanded by the respected Generalmajor Ludwig Crüwell, the 11. Panzer-Division had been part of the invasion of Yugoslavia in the spring of 1941 and was then allocated to Heeresgruppe Süd, where it was part of Panzergruppe 1 within XLVIII Armeekorps (mot).[158] The core of the division were men wearing the black, double-breasted uniforms with their pink piping of the tank units of the Panzerwaffe and Panzer-Regiment 15.

Between February and December 1941, Panzer-Regiment 15 was commanded by the skilled, popular and brave Oberstleutnant Gustav-Adolf Riebel. Riebel left his mark on the regiment, and it was a skilled tank unit with a considerable reputation before, in January 1942, the commander moved on to help lead and rebuild Panzer-Regiment 24 as part of 24. Panzer-Division.[159] One of the members of Panzer-Regiment 15 was Unteroffizier Gustav W. Schrodek, a tank commander. In *Panzer Warfare on the Eastern Front* by Hans Schaufler, published in 2012, an extract from Schrodek's diary gives a vivid impression of what the 11. Panzer-Division had been going through in December 1941 in front of Moscow. Diverted north in the southern push to encircle Moscow, 11. Panzer found itself locked into increasingly violent battles as the Russians fought hard to defend their capital city. Schrodek wrote:

'I saw a traffic sign – Moscow 18.5km …

'Our ranks were getting thinner. A couple [of tanks] got hit every day. When would it be our turn?

'The trust of the troops in the senior leadership dwindled; the morale had been battered.

'It was clear to everyone that we could expect no mercy from the Russians. Ever since 9th December, we had been ordered to conduct a "scorched earth" policy. [designed to deny the enemy any cover from the freezing temperatures].

'The graves of our dead were supposed to be flattened. Easier said than done. We limited ourselves to taking the grave markers, so as to deceive the Russians about our heavy losses and to keep the troop elements of the dead secret.'

He then commented on the impact of winter:

'Whatever was not operational – unfortunately, that included a few tanks – had to be left behind and blown up.

'Around 11.00 hours, the Russians attacked so suddenly that the motorised riflemen had been overrun. The constant staying outdoors in the cold and the lack of rations and sleep had paralysed alertness and the ability to resist.'

He also wrote about the Russian T-34 tanks:

'They [the riflemen] ran up to us and asked us to move out against the Russian tanks. No way! They still believed in fairy tales and thought we could scare away the T-34s with our old crates …. the T-34s were able to churn through anything. In contrast we immediately bottomed out. [The Panzer Mk III and IV were low-silhouette tanks and low on the ground, whereas the T-34 was high and proud, able to move over mud and soft ground. Their armour was also far thicker and easily able to stand hits from the earlier German tank types].

'The other tank from my company had been knocked out. By then, we were moving past another knocked-out tank. We no longer had any way on our tank to provide aimed fire. Everywhere you looked there were Russian tanks, which were completely unaffected by our main gun.'[160]

From December 1941 to February 1942, Russian attacks occurred almost daily along some parts of the line. German units were exhausted, with casualties to the Russian winter often exceeding those lost to enemy action. In all, some 750,000 German troops had so far been either killed, wounded or gone missing in action (many being captured). If the Wehrmacht was to mount any sort of offensive in the spring of 1942, then whole new units and vast numbers of replacements would be needed – but there was no substitute for combat experience. To give an example, on the southern front, Oberleutnant Grossjohan recalled that, by the end of 1941, his 198. Infanterie-Division had lost 203 officers and 5,426 enlisted men killed, wounded or missing – 50 per cent of its strength. (161)

The combat condition of the 11. Panzer-Division, May–June 1942

The German Army had exhausted itself in the second half of 1941 trying to win a war against Russia, with operational flexibility increasingly tied by Hitler's growing interference, some serious miscalculations about the strength and morale of Russian forces and disagreements on the main objectives. The winter of 1941–1942 depleted what was left of experienced NCOs and good equipment. Indeed, by May 1942, 'Most of the infantry divisions in Army Group South stood at about 50% strength.'[162] Although the Heer worked tirelessly to re-equip the Panzer and infantry divisions, there was no substitute for experienced leaders. To prepare for the new offensives in July 1942, Hitler reached out to his military allies to give him the extra troops he would need to protect his German divisions when they made their next set of thrusts into Russia, both to the north and into the Caucasus to the south. By August 1942, thirty-six new divisions from Hitler's allies were positioned carefully along the Eastern Front, but fresh problems arose with logistics, communications and orders as Hungarians, Italians and Romanians all insisted on individual commands.

In terms of personnel, Balck was often regretful at how the quality of NCO leadership and officers declined through the near constant erosion of battle:

> 'Since the turn of the century, and in accordance with the idea of decentralised command, NCOs formed an essential part of German low-level leadership, normally leading platoons, groups, and individual heavy weapons. This is clearly pointed out in "Guidelines for the training of the NCOs at the Field NCO Schools".'[163]

Nonetheless, 11. Panzer-Division had preserved a good number of quality officers and junior combat leaders, who were spread across its many units. There were numerous already decorated men, who had survived and served well in Poland, such as Oberfeldwebel Lorenz Harthan, who was part of motorcycle Kradschützen-Abteilung 61. Harthan had already been wounded four times before Balck arrived to take command of the division, and he would eventually receive the Knight's Cross and the Close Combat Clasp in Gold, marking him out as an exceptional soldier in the division.[164]

After Crüwell left for North Africa to take command of the Afrikakorps, he was eventually succeeded by Generalmajor Walter Scheller, who took command until Balck's appointment in May 1942. Scheller never lived up to the popularity of Crüwell, and Balck faced a unique problem in terms of his officers upon his arrival:

> 'Making matters difficult, but in some ways easier, was the fact that my predecessor had so thoroughly alienated all his subordinate commanders that twenty-two regimental and battalion commanders were then home on sick leave.'[165]

After leaving 11. Panzer, Scheller went on to a number of successful commands and was promoted to Generalleutnant and awarded the Knight's Cross in April 1943, so whatever was wrong with his relationship with the officers of the division may not have been all his fault.[166]

Order of Battle for 28 June 1942, and Case Blue

Panzer-Regiment 15 formed the core tank unit of the 11.Panzer-Division and was re-equipped in preparation for the expected June offensive of 1942. The OKH had shuffled their tanks around to make sure the armoured divisions were in place for Heeresgruppe Süd's offensive, known as Fall Blau ('Case Blue'). The summer offensive was structured in phases. Phase I would see 4. Panzerarmee and the 2. and 6. Armees break through towards Verozneh and the upper Don River, encircling Soviet forces as they went. In Phase II, the 6. Armee would pivot southwards towards the Donets River and the Caucasus Mountains, where it was to seize crucial oilfields – Stalingrad was not the main objective.

The 11. Panzer-Division under Generalmajor Hermann Balck was part of XXIV. Armeekorps (renamed XXIV. Panzerkorps in July 1942), commanded by the recently promoted General der Panzertruppe von Langermann und Erlencamp, which in turn was part of Generaloberst Hermann Hoth's 4. Panzerarmee. Now expanded back to three tank battalions, according to the Niehorster tables, the order of battle for 11. Panzer-Division was as follows:

Divisional Headquarters (Divisionstab).
Panzer-Regiment 15 made up of three Panzer Battalions (Abteilung), I, II and III. The total number of tanks was 221 (compared to the 160 that they began with at the start of Barbarossa in June 1941), and these composed six light tank companies and three medium tanks companies (there were as yet no heavy tanks in production and ready to be sent to the front). Within the nine Panzer companies were spread the following number of armoured vehicles:

Panzer Mk II	74	With its thin 30mm armour, 20mm gun and weighing 10 tons.
Panzer Mk III	106	The 20-ton variant, with 50mm armour, was still very vulnerable to the 76.2mm gun of the T-34.
Panzer Mk IV	30	The new backbone of the armoured divisions but still coming off the production lines. It had thick frontal armour, could take on the T-34 with its 75mm gun, was good across country and had a crew of five.
Bef-Pz Sd.Kfz. 265	11	The Sd.Kfz. 265 Panzerbefehlswagen was a light armoured command vehicle. Only 190 were built, and as the war progressed they were steadily destroyed and not replaced.

The regiment also had its own tank recovery and repair workshop.

The 11. Panzergrenadier-Brigade was composed of:

Panzergrenadier-Regiment 110, with two motorized battalions commanded by Oberstleutnant Albert Henze.

Panzergrenadier-Regiment 111, with two motorised battalions.

Panzerjäger-Bataillon/Abteilung 61. Every Panzer division valued its anti-tank regiment very highly. Often armed with the outstanding 3.7cm Pak 36 or 5.0cm Pak 38, which were also motorized, these were the 'Tank Hunters' and could be used for a hasty defence against swarms of T-34s or in ambush situations – either way, they were a vital part of both the offence and defence against a Red Army dependant on tank power. Later in 1942, the tank destroyers began to arrive in greater numbers to assist in the job of eroding Red Army tank brigades.

Kradschützen-Abteilung 61, complete with two companies of motorcycle troops and mortars.

Aufklärungs-Abteilung 111, an armoured car reconnaissance unit usually equipped with six- and eight-wheeled heavy armoured cars such as the Sd.Kfz. 231 or 232 and the Sd.Kfz. 234.

Panzer-Artillerie-Regiment 119. In 11. Panzer-Division in June 1942, the regiment contained three battalions of guns.

Heeres Flak-Abteilung 277, an anti-aircraft unit.

Nachrichten-Abteilung 341, a signals unit composed of an armoured radio and signal company.

Panzer-Pionier-Abteilung 209, the engineers (or pioneers) of the 11. Panzer-Division, which included three units of bridging companies.

Feldersatz-Abteilung 61, an interesting unit where new recruits were acclimatized to the conditions at the front while being kept behind the lines. A Feldersatz battalion would learn how to survive in the field, get used to the sound of heavy gunfire, acclimatize to the need for camouflage and then would be called into the mother unit as replacements. They were increasingly used to guard rear areas from partisans, but as the war went on, the rear areas often very quickly became the front lines.

Kraftwagentransport-Regiment 61 (dealing with motor transport and supply matters).

Finally, of company size, there were a range of smaller units to cover off all the necessary tasks that made a Panzer division a totally independent unit, just as Guderian, Balck and others had envisioned during the 1920s and 1930s. There was a butchery unit for providing meat for the cooks, a commissary to ensure men were paid and private matters were dealt with (such as pensions and payments to families), a field post office, two medical companies, three ambulance columns and two platoon-strength units of military police. The divisional bakery provided as many loaves of bread as possible every day to feed 15,000 men of the division. Some divisions even had their own carrier pigeon unit. [167]

Under Hermann Balck's command, the 11. Panzer-Division stood ready to go for the new offensive in southern Russia in late June 1942 with around 15,000 officers and men.

Some of the personalities of 11. Panzer-Division in May 1942

We are fortunate to be able to identify a few of the personalities who would have welcomed their new commander into the division in May 1942. Oberstleutnant Theodor Graf von Schimmelmann, who had taken over command of Panzer-Regiment 15 with the departure of Oberstleutnant Riebel in January 1942, was commander of Balck's three tank battalions. Von Schimmelmann was an experienced tank officer and had served as a Major in 1941 in the Kursk-Oboyan Operation and the advance on Moscow. Vital to the success of the division was the relationship between the divisional commander and his senior tank officer, one of mutual respect and harmony of thinking. Von Schimmelmann already held the Iron Cross 1st and 2nd Class from the Great War, and by the time Balck took over command had been awarded the Ritterkreuz des Eisernen Kreuzes (Knight's Cross of the Iron Cross) as commander of the II. Bataillon in May 1941.[168]

Von Schimmelmann now had not two but three battalion commanders, as Case Blue decreed that all Panzer divisions would have a third tank battalion if resources allowed. Of the three tank Abteilung within 11. Panzer and Panzer-Regiment 15, Hauptmann Karl Lestmann commanded the II/15 Abteilung and would later distinguish himself in the winter fighting, while Hauptmann Edel-Heinrich Zachariae-Lingenthal led I/15 and, by early 1943, Hauptmann Klaus Piontek commanded the III/15.[169]

Balck would also have met Feldwebel Alois Assmann of the 1. Kompanie of Panzerjäger-Abteilung 61, who was awarded the Iron Cross in July 1941 for his bravery and skill with the Pak anti-tank gun. Zugführer – Platoon Leader – Gerhard Hensel was a member of the 2. Kompanie of the I. Bataillon of Panzer-Regiment 15. Hensel had been decorated with the Iron Cross 1st and 2nd Class, as well as the Panzerkampfabzeichen for fifty of more battle engagements. In the fighting near Moscow in December 1941, Hensel was also awarded the Knight's Cross for outstanding bravery.[170] Another member of Panzer-Regiment 15 was Unteroffizier Gustav W. Schrodek, a tank commander. The commanders of both Balck's Panzergrenadier regiments, the 110. and 112., were experienced officers, and he also had the very dependable Hauptmann Paul Freiherr von Hauser commanding the Kradschützen-Abteilung 61.[171] The motorcycle infantry were still invaluable units for forward reconnaissance and quick attacks which disorientated the enemy front lines, as well as providing intelligence of movements of enemy tank formations in the wide-open plains of the Ukraine and River Don basin.

Arriving in May 1942 at the divisional headquarters near Smolensk, Hermann Balck immediately asked for an update on all aspects of the fighting ability of the 11. Panzer-Division. He found that the refitting of tanks had gone exceedingly well in all areas, but motor transport still needed far more vehicles, being only at 40 per cent of its establishment.[172] The 11. Panzer had been re-equipped with the new longer-barrelled Mk IV tank, which put them in a far better position to destroy the T-34. Generalmajor F.W. von Mellenthin, Balck's future chief of staff, wrote in his memoirs:

> 'In 1941 we had nothing comparable with the T-34, with its 50mm maximum armour, 76mm high-velocity gun, and relatively high speed with splendid cross-country performance. These tanks were not thrown into battle in large numbers until our spearheads were approaching Moscow.'[173]

In 1941, although production of Mk III and Mk IV tanks with improved armour and a larger gun had increased, around 28 per cent of every Panzer division's tanks still comprised the old and inadequate MkI and Mk II models, which stood little chance against the T-34 and Russian anti-tank fire. Sending these light tanks into battle in Poland, France and the Balkans had been acceptable, as the armies they faced were not able to contend with Blitzkrieg and the German tank formations' *Auftragstaktik*. In Russia, however, things were very different. Hitler saw that tank warfare of the future belonged to far heavier leviathans, such as the T-34, and in response German had begun new tank designs for the Tiger Mk I and Mk II, plus the Panther, with their heavier armour, wider tracks and larger guns. Nevertheless, the fact that the 11. Panzer-Division had been re-equipped at all was a miracle in itself. According to Balck, this was fairly typical of all the formations around them. Even if the division did still have more than seventy largely obsolete Mk II tanks on strength, these were still fast and manoeuvrable on the hard ground of summer, and hopefully 1942 would be the last summer they would be needed in Russia. As well as creating two totally new tank formations – the 22. and 23. Panzer-Divisions – the OKH and OKW had also rushed whatever tank and weapon production they could muster over the hundreds of kilometres to the front lines into the many new SS-Panzer divisions that were also being developed.

Supplying the front lines in Russia

In their 2018 analysis *The German Army on the Eastern Front*, Jeff Rutherford and Adrian Wettstein provided a detailed assessment of the supply issues facing the OKW and OKH from 1941 onwards.[174] Going into any conflict requires a series of steps within the logistics set-up to ensure a steady flow of the essentials to maintain a division, corps or army. German domestic production needed to create an adequate supply, but these supplies had to get to the front lines safely and in the correct places. Barbarossa having failed, the peculiarities of a Western European army taking on Russia once more dramatically affected the chances of winning. The huge distances from depots, factories and railyards to an ever-advancing front line created massive challenges. All forms of transport were used – road, air and by sea – but it was the performance and capacity of the railways upon which all hopes were pinned. There was also the major issue of having gone into war from 1939 with forces which were only partially ready, and the use of captured tanks, trucks and artillery was the sticking plaster which the Russian campaign would expose as insufficient for what was ahead.

The infrastructure of the rear-echelon units was spread over huge areas, and they needed to maintain headquarter traffic, ensure a steady flow of communications with their combat units and order resupply requests for equipment, food, fuel, ammunition and spares for motorized units, and channel these through to front lines that were always moving – both backwards and forwards. Added to these hugely complex tasks was the administration of the army – records, decorations, sick and home leaves, disciplinary issues, promotions and appointments, all of which required a highly organized and disciplined approach. Often, all of these rear operations were carried out under the threat of partisan attacks – especially as the supply lines became over-extended – as well as bombing raids by enemy aircraft. Partisan actions were often dealt with by rear units of the SS or police battalions, with the consequent atrocities and massacres associated with their strategies. However, large numbers of infantry were also required to police the supply routes as best they could.

The German Army had two significant problems that consistently undermined its logistical support capability. The first was that the acute shortage of motor transport needed for such a vastly expanded army meant that there were not enough trucks to move supplies to the front – coupled with the fact that over

20 per cent of the existing transport in 1941 comprised either captured vehicles or civilian ones commandeered in Germany. There was a further problem in that wheeled transport stood no chance of being able to move on the few and muddy roads of Russia after September each year. In his report on his unit's performance in Greece earlier in 1941, Hermann Balck had stated that the only vehicles that could move over difficult ground and through shallow rivers were tracked or half-tracked ones. In a peak of fanciful thinking, Balck recommended that all wheeled vehicles in Panzer divisions were replaced with tracked ones.[175] Yet it was the Eastern Front of 1941 that fully exposed the Wehrmacht's paucity in tank and half-track production and the dilemma that German industrial oligarchs had wreaked upon Hitler's plans for a quick victory in Russia.

The ability of the repair and service workshops to cope with large numbers of vehicles that had been in combat since 1939 – many of which were foreign-made – meant that the workshops were dealing with maintaining worn-out vehicles and many that required Czech, French or Polish spare parts.[176] The same was true with weapons, as revealed by this examination of the variety in use by V. Armeekorps:

> 'It [V. Armeekorps] commanded the German 9th, 73rd and 125th Infantry Divisions, as well as the 3rd Romanian Mountain Division ... The 9th Infantry Division fielded several batteries of Light Field Howitzer 16, 10.5cm guns as the German standard gun Light Field Howitzer 18, but with different shells. The 125th Infantry Division had a few 4.7cm ATG's of Czech origin and 7.5cm ATG 38/97, the barrel of which was of French origin and needed different shells than the usual 7.5cm ATG 40. All three divisions had 7.65mm hand guns, which added a further type of ammunition to be delivered. The 3rd Romanian division had few weapons compatible with German munitions, which meant dozens of additional types of ammunition were required ... the Vth Army Corps quartermaster staff had to manage the administration and distribution of far more than 100 types of ammunition and to ensure that the right type of shells reached the right guns in time.[177]

Another significant challenge was the railways, specifically the shortage of rolling stock and the different gauges between the German and the Russian rail systems. In reality, this meant that long supply trains of the Deutsche Reichsbahn (German state railway) had to be unloaded at the old border and reloaded onto captured Russian rolling stock before they could be sent on to parts of the front. Yet that was only one of the problems the supply staff faced. According to Rutherford and Wettstein, to man and run the Reichsbahn in Russia, an additional 112,000 employees were needed for signalling, communications, repairs of track and engineering depots, plus more than 600,000 Soviet auxiliaries.[178] Traffic hubs in towns and cities became vital military objectives, as these linked up the comparatively small number of railways routes and avoided the use of roads and the lack of vehicles, but they needed to be captured fast and intact. During 1941, the German management of the new railway system was, at times, chaotic, but matters improved in 1942.

One other aspect should be factored into any thinking regarding the performance of German forces in Russia: how the strategic use of tanks impacted on logistics and supply. With a Heer containing over twenty armoured divisions, plus the new SS-Panzer divisions, and the now accepted strategy of *Schwerpunkt* followed by deep-penetration breakouts, the tanks could be in one place in the morning and 70km further away by the evening, and yet the supply systems were expected to keep up with them. One way this issue was partially solved was for the Panzergruppen to have mobile depots containing supplies, spare parts (when they were available) and engineers to complete repairs and service.[179] This aspect of the war in the East has yet to be fully studied, but the officers and men who provided these services performed daily miracles in all weathers to keep the armoured formations moving between 1942 and 1944. When we add in the tactical angle of *Auftragstaktik* and the encouragement of local commanders in the field – men such as Hermann Balck – to make their own decisions, then the situation could change even more rapidly. Forces could thus end up in completely unknown sectors of the front, waiting for food, ammunition and fuel to arrive overnight.

The Red Army and the Bryansk Front

Facing Balck across the front line of the Bryansk (very shortly to become the Voronezh) Front were the forces of Lieutenant General Filipp Golikov and Marshal Semen Timoshenko. By the spring of 1942, Stalin looked at the continuing siege of Leningrad in the north, the German forces still in front of Moscow, the loss of eastern Crimea and a disaster at Kharkov, and tried to predict what would happen next. Although he expected another assault on Moscow, he was not surprised when on 28 June the German 4. Panzerarmee under Generaloberst Hermann Hoth launched Case Blue between the cities of Kursk in the north and Kharkov further south, and headed all out for the Don River. The Red Army formations now in front of Hoth's Germans were those of the 3rd, 13th, 40th and 48th Armies, together with the 5th Tank Army. Golikov had assumed command of the entire Front on 2 April 1942, and he would remain in his post until 7 July. It would be his 40th Army, under

Lieutenant General Mikhail Parsegov, and the 13th Army, commanded by Major General Nikolai Pukhov, that would bear the brunt of the attack that was about to begin.

Fall Blau and the attack on Voronezh, 28 June – 7 July 1942

As the German Army emerged from the freezing cold, death and huge losses of the winter of 1941–1942 and looked forward to the coming spring, it was clear that Barbarossa had failed. The Red Army had suffered but survived, proving itself to be a stubborn and formidable fighting force, and was still holding defensive lines across the three main Heeresgruppe fronts.

Strategically, Hitler knew that he could only win what was now a war of attrition if his economy was strong enough to support him, which meant that he needed oil. The plans for the summer offensive took shape during February and March 1942, with Hitler promising Dr Joseph Goebbels that by October, Germany would be in a position to fight a 'hundred years' war in the east' and to cope with global conflict.[180]

As the front line began to thaw, the strategic situation showed itself in more detail, and it was clear that the defensive lines on both sides – that had been frozen in place by minus 40-degree temperatures – offered both weaknesses and opportunities. In southern Russia at least, the German target was clear – the oil fields of Baku, Grozny and Maikop. In Fall Gelb (Case Blue), Hitler reversed the dictum of von Clausewitz that first one must defeat the enemy in the field and then control their raw materials. The Führer did not have time, or the capacity, in 1942 to destroy the Red Army, but he did need resources in order to continue the war until achieving victory.[181]

If the Caucasian oil fields were now the main objective, then it was Heeresgruppe Süd that would be tasked with the main summer offensive, taking Case Blue forward with its consecutively unfolding phases. Originally, Generalfeldmarschall Walter von Reichenau was to be in command, but when he succumbed to a stroke and died on 17 January 1942, Hitler once again turned to von Bock – whom, it should be recalled, he had sacked the previous December for advocating a retreat in front of Moscow. Under von Bock's command were some of the most powerful forces ever assembled – the Panzer divisions had been enlarged with an additional tank battalion – and they were all set loose on 28 June.

Balck recalls how all was quiet just before his regimental artillery opened fire at 0215hrs on 28 June. As part of XXIV. Armeekorps, commanded by austere imperial cavalryman Willibald von Langermann und Erlencamp, 11. Panzer-Division moved forward at speed. The tanks and motorized troops of

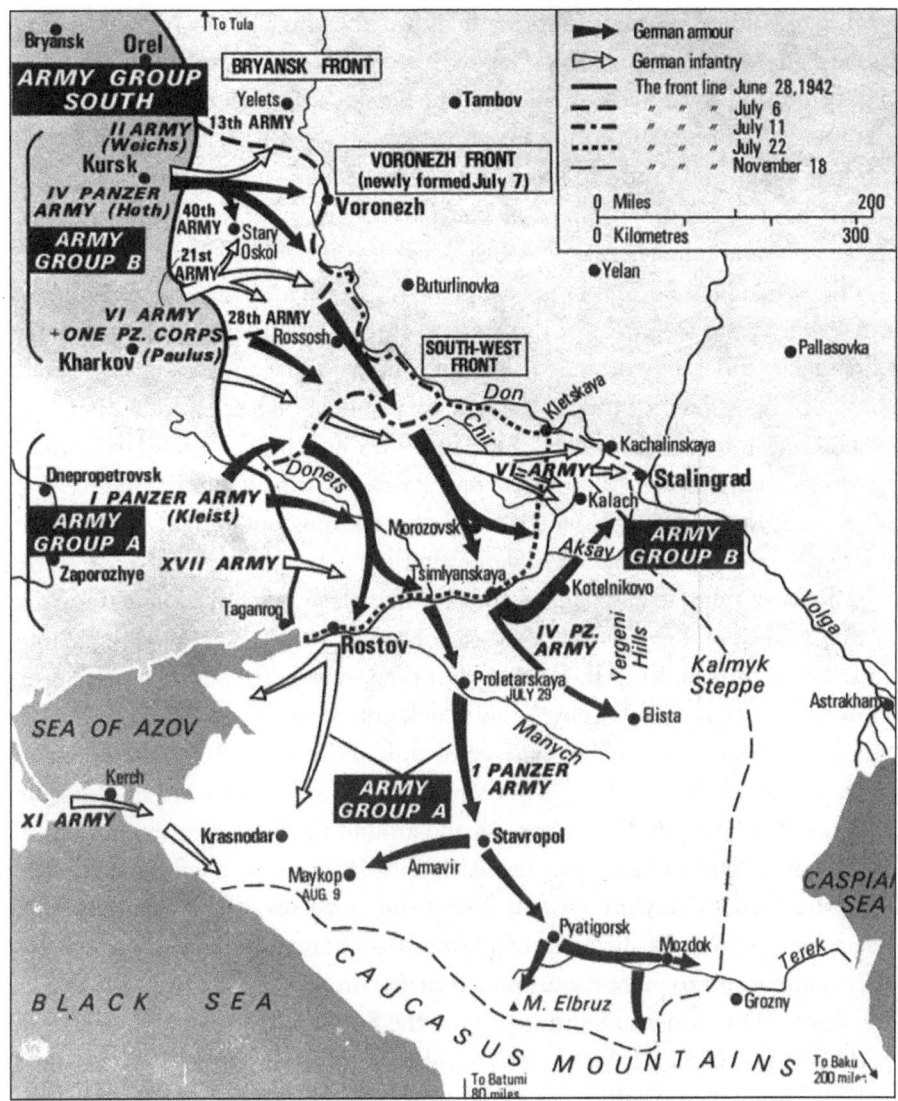

Map 2. Case Blue – Hitler's pivotal decision to divert Heeresgruppe Süd (South) into the Caucasus, June 1942.

Panzer-Regiment 15 crashed through the defences of the Red Army 15th Rifle Division, part of the Soviet 13th Army. Balck narrates the opening hours of the assault with descriptions of soldiers and NCOs leaping up under enemy fire to salute him as he walked or drove by in his Kübelwagen, and he felt that from this moment onwards he really was in command of the division.[182] This heroic style suited the Prussian part of Balck's character well, sharing the privations and dangers with his men. There is no doubt that he was enjoying and relishing this return to combat after the enforced break in Berlin. It is a common feature of soldiers to enjoy battle – the noise, the adrenalin, comradeship and bloodshed – but of course some enjoy this more than others. 'Intoxicating' is not a common word used by soldiers, but Balck uses this term to describe his elation and happiness in seeing his tanks advancing over a low flat plain, with a Stuka squadron in the sky above.

It is hard to locate an image of Hermann Balck wearing his steel helmet. Always photographed in his grey cloth forage cap, he was lucky not to have been wounded or killed on numerous occasions, especially as the 11. Panzer broke through into the rear areas of the Russian forces. Whether this was just force of habit, a deliberately designed show of elan or propaganda, or even a public display of his contempt for his Russian enemy, Balck never tells.

The division was soon over the River Tim and built a bridgehead from which to emerge, and within three days Balck was already struggling to keep his Panzer-Regiment 15 moving as they were running out of fuel. At one point the regiment was two hours ahead of even their commander, and had to pause to wait for supplies to catch up with them. The distances were simply immense as they pushed on towards the north of Voronezh. The newly fitted long 50mm and 75mm guns on the Mk IV tanks put the German Panzer on a more even footing with the T-34, and by 6 July Balck noted that his division, through a mix of anti-tank and tank-to-tank combat, had destroyed 160 Russian tanks, 'with minimal losses'.[183] The Soviet tanks were mostly those of Major General Mikhail Pavelkin's 16. Tank Corps in and around the Kshen' River, part of 5th Tank Army. Pavelkin had begun the battle with 180 tanks and left the battlefield with less than a company's worth. Burnt-out carcasses of both the huge KV heavy tanks and T-34s littered the landscape for days afterwards.

It is important to place these losses inflicted on the Russians in context. The 11. Panzer-Division was fighting against the Soviet 1st and 16th Tank Corps, part of Major General Alexander Lizyukov's 5th Tank Army. Lizyukov had only recently taken up this post and had been promoted from colonel only in January 1942, when he had commanded a division. The speed of his promotion to command a Tank Army with two entire corps was clearly an overpowering challenge, and his formations met the concentrated expertise of 11. Panzer in waves of uncoordinated counter-offensive attacks which were repelled by the Germans with huge losses. By the middle of July, 5th Tank Army had lost 8,000 men and only had 27 per cent of its tank force still intact.[184] Lizyukov was demoted to a corps command and was killed in action on 23 July while fighting in the front lines to redeem his honour. Overall, the Russians lost four tank corps on the Bryansk Front alone, with 1,200 of their tanks destroyed, and 73,000 men were taken prisoner. Across the Eastern Front, a further 650,000 Russian troops had been captured. In his biography of Balck, Robinson comments on why Russian commanders were failing so often:

> 'At this stage of the war, most Red Army tank generals struggled to command armoured forces larger than brigades and, therefore, their attacks were not effectively synchronised.'[185]

This is hardly surprising. The huge purges of the Red Army officer corps during the 1930s had seen hundreds of very senior and experienced commanders replaced with lower-ranking officers whose patriotic and political fervour, Stalin hoped, was more than enough to compensate for any military and tactical inexperience. Additionally, the vast expansion of the Red Army now meant that officers were asked to command larger and larger forces, without any training on how to establish command and control over units spread across hundreds of miles. Even Balck would have struggled to go from a divisional to army commander within weeks.

The advance on Voronezh continued, and Hoth's 4. Panzerarmee arrived at the outskirts of the city on 7 July. The Russians did what Hitler and the OKH and OKW had hoped, rushing reinforcements to hold the city, not realizing that the whole attack was a diversion away from the main objective to the south and the oilfields of the Caucasus. In what was a practice run for Stalingrad later in the year, street-by-street fighting broke out despite Hitler's orders not to become bogged down in Voronezh. Meanwhile, the renamed XXIV. Panzerkorps under Langermann, and especially the 9. and 11. Panzer-Divisions, had excelled themselves. Not only had they defended the left flank of the advance towards Voronezh, but they were distinguished by the speed of their advances. No doubt it was the ability to get troops under him to perform with such speed that had seen Langermann promoted to Generalleutnant and then General der Panzertruppe in short order.[186]

Von Bock was already receiving reports of his advance units engaged in house and street fighting in the outskirts of Voronezh, and he was concerned that, without securing this sector, his flank could be vulnerable. What Balck was unaware of was the vacillation that could now develop in Berlin as events outpaced strategy, and the degree to which Hitler now controlled the OKH on an almost daily basis. Concerned that too much time would be spent in Voronezh, and certain – through his self-professed divine guidance – that Russian forces had either already been annihilated or were in disarray, the Führer flew to visit Bock at his headquarters in Poltava on 3 July to personally order him to bypass Voronezh. All that resulted was confusion between senior generals, whose instincts told them to do one thing, and a Führer with his God-given visions and experience as a corporal during the First World War, telling them to do another. The combination of Hitler's psychological need for deference to the old Prussian elite with his fits of rage about their resistance to his demands created fatal contradictions in strategy. When combined with Stalin's increasing stubbornness and a lack of fuel and supplies to continue the German advance, this created a perfect storm that crippled the Wehrmacht's ability to win this war.

Stalin was attempting to defend everywhere, while at the strategic level, Hitler and the OKH were trying to move Stalin's forces to defend against what were essentially feint attacks, thus creating gaps in the line through which the main attacks could take place. A good example of this was around Voronezh, in the northern part of the Heeresgruppe Süd front. For Hitler, the attack on Voronezh was a bluff that XXIV. Panzerkorps was part of to draw Soviet forces northwards, away from the 6. Armee and 1. Panzerarmee's drive southwards – the second phase of Case Blue. According to historian Stephen Fritz:

> 'Bock was surprised to learn on 2nd July that Hitler and Halder now placed no importance on the capture of Voronezh, and instead urged him to wheel his mobile units south.'

Meanwhile, the field commanders got on with their job. The southern wing of 4. Panzerarmee linked up with 6. Armee to the south of Voronezh, and the city was taken on 5 July. Hitler had been fuming since their meeting on 3 July; ten days later, on 13 July, his patience broke and Bock was sacked for a second and final time, for what Hitler regarded as intransigence but Bock felt he had himself acted with sensible precaution.

A sign of things to come, 7–10 July 1942

Stalin watched the Bryansk Front collapse and created the Voronezh Front in order to stem the penetration by the Panzer divisions. One week before Bock was sacked, on 7 July, Balck and the 11. Panzer-Division faced what were their most serious Red Army attack so far when Lizyukov ordered 7th Tank Corps, commanded by Major General Pavel Rotmistrov, to attack at 0600hrs. Balck had created two Kampfgruppen within 11. Panzer, and it was one of these – containing around fifty Panzers – that suddenly saw the Soviet 67, 87 and 59 Tank Brigades heading towards them in a mass assault towards Krasnaya Polyana, 50km to the north and west of Vorozneh – in total, some 200 Soviet tanks. Balck reacted by immediately ordering the Kampfgruppe to withdraw over the Kobylia Snova River, where their bridging engineers had constructed bridges capable of bearing tanks, then ordered in strikes from local air support units. Bombing by the Stukas and anti-tank fire broke up this first attack. However, sensing some backward movement, Lizyukov ordered more tanks into the attack, and on 8 July, both the 11. Panzer Division and the 9. Panzer, which was supporting their right flank, withdrew another 6km and over another river, the Sukhaya Vereika. This time, a combination of 11. and 9. Panzer artillery fire, anti-tank units and another series of Stuka dive-bombing sorties again stopped the Soviets making a breakthrough.

During these tank actions, Feldwebel Alois Assmann in Panzerjäger-Abteilung 61, with his new and deadly Pak 50mm anti-tank gun, was one of those who scored many kills on Soviet tanks. A third attack began on 9 July, with forces from Popov's 11th Tank Corps. At one point, the 11. Panzer-Division's defensive line broke, but the hole was filled by a stubborn defence spurred on by Balck and his senior officers. It was a close-run thing, but the Russian attack faltered and failed, with terrible losses in men, tanks and artillery pieces. Lizyukov paid the price with his job and his rank. The new Voronezh Front would now be commanded by Lieutenant General N.F. Vatutin, but even as Stalin made these changes, the German forces were turning south and Voronezh was left behind as the bluff that it was.

The 9. and 11. Panzer-Divisions were now give the task of assisting in straightening the right flank of Heeresgruppe Mitte to the north and further confusing the Russians as to where the main assault was taking place. They were withdrawn from the front line and replaced by the 340. Infanterie-Division on 10 July, but all was not as well as it seemed. The Russian forces had suffered badly, but as many formations – if not more – had been able to pull back, with Stalin's blessing, and five new armies were being hastily assembled along the Voronezh Front. At the OKH, Halder pressed Hitler to maintain a single advance and take Stalingrad in Phase Two of Case Blue before turning his forces south to the Caucasus. Halder was acutely aware that the Russians had saved many of their divisions, and that reinforcements continued to build behind their lines. Instead, Hitler did the unthinkable – he divided Heeresgruppe Süd in two, and would now attempt to take Stalingrad with one and the Caucasus with the other, which would link up with Erich von Manstein's forces in the south, who were battling their way, at huge cost, through the Crimea. Hitler's views were expressed thus:

'In a campaign which has lasted little more than three weeks [suggesting that he believed it was over] the broad objectives outlined by me ... have largely been achieved. Only weak enemy forces ... have succeeded in avoiding encirclement.'[187]

Hitler was in denial. A tyrant blinded by his own verbosity, he believed the world would move in the way he ordained. Moreover, the Führer had decided that the Russians were poor soldiers and their leadership was even worse. Unfortunately, these views were not anchored in any sort of reality, as the Russians were getting better at understanding German Panzer tactics and pre-empting them. In Berlin, Halder tried repeatedly to persuade Hitler to take Stalingrad first, while the Russians were still obviously re-forming along a new front, and not to undermine the 6. Armee of Paulus, who needed the entire strength of Heeresgruppe Süd behind his efforts – not half of it, as Hitler now ordered. In his diary for 23 July – the day Hitler made his decision to divide Heeresgruppe Süd – a furious Halder wrote:

> 'The chronic tendency to underrate the enemy capabilities is gradually assuming grotesque proportions and develops into a positive danger ... this so-called leadership is characterised by a pathological reacting to the impressions of the moment.'[188]

It was a decision that changed the course of the entire war in the East.

The Rzhev–Sychyovka offensive, August and September 1942

The impact on Balck and the 11. Panzer-Division was serious. Heeresgruppe Mitte came under heavy and repeated attacks from Marshal Zhukov, in what the Russians called the Rzhev– Sychyovka offensives, from 30 July onwards. These constant attacks on German positions petered out by 23 August, but the 11. Panzer was not withdrawn from the line until 9 September.

Holding back these offensives resulted in German manpower and equipment being depleted on an epic scale, with much of the new equipment and reinforcements that had arrived in the spring during the build-up to Case Blue being destroyed. Balck had led his division north (rather than south towards the Caucasus, where he had expected to be by September) and began what would be a month-long period of attack, defence and counter-attack for the 11. Panzer. The newly promoted Obergefreiter Alois Assmann appears again in the divisional records for one particular action during this period:

> 'In August 1942, 61st Panzerjäger-Abteilung had just been supplied with brand new anti-tank guns when a Soviet tank attack began. Preceded by a very heavy artillery bombardment, the rest of Assmann's companions were killed and injured. At that moment Assmann, completely alone, with great

determination and courage, began firing the piece in a rapid and deadly succession, managing to knock out nine enemy tanks.[189]

Awards of the Knight's Cross were far from common, but Hermann Balck had every reason to be proud of the number awarded to his division, including that announced for Alois Assmann on 18 September for his action to the north of Voronezh.[190] The Pak 38's 50mm rounds were easily able to penetrate T-34 armour; hard tungsten carbide core rounds were also fired, that could sometimes destroy even the larger and more heavily armoured K-series tanks. These latter Soviet tanks generally only fell prey to either transmission failures on the battlefield – in trying to move 50 tons around – or the deadly German 88mm Flak guns that were turned into anti-tank weapons.

Hermann Balck's diary for this period pays considerable homage to Kradschützen-Abteilung 61, which, under the command of the 'tough Austrian' Hauptmann Freiherr von Hauser, faced forty-two enemy attacks on their positions. Some of the Soviet tanks broke through, requiring the motorcycle detachment to counter-attack no less than twenty-three times, launching eight attacks of their own. At the end of August, Dr Hellweg, the battalion's surgeon, wrote:

'The health conditions of the troops has deteriorated drastically. The troops are extremely exhausted. Their leaders can no longer motivate them. Everywhere there are cases of total exhaustion and weakness. Since food can only be brought forward at night, the troops have not had a warm meal in weeks. Add to that the effects of hypothermia in the trenches and foxholes. Infectious colds of the bladder and diarrhoea are extremely common, without the possibility of treatment. Since the beginning of operations on 11 August the troops have not been able to wash themselves. They are dirty and covered with lice.'[191]

After this punishing period in the front lines, 11. Panzer-Division was pulled back to Bryansk to rest and refit – close enough to be on hand should there be a breakthrough. In relatively clean quarters, this was a time to sleep, wash, tend to wounds and illness, and think about home. It was also a time to reflect on the comrades they had lost, wonder how they had survived and reimagine the horrible images of war and death that they had just experienced; they were now a battle-hardened division. Balck records that there was no brothel nearby to the men's quarters, as twenty-eight of the thirty unmarried young women employed in their sector were virgins.[192] it is an interesting statistic, but quite how Balck was so certain of this figure he does not say. What Balck fails to mention is that there would be no virgins in the sector if the Russians overran their position. Further statistics are revealed in Balck's memoirs. One was that a staggering 501 Russian tanks had been destroyed by 11. Panzer-Division since the opening of Case Blue in September. However, the cost had been severe, with only nine Panzer Mk IVs still operational.[193]

Whilst it was recovering, the division received a unit citation that stated: 'Faithful to the reputation that preceded it for outstanding combat accomplishments, gained in countless battles, the division once again has conducted itself in an outstanding manner.' This was from the commander of the 2. Panzerarmee, Generaloberst Rudolf Schmidt, whom Hitler personally chose to replace Guderian when he was sacked in December 1941. Interestingly, Schmidt was one of numerous senior figures in the Heer who was privately very critical of Hitler's conduct and decisions in running the war, writing down such thoughts in letters to his brother. This would have been at the same time that he was commanding 2. Panzerarmee, evidence of the enormous emotional conflicts that so many officers had to battle with. Schmidt's brother was arrested by the Gestapo in April 1943 for spying for the French, and the letters were discovered. Schmidt was relieved of his command and put on trial. Fortunately for him he was acquitted and moved to the Führerreserve, but he never commanded a unit again.[194]

The Black Hole of Stalingrad – October and November 1942

From Bryansk, 11. Panzer-Division was ordered north to remain in the rear of 'sensible' General Hans von Salmuth's 2. Armee.[195] By early October it was resting and refitting near Roslavl.

Strategically, Hitler was now facing what he had always feared most – wars on more than one front. In North Africa, the mercurial and often disobedient Rommel had lost momentum and was now awaiting General Bernard Montgomery's attack near El Alamein. Hitler's allies in Italy looked vulnerable, while the Dieppe raid in northern France – although repulsed – had merely confirmed in the Führer's mind the inevitability of an allied invasion in 1943. Hitler became increasingly intent, if not obsessive, about taking Stalingrad quickly. Heeresgruppe Süd had taken a battering during the summer, suffering heavy losses, and was now split into two parts – known as Heeresgruppe A and Herresgruppe B – neither of which were strong enough to take their objective. Stalingrad was becoming a bloodbath, while the Caucasus Mountains with their vital sources of oil seemed out of reach. This dilution of Heeresgruppe Süd made it very vulnerable to the steadily building Russian forces it faced.

With the fighting in Stalingrad unfolding like a slow nightmare, the 11. Panzer-Division was ready to be sent back to the front. Despite the huge challenges of distance, new officers and men had arrived and it was time for a clear-out of anyone physically and mentally not up to the job of fighting through what was going to be another terrible winter. Hitler had his own clear-out; on 24 September, Halder had gone from the OKH and was replaced as chief of staff by the committed Nazi and disciple of Hitler, General der Infanterie Kurt Zeitzler. The policy of appointing greater numbers of overtly zealous Nazi commanders now began in earnest. Exhausted from his role, the losses and the fights with Hitler, Halder was probably relieved to be placed in the Führerreserve, which was becoming more like a convalescent home for emotionally crushed former Wehrmacht officers destroyed by Hitler. Balck records that he too removed the commander of one of his regiments and another unnamed battalion commander.[196]

Before 11. Panzer returned to the front, an anti-partisan operation was required in its rear area. While Balck treats this very superficially in his memoirs, he admits that the war against the partisans was 'conducted with a great deal of cruelty'. One suspects that the brutality and executions common in such measures by the SS were employed just as much by his own troops.[197]

One of the first presentations that Zeitzler made to Hitler concerned the perilous position of the front line between Voronezh and Stalingrad. Calling it 'an enormous danger that must be eliminated', Zeitzler pressed for 6. Armee to begin a withdrawal from Stalingrad. This area contained a large concentration of allied Axis forces such, as the 8th Italian Army in Russia – known as ARMIR – which was commanded by General Italo Gariboldi. The Italians came under the direction of Generaloberst Maximilian von Weichs and Heeresgruppe B, and sat on the left flank of the German 6. Armee between Hungarian and Romanian formations. Thus, some 250km of front line on the River Don, north-west of Stalingrad, was held by much-weakened German divisions and large numbers of very dubious allied formations. Additionally, the frozen ground prevented any sort of deep defences being dug. What anti-tank weapons the Romanians had were in short supply, lacked firepower to penetrate the T-34 and certainly the KV-1, and ammunition stocks were limited. Communications between German forces and the Italians were especially difficult, such was the level of mistrust between the allies that German signals units were sent to all positions to report back on what was being done.[198] But this was not the only problem north-west of Stalingrad. It was reported to the OKH that as many as six German infantry divisions in this area were 'no longer fully reliable even for limited defensive purposes and that heavy defensive fighting might well stampede them. Unless they could be pulled out of the line for rest and rehabilitation, these divisions, which accounted for nearly half of Second Army's total strength, could only be trusted in the defence of small, quiet sectors.'[199]

There was thus a very precarious situation along the River Don front to the north of Stalingrad and the 400 miles north up to Voronezh during October and November 1942. The front was manned by an amalgamation of weakened German infantry divisions, torn apart by the fighting in the autumn of 1942, and a collection of allied armies unwilling to defend themselves and lacking any defensive spirit. Zhukov sensed this weakness and vulnerability. In Berlin, Hitler's reaction to Zeitler's presentation in September had been merely to wave his hand across the map and dismiss such concerns, but by October even the Führer had to accept the constant stream of intelligence reports of a large Soviet build-up to the east of Stalingrad. Hitler now pored over the updated situation maps for hours each day – and night. His problem was what to do about it. His intuition told him an attack was coming and he knew full well what might happen to 6. Armee, now fully sucked into street fighting in Stalingrad. Yet other than pulling out of Stalingrad and following advice to withdraw from generals he regarded as weak and non-Nazi, or stripping German forces from elsewhere, there was little he could do, other than filter in some newly raised Luftwaffe field divisions in between the Hungarians, Italians and Romanians. The next challenge for 11. Panzer-Division now lay ahead.

The *Dolchstosslegende* (the stab in the back of the German Army) was an anti-communist and antisemitic conspiracy theory that was all pervasive throughout Germany in the post-1918 period and affected the international perceptions of many young army officers.

Rittmeister – Hermann Balck as Captain of Cavalry, signed and dated October 1929 while serving with Kavallerie-Regiment 18, 3. Kavallerie-Division.

Oberst Hermann Balck, commanding 1. Panzer-Brigade, which was now part of the new 1. Panzer-Division formed out of the 3. Kavallerie-Division, presents a set of captured French colours to General Heinz Guderian in June 1940. These are likely to have been captured in the fighting around Sedan or Belfort. Balck received the Knight's Cross on 3 June 1940.

A very rare image of Hermann Balck in his characteristic forage cap talking to panzer troops of 1. Panzer-Division in June 1940. This image can be dated as you can see the French colours sticking out of Balck's staff car – no doubt he was on his way to meet with Guderian.

These Panzer Mk III tanks are part of Hermann Balck's Panzer-Regiment 3 of 2. Panzer-Division when he was commanding it during the invasion of Greece in April 1941. With so many roads almost impassable, it was quicker for Balck's panzers to use railways lines – for example in the advance on the Vale of Tempe. (*Image courtesy of the Bundesarchiv*)

Oberst Hermann Balck in his black panzer tunic, mounted on a Panzer III Ausf E near Panteleimon in Greece during Operation Marita in April 1941. As his command panzer for Panzer-Regiment 3, Balck would have had a long-range radio and operator as part of the crew to communicate with his tank companies. Note the additional tank track on the front of the hull for extra protection and as a spare – plus the 37mm main gun and twin MG-34 machine guns mounted in the turret. There is also a captured New Zealand POW sitting on the back. (*Image courtesy of Alifrafikkhan*)

General der Infanterie Rudolf Schmundt, Hitler's senior adjutant and close confidante of Hermann Balck, provided a direct route through to the Führer. Hitler promoted Schmundt to General as he was one of the very few officers he trusted. Leading the Army Personnel office, Schmundt had control over all promotions and dismissals and who to allow through to see the Fuhrer personally - this often included Hermann Balck. Schmundt was seriously injured in the July Bomb Plot explosion and died a few days later in hospital.

'The 61st Motorcycle Infantry Battalion had been engaged in combat action for three continuous weeks without relief. Within six days it destroyed eighty-five enemy tanks' (*Order in Chaos*, p.257). Often overlooked, in the early stages of Blitzkrieg it was infantry mounted on their BMW R75 motorbikes and sidecars that were the eyes, ears and striking force of the German Army. Hermann Balck was full of admiration for the Bataillon 61 in 11. Panzer-Division, commanded by Paul Freiherr von Hauser. Note the white 'Ghost' emblem on the side car which helps to identify this man and his cycle as from 11. Panzer Division – 'The Ghost Division'.

Oberst Theodor Graf von Schimmelmann, 'The Graf', was Hermann Balck's bold and nonchalant but talented commander of 11. Panzer-Division's Panzer-Regiment 15. He is seen here in his command tank, wearing his reversible Russian winter smock, at some point in the Russian winter of 1942.

Commander of Russian Fifth Shock Army, General Markian Mikhaylovich Popov. It was Popov's divisions which encountered Hermann Balck during one of his impressive periods in late 1942 in the Chir River battles.

Generalmajor Hermann Balck, commanding 11. Panzer-Division, discussing strategy with Colonel von Schimmelmann, commander of Panzer-Regiment 15 in the Don River region, during the winter of 1942–1943 when engaged against Popov's Russian Fifth Shock Army. Balck was tasked with trying to break through to Stalingrad as well as holding the southern front together.

'…the main credit must go to the courageous men in the front lines. Above all, it was Lieutenant Piontek, the adjutant of the 15th Panzer Regt., who led the tanks of the divisional reserve from one successful action to the next.' Piontek was killed at Kharkov in 1943, and his men are shown standing guard over his coffin in a Russian Orthodox Church prior to his burial.

Tatsinskaya airfield before the Russians arrived. Note the variety of models of Luftwaffe aircraft still there and left exposed – around 150–200 would be destroyed. In December 1942, Hermann Balck and 11. Panzer-Division were tasked with the protection and relief of the vital airfield of Tatsinskaya, which supplied Stalingrad as best it could, and was threatened by the Russian 24th Tank Corps, which eventually captured the airfield. Many atrocities were uncovered there when the airfield was retaken by German forces. Balck received the Oak Leaves to his Knight's Cross on 20 December 1942.

Hermann Balck's brief deployment with Panzergrenadier-Division 'Grossdeutschland' came with his promotion to Generalleutenant. Balck is seen here in a Mercedes L1500 A 1.5-ton 4x4 troop carrier from Grossdeutschland in the Kharkov region at some point in May or June 1943. (*Image courtesy of Alifrafikkan*)

Generalleutnant Balck receiving a briefing from Major Walter Pössl, who commanded Panzer-Regiment 'Grossdeutschland', at some point in May or June 1943. Pössl is wearing the Knight's Cross that he was awarded for destroying fifty Soviet tanks with his unit in April 1943, which helps to date this picture. Pössl would be killed in action in Warsaw on 25 September 1944. (*Image courtesy of Alifrafikkan*)

Taken in late 1943, this image shows Hermann Balck as General der Panzertruppe and commander of XLVIII. Panzerkorps, with some of his staff on the Russian Front near Zhytomyr. Note that Balck now wears the Oak Leaves to his Knight's Cross, which he had received on 20 December 1942, and the Swords, which he was awarded on 4 March 1943. From the left: Major Johannes Erasmus (1a Staff Officer, XLVIII. Panzerkorps), Hermann Balck (Commander, XLVIII. Panzerkorps), Major Günter Kaldrack (IIa and Personnel Officer, XLVIII. Panzerkorps) and Oberst Friedrich von Mellenthin (Chief of Staff, XLVIII. Panzerkorps).

A dinner held at some point in January 1944 when 1. SS-Panzer-Division 'Leibstandarte SS Adolf Hitler' was part of XLVIII. Panzerkorps. Seated on the left is SS-Rottenführer Balthasar 'Bobby' Woll, of SS-Panzer-Regiment 1 of the Leibstandarte, on the occasion of the award of his Knight's Cross. Balck is seated next to an unknown soldier with the Close Combat Clasp in Gold. Woll became synonymous with the Tiger tank as the gunner for panzer 'ace' Michael Wittmann.

Another image of Hermann Balck with members of the SS-Leibstandarte, here walking with SS-Standartenführer Rudolf Lehmann – later chief of staff to I. SS-Panzerkorps.

This image was taken in September 1943 during Balck's temporary command of XIV. Panzerkorps on the south-east coast of Italy. Balck (centre) is shown with his chief of staff, Oberst Bogislaw von Bonin (left), and Generalmajor Rudolf Sieckenius (right), who commanded 16. Panzer-Division and was later killed in action on 29 April 1945.

The family of Hermann Balck put his entire medal collection up for sale and it was sold to a private collector. This image shows Balck's well-worn Second World War Wound Badge in Gold. (*Image courtesy of Michael Autengruber of Fritz Kunker GmbH, Germany*)

A few days after the 20 July assassination attempt on Adolf Hitler, the army salute was replaced by the Nazi salute, which dates this image of Hermann Balck giving the Nazi salute to panzer troops – probably of the 11. Panzer-Division – to the late summer of 1944.

Lieutenant General Filipp Golikov, commander of the Voronezh Front, led the attacks on Kharkov in February 1943. He was later dismissed by Stalin – but not executed.

Hermann Balck pictured receiving the Diamonds to his Knight's Cross from Adolf Hitler outside under the pine trees at Rastenburg on 21 September 1944. Pictured (from the left) are Generaloberst Josef Harpe, Oberstleutnant Erik von Amsberg, Generalfeldmarschall Keitel and SS-Hauptsturmführer Otto Günsche.

The original Oak Leaves, Sword and Diamonds of Hermann Balck's Knight's Cross, one of only twenty-seven sets ever awarded by Adolf Hitler. (*Image courtesy of Michael Autengruber of Fritz Kunker GmbH, Germany*)

A rare close-up of Hermann Balck, exuding charisma and swagger with a group of young, fresh-faced German infantrymen, probably on the Western Front as commander of Heeresgruppe G in late 1944.

Generalmajor Gerhard Schmidhuber, the very humane and courageous commander of 13. Panzer-Division who committed suicide rather than be taken prisoner by the Russians after the destruction of his division in Budapest.

SS-Obergruppenführer Karl Pfeffer-Wildenbruch commanded the doomed IX. SS-Gebirgskorps in Budapest and appealed for help from Hermann Balck in the breakout from the city on 11 February 1945.

A smiling Hermann Balck meets with the 'decent but stupid' SS-Oberst-Gruppenführer Sepp Dietrich, probably around early March 1945 during preparations for Operation Spring Awakening at Lake Balaton, when Dietrich commanded the 6. SS-Panzerermee and Balck commanded 6. Armee.

A rare image of Hermann Balck in old age, taken at his home just before his death on 29 November 1982.

Hermann Balck's grave in Osnabrück, Lower Saxony. (*Courtesy of Rob Hopmans*)

A very rare image of Balck and von Mellenthin together once more in the 1970s, perhaps in the USA. The two men shared a rare emotional connection and a mutual professional respect for each other until the end of their lives.

The most often used image of Generaloberst Hermann Balck, at work in his headquarters as commander of Heeresgruppe G and at the height of his professional career. The Knight's Cross with Oak Leaves, Swords and Diamonds around his neck dates this photograph to September or October 1944.

Chapter X

The Planet Suite and the Chir River Battles, November–December 1942

'Quantity has a quality all its own'

(Joseph Stalin)

The Red Army of 1942 was a different beast to that of 1939 – and even of 1941 – in terms of leadership, ambition and tactics. Yet one essential strategic belief that remained constant was that quantity would always eventually defeat quality. Soviet tanks were designed to be easy to use – a Russian tank crew took only three weeks to train before they could take their T-34 into battle, while the crew of a German Tiger tank, because of the technological capability and design of the Panzer, could take up to three months. The Russians attacked in volume, not because they did not care about human life but simply because they could – their reserves of manpower were almost endless. Whereas German leadership concentrated on leading right down to the smallest group of soldiers, Russian leadership focussed on how to manage large masses of men and materials and get them into battle quickly to overwhelm the enemy. What Balck and other German officers perceived as inhuman hordes of men thrown against machine guns was to completely miss the essential point; Russian soldiers did care, Russian officers did grieve and Stalin did feel a conscious guilt over the losses, but this was the Russian way.

Uranus – the envelopment of 6. Armee

During October 1942, Marshal Zhukov was planning a major offensive, or rather a suite of three offensives, set to begin in the third week of November and all named after planets. The first of these, Operation Mars, would attack across the front of Heeresgruppe Mitte and cut through to the city of Rzhev, designed to stop reinforcements being moved south to support their compatriots in Stalingrad against what would be the second operation, named Uranus. The Uranus offensive would be led by the experienced Colonel General Nikolai Vatutin and was designed to encircle and suffocate the German 6. Armee in Stalingrad. Finally, Operation Saturn, led by the 1st Guards Army, would drive south to attack and liberate the city of Rostov, thereby cutting off all the German formations that had driven deep into the Caucasus Mountains and south of Rostov. This constellation of operations was bold, ambitious and brilliant – contrary to Hermann Balck's observations on Soviet military leadership.

Any attack to encircle Stalingrad would first have to carve its way through allied formations, and it would be the 3rd and 4th Romanian Armies and Italian 8th Army that would bear the brunt of the winter offensives of 1942. Formed up against the 3rd Romanian Army were Vatutin's 5th Tank Army, the 21st Army and the Don Front's 65th Army. To the south of Stalingrad, the Soviet 51st and 57th Armies would face the Romanian 4th Army, and then the two pincers would link up at the city of Kalach on the Don River.

On 8 November, Hitler's rhetoric at his annual speech in Berlin's Löwenbräukeller to his cronies, disciples and hypnotized old comrades was a show of bravado and self-promotion to quell the nerves of the faithful. He knew what he was doing – Churchill, Roosevelt, Mr Stalin, the Jews, they had all learnt the hard way that the new National Socialist state had an iron will. Even the Wehrmacht was now increasingly politicized and radicalized in their

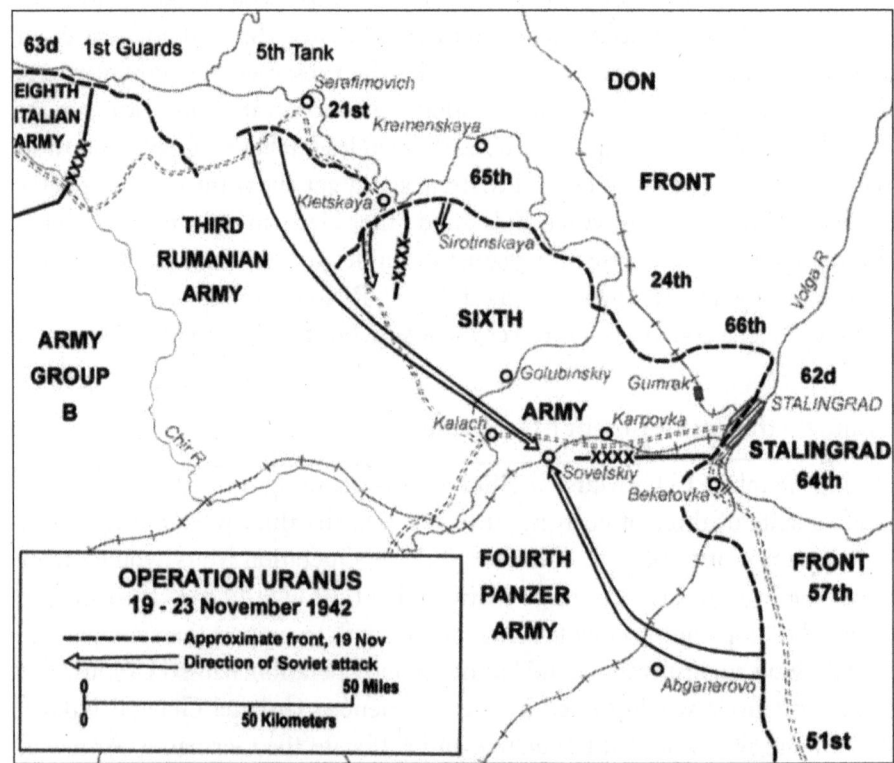

Map 3. Operation Uranus and the encirclement of Stalingrad, 19–23 November 1942.

National Socialist fervour, and the Führer believed this could have but one outcome – ultimate victory:

> 'Today the National Socialist community of the people goes to the front, and you will perceive from many things how this Wehrmacht grows more National Socialist from month to month, [and in a deep, cutting dig at the hierarchy of the Army] how it constantly takes on more and more the imprint of the new Germany, how all privileges, class prejudices and so on are being eliminated more and more.'

Hitler went on to justify his interest in Stalingrad not as an obsessional and frantic desire to defeat Stalin in the city named after him, but because it was a 'gigantic transfer point' that he would take by 'small, targeted thrusts' – Hitler said he did not wish to create another Verdun. However, with an entire army now almost trapped in the noose, something clearly was not right. Within days, trust in the Führer's messianic leadership would be shaken. Less than a fortnight after the smoke-filled Löwenbräukeller had been cleared of tables and chairs – where Göring, Goebbels and Himmler had sat in adoration of their leader – Operation Uranus began on 19 November. It took only four days to smash through the Romanian units manning the front and for the two pincers to meet at Kalach, due west of Stalingrad, sealing the Operation Uranus trap and 6. Armee's fate.

Both the OKH and OKW initially struggled to gauge the strength of the Russian attacks. It seemed impossible that the massive Soviet losses of earlier in 1942 had simply been replaced by more troops and tanks. The German High Command's reaction was foggy in the early stages, as Antony Beevor pointed in his excellent book *Stalingrad*.[200] In panic and desperation, Hitler first issued orders preventing any breakout by 6. Armee. He was convinced a relief force from Heeresgruppe B would come to the rescue, while in the meantime, Göring had reassured him the Luftwaffe could resupply 6. Armee by air. From now on, Stalingrad would be turned into a *Festung* (fortress). Hitler also turned to Generalfeldmarschall Erich von Manstein to deal with this crisis as commander of a newly and hastily formed Heeresgruppe Don. The 11. Panzer-Division received immediate orders to join XLVIII. Panzerkorps on 25 November in preparation for Operation Winter Storm – the attempt to relieve 6. Armee –and on 29 November a new chief of staff also arrived at the headquarters of the Panzer corps.

Oberst Friedrich von Mellenthin already had a fine wartime record. He had been with Guderian on his staff in France and worked with Rommel as operations officer in North Africa. Suffering a severe illness in the desert, von

Mellenthin had returned to Germany to recuperate and found himself reporting to the new OKH chief of staff, General Zeitzler, on 27 November 1942. Von Mellenthin recalled standing in Zeitzler's office in the Führer's headquarters near Rastenburg in East Prussia:

> 'He [Zeitzler] informed me of my new appointment as chief of staff to the 48th Panzer Corps, and gave me his appreciation of the situation around Stalingrad. It was my impression that Zeitzler did not think it would be possible to relieve Sixth Army, and that Paulus' only chance was to break out.'[201]

Before he left Rastenburg, von Mellenthin visited the Operations Room, where he saw that German intelligence units now showed that the Russian breakthrough was formed of three armoured corps, two cavalry corps and twenty-one rifle divisions. They had opened a 20-mile breach in the Romanian lines – this was the opening of Operation Little Saturn – to tie up potential German relief forces for Stalingrad and to force a breakthrough towards Rostov-on-Don and cut off all German troops that had moved south into the Caucasus.

Little Saturn – forcing a breakthrough to Rostov

The Romanian forces and 13. Panzer-Division nearby had been slow to react, partly because tank lighting flexes had been eaten through by mice and rats living in the warm engines of the tanks, but also because of apparent indecision at XLVIII. Panzerkorps headquarters. It was this inaction that led to the sacking of the commanding general, Ferdinand Heim, and his chief of staff, and von Mellenthin's new appointment.[202] In reality, Heim was no doubt desperate to do what he could – he had been the successful commander of 14. Panzer-Division during the summer advances and had been awarded the Knight's Cross on 30 August 1942. When he was promoted to command XLVIII. Panzerkorps, it had already been stripped of its forces – the 14. and 24. Panzer-Divisions had been moved to another corps, and by the time von Mellenthin arrived, all that was left were remnants of the 13. Panzer and 1st Romanian Armoured Division, which had withdrawn to hold the Chir River as best they could. There is little doubt that Heim was very badly treated by Hitler. Nevertheless, the XLVIII. Panzerkorps was put under the temporary command of Oberst Hans Cramer pending the arrival of its new commander.

Von Mellenthin remarked how he flew over the 'endless spaces of Russia' – the 1,500 miles from Rastenburg to Heeresgruppe Don and von Manstein's headquarters at Rostov in a Ju 52 transport plane – and then met the army commander and received a briefing from his intelligence officer, Oberst (later General der Infanterie) Theodor Busse. When new units arrived from the south, taken from the Caucasus Front, the dual aim was to reinforce the battered 4. Panzerarmee under Hoth and then that force, including XLVIII. Panzerkorps, would strike towards Stalingrad to try to relive 6. Armee. This movement was to be codenamed *Unternehmen Wintergewitter* (Operation Winter Storm).

Orders flowed in and out constantly, by day and night, as each day counted. Von Mellenthin then flew to XLVIII. Panzerkorps (flying at tree-top level in case they went over the wrong side of the lines) in a small Storch two-man reconnaissance plane. The situation there was dire. The corps was battered and fragmented, but elements of the 13. Panzer-Division were still effective and this made up for the terrible state of the Romanian forces, with their outdated equipment and shock at the fighting conditions and their losses.[203] Holding the Chir River position looked a difficult task. Apart from the scattered remnants of the Romanian divisions forced backwards by the northern pincer of the Russian offesive, Wray describes the Chir River defences as being held by 'a rabble':

> 'The Chir River line was held by whatever forces could be scraped together. Initially, these forces consisted of mixed combat units swept aside by the Russian offensive, alarm units called out from various support units, service troops, rear area security forces, convalescents, and casual personnel on leave. All these were formed into ad hoc battle groups and plugged into an improvised strongpoint defence along the Chir "like pieces of mosaic".'[204]

Thankfully, the Russians seemed to be showing little desire to press home their advantage, which opened a slight window to reform the XLVIII Panzerkorps to get it into position. By 3 December, a fully refitted 11. Panzer-Division had begun to arrive at the new headquarters of the Panzerkorps, Nizhne Chirskaya, closely followed by the 336. Infanterie-Division, commanded by Generalmajor Walther Lucht. An additional division was also gratefully received, the 7. Luftwaffe Feld-Division, which gave the corps a more stable shape.[205]

The 7. Luftwaffe Feld-Division had been hastily raised and equipped in October 1942 as part of the OKH suggestion that personnel could be farmed by exploiting the huge manpower reserve of the underemployed Luftwaffe. These troops were not of the same quality as the exceptionally trained Fallschirmjäger (paratroops), but instead were poorly trained in infantry skills and led by an amalgam of retired army officers brought back into service and Luftwaffe ground crew officers pressed into an infantry role. The commander of this division was Generalmajor Wolf von Biedermann. He had served as an infantryman in the First World War, so commanding a ground combat unit was not totally new to him, but he was primarily a pilot as he had been a member of the Luftwaffe since 1934. Promoted to Generalmajor, he took charge of the 7. Luftwaffe Feld-Division in September 1942, which must have come as a shock to someone who was, up to that point, commanding a small airfield in Saxony.[206]

The replacement commander of XLVIII. Panzerkorps was General Otto von Knobelsdorff, whom von Mellenthin greatly admired. Knobelsdorff had been a Generalmajor at the outbreak of war and had commanded the 19. Infanterie-Division in France; when the division was converted to a Panzer division, von Knobelsdorff was promoted to Generalleutnant and took it through Barbarossa to the gates of Moscow. Von Knobelsdorff was commanding XXIV. Panzerkorps before being ordered to take over and reform the XLVIII. Panzerkorps.[207] Von Knobelsdorff noted in his statements to the Americans after the war:

> 'I arrived at the command post of the XLVIII Panzer Corps in Nizhne Chirskaya at approximately 15.00 on 5th December, 1942 ... I immediately assumed command of the XLVIII Panzer Corps. The Corps Chief of Staff was a certain Lieutenant Colonel von Mellenthin, GSC, who himself had joined the Corps a few days before.'[208]

Von Knobelsdorff noted that one of the ad hoc units that had been hastily put together in the corps defensive area was that of artillery officer Generalmajor Hans Joachim von Stumpfeld and a colonel of engineers named Schmidt, which consisted mostly or rear units and military police formations. Von Stumpfeld's group also included remnants of the 213. Infanterie-Division. He would fight through to the end of May 1943, when he was among those dismissed from the Wehrmacht for his 'failure' at Stalingrad.

Sowchos 79 – 8 December 1942

If there is one period in Hermann Balck's military career that typifies his battlefield prowess, it is the battles around the Chir River sector. Between 3 and 7 December, 11. Panzer-Division, the 7. Luftwaffe Feld-Division and 336. Infanterie-Division were moving up to new positions along the Chir River salient. The most advanced German positions in this area were only 20 miles from the outskirts of Stalingrad and their surrounded comrades of Gruppe Adam (Oberst Wilhelm Adam, adjutant to Paulus), with whom they could communicate by radio.

By 7 December, von Manstein was preparing his final orders for the start of Winter Storm, which was scheduled to begin on 12 December. In his memoirs *Lost Victories*, von Manstein writes that he had expressed his opinion to the

OKH and Hitler that there was still a way of regaining control of the initiative, even with the unfolding nightmare of the trapped 6. Armee in Stalingrad. The problem was that he advocated a strategic withdrawal, proposing that 6. Armee break out of the encirclement and taking Heersegruppe Don and Heeresgruppe A back as far as the Lower Don and even the Dnieper, where they could regroup and then counter-attack the flanks of the advancing Russian juggernaut, by which means he felt 'a grave crisis could have been turned into a victory!'.[209] Given Hitler's obsession with National Socialist principles and his growing belief in his disciples in the new and superbly equipped SS divisions, any possibility of a strategic withdrawal was dismissed. It was probably already too late to save the forces in Stalingrad, now that they had been encircled. The Führer's steadfast refusals to allow Paulus to withdraw would show that Hitler was actually prepared to sacrifice 6. Armee in order to tie down Russian forces while he slowly extricated Heeresgruppe A from the Caucasus, having over-extended his reach.

The 336. Infanterie-Division had arrived by 6 December and set up defensive positions close to the Chir River. Amazingly, its units discovered a small bridgehead on the eastern bank still held by an amalgam of German elements commanded by the heroic Oberst Wilhelm Adam. Adam had been holding out there since mid-November to provide a route out and across the river for 6. Armee. While aware that Hitler had forbidden any such move, Adam still hoped that Paulus would ignore the order. Awarded the Knight's Cross on 17 December, Adam and his exhausted butd courageous soldiers eventually surrendered to the Russians with the fall of Stalingrad on 31 January 1943.[210]

Out ahead of his leading elements, wrapped in a warm officer's winter coat, Balck was at this time reconnoitring in a half-track through the frozen ground and snow for the best places to position his units to fulfil his mission, which was to cross the Chir and then support Winter Storm. Nevertheless, Zhukov could see the Stalingrad relief force gathering and decided on a pre-emptive strike across the Chir to disrupt the German plans and maintain the Soviet grip around Stalingrad. Thus, Generalmajor Lucht and his 336. Infanterie-Division hardly had time to draw breath on 7 December before a huge dawn artillery bombardment rained down on his men. Meanwhile, some 200 tanks of the Soviet 1st Tank Corps led by Major General Vasilevich Butkov – themselves part of 5th Tank Army commanded by Lieutenant General Prokofy Romanenko – cut a swathe through the fragile left wing of the 336. Infanterie-Division and the right wing of the 7. Luftwaffe Feld-Division and swept onwards to Sowchos 79. A Sowchos (pronounced Sovchos) was a large state-owned and numbered farm. According to Robinson, Butkov's 1st Tank Corps contained only five 50-ton heavy KV tanks, but had seventy-five T-34 medium tanks and sixty-six T-70

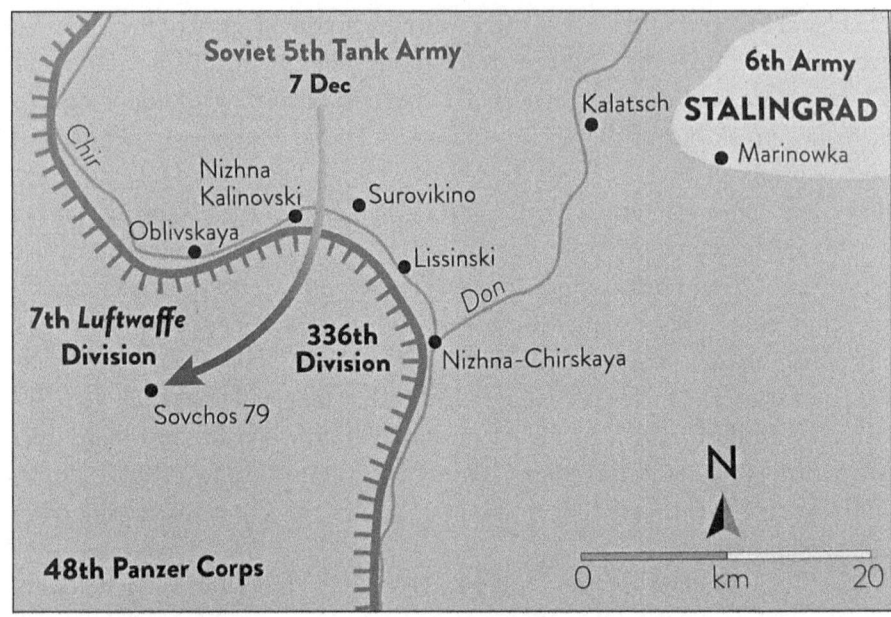

Map 4. Soviet Fifth Tank Army's advance on Sovchos 79, 7 December 1942. (*From Robinson, p.212*)

light tanks.[211] Two days later, on 9 December, Romanenko planned to launch a second attack across the Chir with another 200 tanks, this time from Major General Mikhail Volkov's 5th Mechanized Corps.

Coming up immediately behind the 336. Infanterie-Division were the leading elements of 11. Panzer-Division, and before all of his formation had arrived, Balck was ordered by von Knobelsdorff to 'throw them [the Soviets] out' of this position and the Chir battles thus began. This was to be the first in an exhausting and costly series of confrontations between two full-sized Soviet tank corps and what was a hybrid German Panzerkorps of two elite German divisions plus a useful but hardly effective Luftwaffe Feld-Division. The coming battles would show how the leadership expertise of fire control and movement of the German forces under Balck, Lucht and their corps commander, von Knobelsdorff, compared with the far larger and courageous Red Army attacks under their corps commander, Butkov. At this time, Balck had between seventy and seventy-five tanks that were operable, and the XLVIII. Panzerkorps around 30,000 men from various units and of widely differing experience. The Soviet 5th Tank Army had approximately 85,000 men and between 280 and 400 tanks at any one time. However, Balck also had the highly efficient divisional artillery commanded by Oberst Schmidt, which 'always knew how to mass fire quickly on the decisive point, thereby contributing to the success of the division time after time'. Schmidt would not survive the war.

Balck immediately did something unique, setting up his command post alongside that of Lucht in the village of Verchne Solonovski.[212] This was unusual in that German divisions tended to be separate and only talk to each other through their signals units, but this close co-operation allowed both commanders to be able to react immediately, and in tandem with each other, without the usual delays. The situation was dangerous. This was only the opening phase of Operation Little Saturn, and already Sowchos 79 was 12 miles into the rear of the front line of XLVIII. Panzerkorps. Balck remained cool and focussed on how to eliminate the Soviet tank position, but so did the experienced and perceptive Lucht – the latter had wanted an immediate frontal assault, but Balck had already seen in his reconnaissance that the ground was not suitable for his tanks and he wanted to prevent any type of breakout by the Red Army armoured units. Overnight, and with great skill using the many snow-covered ravines to shield their movement, Balck's Panzer-Regiment 15 of three Abteilungen commanded by Oberst Theodor Graf von Schimmelmann, along with Oberstleutnant Alexander von Bosse's Panzergrenadier-Regiment 111, moved southwards away from State Farm 79 and then arced around to the north-west, cutting off any chance of a withdrawal back across the Chir River.[213] Balck then moved Oberstleutnant Albert Henze and his Panzergrenadier-Regiment 110, to the west side of State Farm 79, while his deadly and experienced 61st anti-tank and Flak gun units moved towards the south. Moving at night with an infantry screen all around, Balck did not have to contend with Russian air attack, which was a crucial advantage moving over the empty snow-covered ground. In the early morning of 8 December, the artillery regiment of the 336. Infanterie-Division opened fire on the farm. In the attack that followed, the Soviets first started up their tanks and headed south and east, towards German infantry fire, not realizing that the battle-hardened Panzer-Regiment 15 was coming in at full speed into their rear.

Von Mellenthin paints a vivid picture of the merciless destruction meted out by 11. Panzer-Division:

> 'The Russian fought bravely, but their tanks were caught in a circle of fire from which they vainly attempted to escape. When the short winter day drew to a close the Russian 1st Armoured Corps had been completely bowled over, and fifty-three of its tanks were knocked out.'[214]

The black, flaming carcasses of between fifty and seventy-five Russian tanks and their crews littered the area, the acrid smell of burning oil covered the battlefield. Clearing out State Farm 79 on 9 December was merely the precursor to a whole series of now-famous battles, where Balck and his 11. Panzer became synonymous with the names *Gespenster-Division* ('Ghost Division') and *Die Feuerwehr* ('Fire Brigade').[215] But before Balck launched his attacks in earnest, he reveals that he drove through Sowchos 79 and witnessed at first hand the brutality of their Russian enemy. The German invaders were far from strangers to committing atrocities, the Einsatzgruppen having murdered hundreds of thousands of people as they crept in the rear shadows of the fighting formations. But here at Sowchos 79, the Russians had retaliated:

> 'As I drove through Sovkhos 79 a horrible picture unfolded before me. The supply units of the 336th Division had been staged there. By the hundreds our brave soldiers had been brutally slaughtered. They had been surprised and destroyed by the Russians in the early morning hours.'[216]

The Russians had not only fallen onto and ravaged this lightly armed supply column; they had also shot hundreds of German prisoners in cold blood. Balck saw not just the corpses of a fire-fight but also rows of bodies of officers and men who fell in lines as they were machine-gunned down. This was just another atrocity in a war full of atrocities.

New forces and new motivations – The Russian 5th Shock Army, 9–12 December

Lucht agreed that his 336. Infanterie-Division would form what Balck called the 'shield and pivot' for future defensive operations on the western bank and bend of the Chir River Front. Operation Little Saturn was now in full swing.[217] With Lucht and his battalions holding fast and never retreating – often being run over and through, but never retreating – a desperate struggle now unfolded. The Russian forces attempted daily assaults across the Chir, and Hermann Balck and his Panzer-Regiment 15 commander, Oberst von Schimmelmann, acted as the *Feuerwehr* across the sector. This required a very careful and cool-headed use of force – concentrated and timed with precision through von Schimmelmann and on to the three battalion commanders. To commit only partially might mean disaster and a total breakthrough, while committing too heavily could leave a door open elsewhere. This was the genius that Balck now showed in being able to make the right decisions in terms of the weight and purpose of each movement, getting the timing perfect so that units were able to destroy the enemy, withdraw and regroup, ready to move somewhere else along the line.

Facing the weakened XLVIII. Panzerkorps were the already battered units of the 5th Tank Army and the stressed and under-pressure Romanenko, whose men had the unfortunate experience of running up against Balck and his 11.

Panzer. But there was also a new Soviet commander in the area. Lieutenant General Markian Popov commanded the newly raised – actually thrown-together – 5th Shock Army. Popov was tough, part of the new breed of Russian generals promoted during 1941, with increasingly acute tactical sense and new formations keen to destroy an enemy that was there for the taking. Much of the original Red Army had gone in the massed encirclements of 1941 and the huge losses defending Moscow. Popov led new divisions for whom the motivation was no longer the defence of the Motherland, but the destruction of Germany. He was there to support the efforts of 5th Tank Army, which seemed to be losing the momentum that the Stavka (the Soviet High Command) wished to maintain.[218] According to historian Catherine Merridale:

> 'To write about an army 30 million strong, after all, is to take on an entire society, albeit one that faced extreme crisis. And this army, like the society from which it sprang, did not remain the same over four years. Where panic and despair had reigned in 1941, a dogged stoicism would emerge by the time of Stalingrad, and this in turn gave way to something like professional confidence. One reason was that the bulk of the army died (or was captured) and was replaced several times – at least twice – in the course of the war.'[219]

The 5th Shock Army that Popov commanded was formidable, composed of a series of reconstructed divisions but also brand-new ones raised and trained in the east and eager to use their weapons delivered straight from the factories. What was impressive about this new army was that not only did it demonstrate the vast reserves of manpower and new equipment available to Stalin, but also that it was formed and brought together in just four days, between 9 and 12 December. Many of the rear echelons had never been in action before, but they were keen to show that, this time, the Russian Army would reign supreme. Their target was the Chir River area and the potential for the XLVIII. Panzerkorps to support von Manstein's Operation Winter Storm to relieve Stalingrad. Popov exuded professional competence – he had been a commander on the Leningrad Front and had the confidence of Zhukov as a field commander, which in turn, just like with Hermann Balck, permeated down to his huge mass of fighting units. There was a chance, so Zhukov hoped, that this new 5th Shock Army, combined with the existing 5th Tank Army, could turn the German tactical defeat in Stalingrad into a larger strategic Soviet victory in southern Russia.

For the XLVIII. Panzerkorps, the strategic situation had developed whereby advance seemed impossible and retreat meant death and destruction. In such circumstances, fear is replaced by the desire to kill and to survive. They were also fighting for the salvation of the men of 6. Armee, and the longer the Russian 5th Tank Army was fighting them here, the fewer Russian troops were available to try to stop Winter Storm. Von Manstein's operation was well under way to their south-east, striving to break through to Stalingrad, led by Hermann Hoth's 4. Panzerarmee. Furthermore, these men were responding to the success that their commander was giving them. While it was hard and brutal, with constant night movements, heavy losses and exhaustion, they could relish each small victory and see the results of their success in the hundreds of burning Soviet tanks in front of them. On top of all this, it was obvious to them that the Russians sought to destroy Germany. The cold-blooded executions of the men of the 336. Infanterie-Division at State Farm 79 showed that they were now fighting in a war not of conquest, but of survival and for their homeland. Balck had made that clear in a rare order of the day to his men just after the discoveries at Sowchos, part of which read:

> 'Comrades, the tough days of fighting that are behind us now show us anew that this is about the existence or non-existence of our people. If in the future you waver in your courage, should you grow weak during the bitter fighting, always remember the Anglo-American hate tirades, the slogans of the 157th Russian Tank Brigade, the horrible sights at Sovkhos 79 that prove to us without a doubt the fate that will await us if we do not win this fight.'[220]

To what extent the men of 11. Panzer-Division used these words as their mantra we do not know, but what is certain is that until 23 December, 11. Panzer would fight like lions and defeat attack after attack from both Romanenko's 5th Tank Army and Popov's 5th Shock Army.

While throughout his memoirs, Hermann Balck remains steadfastly of the opinion that the Red Army was just a horde of disposable soldiers, poorly led and without any moral compass, the reality was very different. To continue to see the early Russian Army as the same animal as the emerging Soviet Army was myopic and stereotypical. Catherine Merridale comments:

> 'Another [change in the Russian Army] was the changing mood of the people – soldiers – as the army's own culture and fortunes changed. Generalizations about Ivan, in other words, are either crude shorthand or cruder racism.'[221]

On 9 and 10 December, fresh attacks occurred on the Chir River front. At times, the Russian tanks of the 159th Tank Brigade, supported by infantry, penetrated in numerous places such as Surovikino and pushed ahead to Nizhna Kalinowski. No quarter was given, the Russian tanks driving straight over infantry trenches and returning to spin their tracks to bury their occupants, before themselves then being caught by ambush fire or outmanoeuvred in the rear by the careful use of Panzer-Regiment 15's tanks. Balck cleverly employed his Kradschützen-Abteilung 61 motorcycle infantry and encouraged von Hauser to be bold and surprise the enemy by appearing all over the battlefield. On 11 December, another series of Soviet attacks began, led by the Russian 5th Mechanized Corps, and both Bosse and Henze drove and encouraged their companies onwards in Panzergrenadier-Regiment 111 and 110 respectively.

Between 13 and 15 December, the Russians mounted attacks to the north of the Chir River salient as well as in the south, and the 11. Panzer 'fire brigade' chased – overnight and every night – to suddenly appear where the Russians thought it was impossible. Each time, Lucht and Balck liaised regarding where the best place to attack first would be, then artillery fire was co-ordinated with their attacks. On 13 December, the 5th Shock Army launched new attacks, using the 7th Tank Corps command by General Pavel Rotmistrov, and they quickly overran the German positions at Rychkovskii and Verkhne-Chirskii. Rotmistrov prematurely observed to his Army commander, Popov: 'The Germans in Rychkovskii are kaput!'[222]

Balck and 11. Panzer-Division were also now fighting Russian infantry from the two Russian armies in front of them, and von Knobelsdorff, von Mellenthin, Lucht and Balck all knew that any remaining hopes of XLVIII. Panzerkorps being able to take part in Winter Storm were over. They were facing their own storm of Russian power, fighting to survive being overwhelmed.

Instead of just massed tank attacks, waves of company- or regimental-sized Russian infantry also tried to overpower the defensive lines of the 336. Infanterie-Division. The fighting was intense and brutal. Wray tells us that during this period, one German battlegroup holding a bridgehead on the Chir lost eighteen officers and 750 men in ten days of combat.[223] Balck was helped by the Russian tactics, in so far as they continued to attack not only at different points of the Chir River line but also at different times, although this was not necessarily because of poorly co-ordinated communications, as Balck liked to think. In the Russian mind, smaller and multiple attacks at different places and at different times had some real advantages in keeping the enemy constantly guessing where the next assault would come, unnerving their German opponents and wearing them down by attrition. What they did not factor in was the ability of a commander like Hermann Balck, whose deep reserves of determination, physical stamina and willingness to fight in the front lines were a perfect foil to the tactics of multiple attritional attacks. As Balck himself admitted, had the Russians paused and instead co-ordinated a single advance along the line, then the weakened German forces would certainly have been overwhelmed; even the Ghost Division could not be everywhere at the same time. As long as they continued fighting, the men of the 11. Panzer felt that they were at least helping to drain the Russian forces of units able to help in the encirclement of Stalingrad. Major airlifts to the encircled 6. Armee had begun in November from airfields held by the Germans at Tatsinskaya and Morozovsk, and there was still a chance the flying in of supplies by the Luftwaffe's VIII. Fliegerkorps and the attack of 4. Panzerarmee in Winter Storm could release 6. Armee from the trap.

Yet more attacks – the Red Army 5th Mechanized Corps, 17–19 December 1942

By 16 December, the troops of 336. Infanterie-Division were exhausted and could no longer hang on, even with the constant help of 11. Panzer. Balck's men were drained, their vehicles constantly on the edge of breaking down. Fuel, food and ammunition supplies were low, and the freezing temperatures and snow made everything much more difficult.

On the Russian side, the overall commander of the Southwestern Front was still General Nikolai Vatutin. Nicknamed the 'Grandmaster', Vatutin was playing out his chess game of strangling the 6. Armee at Stalingrad, defeating Generalfeldmarschall von Manstein's plan to relieve the surrounded city (Winter Storm) and hoping that his 5th Tank and 5th Shock Armies might be able to force an entirely new breakthrough in the Chir River area. Vatutin ordered Romanenko to continue to attack to ensure that the 11. Panzer-Division and LXVIII. Panzerkorps were both tied down and if possible broken.

Thus, from 17–19 December, Major General Volkov ordered his 5th Mechanized Corps alongside a rifle division – the 321st – to attack out of the Nizhna Kalinowski bridgehead and force through to Surovikino. Balck had recently moved his troops away and this sector was held by a smaller force of battalion size – Kampfgruppe Wagner – composed mostly of men from the 7. Luftwaffe Feld-Division.

This heavy attack was serious enough for von Mellenthin to tell Balck he needed to break off another fire-fighting action to the east of the line and move immediately to stop what was a 20km intrusion into the rear lines at Nizhna Kalinowski by 5th Mechanized Corps. Issuing 'prepare to move' orders straight away, after an overnight march with headlights on for speed of movement, most of the 11. Panzer Division moved into new positions. By 0500hrs, it awaited the arrival of the first Soviet tanks. Balck had placed Oberstleutnant Henze and his Panzergrenadier-Regiment 110 to the south of the expected Soviet route, and

Bosse's Panzergrenadier-Regiment 111 to the north, with three tank battalions from von Schimmelmann's Panzer-Regiment 15 in the centre.

As they watched and waited from the deep cover of the ravines, dozens of tanks rolled by. Robinson writes that these were mostly British-made Valentine and Matilda models which had been sent to Russia. Von Schimmelmann and his three battalions from Panzer-Regiment 15 sat with the guns of their Mk III and IV tanks loaded with high explosive shells. He then ordered his Panzers to start their engines and spread out into a wide arc – moving first north then north-west, then west and due south into the rear of the Soviet tank force, which had no idea that the tanks behind them were in fact German. With Hauptmann Karl Lestmann and Abteilung II/15 in the lead, von Schimmelmann gave the order to his Panzers to open fire. Balck recounted:

> 'Just like in a training area, our tanks pivoted around and followed the Russians. The Russians had no idea that the tanks following their columns were German. In just a few minutes Lestmann's [of Abteilung II/15] twenty-five tanks destroyed forty-two Russian tanks without any losses. Then they disengaged and prepared in the hollow of a valley for the second Russian wave.'[224]

The second wave duly arrived, oblivious to the danger. This time the Soviet tankers were caught in a cross-fire, and another sixty-five Russian tanks were destroyed – or more precisely, tanks driven by Russian crews were destroyed. As the German crews took aim, they would have seen the back end of mostly British Mk III Valentine tanks, and possibly some Matildas too, which formed a large percentage of 5th Mechanized Corps' tanks. Described by Boris Koshechkin, the commander of a Valentine platoon at the Battle of Kursk in the summer of 1943 as being 'roomy like a restaurant', the British Arctic convoy routes had lost hundreds of Valentine tanks to U-boat actions during the autumn of 1941, but many also made it through. The Valentine Mk III could be found in numerous Russian tank units by the winter of 1942. A year after the end of the war, the British House of Commons heard the full extent of the assistance that Britain had given to Russia during the conflict in terms of tanks. The then Prime Minister, Clement Attlee, reported that for the period from 1 October 1941 to 31 March 1946, Britain had supplied 5,218 tanks to Russia (complete with ammunition), of which 1,388 were sent by Canada.[225]

Despite the vulnerability of the Valentine Mk IIIs to German high explosive shells, Russian crews reported that they liked the simple manufacture and functions of the Valentine, even though they lacked speed over difficult ground, only carried light armour and had an even lighter 2-pdr gun. In November 1941,

German after-action reports from the advance on Moscow reported that they had destroyed a number of British Valentine tanks, and it was evidentially a large number of these same types that 11. Panzer had now also destroyed during the attack of 19 December 1942.

Resisting Operation Little Saturn had been exhausting and costly for XLVIII. Panzerkorps. Balck put forward the names of a number of men from 11. Panzer-Division for awards for bravery in these battles, including mentions in despatches, Honour Roll Clasps for those already holding an Iron Cross – the *Ehrenblattspange*, which was pinned on their medal ribbons on the buttonhole – new Iron Cross awards and even a Knight's Cross. One such *Ritterkreuz* was awarded to Hauptmann Karl Kurt Max Wilhelm Lestmann of Panzer Abteilung II/15 on 25 January 1943. A newspaper excerpt from the following day stated that 'Hauptmann Lestmann and his Panzer-Abteilung destroyed 48 Soviet tanks'.[226]

Also fighting in these actions were the tanks of Pz Abt III/15 commanded by Hauptmann Klaus Piontek. He too would have gloried in this victory, but not for long as he was killed in action on the Eastern Front on 23 March 1943.[227] Such was the rate of attrition for front-line units such as 11. Panzer-Division. Oberst von Schimmelmann must have deeply mourned the loss of tank officers whom he worked so closely with. Tough, experienced and decorated commanders were almost impossible to replace, and new names were constantly filling the divisional manpower lists as others were being removed and their personal belongings packaged up and sent home.

Both German and Russian forces came to a complete halt in their ability to either attack or defend around 23 December. The battles along the Chir River had been a masterpiece of improvisation and tactical brilliance by Lucht and Balck, working together in harmony, aided greatly by the expertise of the officers and men under their command. But it was the skilled use of Panzers in concentrated force that proved decisive,[228] alongside simple and fast communications between the two divisional commanders, a cool head from both and synchronized, mutually supportive artillery actions. It was in many ways a perfect example of *Auftragstaktik* in operation, with immediate decision-making on the front lines and no interference from XLVIII. Panzerkorps headquarters. The combination of the 336. Infanterie-Division and 11. Panzer-Division was in truth an enlarged Kampfgruppe, with artillery, anti-tank weapons and infantry battalions working in close harmony. Back described the all-important communications aspect of success in the field:

> 'My General Staff officer, Major Kienitz, sat in one position a little toward the rear and maintained radio contact with me, the higher headquarters,

and everyone else. I remained highly mobile, moving to all the hot spots. I usually was at every regiment several times a day …. After communicating by phone with Kienitz, I drove to each regiment and gave them the next day's order personally. Then I drove back to my own command post and spoke by phone with the chief of staff of the XLVIII Panzer Corps, Colonel von Mellenthin.'[229]

The cumulative impact of 11. Panzer-Division's victories along the Chir River were ideal for the German propaganda machine, and news spread along the entire Eastern Front of the exploits of Generalmajor Hermann Balck and his men – less so for the troops of the not-so-cavalier 336. Infanterie Division, who were, in their own way, just as deserving. But in the cold light of day, these victorious defensive battles were limited in their impact. The Russians had achieved their aim of not allowing XLVIII. Panzerkorps join in Winter Storm, as von Manstein had hoped for. The attritional nature of the fighting did not allow either side to gain a tactical advantage. The rock-hard fields and ravines around the 30-mile stretch of front were strewn with decaying bodies, burnt-out tanks and hastily improvised cemeteries (which the Russians simply bulldozed over with their tanks once they discovered them). An entire division had been effectively lost. In all the chaotic and unconventional fighting, the naïve, ill-equipped and poorly trained officers and men of the 7. Luftwaffe Feld-Division simply disintegrated, the division losing all shape and structure during the fighting. Otto von Knobelsdorff, the Panzerkorps commander, commented in his after-action report:

> 'The furthest advanced air force infantry battalions had been assigned their respective sectors by their division headquarters. However, the division had quite apparently neglected to inform the battalions sufficiently well on the serious nature of the situation. It had failed to give them detailed instructions and orders on how to effect an undetected night time relief. The battalions therefore drove right into the outpost lines. They rumbled along with their trains [supply convoys] without providing for security on the march, without reconnaissance … until they were right in the middle of the Russians where they were duly and promptly wiped out without firing a shot. This was a terrific shock to the division – so terrific, as a matter of fact, that it was for the moment in no shape to be sent into combat as an effective unit.'[230]

Tragically, both the OKH and OHW recognized that the fighting, heroism and sacrifices along the Chir River were 'but a minor hiccup in an otherwise widely unsuccessful general offensive'.[231] In other words, these were tactical successes within the framework of a general operational defeat. For the Russian forces involved, the high casualties in terms of tank crews were replaceable, as were the huge losses in tanks, which explains the way in which they kept attacking en masse. What would be irreplaceable was the huge boost in Soviet morale that would be gained from destroying the 6. Armee in Stalingrad. Stalin was willing to sacrifice whatever forces he needed to in order to ensure that the 'Hitlerites' were delivered this crushing blow. To achieve this huge propaganda victory, constant and costly attacks on XLVIII. Panzerkorps were necessary to prevent 11. Panzer from relocating and contributing to Winter Storm.

Oakleaves and applause

For Generalmajor Balck and the 11. Panzer-Division – or what was left of it – orders could not arrive soon enough to pull back from the front lines. By 20 December, Glantz records that the divison had only thirty-one operational tanks left in Panzer-Regiment 15. However, Balck was still in offensive mood, ordering both Bosse and Henze to advance with Panzergrenadier-Regiments 110 and 111 either side of Panzer-Regiment 15 in a bid to push the Russians back to the northern bank of the Chir River. The advance started well but then faltered as the Russians counter-attacked. It was obvious that 11. Panzer no longer had the capacity to force any sort of successful attack, and Balck finally ordered a withdrawal and stabilization of the front lines. The days of seeing a Panzer division sweep across the fields and wipe out an enemy were over. The Chir River battles of December 1942 had been harsh and exhausting, and the impact was almost terminal for the division. The same day as his attack had failed, Hermann Balck received news that he had become the 155th recipient of the Oakleaves – *Eichenlaub* – to his Knight's Cross:

> 'Awarded for holding the Chir River line with his 11. Panzer-Division during late 1942. In this time his division smashed all the corps of the Soviet 5th Tank Army one after another.'[232]

In addition, the OKH recommended Hermann Balck for the *Wehrmachtbericht* award (which literally translates as the 'naming in the armed forces report). This was a relatively new and noon-wearable award, which had first been instituted by the then head of the German Army, von Brauchitsch, following the invasion of Norway and just prior to the attack on France. It was not normal for individual soldiers to be directly named in official army reports on the basis that all men were fighting equally bravely. However, von Brauchitsch said in the spring of 1940 that this situation would change: 'In future the names of soldiers who excelled themselves at combat actions in an outstanding way will be named. This is a very special honour. Thus, only deeds which call such special attention from others will be recognised to justify public mention in front of the German people.'

This new 'naming' was a real asset to Dr Joseph Goebbels and his Nazi propaganda machine, as they were now able to throw their media resources into creating new heroes of the Reich and magnifying the triumphalism associated with military exploits for the nation to see and hear. The daily Army Reports threw up regular opportunities for Goebbels to approve their inclusion in news broadcasts in cinemas and on the radio to ensure that the Army's own propaganda machine exploited every victory to the full. For Hermann Balck, this meant that his name was spread across all arms of the Wehrmacht as the heroic defender of the Chir River in the face of constant and almost overwhelming enemy superiority. This drip-feeding of virtuous sacrifice was all part of the far greater cynical deceit of the German people regarding the crimes of the Nazi regime, which historian Wolfram Wette discusses in his 2006 work *The Wehrmacht: History, Myth, Reality*. In the notion of the 'clean Wehrmacht', the myth was that it was the SS that bore sole responsibility for atrocities in the war.[233]

So while in the post-war period Balck drifted into anonymity in the Western world in terms of historical recognition – becoming one of Hitler's 'forgotten generals' – within Nazi Germany during the course of the war, he became famous for his achievements during 1943. It is common to see Hitler smiling in photographs whilst in the company of Balck. It can be assumed that the Führer, always searching for the 'true German general', loyal only to him, would have had a smile on his face when he realized that Hermann Balck's name was now seen as a hero of the Nazi regime, a talented follower full of self-sacrificing principles and, even better, someone not from the Prussian elite but a soldier's soldier. There is no doubt that this credit was merited, as von Mellenthin's appreciation of Balck as a tank commander stated:

> 'I must pay tribute to General Balck, a born leader of armour. Throughout the fighting his panzer division had acted as the "fire-brigade". Moving behind two infantry divisions [7. Luftwaffe and 336. Infanterie] to quell one dangerous conflagration after another. When the infantry found it impossible to deal with the larger Russian bridgeheads, Balck came tearing down on the enemy with the whole weight of his armour.'[234]

But the Russians knew nothing of all these developments behind the German lines, nor did they care, and as Balck was sleeping in the early morning of 21 December,

> 'at 02.00 hours Kienitz woke me up. All hell had broken loose from all directions. The 110th Panzergrenadier Regiment had been penetrated and the 111th Panzergrenadier Regiment overrun. The 15th Panzer Regiment radioed that the situation was very critical. In the bright light of full moon the Russians had attacked with tanks and infantry right at the seam between the two Panzergrenadier Regiments.'[235]

It would take seven hours for the Russian attack to be stopped and the gap in the line restored to German control by 0900hrs. According to Balck, 'there were times when I thought that the division had actually ceased to exist'. In the process, more experienced, committed and brave soldiers of both sides were killed. Hundreds of dead Russian soldiers were mown down by machine-gun fire from Hauser's Kradschützen Abteilung – which had been rushed to the scene – and many dozens of men from 11. Panzer-Division would now not see the new year. Some German wounded had been deliberately crushed by Russian tanks and lay frozen in contorted and grotesque shapes. Their bodies had to be carefully peeled from the ice, identified and laid in temporary graves, dug with the use of hand grenades, eventually to be left behind in what would soon become the Russian lines.

Chapter XI

11. Panzer-Division, December 1942–February 1943

'Stalinus afflavit ac dissiparti sunt' (Balck, *Order in Chaos*, p.273)

(A play on Queen Elizabeth I's supposed words upon the destruction of the Spanish Armada in 1588 – instead of 'He blew with his winds and they were scattered', Hermann Balck describes the scene that met his eyes when he arrived in a new section of the front where German forces had been dispersed: 'Stalin blew and they were scattered'

Tatsinskaya airfield

The morning of 23 December 1942 brought news that the 11. Panzer-Division was to be transferred immediately to the north-west, towards part of the line held by the Romanian 3rd Army and Heeresgruppe Hollidt. A number of fierce battles were now raging ever closer to the two key airfields of Tatsinskaya and Morozovsk, which were vital in attempts to supply the stranded 6. Armee in Stalingrad from the air. New Russian assaults had been launched to the north of the Chir bend as part of Operation Little Saturn, the extension to Operation Uranus and the encirclement of 6. Armee. Marshal Zhukov had already prepared for the destruction of General der Panzertruppe Friedrich Paulus' forces at Stalingrad, and it was he who also oversaw operations further to the north, to the west of Moscow, and pushing towards Rostov – both of which were designed to draw as many German units away from the relief of Stalingrad as possible:

> 'Zhukov reports that the westward thrust in front of Moscow against the Wehrmacht's army Group Centre was to confound the enemy – to make the German command think it was precisely there and nowhere else that the Red Army was preparing for a major winter offensive.'[236]

This new effort was designed to strangle any air or ground assistance to Stalingrad and further erode German forces trying to stabilize the line and thereby prevent a breakthrough to Rostov.

The assault towards the airfields by the Third Guards Army had begun on 16 December. By 22 December, 24th Tank Corps, commanded by Major General Vasily Mikhailovich Badanov, had been ordered to follow through the breeches in the German front lines, then reach and destroy the two airfields. With German forces spread so thinly, a serious breakthrough – even beyond Tatsinskaya and Morozovsk – could occur at any moment.

Defending the area between the airfields and the front lines fell to a mixture of units that had been able to escape the trap sprung on 6. Armee. They had been swept up together and placed under the command of Generalmajor Karl-Adolf Hollidt, to be known as Heeresgruppe (or Gruppe) Hollidt. During Barbarossa, Hollidt had commanded 50. Infanterie-Division and, like Balck, liked to lead from the front. Hollidt had been decorated with the Knight's Cross on 8 September 1941. He remained a valued infantry commander during the battles of 1942 and, as part of Paulus' 6. Armee, had been promoted to command XVII. Armeekorps, which only just managed to avoid the Uranus trap. Although Hollidt was now supposedly commanding a Heeresgruppe, its title was just wishful thinking on the part of the OKH; his mix of understrength units were under severe pressure in the slowly collapsing front, with the Romanians about to buckle just as 11. Panzer-Division arrived.

The memoirs of Hermann Balck tell us that he was ordered to move urgently, but before he departed he made sure personally to say goodbye to both Generaleutnant von Knobelsdorff, his commanding officer of XLVIII. Panzerkorps, and the heroic but exhausted Generalmajor Walther Lucht of the 336. Infanterie-Division. Lucht would also receive his Knight's Cross in just over a month's time, on 30 January 1943 (he would become the 691st recipient of the Oak Leaves on 9 January 1945 as commander of LXVI. Armeekorps).

As the 11. Panzer withdrew from the line, the men spared a thought for what they had gone through in the previous three weeks – which must have felt like a lifetime. No doubt some had time to pay their final respects to dead comrades lying in the temporary cemeteries in frozen earth along the Chir River bend before joining their transport and moving off. Balck's two Panzergrenadier commanders – the 'quiet, calm and steadfast' Albert Henze, who commanded the 110. Regiment, and the 'Russian educated and fluent' Alexander von Bosse of the 111. Regiment, had both lost many men both killed and wounded during December 1942 and early January 1943. They would remain outstanding regimental leaders, Balck relying heavily on both of them, speaking with and visiting them personally almost every day.

The editor of Hermann Balck's memoirs was Major General David T. Zebecki. Fulsome and helpful though his footnotes are throughout the text, I would venture to amplify on his footnote on p.273 that 'Hitler ordered Morozovsk held at all costs', stating that 'Morozovskaya was an important railroad station'. In fact, Hitler was not at all interested in a railroad station. Morozovsk was then, as indeed it is now, a vital airfield; together with Tatsinskaya, it was one of the two main airfields still airlifting supplies into Stalingrad – only an hour away by plane. Tatsinskaya was the main supply base using Ju 52 transport aircraft, while Morozovsk was home to He 111 bombers which had lost their bomb bays and were also now being used to fly and drop supplies into 6. Armee. It was to protect both these airstrips from the Russian advance that 11. Panzer-Division, and indeed 6. Panzer-Division too, had been ordered to move so quickly.

The area that Balck was moving towards was some 90 miles away and was littered with the remnants of numerous German units that had been broken by initial assaults across a wide part of the front. Further behind the German front, large Russian tank forces had exploited the jumble of German elements to head for the two main airfields. In his formidable and still worthy book from the 1970s, Abert Seaton described Heeresgruppe Hollidt thus:

> 'Group Hollidt consisted of Hollidt's own 17 Corps, parts of five infantry divisions and elements of five Romanian Divisions – to which would be added von Knobelsdorff's 48 Panzer Corps.'[237]

We know that XLVIII. Panzerkorps was as weak as those they were going to support. In Panzer-Regiment 15, Oberst von Schimmelmann only had around twenty tanks and two battalions of infantry out of the original six, the 336. Infanterie-Division was on its knees and 7. Luftwaffe Feld-Division was a division in name only, merely a collection of leftover units, which was typical of the whole front. It was impossible to know what was still intact by way of fighting units, communication links were in tatters and there were gaps in the line everywhere.

With 6. Panzer-Division also being ordered north-west to help plug the many gaps in the line, any realistic hope that von Manstein had of reaching Stalingrad was over. As Balck arrived, the 6. Panzer was still some way off; he immediately saw that the only realistic option was to try to restore some control over the battlefield with what he had at his disposal.

The Soviet offensive towards Tatsinskaya by 24th Tank Corps, under former teacher Major General Vasily Badanov, had begun on 19 December 19 and had successfully routed the Italian forces holding that part of the line. Some 15,000 Italians were taken into captivity and the attack developed into a major breakthrough, with an advance of 240km within three days. As they neared the town and airfield at Tatsinskaya, German resistance stiffened. Nevertheless, Badanov pressed his tank divisions onwards and at 0730hrs on 24 December, a Katyusha rocket barrage was the prelude to an attack on three sides of the airfield. Balck, using a forced march to get to the area, decided on a bold flank attack with his understrength 11. Panzer-Division to relieve pressure on the ever-weakening Heeresgruppe Hollidt.[238]

The Romanian commander, Lieutenant General Dumitrescu, supported Balck's desperate plan, as did the attached former staff officer of 1. Panzer-Division and later defender of Berlin, Oberst Walther Wenck. With intelligence fragmented about what units were still intact, Balck decided on 24 December to gather the remains of his division (it now had only twenty tanks running and just one infantry battalion remained, the rest being dead, wounded or missing) and see what developed, following Napoleon's alleged maxim '*on s'engage partout et en voit*' (which roughly translates as 'jump into the fray, then figure out what to do next').

Hill 175 and the cauldron

Heading north-west between Morozovsk and Tatsinskaya, Balck at least had most of his hard-worked divisional artillery intact. His artillery commander, Oberst Schmidt, remained in post and was still frantically trying to keep his guns and crews together and making sure ammunition supplies were reaching them. In his established style and still wearing a cloth forage cap instead of a helmet, following behind the lead tank, Generalmajor Balck inspired his men forward into the unknown.[239] However, while 11. Panzer-Division was on the move, Badanov's 24th Tank Corps had already smashed its way into the airfield of Tatsinskaya on Christmas Eve.

The Luftwaffe formation tasked with supporting those trapped in Stalingrad was VIII. Fliegerkorps, commanded by Generalmajor Martin Fiebig. Earlier that month, Fiebig had already protested to Göring and the OKW that the Luftwaffe alone could not save the 6. Armee and that Paulus' forces should be allowed to break. When his suggestion was turned down, Fiebig asked Göring directly for permission to evacuate Tatsinskaya airfield and save the planes, their aircrews and ground crews. Again, Göring refused.

Fiebig was one of the few who managed to escape the destruction around the airfield. Reports vary on how many aircraft were captured or destroyed by Badanov's corps, with numbers ranging from fifty to as many as 200, mostly transport planes intended to airlift vital supplies into Stalingrad.[240] Many were rammed by Soviet tanks to save on ammunition, whilst others were still to be unloaded from railway cars, having made the long journey from Germany but never having been in action. One Russian officer described the chaotic scenes as the Russian tanks suddenly broke through the perimeter defences:

> 'Our tank detachments unexpectedly broke into Tatsinskaya military airport. First to penetrate the enemy's territory was Captain Nechaev's battalion. A tough fight between tanks and enemy anti-aircraft artillery began [this must mean German 88mm anti-aircraft guns were turned on the Russian tanks]. Germans were shooting grenades at the Russian tanks and managed to blow up several of them. However, the Soviet tank crews broke the Nazi defence. After they destroyed patrol forces, Russian soldiers started shooting German pilots that rushed to their planes desperately hoping to save their lives.'[241]

The airfield's defenders must have had some warning that the Russian tanks were heading towards them. Alongside the 88mm Flak guns that were turned on the tanks, there was also the Romanian Air Force's 4 Anti-Aircraft Brigade with Vickers 75mm anti-aircraft guns, and reports state that they destroyed five Russian tanks before they too were overrun.[242]

It is unlikely that any prisoners were taken, and precious few survivors from this episode lived to record the events. Most of the the Luftwaffe ground crews died in the trenches alongside their infantry protectors, and the men of the anti-tank units were wiped out. One person that did escape was German pilot Kurt Schreit, who described the terrible scenes he witnessed at the airfield on the morning of 24 December:

> '[A] faint dawn broke in the east, illuminating the still grey horizon. At this moment, Soviet tanks, firing on the move, suddenly burst into the village of Tatsinskaya and the airfield. The planes flashed like torches. Flares of fires raged everywhere, shells exploded and stored ammunition flew into the air. Trucks darted across the take-off field, and between them screaming people rushed about. Who will give the order where to go to the pilots? Take off and leave in the direction of Novocherkassk – that's all that General Fiebig managed to order. Shaped madness begins. Planes leave and take off from all sides on the runway. All this is happening under enemy fire and in the light of the flaring fires. The sky stretched out like a crimson bell over thousands of dying soldiers, whose faces expressed madness. Here is one Ju-52 transport plane [which], not having time to rise into the air, crashes into a Soviet tank and explodes with a terrible roar. Already in the air "Heinkel" collides with "Junkers" and are scattered

into small fragments together with their passengers. The roar of aircraft engines and tank engines mingles with the roar of explosions, cannon fire and machine gun bursts to form a monstrous symphony of music. All this together creates in the eyes of the viewer of those events a complete picture of [...] hell.'[243]

Yet that was not all that happened once the air base had been overrun. In *Panzer Battles*, Friedrich von Mellenthin mentions the fall of Tatsinskaya airfield:

'On Christmas Eve the Russians overran a large airfield to the west of the town [of Tatsinskaya], which was being used to supply the Stalingrad garrison. Terrible atrocities were committed there, and when the airfield was retaken, we found the corpses of many of our comrades, with eyes gouged out and ears and noses cut off.'[244]

Von Mellenthin references the work of R.T. Paget, who recorded that 'The Slavs, particularly when drunk, appear to have a taste for fantastic mutilations.'[245] The men of Hermann Balck's 11. Panzer-Division later retook the airfield, but strangely there is no reference of the barbarity committed at Tatsinskaya that was reported to von Mellenthin at the headquarters of XLVIII. Panzerkorps.

Map 5. Tatsinskaya Airfield, 23–25 December 1942.

By nightfall on Christmas Eve, after a heavy fire-fight at Skasyrskaya, and through a combination of skill and luck – which included intercepting and translating Russian radio communications – Balck had encircled the Russian 24th Tank Corps on Hill 175, adjacent to the airfield of Tatsinskaya.[246] Determined to inflict maximum damage on the Soviet armoured force, Balck and the gunners of his Panzerjäger-Abteilung 61, under the command of Oberst Schmidt, shelled what was an increasingly small pocket between 25 and 28 December. But even with the arrival of additional units from 6. Panzer-Division, including an assault gun Abteilung, Balck could not break through the Russian defences. To prevent any Soviet relief force reaching them, a mixed Kampfgruppe had been positioned to block the main route to the airfield. On 27 December, further elements of 6. Panzer, led by the experienced Generalmajor Erhard Raus, arrived ay Tatsinskaya and applied even more pressure.

For the Russians, the encirclement of the 24th Tank Corps was a mini-Stalingrad in reverse. Always fearful of any negative propaganda, the supreme headquarters of the Stavka, Front commander Vatutin and Marshal Zhukov himself insisted to Badanov that the 24th Tank Corps either be relieved or launch a breakout back to the Russian lines. With scant regard for the cost in lives or equipment, Badanov consequently ordered a last-gasp breakout; on the 28th, the Russians 'exploded' out of the north-west corner of the pocket and headed back to their own lines.[247]

Looking at the bigger picture, the actions around Tatsinskaya had deprived the German forces driving towards Stalingrad in Operation Winter Storm of two Panzer divisions, a large number of transport aircraft and probably all of their crews. From the Soviet viewpoint, a sustained operation to disrupt the enemy's rear had been successfully completed, despite heavy losses. The previous year, perhaps Badanov would have been relieved of his command – or worse – for giving up ground. But in January 1943, with the imminent collapse of Stalingrad, the Russian High Command did not want this immense victory marred by any bad news, so Zhukov duly proclaimed Badanov a hero.

In a perverse act of patronizing deference to the views of Fiebig, whose prophecies of doom had been proven correct, Göring ensured that the commander of VIII. Fliegerkorps was awarded the Oak Leaves to add to his Knight's Cross on 23 December – the day his airfield and his men were destroyed.[248] It is clear that this disaster could have been avoided, with the men and aircraft moved further inland, away from the inevitable Russian advance, but Hitler's intransigence again cost many lives and sealed the fate of hundreds of thousands more at Stalingrad. Despite escaping the Russians, Generalmajor Fiebig would be hanged in Yugoslavia in 1947 for war crimes, while Tatsinskaya airfield fell back into Russian hands by 31 December 1942.

A few days of calm followed, which allowed Balck to reform what was left of his division. He once more created two Panzergrenadier regiments, though now of only one Abteilung each. The 11. Panzer had just twenty tanks left, and the courageous Panzerjäger-Abteilung 61 that had destroyed some 700 Russian tanks over a one-month period was dissolved; such was the savagery of the fighting that the unit only had one gun left.

The Russians had one final New Year's gift for Hermann Balck: during the night of 31 December and on into 1 January 1943, more Soviet attacks came in as the 33rd Guards Rifle Division crossed the Don River and headed west, while the 2nd Guards Mechanized Corps also advanced west towards Tormosin. The race towards Rostov had resumed before any new reinforcements had been able to reach the embattled German units.[249] Balck and his 11. Panzer-Division yet again moved to intercept, and managed to hold up the Russian advance for three days.

With their attackers fuelled by vodka and shouts of the unnerving '*ooorah!*', at one point even Balck thought that the 11. Panzer had ceased to exist, with all units reporting to the divisional headquarters that they were being overrun. Yet again, however, cool leadership down through the ranks allowed them to understand the situation they were in trouble, the units reorientating themselves to meet the threat and force the Russian attackers apart into small groups, which they destroyed Balck recalled:

> 'When we were able to assess the battle damage we found that nothing much had actually happened, except that the Russians had suffered senseless losses. Alcohol in a good unit is totally harmless; in a poorly led one it spells catastrophe.'[250]

That same day, Hermann Balck was promoted to Generalleutnant, although it took three weeks before his new rank was officially published on 21 January 1943.

Rostov and the withdrawal of Heeresgruppe A – January 1943

All through early January 1943, the German front lines were moving westwards – either through sensible withdrawal or being forcibly redrawn by the continuous Russian assaults. Consequently, each day also moved any hope of survival further away from Paulus and the doomed men of 6. Armee at Stalingrad. In Berlin and his headquarters at Rastenburg, the arrogant, meandering, hubris of Hitler's 9 November 1942 speech and its rapturous, sycophantic applause had, by January 1943, been forgotten. Deference to the Führer was still strong, but the atmosphere among his generals was now one of deep depression and panic over Hitler's military leadership. In the East, the numerous small cemeteries of the men of the 11. Panzer-Division in the Chir River bend were now well behind enemy lines – some in fields covered by snow, others in small corners of towns or villages, and even in churchyards. Months later, the body of Hauptmann Piontek, commander of the 11th Abteilung in Panzer-Regiment 15, lay in state in a Russian Orthodox Church near Kharkov after he was killed in action in March 1943. The bodies of dead comrades would never be seen again, either being scavenged for plunder, dug up in a search for information about unit details or churned by the tank tracks of Soviet T-34s.

The next unnerving development for the Germans on the Eastern Front was the bottleneck being created between Rostov and the advancing Russian lines, which, if not kept open, would seal the fate of Heeresgruppe A and trap them in the Caucasus. Hitler's great strategic gamble had failed, the oil had not been secured, and the Russians were now going all out for Rostov to create an even more devastating situation for the Wehrmacht than Stalingrad. To prevent that happening, von Manstein was faced with what von Mellenthin described as 'strategic problems of a magnitude and complexity seldom paralleled in history', and throughout January he worked his forces tirelessly to navigate a controlled strategic withdrawal.[251] The strategic initiative had clearly shifted to the Russians; at senior command levels, they were a completely different force to those that faced the Germans in 1941 and 1942. The OKW and OKH were having to deal with a far more tactically advanced enemy, as historian Albert Seaton explained in his examination of the struggle on the Eastern Front:

> 'The strategic planning and execution of both the Uranus and Saturn offensives were of the highest order and demonstrated for the first time in the war the ability of the Soviet High Command and higher headquarters to command-and-control fast-moving massed tank and motorised formations. Yet the education and tactical ability of the lower field commanders, particularly those of divisions and regiments, was still poor and the training of the air and tank arms remained much inferior to that of the Germans.'[252]

The battle to keep the bottleneck open was to be the next fight, and there was little hope of 11. Panzer-Division getting out of the line just yet, even though it was critically depleted in men and equipment. The leadership of Generalleutnant Balck was critical at this juncture as he continued to display his customary ebullient, self-disciplined and energetic style. He was still leading from the front, despite the enormous physical and emotional strain that had broken many commanders in similar positions.

While XLVIII. Panzerkorps was reinforced with new units – such as the 302. Infanterie-Division and the 6. and 7. Panzer-Divisions – Balck and 11. Panzer were detached from the corps and ordered south-eastwards towards the Don River, where they were to assist 4. Panzerarmee in protecting the Caucasus bottleneck. They had a daunting task ahead of them. On what the Russians called their South-Western Front, an Army Group composed of First and Third Guards Armies, Fifth Tank Army and Fifth Shock Army had been assembled. Many of the corps and divisional commanders had fought against 11. Panzer on the Chir River, and now hoped to extinguish Balck's hated division altogether in the drive to reach Rostov. One of the Russian commanders was Lieutenant General Markian Popov and his Fifth Shock Army, which had been on the receiving end of more than one of Hermann Balck's fire-brigade missions on the Chir River in mid-December 1942.

North of Rostov were the slowly disintegrating and retreating forces of the Italians and Romanians, and Hitler was receiving almost hourly reports of further collapses in the line between Heeresgruppe Don around Rostov and Heeresgruppe B to the north. By 21 January, Generaloberst Maximilian von Weichs, commander of Heeresgruppe B, was faced with the unenviable task of telling Hitler the truth about a 200-mile gap in the front with little possibility of preventing a permanent Soviet breakthrough and total collapse of Axis forces. Notoriously, Hitler hated bad news, and von Weichs would soon join those to be relieved of his command as the Führer searched for generals with more National Socialist passion and zeal. Depressingly for the Führer, von Weichs was right. Hitler's reluctant withdrawal from lands gained in the south meant that von Manstein was working with his hands constantly tied behind his back to save what he could of the German forces that Hitler had diverted south the previous summer.

For Generalleutnant Balck and what was left of 11. Panzer-Division, the sacrifices were not over. Between 8 and 10 January, he drove his men at right-angles, counter-attacking the regular Russian thrusts towards Rostov. Panzer-Regiment 15 and its fine commander, Oberst von Schimmelmann, was still intact, as was Kradschützen-Abteilung 61 led by Oberstleutnant von Hauser, but both now very weak and it was only by tactics of fire and movement that they were able to remain effective forces – any full-frontal encounter would have seen them completely destroyed. In his journal, Balck noted how, in order to give some breathing space to a worn-out and desperate German infantry division on his left, he advanced his men 16km into the Russian lines, 'overrunning everything in their way'.[253] The extent to which the fighting exhausted some generals is indicated by this journal entry for 8 January:

11. Panzer-Division, December 1942–February 1943   145

'There was some concern whether or not "Division G" could hold [Balck clearly did not wish to identify this commander or the division concerned]. I had talked to G for about an hour today. He was like a sick horse. He was finished. Even though he was senior to me, he was asking for orders. I referred him to his corps commander.'[254]

The motorcycle infantry of Kradschützen-Abteilung 61 had lost many of their bikes and men over the past six weeks, and could now field only two partial companies, but on 10 January they had to repulse a direct attack by a Russian infantry regiment. Their MG42 machine guns raked another rich harvest in Russian dead, almost wiping out an entire battalion in short order. Balck caught up with them in the front lines, littered now with hundreds of frozen, snow-covered Russian bodies, to congratulate and inspire his men, later reporting:

'They looked audacious, unwashed and unshaved. For days they had been sleeping outside in sub-zero Fahrenheit temperatures but they were quite alive and feisty.'[255]

On 10 January, Balck also recorded that Oberst Helmuth von Pannwitz passed through his command headquarters 'on his way to Hitler's Headquarters to receive his Knight's Cross'. Von Pannwitz had been leading elements of the Romanian forces during December 1942 and played a key part in keeping them together. In fact, von Pannwitz had already received the Knight's Cross for his leadership in the battles around Pinsk during Operation Barbarossa – his award is dated for 4 September 1941.[256] This simple error on the part of Balck is understandable, as von Pannwitz was actually on his way to Hitler to receive the Oak Leaves to his Knight's Cross. With the practicalities of getting so many individual soldiers and officers into the personal space of the Führer, it is no wonder that many awards were sent to families posthumously; it was important to get the recipients in front of Hitler quickly.

Ordered north to cut across the advances of the 3rd and 4th Guards Tank Corps of Popov's Fifth Shock Army, 11. Panzer-Division engaged in bitter fighting around the town of Kramatorsk. Interestingly, both sides thought that they were encircling the other, and a merry and macabre dance was played out on combat maps in the confusion of who was attempting what. Balck was frustrated that he could not take Kramatorsk, and this was perhaps his first major defeat in Russia. This annoyed him, as his memoirs indicate, but with such weakened forces at his disposal, he had no right to assume that his single division was capable of destroying two entire Russian tank corps. Discussions with the headquarters of 1. Panzerarmee – now commanded by Generalleutnant

Eberhard von Mackensen, a former colleague of Balck's in the cavalry inspectorate in the early 1930s – concluded that 11. Panzer should withdraw and then strike at the rear of Fifth Shock Army. On 18 January, 11. Panzer duly pulled back.[257]

Moving into Novotroitsk, a moment of humour amongst the chaotic savagery of battle in Russia emerges from *Order in Chaos* as Balck recalled a mission of shuttle diplomacy by Major Otto Kaldrack, his adjutant, whereby Balck ordered Kaldrack to bring the regimental commander, Graf von Schimmelmann, to his Kübelwagen.[258]

Kaldrack: 'Sir, the Graf said that there is still heavy fighting going on in the village, and whether you would not rather join him in his tank.'

Balck: 'Nonsense, you cannot see anything from a tank. I want von Schimmelmann to come with me.'

Kaldrack: 'I am supposed to report from the Graf that if the general does not behave and come forward with him in his tank, he will not go.'

Balck took all of this in the spirit in which it was meant, and got on board von Schimmelmann's tank![259]

In the fighting that followed, Balck and the 'Graf' surprised, harried and shot their way through numerous combat groups from Fifth Shock Army, and could eventually claim to have completely destroyed its 4th Tank Corps.

On 22 January, 11. Panzer arrived in Rostov and had two days of rest. Balck's men had already played a key part in disrupting the determined Russian attack towards Rostov, which had bought time for further elements of 1. Panzerarmee to move north through the bottleneck and out of the closing trap. But there was little respite. As divisional commander, Balck would perhaps have had time to sign off numerous documents presented by his adjutant, Kaldrack: reports on action to von Mackensen at 1. Panzerarmee headquarters and promotions within the division, such as eventually moving Major Kaldrack to command Panzergrenadier-Regiment 111. There were many decoration requests to be sent to corps and army headquarters, such as for *Der Kriegsorden des Deutschen Kreuzes* (the War Order of the German Cross in Gold), which sat between the Iron Cross and the Knight's Cross. Eligibility for this cloth or enamel cross, worn on the right breast pocket, was having taken part in frequent actions against the enemy – normally around eight; during the course of the war, 140 such awards were made to troops of the 11. Panzer-Division.

Over the eleven-month period of Balck's command of 11. Panzer, award ceremonies would occur at any time that Balck's adjutant or staff officer, Kienitz, could get the awards and the men together. These were important official events within the life of the unit, and essential for recognition and appreciation of the efforts of the troops. In the winter, the ceremony would almost certainly be in the command tent, while in the summer it would be outside in a bunker; such was the case with the German Cross in Gold presented to Leutnant Dieter Mund of 1/Panzerjäger-Abteilung 61 on 15 June 1942. (Mund was KIA on 23 November 1943.) Hauptmann Ernst Otto Schaeffer of Panzer-Regiment 15 received his award from Balck on 25 September 1942.[260] Apart from decorations, there were personal letters to be written to family, friends – making sure that the snooping Gestapo was given no cause to interview Balck or his family for lacking Nazi values – and those who had lost loved ones, who also received a letter from the commanding officer. There were also orders of the day and 'prepare to move' orders almost every day, but one of the most important of Balck's tasks was assessing the situation reports on the strength of the divisional combat equipment, especially vehicles, tanks and fuel.

A Note on what constituted a wreck

The fact that there were ten transmissions and engines for Panzer Mk IIs still distributed in spare part depots in February 1945 says much about the lengths to which the Wehrmacht was prepared to go to keep running every tank it could for as long as possible. For every divisional tank commander, a vital task was ensuring that his workshop was never too far away from the front lines so that damaged vehicles could be recovered – sometimes under fire – and taken out of the line for repair. Sometimes, however, there could be 100km or more between a fast-moving motorized tank formation and its workshop. The workshops were also very vulnerable to attack from the air and ground, and to lose the divisional workshop was a serious matter.

Nothing much could happen without the constant supply of spare parts, but given the huge distances, it was often a case of cannibalizing the worst-hit vehicles in order to keep others running. What actually classified as a wreck and total write-off differed between divisional workshops, but in reality, a tank had to be completely destroyed and burnt out to have no chance of repair. Any tank that had been hit by a shell, with its crew blown to pieces on the inside, but was still moveable, was cleaned out, repaired and given to another crew. As Albert Ganz wrote:

> 'The Germans experienced very few instances in which it was not considered worthwhile to recover a disabled tank. The guiding principle was that no tank would be abandoned unless it was blown to bits or completely burnt out. In every other case, recovery was mandatory, even though cannibalisation was often the only possible use.'[261]

Ganz also stated that 'Among the armed forces in Russia there was a strong aversion to allowing a disabled tank to leave the regimental area.'[262]

Balck expected his maintenance team to be able to repair a tank within fourteen days – more than that and it would have to be moved deeper into the rear lines to a corps workshop, where more mechanics and spares would be available. Two senior leaders stand out from the 150 men of the tank maintenance and repair company – Leutnant Ruhmkorf and Feldwebel ('Sergeant') Schrodek. Without these men, 11. Panzer – or any other armoured unit – simply would not have been able to function.[263]

Logically, the simpler the tank design, the easier the repair – something that never appealed to German tank designers, which meant damaged or broken-down Panzers needed more time being worked on to get back in running order. Furthermore, regular divisional withdrawals due to enemy attack naturally disrupted the replacement and repair timetable, hence the divisional workshops preferred to be well behind the lines before they once more started work, having to take all their disassembled tanks with them. For both von Schimmelmann and Balck, tank capability and crew availability would have been discussed on a daily basis while in the front lines.

Manychskaya

The short refit in Rostov that had begun on 22 January was over and the pressure mounted once more as a new Soviet offensive had begun along the Manych River, with the objective of breaking through to Rostov. Major General Pavel Rotmistrov, commander of the 3rd Guards Tank Corps, urged his men forward, and as 11. Panzer-Division arrived in Rostov on the 22nd, the Russians reached the confluence of the River Don and the Manych, which was only 20km northeast of Rostov itself. The Red Army had forced a road bridge and formed a small bridgehead on the western bank in and around the town of Manychskaya, so once again the 1. Panzerarmee commander, von Mackensen, ordered 11. Panzer into the line. During the night of the 22nd, Balck briefed his senior command team on how they were going to clear the town and destroy this bridgehead to give 1. and 4. Panzerarmee a few more days to get out of the Caucasus net that was being closed.

With the arrival of a typically freezing cold and grey morning, 11. Panzer-Division – its planned refit interrupted by the actions of the 3rd Guards Tank Corps – attacked the town of Manychskaya and was quickly in control of the outskirts. Russian resistance stiffened, trying to protect the small bridgehead, as being forced back across the Don may well have ended Badanov's tenure as commander of the 24th Tank Corps. Fighting continued through the night, and by the morning of the 23rd, the Russians had repelled three assaults by 11. Panzer. The fighting was extreme, with the men exhausted, filthy, hungry and becoming smaller in number. The 3rd Guards Tank Corps seemed to have learned a lot by way of tactics from Balck – they had already fought each other as 7th Tank Corps at Voronezh and on the lower Chir River trying to stop the advance of Case Blue. In Manychskaya, Balck reported that Russian tanks drove up and down the main street, 'constantly shifting superior forces into position at the right time and frustrating every attempt to break in', which sounds very similar to the actions of Balck's 'fire brigades' – he must have recognized the irony.

Far to the north of Rostov, the Germans evacuated Voronezh on 25 January. Voronezh was where Fall Blau had opened in late June 1942 and where 11. Panzer had been so successful, charging through the open steppes and encircling Russian divisions one after the other. Some seven months later, 11. Panzer was now a badly weakened and exhausted division, constantly launching defensive operations before another entire German army was captured, this time in the Caucasus. As the German forces streamed out of Voronezh, 25 January was also the day that would herald a sophisticated and multi-faceted attack on Manychskaya by 11. Panzer-Division, co-ordinated by Balck to lance the awkward boil which was the wrong side of the River Manych. The plan was simple but required perfect timing.

An early morning feint attack by the Panzergrenadiers of the 110th and 111th Regiments was launched to the north of the small town with what half-tracks and remaining armoured cars were available from Aufklärungs-Abteilung 231. Covered by smoke, they made enough of an effort to draw Russian tanks out of their dug-in positions in the south of the town to support the northern end of their defences. When Balck saw them move out and head north, a force of Stukas was ordered to circle the area and then dive-bomb Russian positions in the south, where, supported by the divisional guns of Panzer-Artillerie-Regiment 119, a deluge of fire wreaked havoc in the Russian defensive positions. The Russians had already defeated numerous attacks in this sector of the town, so were convinced by logic that this assault at the other end of town must be real. Oberst Schmidt had to be precise with his artillery fire – at one moment laying a diversionary barrage of smoke and light rounds in front of the advancing feint attack, then switching all his guns to heavy explosive rounds to fire on the southern part of the town to ensure there was no defence left as the Panzers rolled through.

Balck ordered von Schimmelmann forward with what was left of Panzer-Regiment 15. Leading the attack was Hauptmann Lestmann, who commanded the II. Bataillon and would be awarded the Knight's Cross for his actions on this day.[264] The brave and popular Lestmann had already been awarded the Iron

Cross 1st and 2nd Class in 1941, as well as the German Cross in Gold on 20 September 1942 – when he was an Oberleutnant in the I./15. He would die of wounds the following month on 26 February.[265]

The attack worked and a subsequent report detailed that Lestmann and his Panzer had driven through the south of the town and caught up with the rear of the Russian tanks, in what was now a common manoeuvre for Balck's Panzers, destroying 'approximately twenty-two' Soviet tanks. The rate of fire must have been very fast to catch so many Russian tanks in their poorly armoured engine areas before they could turn around, and the phrase 'shooting fish in a barrel' seems appropriate for these actions. The 3rd Guards Tank Corps had been mauled and the temporary bridgehead destroyed. Only one man from 11. Panzer was killed and fourteen wounded. Von Mellenthin paid his own compliment to Balck for this action:

'This battle showed in the clearest way how an action can be conducted with a minimum of losses, provided the attacking forces are well coordinated and can turn the enemy's dispositions to their own advantage. In this case General Balck decided to break in at the very point where our previous attack had failed; thus his feint attack completely fooled the Russians.'[266]

These defensive actions, along with others elsewhere, helped save the 1. Panzerarmee, and both Hoth and von Mackensen would later show their appreciation for the commitment of 11. Panzer. Before that, and on the very next day – the 29th – 11. Panzer-Division was transferred to LVII. Panzerkorps, which was in danger of becoming encircled. The LVII. Panzerkorps was commanded by General der Panzertruppe Friedrich Kirchner, an acquaintance of Balck's from the earliest days of the first Panzer divisions. They had not got along well then, and even now there was friction.[267] Balck recalls that he planned an assault against the encircling Russian forces near Zernograd, 70km south-east of Rostov, on 29 January, and was driving to locate where he thought his Panzers, commanded by Hauptmann Lestmann, should be, but they were nowhere to be found. After some time, the Panzers appeared – as did 'the Graf' in a staff car to report that Lestmann, who had just received the Knight's Cross, was still hugely drunk, as were many of his tank commanders. It was down to Balck and von Schimmelmann to lead the tanks to the point of the attack, the village of Kamenyi, where the Soviet 248th Rifle Division and two partial rifle brigades were encircled by German forces. It was another massacre as the Russian infantry streamed out, attempting to overwhelm the 11. Panzer-Division by force. By nightfall, 1. Panzerarmee headquarters wanted Balck to move onto another part of the line, but he forcefully persuaded them to let him finish the job, which he did on 30 January, capturing large amounts of men and equipment. According to Balck: 'The members of the enemy divisional staffs tore off their rank insignias or committed suicide.'[268]

On 2 February – at last – 11. Panzer-Division was pulled out of the line. It had endured a record-breaking period of fighting at the front, with an action of some sort virtually every day since early December 1942. Many fine soldiers had been killed or wounded, and the division was at less than 30 per cent of its starting compliment. Recognition for its part in the Chir River battles had already been received, but the battles to protect Rostov and allow time for both the 1. and 4. Panzerarmee to withdraw was yet another significant and historic achievement within the Panzerwaffe generally and for Hermann Balck specifically. He had proven to be Germany's most able Panzer commander of this stage and front in the war.

Hoth would write to Balck in February 1962 stating that 4. Panzerarmee would not have evaded capture if it were not for Balck and 11. Panzer-Division. As 11. Panzer left the front and the control of 1. Panzerarmee in February 1943, von Mackensen wrote an open letter to the division:

'Panzer High Command Teletype 11th PR Div.,
The 11th Pz.Div. is now leaving the 1st Panzer Army after 4 weeks of the toughest winter offensive fighting, having been called to a new task.

I see the departure of this outstanding division and its tried and tested commander with the greatest regret. The brave division has once again had success after success in this winter battle, fulfilled all of its assigned tasks and demonstrated its full performance capabilities. The division was committed deliberately by me and its commanding general to the critical points of the operation. It was therefore the soul of the attack of this army, specifically securing not only the necessary space, but also destroying the enemy forces. The 11 Panzer Division has proven itself repeatedly to be the master of such situations. It is with great pride that I express my high and grateful appreciation of the division and I wish it and its commander further battle success in the name of the whole Panzer army. And most especially I personally salute you with the words,

Farewell until we serve together again.
Von Mackensen
General of Cavalry'

Chapter XII

Remodelling Panzergrenadier-Division 'Grossdeutschland', April–September 1943

The 11. Panzer-Division was now ordered to move to Kharkov, where a new and decisive battle to stop the Russian advance would be fought. The battered and worn-down elements of the division began moving out on 4 February.

The rest and refit period allowed the survivors of the front to catch up with their lives, but the backdrop of the fall of Stalingrad came hard to everyone. With this in mind, the German propaganda machine began to play a new record – that the entirely avoidable annihilation and surrender of the 6. Armee was all part of the great Führer's plan to sacrifice one to save the many. Members of the 6. Armee were now heroes of the Reich, not the sacrificial lambs of Hitler's intransigence and hubris. At the OKH and OKW, a certain crisis of trust and confidence in the military leadership of the Führer had infected even the most die-hard of committed National Socialist generals and officers, as Major Kaldrack reported to Balck on a return trip to the OKH.[269] The nature of complete subservience to the vision of Hitler as a Messiah and genius was also affected; as confidence fell within the German Army, the speeches of Minister of Propaganda Goebbels became even more fanatical, as demonstrated by his 'Total War' speech in February 1943. It was Goebbels who also noted that a decline in confidence went both ways. Fritz writes that in an 8 March discussion at Hitler's headquarters at Vinnitsa, Goebbels commented on how Hitler

> 'vented his rage at his generals. Although especially scornful of Göring and the Luftwaffe leadership, virtually all of his military advisers came in for criticism, with the notable exceptions of Zeitzler and, perhaps surprisingly, Jeschonnek, who was praised expressly for being a "fanatic about the truth; he sees the situation clearly and makes no false representations." Hitler was, Goebbels noted, full of contempt for his officers. "The experiences which the Führer had with the army generals have embittered him utterly." According to Hitler, they fawned over him and then lied to him, fed him false statements that insulted his intelligence, and lacked technical

knowledge …. Still he was forced to conduct the war "with the present corps of Generals".'²⁷⁰

In this context, Hitler was looking out for individual generals who did not fawn, who seemed honest and brave enough to contradict him and were personally courageous. Hitler was under no illusion that he was surrounded by sycophants, which is why general officers like Rommel, Adelbert Schulz, Gille, Dietrich, Hube and Hermann Balck were such a relief for him, and why he seemed so animated in their presence. It was a serious problem for Hitler to know whom to trust and whose advice was worth relying upon. It is a true mark of respect for Balck that Hitler would shortly reach out to him for exactly that.

Generalleutnant Balck, his Knight's Cross with Oak Leaves around his neck, now had time to reflect that he too had seen Hitler become hesitant, stubborn and insecure.²⁷¹ Balck's time as a front-line commander was inevitably coming to end. With the record of achievements behind him of the last few months, a period of rest was deserved, as was a new and probably higher command allocation from the OKH. On 13 March, Balck departed 11. Panzer-Division and was replaced by Generalleutnant Dietrich von Choltitz (the future commander of the Paris garrison in June 1944). Balck was placed in the Leaders' Reserve (Führerreserve), ostensibly to rest and refit himself.

Once again, Balck went through his ritual of saying farewell to the surviving officers of the division, such as his key Panzer commander, Theodor Graf von Schimmelmann, adjutant Major Kaldrack, 1a and operations officer Major Kienitz, trusted and capable artillery commander Oberst Schmidt, Panzergrenadier-Regiment 111 commander Oberst Alexander von Bosse, Panzergrenadier-Regiment 110 commander Oberstleutnant Albert Henze and Oberstleutnant Paul Graf von Hauser, the steadfast commander of Kradschützen-Abteilung 61.

Between 13 March and 4 April, Balck was able to garner a few days of rest, but before he left he made contact with both von Manstein and Hitler. In his own words, this was to 'notify' them that he was leaving, but it seems more likely that he wanted to prompt them both into meeting him; his efforts were rewarded on both counts. Hardly indicative of a person disaffected in any way with the leadership of the war, the nudge to Hitler to meet with him smacks of fawning to meet with the supreme leader in the knowledge that he would himself be receiving considerable – and indeed deserved – praise.

Balck found Hitler in 'plaintive mood', with a suggestion that his melancholy was borne out of his heavy workload of concerns and worries – for example about the economy or war leadership – both of which Balck felt were 'beneath' him, when in fact it was the Führer himself who immersed himself in all aspects of running the war and not some functional problem with the state. Balck's blind spot for Hitler is very apparent here and he is clearly emotionally affected by and sympathetic to the mournful atmosphere of their meeting and the burdens Hitler was feeling. Balck concludes by stating in his memoirs: 'He [Hitler] should be above all that.'[272] The display of emotion by Hitler to Balck seems personal and real, and is another mark of the respect that Hitler seems to have had for him as one of the very few whom he could rely upon. Balck responded in kind. The Führer could indeed rely upon him, but the relationship would deepen further still.

Had Balck been aware of the degree to which Hitler had assumed total control over the war, then he would have been even more shocked. A pertinent example comes from Generalleutnant Walter Warlimont's diaries for the midday conference on 12 December 1942, held at the *Wolfsschanze* in East Prussia. The context is a briefing by the OKH chief of staff, General der Infanterie Kurt Zeitzler, and discussions with Hitler about the situation on the southern part of the front and 11. Panzer. I paraphrase:

Zeitzler: 'We had hoped to put 11 Armoured Division in here. That would have been more or less all right.'

Hitler: '17 Division's not worth much.'

Zeitzler: 'What about 11 Division then?'

Hitler: 'That's only got 45 tanks.'

Zeitzler: 'It's had 49 up to now. There are some unserviceable. It had to leave one battalion up here; as an emergency measure.'

Hitler: 'When did 11 Division lose all these tanks? Up there it had 70 or 80.'

Zeitzler: 'As far as I know it arrived with 49 tanks.'

Hitler: 'And now there are more unserviceable.'

Zeitzler: 'Of course there are always some temporarily unserviceable. The figure always goes up the day following bad weather.'

Heusinger [Oberst Adolf Heusinger, operations chief of the general staff]: 'At one time 11 Armoured Division had 57.'

Hitler: 'It moved from up there with 73 or 75.'

Zeitzler: 'I'll look into it again. I haven't got the figures in my head. In my experience one must always reckon with ten to twenty tanks unserviceable owing to the weather.'

Hitler: 'I'd like to hear the whole situation first and we will come back to this business at the end.'[273]

What are we to make of this exchange? It is a minute snapshot of a conversation that must have been indicative of every conference, Hitler steeped in the detail of individual units, arguing about exactly how many tanks it had and why the numbers did not add up instead of concerning himself with the strategic situation and how to end the war. We can compare this with Stalin and Churchill, neither of whom had any notion of the strength of individual units, even less any interest; their role was to set the objectives and leave matters of detail to generals. Hitler was trying to run the war himself as well as deal with every other aspect of the German state. Being able to impress Balck by his knowledge of the 11. Panzer-Division was simply the result of a fanatical desire to control all knowledge, an inability to delegate – except in areas in which he had no interest, such as the minutiae of the Final Solution – and a fantasy that he should have been a general, not a corporal, in the First World War. None of these were the marks of a great statesman.

There is no mention of what passed in the meeting with von Manstein, other than a slightly vindictive and sarcastic comment that 'von Manstein was in the process of analysing past operational possibilities'. Perhaps von Manstein did not indulge in praising individuals in the charismatic and sycophantic way that the Führer enjoyed, hence the nasty taste of Balck's comment.

A few days at home with his wife, Marianne, saw Hermann Balck reunited with his family. Balck and Marianne were close correspondents all their lives, with letters regularly flowing through the field post offices trying to find their way between them. He had been moved to the Führerreserve for a long rest and evaluation for his next command – this was supposed to be a period of around three months. After the loss of their son in Russia and his experiences at the front, one can only imagine how the feeling of a soft bed, the security of home life and a garden must have felt with his wife, about whom we know precious little. We have to imagine these feelings as Balck completely ignores emotions at this stage of his memoirs. However, before he could set off for a vacation in German-occupied Slokavia, he was called from the train and ordered back to Russia.

The OKH wished Balck to take temporary command of the Panzergrenadier-Division 'Grossdeutschland' – one of the premier fighting divisions of the Wehrmacht, expanded from a regiment the previous April – and by 4 April 1943, he was back in Russia at Poltava. It seems that Balck had been posted there quickly for a number of reasons. Firstly, the OKH was preparing for a major battle and offensive at Kursk for the spring of 1943. It was here that von Manstein hoped to deal a decisive blow to the Soviet tsunami that at the time showed no signs of running out of energy. Secondly, the 'Grossdeutschland' was slated to become part of a so-called 'super-Corps' for the Eastern Front, a sort of super-enlarged *Feuerwehr* (fire brigade), so who better to prepare the formation for this than Hermann Balck? Lastly, Balck had been earmarked to command the division and the whole *Feuerwehr* in the coming battle.[274]

As might be expected, Balck quickly applied himself to the task of assessing the current capabilities of what was already a 'super-Division'. With the infantry compliment of a regular infantry division but more tanks and vehicles than a normal Panzer division, Balck noted from the start that the 'Grossdeutschland' (GD) was unwieldy for the sort of war that he had been fighting in Russia. Hitler still had not grasped that Germany could not win the war trying to go toe-to-toe with the Russian armies. The German armed forces were unable to succeed by attrition; what was needed were smaller, heavy-hitting and very mobile units – something on which Hitler did not look favourably.

By now, the first generation of the heavy Tiger Mk I tanks were in the front lines, and GD had more than most in company-sized units. Balck's suggestions were controversial. He intended to break up the division in to three Kampfgruppe-style, brigade-level formations, with the combined arms design that he had used so well with 11. Panzer. They would move over the battlefield separately but fight as a combined single entity with different objectives. He also wanted to dispense with the new generations of heavy self-propelled guns. In Balck's opinion, these tank destroyers (Jagdpanzer, or JgPz) were easy prey for enemy ground-attack aircraft and their chassis would not cope well with the Russian landscape; when their tracks failed, the gun was lost. However, towed artillery could be kept moving. Lastly, he aimed to expand the Tiger component to battalion level and place each one within a separate brigade. Given that Balck arrived with GD on 4 April and his report was submitted to the OKH on the 14th, it clearly did not take long for him to completely remodel this super-sized division on the Russian battlefields. It was not a popular view. He later expounded on his thinking:

> 'I considered the overstuffing of the division with equipment to be a mistake. The excess was easily destroyed by enemy fire without increasing the division's effectiveness, and that excess equipment was not then available elsewhere.'[275]

With the fall of Stalingrad in February, Hitler had recalled Heinz Guderian from the wilderness and appointed him Inspector General of Armoured Troops. Guderian had lobbied hard on his own behalf and managed to reassure Hitler that he was back onside as a National Socialist. It was Guderian who favoured the tank-hunting JgPz, and he agreed with Hitler's wish to allocate more and more resources to the Waffen-SS divisions than to the Panzerwaffe of the

Heer. Guderian was also preoccupied with getting new stocks of the Panther tank into front-line formations, and with the training of enough new crews to man them. Consequently, Balck's recommendations fell on deaf ears – even Schmundt, Hitler's adjutant and close friend to Balck, was unable to get his report a positive hearing. Balck was philosophically at a variance with the thinking at the highest levels, and his approach was too pragmatic. Undoubtedly, he did not apply enough politics to his suggestions, which was crucial in Nazi Germany to get anything done.[276] GD would remain unique in terms of its structure and role, being 'neither fish, nor flesh, nor good red herring'.

Throughout May and on into early June 1943, Generalleutnant Balck worked at overseeing the training and build-up of the division, as well as preparing to lead it into battle in Operation Citadel – codename for the massive German offensive at Kursk. Had the start date of the operation not been regularly postponed, then that is what he would have done. The May 1943 entries in Balck's diaries provide an interesting insight into the mind of a German general on the Eastern Front: he wrote that Italy was on the verge of collapse, more good divisions had been sacrificed in North Africa and Tunisia, partisans in the rear of the Eastern Front showed continuing savagery and devotion, and the Kursk offensive was postponed again. Most in higher command positions knew that the war was already lost. Balck's hopes for leading the charge in Citadel came to a sudden end when, on 10 June, the GD's previous commander, Generalleutnant Walter Hörnlein, returned to take command of the division. Balck returned to the Führerreserve and to his wife – but again, not for long.

Part IV

Fighting for Germany 1943–1945

Chapter XIII

Italy – Acting Commander XIV. Panzerkorps, September–October 1943

After his brief time with Panzergrenadier-Division 'Grossdeutschland', Hermann Balck was meant to complete his period in the Führerreserve, but events were moving quickly. Even before Unternehmen Zitadelle (Operation Citadel, the German offensive at Kursk) began on 5 July, the OKH had planned to send Balck to Italy, where their tried and trusted commander of XIV. Panzerkorps – General der Panzertruppe Hans-Valentin Hube – was due a period of leave in September.

Having lost a hand at Verdun in 1916, Hans-Valentin Robert Friedrich Hube had led 16. Infanterie-Division through France in 1940 and what then developed into 16. Panzer-Division in Operation Barbarossa. By January 1942, Hube had been decorated with the Knight's Cross and Oak Leaves, and in September 1942 he was promoted to command his parent formation of XIV. Panzerkorps. As a Generalleutnant, he took his corps into the battle for Stalingrad as part of 6. Armee.[277] It was Hube and his corps that were on the receiving end of Operation Uranus, the Red Army's pincer offensive to encircle 6. Armee. Hube is widely regarded as one of the few German officers to have been able to hold a frank, face-to-face discussion with Hitler, and had told the Führer that he must evacuate Stalingrad. Despite this unwanted advice, Hube was to share, along with Balck, the rare distinction of ultimately being awarded both the Swords and Diamonds to his Knight's Cross.

By March 1943, Hube had been transferred to Sicily, where he commanded a reconstituted XIV. Panzerkorps, the designation having followed the commander rather than the formation itself. In Italy, political and military fires were burning, and the extent to which Mussolini could be relied upon to maintain control was diminishing by the day. In July, Hube was told he must take control in Sicily and hold it for as long as possible, but during August he had actually overseen a successful evacuation of German troops from the island. For the OKH and Hitler, it was vital to have reliable commanders if someone like Hube was on leave, so they turned to Generalleutnant Balck for his first appointment as a temporary corps commander, with orders to be ready to act once again as the leader of the local 'fire brigade'.

In what must have been late June, Balck was summoned from leave to Bendler Strasse in Berlin to meet with his old friend, Generalmajor Rudolf Schmundt, senior adjutant to the Führer, who passed on orders directly from Hitler that Balck was temporarily to replace Hube, with XIV. Panzerkorps positioned around the Bay of Naples. The Allies launched their invasion of Sicily on 9 July, and Italy was teetering on the brink of collapse, their armies having been smashed at both Stalingrad and what was now being called 'Tunisgrad' in North Africa. For Balck, Italy at least had the advantage of a good climate compared to the privations of the Eastern Front – where 11. Panzer-Division was still fighting – but his orders came with an additional requirement. An oral message directly from Hitler to Balck stated:

'Hitler sends you the following message: All military and civilian directorates in Italy are misinterpreting the situation in Italy. Italy is not – as they believe – a faithful ally, but is preparing to defect. Italy will do so combined with an attack on all German troops and staffs. It is your mission to take over command of all available German troops in the event of the loss of your next higher level of command and, disregarding any previously made deals, act to stabilise the situation. There will not be another Stalingrad or Tunis in Italy. [In the event that Italy defects] you have complete freedom to act. You are not authorised to disclose to anybody this special mission, and it is therefore only issued to you orally.'[278]

As Balck took in the gravity of this message, Schmundt further disorientated him when he revealed that he also had a personal question direct from the Führer: 'Do you believe that the offensive near Kursk will be successful?'

Clearly wrong-footed, Balck records that he gave a nebulous response, along the lines of 'why not?'. With the luxury of retrospect, Balck, in a period of post-war reflection, regretted not being far more direct and responding that he did not think Citadel would be successful as the German forces were openly displaying their offensive plans and should rethink what they were doing. Balck reminisced that had he responded in this way, perhaps Hitler would have paused; had he done so, then the Battle of Kursk may have turned out differently, or indeed not taken place at all.

Before Balck took up his new command, Sicily fell to the Allies in mid-August. It was then only a question of time before the Allies would cross the Straits of Messina into mainland Italy and then, in all likelihood, land further up the Amalfi coastline.

Balck landed in Rome on 2 September, and the British XIII Corps, part of Montgomery's Eighth Army, began moving across the Straits the next day.[279]

Italy – Acting Commander XIV. Panzerkorps, September–October 1943

Balck immediately made for Frascati for a briefing from Oberbefehlshaber Süd (Commander-in-Chief South) Generalfeldmarschall Albert Kesselring, who held this position until November 1943. Rommel, meanwhile, was commanding northern Italy, tasked with creating defences north of Rome which would allow German forces to withdraw and hold the shortest line possible across the Italian peninsula. Rommel would be transferred to start work on another wall, this time in France, on 6 November, with Kesselring taking command of the whole of Italy. Thus, while Rommel was away from the front lines and given months of defensive wall-building roles as the poster-boy of the Third Reich, Balck remained in full combat operations, which should be borne in mind when comparing the relative contributions of each man to the German war effort.

Kesselring held discussions with Balck about the role of the German 10. Armee, which was tasked with defending southern Italy. Its two leading formations were the LXXVI. Panzerkorps, which was in the heel of Italy to deal with the British XIII Corps, and the XIV. Panzerkorps, which was designated to meet an expected amphibious assault somewhere along the Amalfi coast and was therefore positioned inland and south of Naples. Balck was told that his mission was simple – XIV. Panzerkorps was to prevent any Allied landings in the area of Gaeta and Paestum to the south of Naples and on the Amalfi coast generally, especially the extensive beach area south of Sorrento and Salerno. There was doubt regarding where a landing, or landings, might come, and Balck was to prepare for all eventualities, including parachute drops by the Allies.

After seeing Kesselring, Balck met with 10. Armee commander Generaloberst Heinrich von Vietinghoff and then travelled south to join his new corps headquarters and meet the chief of staff for XIV. Panzerkorps, Oberst Bogislaw Oskar von Bonin, someone whom Balck liked both on a professional and personal level.[280] After the initial briefing, between 3 and 5 September, von Bonin took Balck on a tour of his units, which included 16. Panzer-Division, the Fallschirm-Panzer-Division 'Hermann Göring' Luftwaffe Division and 15. Panzergrenadier-Division. All three formations were a mixture of experienced men and raw recruits who had never seen action.

With his interests in the classics, Balck was impressed to see both Pompeii and the famous Greek temples at Paestum, at the southern end of the Salerno beach crescent, and was concerned to make sure that neither were in the line of fire from his artillery. On 5 September, Balck's Fiesler Storch light aircraft crashed into some trees at the end of the runway.[281] Partly through pilot error but also engine failure, Balck was nearly killed, but survived with a mass of bruised and broken ribs. The Storch had very little in the way of protection for either pilot or passenger, and there were a few very uncomfortable days for the new commander of XIV. Panzerkorps.

Operations Baytown, Slapstick and Avalanche, September 1943

The fighting withdrawal from Sicily during early August had been mastered with very positive results for German ground forces. In contrast to recent events on the Russian front, many units were withdrawn in good order and in good time to the mainland of Italy with their heavy equipment mostly intact. This included units of XIV. Panzerkorps, in which Oberst von Bonin had played a decisive and positive role. This semblance of order and structure was encouraging as, on 8 September, while Balck was nursing his badly bruised body, Luftwaffe reconnaissance reports arrived at the corps headquarters stating that a large invasion force was massed off the coastline at Salerno.

To disrupt German intelligence units, the Allied command had decided that there would be three landings on the mainland of southern Italy. Two of these were diversionary attacks, codenamed Operations Slapstick and Baytown. Slapstick would see troops of the British 1st Airborne Division take the lead in amphibious landings at the ports of Taranto and Brindisi, while in Operation Baytown, units of Montgomery's XIII Corps would land at Reggio Calabria on the south-western tip of Italy. Both Slapstick and Baytown were designed to draw German forces away from the Naples area, where Operation Avalanche would be the Allies' main thrust, involving Lieutenant General Mark Clark's Fifth US Army. Baytown and Slapstick were initially designed to be launched in advance of Avalanche on 9 September, but Slapstick ended up beginning on the same day as Avalanche. Balck thus had to await events to see which was the main thrust before he decided where and when to launch a counter-attack.

For some weeks prior to 9 September, the Allies' Northwest African Air Force had been conducting ground attacks and preliminary bombing raids on German inland air bases in Italy, destroying over 250 aircraft on the ground – a criminal error on the part of the Luftwaffe, as these valuable planes could have been used against the invasion.[282] Indeed, the huge convoys transporting Fifth Army had left Oran in Algeria at 1700hrs on 5 September and sailed, without being attacked, past Sicily and into the Tyrrhenian Sea. Just twelve minutes before the convoys were to drop anchor 20 miles off Salerno, and their landing craft start for the transport area only 8 miles from the beaches, a message came in from Allied theatre commander General Dwight D. Eisenhower informing the entire Fifth Army that Italy had surrendered but that the invasion was to go ahead as ordered. At 2350hrs on 8 September, the invasion force's flagship, USS *Samuel Chase*, dropped anchor and General Clark was able to survey the landing zones across Salerno Bay.

The US Fifth Army was provided with all the necessary men and equipment required for a decisive and successful amphibious landing under the codename

Operation Avalanche – an appropriate name for an operation that had every conceivable advantage in naval, land and air power over its adversary.[283]

Included amongst the nine fully prepared divisions at Clark's disposal were Lieutenant General Sir Richard McCreery's X British Corps alongside US VI Corps commanded by Major General Ernest Dawley. The experienced and redoubtable McCreery and his X Corps, formed of the 46th and 56th British Infantry Divisions, would land on the northern beaches of the Gulf of Salerno, with US Rangers under Lieutenant Colonel William O. Darby and British No 2 (Army) Commando and No 41 (Royal Marine) Commando tasked with securing the mountain passes of their left flank and the town of Salerno itself. The British commando force was commanded by the very experienced and respected Brigadier Robert Laycock. On the southern beaches, Dawley would land the 36th and 45th US Infantry Divisions of the US VI Corps. Their flank would be secured partly by a parachute drop and special forces units.

Balck, meanwhile, looked at the terrain around the landing beaches which his far smaller XIV. Panzerkorps was to defend and saw only advantages. Salerno's plain was quite narrow and, once on the beach, there was not a great deal of room for manoeuvre before the great wall of mountains hemmed in the coastal flatlands. Dominating features such as Monte Soprano towered some 3,000ft above the southern beaches at Paestum, with its knoll named as Hill 386 a key objective and marker for the US troops, but which also gave the German guns excellent observation and fire control options over the plains below. Equally advantageous were the two principal rivers, the Sele and Calore, which for 7 miles run parallel before their confluence 4 miles from the coast. Both rivers were fordable, but they still provided a barrier between McCreery's forces north of them and Dawley's to the south. There was also the main Highway 18 which ran through Battipaglia, a name about to become synonymous with the hard fighting at Salerno.

Equally legendary in the coming battles would be the villages scattered in the area, such as Eboli, Albanella and Capaccio, which would act like hornet nests for defensive fighting. The Allies' plan to land, cross the beaches, force a way through the mountain passes and capture Naples was daring and bold. It was Balck's job to make sure they did not succeed.

British X Corps v XIV. Panzerkorps – McCreery v Balck

While Rommel was losing North Africa and building defensive lines in Italy and later France, Balck was fighting on the Eastern Front, where he held back and destroyed an entire Russian tank corps with only one division. In Italy, as a corps commander at Salerno, he would almost push an entire Allied army of

160,000 men back into the Tyrrhenian Sea. These are not simply the actions of a talented general; they were pivotal and potentially seismic actions that could have changed the course of the war. Hermann Balck thus deserves a central place amongst the pantheon of the more popularized German commanders of the Second World War. Perhaps had Balck been forced to commit suicide by Hitler, then his name may already have been more celebrated.

Balck's XIV. Panzerkorps was faced with the problem of just how to hold and then defeat the incoming avalanche of over 160,000 US and British troops, plus tanks and artillery with air support. Balck was no stranger to meeting overwhelming force, but the geography of the landscape here did not lend itself to wide and fast-moving fire-brigade tactics as he had employed in Russia. Furthermore, the German forces had to quickly take over all current Italian defensive positions, with their former Axis allies having laid down their arms.[284] Italy's withdrawal from the war was no surprise to anyone: Italian/German relations had been fraying for some months, and there was great mistrust of the Italian officer corps, whom many German officers saw as traitors to be shot at the first opportunity. Generaloberst Jodl at the OKW – in the view of Warlimont, probably trying to impress Hitler – even advocated a second fascist revolution in Italy to purge the nation of all enemies of Germany.[285] Practically, this was simply not going to happen, but the impact of the surrender was immediate. While the collapse of the Italian Army provided additional artillery emplacements to be manned by the German troops, it also forced Balck to commit hundreds of men to static positions on the coastline – men who would have been more valuable as mobile forces in his counter-attack plans.

Balck's tactical discussions with the OKH, theatre commander Kesselring and 10. Armee chief von Vietinghoff were inconclusive, as each proposed a different strategic route to victory for him. The OKH and OKW favoured a general withdrawal north to the defensive lines being prepared by Rommel. In his war diary, Generalleutnant Warlimont described how the OKW was unclear about what the Allies might do and where:

> 'Initially there was no firm view in German Supreme Headquarters as to what the next move by the Allies was likely to be. On the evening of 8th September when the great convoys moving towards the west coast of Italy had been detected some hours before, it was thought that an enemy landing in the Rome area was more probable than in the area of Naples.'[286]

At supreme headquarters, Jodl stated that the prime objective was to get the whole of X. Armee out of southern Italy as soon as possible and behind the defensive fortifications being prepared by Rommel. It was this strategic thinking that prevented the OKW from releasing two Panzer divisions based in northern Italy. Kesselring had asked for these to repulse the Salerno landings, but as he crowed so loudly about his current successes in holding the Allies at bay, he rather undermined his own logic. It was this interplay between the OKW and Oberbefehlshaber Süd that would lay behind the myth, in later years, that Kesselring was left to fend for himself.

Kesselring wished to stay and fight the battles in the south to 'push the enemy back in to the sea'. It was a phrase often used by Rommel in the coming months in France, and perhaps both men agreed that any Allied foothold anywhere meant certain defeat in the longer term. Others such as von Vietinghoff wished to await events and decide on how to react once the landings had begun. At an even higher level, the two theatre commanders were Kesselring in the south and Rommel in the north. Quite why Rommel had been placed there by Hitler remains a subject of conjecture, but the rivalry between the two commanders was real, made worse by the fact that they both reported directly to the OKW. This was becoming typical of Hitler's obsession with not making further mistakes with his appointments to senior command:

In his memoirs, Balck recalled:

'But Hitler at that point [the late summer of 1943] was having a hard time bringing himself to making complete decisions. He also always gave two elements to the same task – "*Divide et impera!*" – Divide and Rule! That, of course, was total nonsense in the realm of military operations.'[287]

One of Montgomery's best senior commanders was Lieutenant General Richard McCreery, who had already enjoyed a distinguished career, being somewhat similar in military command style to Hermann Balck.[288] McCreery was a cavalryman like Balck, and both men liked speed and punch in their attacks. Both were also intelligent and used their abilities well on the battlefield. This would be Balck's first experience of fighting the British in the war, and it would be a memorable one.

One particular strength for Balck was that, although depleted in numbers and tanks, he could rely on three experienced divisional commanders within XIV. Panzerkorps. Commanding the Panzer-Division 'Hermann Göring' was the dedicated Generalmajor Paul Conrath, who had led the unit from regiment to brigade and now divisional level. With their distinctive dark blue cuff titles embroidered on their right sleeves, the core of the division had fought in Russia with great distinction. Even with many new replacements, this was a tough unit ready for the fight, situated inland and to the north of the British landing beaches. Directly inshore from Salerno beach, ready to absorb the main thrust of the X Corps landings, were the 15,000 men of the 16. Panzer-Division. Commanded by Generalmajor Rudolf Sieckenius, 16. Panzer had been divided – by either Hube or Balck – into three Kampfgruppen for the defence of the Amalfi coastline: KG Dornemann, KG Stempel and KG Doering. Major Heinrich Dornemann was commander of Panzer-Aufklärung-Abteilung 16, Oberst Hermann Stempel commanded Panzergrenadier-Regiment 64 and Oberst Bernt von Doering led Panzergrenadier-Regiment 79.

The divisional tank regiment, Panzer-Regiment 2, was composed of four companies, each with twenty-two Pz Mk IVs. The total of eighty-eight tanks, divided up between the three Kampfgruppen, made it a formidable opponent for any invasion force.[289] Partially destroyed in the fighting at Stalingrad the previous winter, some 3,500 had been extricated from the Eastern Front, transferred via Toulouse, and now formed the core of the reorganized 16. Panzer-Division in Italy, which was thus also not without real battle-hardened experience to face the British and American invaders.

The third and final division of XIV. Panzerkorps, the 15. Panzergrenadier-Division, was under the command of Generalmajor Eberhard Rodt. The division was another of those that had escaped from Sicily across the Strait of Messina to form up along the Amalfi coast. Like its fellow divisions in the corps, it was still quite well equipped. Rodt was like Balck a fellow cavalry commander, and with similar battle experience and similar attitudes to leadership. A personnel report from March 1942 from Generalmajor Wilhelm von Apell (available on the 'Lexicon der Wehrmacht' website) stated that Rodt was:

'A balanced, dignified, reliable character with high personality values. Mild and mentally well-disposed. According to the judgment of his former superior, he led his regiment or combat group against the enemy with great success, grit and energy in all operations. Right, determined, clear tactical thinking.'

This, then, was the force at Balck's disposal when the codeword 'OKRAN' was received at 1540hrs on 8 September, putting all German forces in Italy on alert that an invasion was imminent. Three good divisions totalling some 45,000 troops, led by three sound commanders, had relatively independent operational freedom – providing von Vietinghoff did not interfere with Balck's tactical appreciation of the situation. They also had local geography that favoured the defence, giving them all the components to ensure the Salerno landings would become a tough, costly and almost disastrous campaign for the Allies. Furthermore, any hoped-for reinforcements from Montgomery to the south

Italy – Acting Commander XIV. Panzerkorps, September–October 1943

in Calabria wwould hopefully be blocked by around 30,000 men from the 26. Panzer-Division and 29. Panzergrenadier Division.

H-Hour for Operation Avalanche was on the morning on 9 September at 0330hrs, without any preliminary bombardment from either the navy or the air force. This was Clark's way of creating surprise, but quite how he felt that the Germans would be surprised when an entire fleet lay in front of them is a mystery that only he could understand. During a day of fighting, the Allies gained a foothold all along the bay with relatively light casualties, but they were well short of where they expected to be and many units were pinned down on the beaches. Balck states that on the morning of the 10th, he was clear that this was the main assault and he could order his divisions to begin counter-attacking in earnest. A series of bloody engagements broke out along the entire length of the 4-mile long, but very narrow, foothold that the Allies had gained. Luftwaffe air support had been strong, with some 450 sorties flown against the beachhead and task force over the first four days, encouraging the defenders in the bitter hillside and village fighting that developed during 10 and 11 September.

On day one of the landings, although the Rangers and Commandos in the north were able to penetrate and capture their objectives relatively quickly (the Commandos losing only nine men killed in taking the town of Salerno), it was inland of the beaches in the centre and north of the landings, opposite Major General John Hawksworth and the British 46th Infantry Division and the 56th Infantry Division under Major General Douglas Graham, that the really violent engagements broke out. Hermann Balck had ordered the three Kampfgruppen of Generalmajor Sieckenius' 16. Panzer-Division to position themselves 10km apart and 5–10km back from the beaches to avoid naval gunfire. These all-arms groups were able to put up stiff resistance as they could call on immediate fire from anti-tank units, as well as tanks and mortars, to disrupt any Allied moves forward around Battipaglia and the Sele River in the centre of the two invading corps. Further to the south, a fourth Kampfgruppe under Doering directed heavy fire from the hills and mountains around Monte Soprano onto the 36th (Texas) Division, and the 141st Infantry Regiment lost both many men and cohesion as they struggled to move forward in what was their first combat experience.[290] This level of battlefield domination, however, was short-lived once the guns of the cruisers USS *Philadelphia* and USS *Savannah* unloaded some 11,000 tons of shells on the German positions over the next three days.[291]

In the centre and bearing the full impact of the landings, the success of the 16. Panzer-Division Kampfgruppe on 9 and 10 September encouraged Balck to unleash his two other divisions. On 11 September, Balck ordered Generalmajor Conrath and Panzer-Division 'Hermann Göring to attack south towards Salerno. Later that day, he also ordered 15. Panzergrenadier-Division under

Generalmajor Rodt to attack the British 138, 139 and 128 Brigades, which were trying to force a way inland to the east of Salerno and expand their bridgehead.

To add further pressure, the leading elements of the 29. Panzergrenadier-Division, which had been released by LXXVI. Panzerkorps, were also now attacking the American right flank around Altavilla and the eastern bank of the River Sele, putting the 45th US Infantry Division under real pressure to hold their ground. The commander of the 29. Panzergrenadier-Division was the highly respected Generalmajor Smilo Freiherr von Lüttwitz, who recognized the importance of the position he was now in, potentially being able to help Balck and XIV. Panzerkorps push the Americans back into the sea or being cut off and surrounded as the British Eighth Army fought its way up from the south.[292]

By 12 September, it seemed apparent to von Vietinghoff and his two corps commanders that there was a developing gap between the British X Corps and American VI Corps along the River Sele, and that this could be exploited. Von Vietinghoff is recorded as believing that this was a deliberate move on the part of the Allies to enable one or other of their corps to be withdrawn as the landings seemed to be going seriously wrong. Von Vietinghoff reported as much to Kesselring, who, in a ghastly example of 'Chinese Whispers', magnified this assumption in a telex to Berlin, then sulked when the OKW predictably refused the transfer of two further divisions to the south – a distance of 450 miles.

Balck, while urging his commanders onwards, was less than convinced by von Vietinghoff's belief. Balck's characteristic appearances in the front lines were just not possible at this stage; his injured ribs would not stand the pain. The effervescent, charismatic and courageous leader from his time on the Eastern Front only started getting closer to the front on 12 September. He personally congratulated Sieckenius and his officers for seizing Montecorvino, Battipaglia, Pesano and Altavilla. British troops had been allowed into Altavilla, only to be pounded by artillery and tanks as the Germans counter-attacked there and at the tobacco factory near Montecorvino airfield, from where 201 Guards Brigade almost ended up back on the beach. There was also good news further north, where Panzer-Division 'Hermann Göring' was also on the outskirts of Salerno and becoming drawn into the deadly game of house-to-house fighting. For Mark Clark, the Salerno landings were turning from a dream into nightmare; he even contemplated destroying all his stores and equipment and pulling out. Balck had done his job well and the Salerno beachhead was unable to be held or expanded without help. All eyes looked south. Balck needed the rest of 29. Panzergrenadier-Division to arrive, but they were critically short of fuel, while Clark was desperate for Montgomery and his Eighth Army to make an appearance.

Italy – Acting Commander XIV. Panzerkorps, September–October 1943   171

On Monday 13 September, a day widely recorded as 'Black Monday', the situation looked bleak for the Allies. Montgomery was being held up by a skilful defensive withdrawal by LXXVI. Panzerkorps, which was blowing up bridges and demolishing roads, and his men were still 70 miles from Salerno. In London, General Sir Harold Alexander, 15th Army Group commander, had messaged General Sir Alan Brooke, the Chief of the Imperial General Staff:

> 'I am not satisfied with the situation at Avalanche. The build-up is slow and they are pinned down to a bridgehead that has not enough depth. Everything is being done to push follow-up units and material to them. I expect heavy German counter-attack to be imminent.'[293]

General Alexander was right to be worried. On 14 and 15 September, Balck – recovering day by day – recognized a gap in the enemy line and urgently pushed forward Kampfgruppe Krüger (led by Oberstleutnant Walther Krüger of Panzergrenadier-Regiment 71) at Persano, where it overran the 1st Battalion of the US 157th Infantry Regiment, before moving over the fordable River Sele and then virtually wiping out the 2nd Battalion of the US 143rd Infantry.[294] For McCreery of X Corps, the issue had always been a lack of space in which to manoeuvre. As a cavalryman, space provided options, but here, just below the

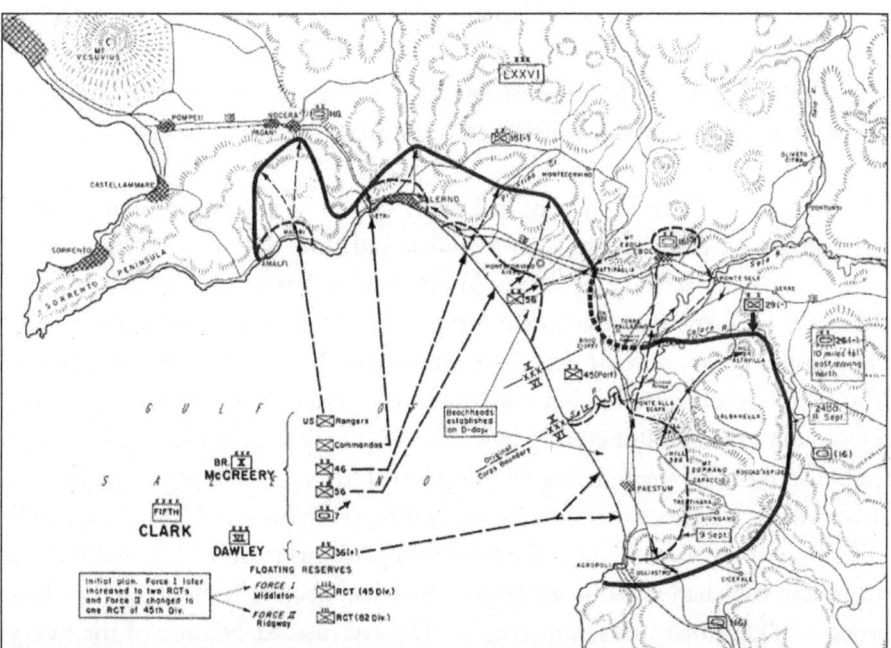

Map 6. XIV. Panzerkorps' counter-attack at Salerno between 12 and 14 September 1943, south-east along the valley of the River Sele. (*West Point Academy*)

mountain passes, space was just not available; his men were forced into frontal assaults, with the casualties that came with them. Balck probably realized that this was the decisive moment of the battle, although his memoirs treat this episode with a very light touch and just a passing phrase:

> 'On 14th and 15th September we had more significant successes, but not enough to reach the point of decision.'[295]

Quite why Balck was so reticent about these actions is confusing. Maybe the men under his command may have been so new and his appointment so short while Hube was on leave that he just did not connect as he had done with his comrades in 11. Panzer-Division. Whatever the case, this does not alter the fact that the attacks by 16. Panzer were successful and critical at this juncture. What Balck is clear about, however, is that the battle could have been won and the whole course of the war in Italy changed had the OKW released the LXXVI. Panzerkorps or other unengaged units in Italy:

> 'My XIV Panzer Corps believed it had fought well. Without concern for its flank and rear security, the corps had thrown all available forces against the enemy's weakest point, the gap between the English and the Americans. Could we have won if it had been possible to bring forward the LXXVI Panzer Corps in whole or even partially? I cannot judge. We certainly could have won if OKW – meaning Hitler – had decided to commit the many divisions that were sitting idly in northern Italy.'[296]

Meanwhile, the British X Corps had really felt the pain of coming up against an experienced commander such as Balck and three German divisions who were motivated, well-equipped and knew how to defend their positions. The ability of the British establishment either to hush up or airbrush from history unpleasant aspects of their experience in warfare has meant that the 'Salerno Mutiny' is rarely mentioned, but it was a serious matter when 200 British soldiers refused to fight and disobeyed orders. The event took place on 16 September in the wake of the savage fighting that developed from the Kampfgruppe Krüger attack where men from the 50th (Northumbrian) Division and 51st (Highland) Division refused to move into the lines to replace casualties. They maintained that when they had sailed from Tripoli, they had been told they were heading home to rejoin their units preparing for D-Day. Instead, because of the heavy losses inflicted on X Corps by Balck and his XIV. Panzerkorps, and General Alexander's concerns about how the landing was going, they were redirected to

Salerno. This was the largest mutiny ever experienced by the British Army, and McCreery had some 200 men shipped to French Algeria for courts-martial.[297]

Withdrawal to Naples

The attacks on 'Black Monday' frittered away through lack of reserves and momentum, and a last stand at the confluence of the Sele and Calore rivers by a mixture of rear echelon troops, supported by naval gunfire, signalled the survival of the Salerno landings. From then on, parachute drops in the southern sector and the arrival of the US 82nd Airborne Division was a sign that the crisis was over there, while the landing of elements of the British 7th Armoured Division began to shore up the northern perimeter. A sustained Allied daylight bomber effort paralyzed the movements of the Kampfgruppen of the 16. Panzer-Division and 29. Panzergrenadier-Division, and they went into a defensive posture, harassing as best they could while preparing to withdraw. Balck admits that his tanks 'suffered heavily under Allied naval gunfire, with which [they] had nothing to counter'.[298] His leadership and tactics had made this battle a very close-run thing, and Balck knew it, despite having no reserves or the support of Hitler at the OKW.

The Battle of Salerno lasted a week – an intensive and bloody time of determined fighting during which the Germans were within reach of a decisive victory, something the Reich propaganda machine could have used well. But Hitler was in defensive posture, and so were his most senior officers, especially with such distressing news from the Russian fronts following the failure of the attacks at Kursk. By 18 September, XVI. Panzerkorps was conducting a defensive withdrawal. The Allies, having been mauled so badly, advanced only very cautiously, licking their wounds and aware that the Germans were going to be tough to defeat in Italy. One unexpected problem for the Germans was the activity of the Italian partisan movement, which would have struck a chord with the troops of all three of Balck's divisions who had fought in Russia and knew how they were dealt with there. With defeat at Salerno for the Germans, losses of good men and now in retreat, the war in Italy started to take a far more ugly turn.

Hermann Balck was now in overall command of Naples and the surrounding area, and he is clear in his memoirs about the very thin line between military necessity – which came first – and the 'justifiable wishes of the civilian population'. Balck explains that he reassured his former commanding officer (as cavalry instructor) and now subordinate, Oberst Walter Scholl, that he would support him in whatever measures he took to fulfil their orders from Berlin. There had already been a substantial rising in Rome, where parts of the Italian divisions refused to be disarmed. Fire-fights broke out with German troops which disabled the city until German forces regained control by 10 September. Scholl had been the commander of the Naples garrison for some time and displayed an uncommon ability to manage the peculiarities of Neapolitan politics and customs. Balck made it clear that he was prepared to go as far as necessary to carry out orders which were essential for the Reich:

> 'What is important to me is that we do not end up with a popular uprising here in Naples, and that you maintain the situation until the decisive moment. If you consider orders and directives as not achievable, then execute whatever you consider to be right. I will cover everything you do.'[299]

The use of the word 'execute' in his memoirs is new for Balck. Nowhere in his autobiography had this been used before. Perhaps it was simply a turn of phrase, but more likely it was a way of introducing the concept of military executions into his diary, as this was to become a new feature of German control over Italy. Exacerbated by what was seen as Italian perfidy, German commanders across the peninsula were becoming far more hostile to acts of resistance; XIV. Panzerkorps was to be no exception, but giving subordinate officers such freedom of action without fear of persecution opened the doors to abuse. The situation in Italy was complicated. The Italian military saw it as their duty to regain control of their country. However, for the Germans, facing certain defeat, the emotional costs of losing comrades to civilian resistance fighters rather than the enemy coupled with news from home of the increasing night-time bombing raids on German cities by the Royal Air Force (soon to be followed by the USAAF daylight raids) – created a desperate desire for survival and a new dimension in their military spirit: that of revenge against traitors.

One of the best books to emerge in recent years on the remaining months of the war in Italy is James Holland's *Italy's Sorrow: A Year of War, 1944–1945*, which captures the torment and nightmare of violence that was about to begin in this land of beauty and sunshine.

Chapter XIV

Hidden from View – Atrocities in Campania, September–October 1943

Apart from echoing American military historian David Zabecki's assessment in the introduction to his translation of *Order in Chaos* that Hermann Balck's apparent failure to reinforce 16. Panzer-Division at the critical moment at Salerno, when he had reserves that he could have used, was 'one of Balck's few battlefield mistakes', Stephen Robinson sadly has little else to say about the almost seismic impact that the commander of XIV. Panzerkorps could have had on potentially changing the course of the war.[300]

To disagree with Zabecki's assessment is straightforward. In reality, Balck had only a small reserve, which he knew would make no real difference to the battle. Only the arrival of fresh divisions from Rommel in the north or the whole of LXXVI. Panzerkorps could have made such a difference. Balck was well aware that there was no mood in Berlin to commit everything to this battle. In these circumstances, what reserves he had were needed to plug gaps in his own lines in order to hold the Allies for as long as possible; but he was no longer in a position to defeat them. Why should he risk gambling what small reserve he had, only to possibly see his entire line collapse and a breakthrough occur, when both the OKH and OKW were sending signals that they had no desire to strike a fatal blow at Salerno? If we recall the actions between 9 and 17 October 1942 on the Chir River, it was standard tactical procedure for Balck to await events before counter-attacking with a reserve force. This was not a 'battlefield mistake' at all. Instead, Balck made a hard-nosed and pragmatic decision. The OKW had made up its mind that German forces were going to withdraw to the Winter and Gustav Lines, and he had no alternative but to make sure his troops were able to achieve that.

But blame was attributed for the loss of Salerno at the time, and it fell on the head of Generalmajor Sieckenius of 16. Panzer-Division for apparently failing to press home his attacks. In fact, Sieckenius had already argued with von Vietinghoff that such a fight was not winnable, given the devastating localized and off-shore naval gunfire that the Allies would and did bring down on his troops. Nevertheless, von Vietinghoff had insisted that he attack. Both Balck and Sieckenius were fighting against the 'succinct and clear and mathematical' Lieutenant General McCreery, who never seemed flustered by the counter-attacks coming from 16. Panzer.[301] In his very good biography of McCreery, Richard Mead adds further weight to the arguments against Zabecki's judgment on Balck's handling of the battle, pointing out that although Clark was contemplating withdrawal and removing the seemingly overwhelmed Dawley from command of the US VI Corps, the German attack 'found itself in a dead end between the Sele and one of its tributaries, causing their whole offensive to grind to a halt'.[302] Thus, it was less to do with a failure to commit reserves to the battle and more a case of sound judgment on the realities of the situation as the counter-attacks unfolded at both a tactical and strategic level.

Ultimately, and as so often happened in Nazi Germany, it was the loyal, brave and capable local commander, Sieckenius, who was blamed and rather unfairly removed from command; humiliatingly, he was sent on a training course for divisional commanders.[303] Naturally, blame goes down and not up, and both Balck and von Vietinghoff remained above criticism. Balck makes no reference at all to Sieckenius, other than his feeling that 'my XIV Panzer Corps felt that it [16. Panzer] had performed well', which sounds very much like a diplomatic backhanded compliment suggesting that he did not feel the same.[304] Balck apparently believed all the 16. Panzer's officers felt they had done their best in the face of what they were up against, especially US air attacks and naval gunfire, before pulling back (rather too swiftly, in his opinion), but that this was nothing compared to the suffering he had seen on the Eastern Front.

There is a distinct period between Balck's arrival in Naples around 20 September and his departure for the Eastern Front on 9 October which deserves greater attention. Italy was in ferment and torment, the Germans facing the oncoming Allied forces while being surrounded by distrusted and potentially murderous Italian soldiers and civilians. The OKW rapidly moved Balck and his panzer corps northwards into his new sector in the Apennine Mountains north of Rome. This was partly to get the defences in the Gustav Line secure, but also to get the corps away from daily bombing raids by the Allies. Balck reveals that he displayed an increasing level of desperation when he threatened a Luftwaffe officer with court martial and a long prison term, bringing him into conflict with Göring – not for the first time. It is possible that the pain of his injuries shortened Balck's ability to extend clemency, but it seems clear and not unexpected that he was becoming a harder and less tolerant senior commander, willing to do whatever was needed in the face of certain defeat in Italy and the newly aggressive actions of the Italian population.

The growth of Italian resistance and the war crimes of XIV. Panzerkorps, September–October 1943

As the XIX. Panzerkorps prepared to move away from the Salerno front, it was subjected to regular delays, disruptions and more confident partisan ambush attacks, which was unsurprising given the context and background of events. While Balck and his three corps had been battling at Salerno, Italy – as had happened in France – was disintegrating into a mass of political and military groups, all seeking to take over power from the previous fascist regime. Encouraged by *agents provocateurs* and supply drops by British agents and SOE (the Special Operations Executive), sporadic outbreaks of violent activity characterized the rear areas at Salerno and Naples.

Surprisingly, both Balck in his memoir and Robinson in his biography completely ignore the serious rising in Rome on 3 September 1943, when elements of Italian infantry divisions tried to take over parts of the capital and fire-fights broke out across the city involving the German Fallschirmjäger and Panzergrenadier units stationed there. By 10 September, the rioting and fighting had died down, with a final stand in the Porto San Paolo before the Italians surrendered and were either executed or imprisoned. The ramifications of events further south contributed to a full-scale battle between Italian forces and German troops at Piombino in Tuscany on 10 September. More than a hundred German troops were killed, with several ships also sunk, and partisan gangs formed across Tuscany. Then on 13 September, as Balck was counter-attacking at Salerno, the Italian 33rd 'Acqui' Division on the Greek island of Cephalonia defended themselves from a German invasion while negotiations were ongoing. A ten-day battle ensued, culminating in one of the worst military massacres of the war (alongside Katyn in Poland), with 5,155 Italian officers and men murdered by units of the elite German 1. Gebirgs-Division and Balck's own beloved – and so often claimed, honourable – regiment, Gebirgsjäger-Regiment 98, under the command of Major Harold von Hirschfeld.[305]

Balck fails to explore the level of tension in Naples, and is especially silent on the open revolt against German forces that broke out on 27 September. For four days, German troops struggled to contain resistance on the streets of the city. By this time, Balck could claim that the events in Naples and the executions that flowed from it were nothing to do with him, as his corps had already left the area and moved northwards. What Balck could not claim, however, was that he knew nothing about the actions of units within his own command during this period.

New research funded by the German government in 2016 concluded that the number of victims of Nazi war crimes in Italy totalled some 22,000 souls, which was double any previous estimate. These were mainly Italian civilians, most often murdered in retaliation for partisan attacks under the doctrine of *Bandenbekämpfung* ('bandit fighting'). Within the substantial list of Wehrmacht and SS units that stand accused of war crimes are each of the divisions that formed XIV. Panzerkorps while Balck was still in command, with atrocities taking place across Campania, whose capital is Naples.

The Fallschirm-Panzer-Division 'Hermann Göring' has been identified as one of the major perpetrators of such events, which began with the execution of ninety-three civilians in Naples on 1 October 1943. Given that Balck did not hand command of XIV. Panzerkorps back to General Hube until 8 October, he must not only have been aware of the incident, but failed to mention this in his memoirs, either in an admission or admonishment of the event.[306]

Nine miles north-east of Naples is the town of Acerra. Here, between 1 and 3 October 1943, the centre of the town was set ablaze and a further eighty-eight civilians, including seven children and fourteen women, were executed by men of Panzer-Division 'Hermann Göring'. This was done in reprisal for locals setting up roadblocks and for one soldier being wounded as he was requisitioning vehicles in the town square. The sub-unit in question was a Kampfgruppe led by Major Karl-Heinz Becker of the III. Bataillon, Fallschirmjäger-Regiment 1. Undoubtedly, division commander Generalmajor Conrath would have been aware of this event, and very likely reported it to his corps commander, Generalleutnant Balck, as a simple despatch in the Italian archives summed up what had happened:

'October 2nd 1943
'Clash with Italian gangs in Acerra. The area was completely destroyed and the inhabitants exterminated.' (Canale Pubblicco/Fanpage.It)

A white marble plaque in the town today commemorates the names of those killed in the massacre. However, the Panzer-Division 'Hermann Göring' was not alone in committing such crimes in Italy at this time. Another of Hermann Balck's units, 15. Panzergrenadier-Division under Eberhard Rodt, was also moving north when, on 7 October, it reached Bellona, a small town 22 miles north-east of Naples. Here, Rodt's soldiers shot fifty-four of the town's citizens for their resistance to the German occupiers. Only males were selected this time, including three very elderly men and four young boys. Local records state that:

'[A] German soldier was killed in a clash and another was wounded with a hand grenade thrown by a local civilian to prevent sisters from being subjected to violence by the military aforementioned. On the morning of the 7th, about 100 men were rounded up and led first to the town square and later, to the chapel of St. Michael the Archangel where, chosen by an officer in groups of ten, they were sent to a quarry, located on the border with the neighbouring territory of Vitulazio, and machine gunned there. Seven groups were sent from the chapel, but the last two were brought back. At the end of the executions, some mines that had previously been placed in the quarry were detonated and the soil caused by the explosion hid the bodies, found only a few weeks later.' (From 'Atlante delle Stragi Naziste e Fasciste in Italia 2016', compiled by Giuseppe Angelone.)

One sad footnote to this tragedy is that the family of the man who threw the grenade to defend the two girls in Bellona, Francesco Cafaro, were ostracized within the town for the rest of their lives. Another is that amongst those selected for execution were four Italian soldiers, a Vice Brigadier of Police and the 67-year-old parish priest, Fr Rovelli Andrea, and six of his church assistants.[307] Given that Balck was about to hand command back to General Hube the next day, it is possible that he never read or received any reports of this massacre, but neither is there any evidence that he issued any command forbidding the execution of civilians. The 2016 joint research reports between the German and Italian governments on war crimes in Italy identified the area commander as Oberst Wolfgang Mauke, who was based in the town at that time and almost certainly gave the execution order to Hauptmann Hans Sandrock.[308]

The third and final example of war crimes by units of XIV. Panzerkorps under the command of Hermann Balck came two days earlier on 4 October, when men of 16. Panzer-Division, commanded by Generalmajor Sieckenius, arrived in the town of San Clemente di Caserta. Unlike the planned executions by their fellow divisions, it appears from the records that during the morning of the 4th, various homes along the Via Galantina were emptied of their residents and then blown up to block the roads against the expected Allied advance. However, around 1600hrs, troops of Panzergrenadier-Regiment 64 of the 16. Panzer were responsible for another sudden and unexpected explosion, which ripped through a number of houses where the residents had not been warned; twenty-five civilians were killed, with bodies of men – including four very elderly – women and seven children strewn across the streets.[309]

Exactly what Balck was aware of, and what role he played in allowing these atrocities to go unpunished, are matters of historical conjecture. Given the strict disciplinary structures of the Wehrmacht, it is almost unthinkable that reports of these actions did not reach Balck before he departed on 9 October. What is known for certain is that all three of these events were ignored completely by Balck in his memoirs, and indeed by his only biographer to date. Post-war, Balck was certainly singled out for punishment and retribution at war crimes trials before the Landgericht Stuttgart in May 1948, but this was largely for further accusations of events that took place in 1944 rather than those discussed here in September and October 1943, which should have been added to the list of his war crimes.[310] The fact remains that Balck was found guilty of all charges for actions in 1944, and it was perhaps only by good fortune that these war crimes in Italy had not come to light by that time and he was spared further charges.

Chapter XV

Commanding XLVIII. Panzerkorps in Russia, November 1943–August 1944

'Several beautiful days followed my return to Germany. After our home in Berlin had been bombed out my family found new accommodations in Silesia, in Wildschütz (now Vlcice) near Breslau-Oels (now Wroclaw Olesnica), where we lived in the castle of Count Pfeil.' (Hermann Balck, *Order in Chaos*, pp.311–12)

In Russia, Unternehmen Zitadelle had failed. While the OKW and OKH had moved Hermann Balck to Italy and left him on leave during July 1943, the all-out German offensive at Kursk had come to a disappointing halt. By the time General der Panzertruppe Hans Hube had resumed command of XIV. Panzerkorps on 8 October, Balck was again on leave trying to repair his battered body.

With the corpses of the numerous atrocities in the Italian villages of Campania still warm, Balck flew out from Italy, this time with a safer pilot, on 9 October. The rest of the month was spent with family on sick leave in and around Breslau, where Balck's former unit from 1915–1916, the 22. Jäger, hosted a dinner, no doubt to talk about old times and the challenges of current ones.[311] Balck still needed time to heal the damage to his ribs, but by early November the call came for him to return once more to the Eastern Front, where the Germans were in a desperate position. A succession of Russian offensives had continued to erode what was left of the flower of the Wehrmacht, while the OKH struggled to maintain a flow of reinforcements to the front; but it was good commanders they really lacked.

Balck had a happy reunion with Oberst Friedrich von Mellenthin as he took over command of XLVIII. Panzerkorps in mid-November, having already been to meet with Heeresgruppe Süd commander von Manstein. Without a shadow of humility, Balck records in his memoirs that von Manstein told him:

'I have just spoken on the phone with Schmundt [still Hitler's adjutant]. You will take command of XLVIII Panzer Corps near Kiev. That's where the point of decision will be and that's where I need the best Panzer leader.'[312]

LXVIII. Panzerarmee was in trouble. Repeated Russian advances during October had forced the German front line westwards beyond Kiev and the Dnieper, eroding the strengths of most German divisions. Despite the pressure of the situation around Kiev, Balck and von Mellenthin's reunion was a mixture of mutual admiration and affection rarely recorded in military diaries and memoirs. Von Mellenthin regarded Balck's appointment with 'great joy', believing him to be 'one of most brilliant leaders of armour' and 'with strong claims to be regarded as our finest field commander'.[313] History has not viewed Balck as the most gifted Panzer commander of the Second World War, but he does have a very strong claim to be seen as a better battlefield leader than Rommel, whose major accolade was a single thrust against a retreating French Army in 1940, followed by ultimate defeat in North Afrika. The Rommel myth was begun by Adolf Hitler, perpetuated by Adolf Hitler even after ordering his death, and Hitler and Rommel remain entangled together even today.

Balck was equally full of admiration for von Mellenthin, calling their reunion 'an extremely happy marriage'. He elaborated on the depth of their understanding and mutual veneration by saying: 'Never during our years of cooperation was there as much as the smallest disagreement between us.'[314] The phrase 'marriage', when used in the context of two men, does have a homoerotic dimension that is not in the scope of this book to explore. However, to avoid confusion, what we are looking at here is typical of how men coped with the emotional stress of war by leaning on comrades in a working relationship forged by the unimaginable toll of conflict. Hitler displayed these tendencies too as he sought out 'real' men and dominated others: Keitel and Jodl are fine examples of the 'feminized' general that Hitler despised but needed, whereas Rommel, Balck and others represented the Führer's ideal soldier.

As a superb article by Juliette Crose examines, very little in the German Army in this respect had changed since the First World War. But in the militarized setting, allies and enemies who were regarded as weak, dependent or disloyal were seen as feminine and rejected in terms of being worthy opponents, as exemplified in the Japanese attitude towards the surrendering British soldier or the German attitude towards the *Untermensch* ('sub-human') Russian fighter. Conversely, officers and men who were defiant or dispassionate in the face of certain death were seen as heroic, as in Hitler's ideological worship of the Valkyrie, and von Mellenthin and Balck seem to display this hypermasculinity towards each other.

> 'The military embraces stoic men because they are "strong enough" to protect the nation, while simultaneously rejecting those feminised [or in

Balck's case from his early life, men who displayed too much intelligence or sensitivity].'[315]

The strategic position by November 1943 and the attack on Zhytomyr

When Balck had left the Russian front the previous July, the strategic situation was precarious but under control, with the OKH and the Wehrmacht placing all their hopes on a successful and decisive engagement at Kursk. With defeat, the Eastern Front in southern Russia was now in crisis, and LXVIII. Panzerkorps would be needed once again to play a pivotal role if the front was not to collapse entirely. By the time Balck arrived at his headquarters in November 1943, another set of surprise Russian offensives had liberated Kiev, crossed the Dnieper and pushed von Manstein and Heeresgruppe Süd back to a line west and south of Kiev. Across the Dnieper, LXVIII. Panzerkorps held the northern sector or left flank, and was orientated to the north. Despite having only just awarded him the Swords to his Knight's Cross and Oak Leaves, Hitler was furious with Hoth due to his 4. Panzerarmee's line having been broken in so many places. According to Robert Forczyk in his excellent book *The Dnepr 1943: Hitler's Eastern Rampart Crumbles*, although Hoth was left 'humiliated', a by-product of the steam-rolling of his front was that the Red Army had, unwittingly, created a salient that cried out for cutting off by a determined attack northwards to retake the city of Zhytomyr.[316] It was in this context that Balck arrived, taking stock of the forces that now composed his Panzer corps and what the possibilities were for countering the immense Soviet pressure.

As von Mellenthin was able to record, under the strained circumstances of the war in the East, LXVIII. Panzerkorps had been generously provided with a good number of divisions for its new commander, which was of huge credit to both the OKH and the German supply machine. The 1. Panzer-Division and 1. SS-Panzer-Division 'Leibstandarte SS Adolf Hitler' had been refitted, including with the heavy Tiger Mk 1 tank. The 25. Panzer-Division had also been completely refitted, with replacements of men and equipment. Additionally, von Mellenthin recorded that the 68. Infanterie-Division, under the command of Oberst (soon to be Generalmajor) Paul Scheuerpflug, was added to the corps. The SS-Panzer-Division 'Leibstandarte' was commanded by SS-Brigadeführer Theodor Wisch, who had taken over the formation from SS-Oberstgruppenführer Sepp Dietrich in July 1943. The 2. SS-Panzer-Division 'Das Reich', led by SS-Brigadeführer Heinz Lammerding – who had only just taken command the previous month – also joined Balck's corps, but 'Das Reich' at this stage was little more than a weakened Kampfgruppe, given the fighting it had been through holding the line after the Russians recaptured Kiev.[317]

Both the leadership and combat effectiveness of many units were suspect. For example, 25. Panzer-Division was commanded by Generalleutnant Adolf von Schell, Balck's one-time superior when they both worked in the tank production department of the War Ministry in Berlin. Von Schell was not a combat officer, and indeed was suffering from extremely poor eyesight, but was still drafted into the front lines. His 25. Panzer had suffered heavily in the fighting to try to hold Zhytomyr early in October, losing most of its equipment. The division now badly needed time to acclimatize its new officers and recruits to warfare, but the OKH and Hitler seemed to assume that this was unnecessary, given the circumstances in the East. Equally, the 68. Infanterie-Division had suffered over 60 per cent casualties in the same battles in October and was now a shadow of its former combat capacity.

Although Hoth's 4. Panzerarmee had suffered substantial losses, it was still intact and LXVIII. Panzerkorps was now considered its strongest element. Much was expected of Hermann Balck and his ability to shape and reshape the tank battlefield. General Konstantin Rokossoskii's Central Front and General Nikolai Vatutin, who commanded the Voronezh Front, had been attacking and counter-attacking Hoth's army without rest during October 1943 to try to degrade and destroy this key part of the German front lines. However, with their success, the Russians now also presented their flanks, with the creation of a new salient to the south of Zhytomyr which Hoth recognized as an opportunity for a decisive move, the arrival of Balck giving him exactly the right commander to lead the attack. Balck was ordered to pivot LXVIII. Panzerkorp on the city of Fastov, which was still in Russian hands, with the right of the line held by Generalleutnant Arthur Hauffe's XIII. Armeekorps remaining static. Balck would then make a reverse sickle cut, moving north to retake Zhytomyr and then east to regain Kiev.

Generaloberst Hoth had developed this plan himself, but although Balck praised him as one the Wehrmacht's most competent generals, both Balck and his chief of staff, von Mellenthin, disagreed with the strategic concept of first retaking Zhytomyr – which would require a northward then westward move – and then turning 180 degrees to advance eastwards on Kiev. Balck felt that a direct thrust on Kiev with the whole Panzer corps was the best approach to enable the key objective to be taken quickly, rather than a predictable plan which the Russians could and would anticipate and thus be given time to restore their lines and resist.[318] Everything in Balck's concept of warfare depended on surprise, manoeuvre and speed to outfox the enemy, but this plan was predictable and unimaginative. However, registering their concerns gained no traction with Hoth, whom von Mellenthin criticizes in his memoirs for being far too cautious and not seeing the strengths of his subordinate corps commander.

Meanwhile, Balck had displayed no difficulty in adapting to commanding his very large force, which was more than double anything he had commanded in the past, or of identifying the strengths and weaknesses of his own subordinate commands. As a result, he was able to discriminate between his commanders, the allocation of tasks in LXVIII. Panzerkorps reflecting his appreciation of their ability to deliver. The left flank would be held by the already badly mauled 68. Infanterie-Division, together with 7. Panzer-Division now led by the very competent and cavalier Generalmajor Hasso von Manteuffel.[319] The right flank would consist of 25. Panzer-Division and the weakened 2. SS-Panzer-Division 'Das Reich', while the main thrust northwards, at the *Schwerpunkt* of the attack, would be made in the centre by 1. Panzer-Division and 1. SS-Panzer-Division 'Leibstandarte', their objective being to fight through to cut the main Kiev–Zhytomyr railway line. Balck felt very confident in the leadership of Generalmajor Walter Krüger, who had successfully commanded the premier armoured division of the Panzerwaffe, 1. Panzer, since 1941, so much so that he expected him also to influence the 'Leibstandarte' in this operation The early November temperatures were well below freezing, allowing for the quick movement of Panzer forces across the icy hard ground and roads. If Kiev could be retaken before the Russians recovered from the advance on Zhytomyr, then the entire southern front could be stabilized and the Red Army put on the back foot for the first time in many months.

Balck set the advance in motion on 15 November and, with typical dash and determination, the now 'fully equipped' 1. Panzer and 'Leibstandarte' cut their way through to the railway line in only two days. There were some significant fire-fights along the way, with Panzergrenadier-Regiment 1 of the 'Leibstandarte' coming to a halt near Soloviika, 10km south of Brusyliv. The heroic actions of SS-Hauptsturmführer Heinrich Heimann, who commanded the 'Leibstandarte' assault gun unit, forced the Russians out. The courageous Heimann, who was awarded the Knight's Cross for his service on the Eastern Front, was killed in Normandy in the Falaise Pocket in August 1944.[320]

Instead of maintaining the confusion that had been caused amongst the Red Army units facing them and heading direct to Kiev, 1. Panzer, the 'Leibstandarte' and 7. Panzer now followed their orders and turned away from the line of advance to retake the ancient city of Zhytomyr, with its domes and churches. The city had little strategic value, but the battle here was vicious as the 1. Panzer-Division and 7. Panzer-Division locked horns with the Russian 1st Guards Cavalry Corps. Balck ordered constant movement forward to pressurize the Russians into defending the city, and on the night of 18 November an attack led by Oberst Adelbert Schulz's Panzer-Regiment 25 from 7. Panzer-Division managed to break into the suburbs. Von Manteuffel drove 7. Panzer hard – by

20 November, the division would possess only forty-seven tanks, just sixteen of which were serviceable.[321] Balck recorded that his forces 'destroyed two Soviet divisions in Zhytomir and three more in the huge Konstytchev Forest'.[322] As recovered film footage shows, the city was littered with burning buildings, destroyed vehicles and the carnage of war. However, as both Balck and von Mellenthin had predicted, the attack on Zhytomyr would not only take time – five days, in fact – but they had also sacrificed the element of surprise. The recapture of Zhytomyr had come at a cost, every unit having suffered losses that they could ill afford if they were now going to take the inestimably more important Kiev.

The breathing space for the Russian forces defending Kiev was vital, and the Russian High Command, the Stavka, reacted quickly. On 18 November, they charged 1st Guards Cavalry Corps and 5th and 8th Guards Armoured Corps straight at Karostyslev and Brusyliv in an all-out effort to retake both towns. In all, three counter-attacking thrusts were ordered before Balck and LXVIII. Panzerkorps could turn eastwards and resume their attack on Kiev.

According to von Mellenthin, it was at this point, with the Russians unable to force a breakthrough, that Balck displayed why he was regarded by many as having the best battlefield appreciation in the Panzerwaffe. Instead of panicking and consolidating in the face of this rapid Soviet counter-attack, Balck moved like a chess grandmaster and ordered a newly arrived but still incomplete 19. Panzer-Division (in reality only possessing the strength of a weak Kampfgruppe) to take the right wing and immediately attack the Russian forces from the south. Meanwhile, the 'Leibstandarte' attacked in the centre and 7. Panzer-Division created a protective screen to the north to prevent any reinforcements reaching the Russians.

The attack on 20 November was important for two reasons. Firstly, for the first time in the war, the exhausted 'Leibstandarte' failed to fulfil their mission and fell short of closing the pincers with 19. Panzer-Division attacking from the east. Secondly, Balck lost his temper when he realized that both the 'Leibstandarte' and 19. Panzer had paused their assault on the evening of the 21st, ordering a fresh attack immediately to close the pincers, which they did on 23 November.[323] All this cost time and resources for the assault on Kiev, and although Balck had once again destroyed a number of large Russian formations, captured thousands of Russian prisoners and over 150 tanks and 250 anti-tank guns, momentum for the main objective had been lost. The arrival of rain and the consequent deep and thick mud from 26 November ended any hope of reaching, let alone taking, Kiev at this stage.[324] This failure, together with the earlier losses of territory before Kiev, saw Hoth on the receiving end of another Hitler tantrum and accusations of cowardice. Hoth had essentially been relieved of command earlier in November, but on the 30th, Hoth called Balck to tell him that he had now been placed on what was to become permanent 'sick leave'. Hoth's removal was unpopular, especially with von Manstein, who praised his fighting withdrawal in front of Kiev:

> 'Colonel-General Hoth, supported by his admirable Chief-of-Staff, General Fangohr, went about this difficult task with a calm resolution matched only by the versatility of his leadership. He skilfully retarded the progress of the enemy pressing hard on his front without exposing himself to danger by holding any one position too long.'[325]

Hoth paid the price of Hitler's hatred of bad news. His immediate replacement was General der Panzertruppe Erhard Raus, another commander who, like Balck, enjoyed the trust and confidence of the Führer. Details of the changeover between Hoth and Raus are obscure, but the Russian liberation of Kiev in October had ended over two years of murderous occupation by Einsatzgruppen who were responsible for some of the most atrocious war crimes of the entire war, including the massacres at Babi Yar and elsewhere. With the memory of huge losses in 1941 in the battle for the city, the Russians were in no mood to compromise on strategy – their war aim was to destroy all German forces. Was Balck ever aware of the activities of the murderous SS killing squads? If he was – and it is inconceivable that he did not know what was going on – they are never mentioned in his memoirs. The omission of the activities of the murder squads leaves a hole in Balck's credibility as a commentator, merely adding to the myth of the 'clean Wehrmacht' that was established in the post-war period. What Balck did not forget to mention was further self-congratulatory evidence that the Allies regarded Balck as a 'superior commander',[326] before resuming his account of the next stage of events whilst he commanded LXVIII. Panzerkorps.

The Russian Sixtieth Army now dominated the new situation maps around Kiev. The remnants of Russian formations that had pulled out of Zhytomyr were also in the area, as were strong reserves, and this large Russian force not only blocked the route to Kiev but were a potent threat to the flanks of Balck's LXVIII. Panzerkorps and the German XIII. Armeekorps and XXIV. Panzerkorps in the Radomyshl area on the Teteriv River.

At a meeting with von Manstein, commander of Heeresgruppe Süd, and Raus, commander of 4. Panzerarmee, Balck was asked if he felt he could roll up the Zhytomyr–Radomyshl front from the flank with a surprise pincer move.

Radomyshl and the Melini Pocket, December 1943

What developed over the next three weeks exemplified why Hermann Balck should be seen as one of the Wehrmacht's greatest generals of the Second World War. Yet again, in contrast to the vast majority of many far more famous German generals, Balck was to prove that, even in the most challenging of battlefield conditions and against a vastly superior enemy, his tactical vision was unmatched.

Although Zhytomyr had been retaken and the Russians forced back towards Kiev – far enough really to concern Moscow – the job of stabilizing and controlling the front was still unfinished. Equally problematic was that the German LIX. Armeekorps, the northernmost corps in 4. Panzerarmee and the linking unit with Heeresgruppe Mitte, had been surrounded at Korosten and was under siege.[327]

When it came to the science of active defensive operations, Balck had already shown that he was a genius of the flank attack, the frontal attack and defensive pincer movements on the Chir River, where his command of 11. Panzer-Division had been a master class in divisional command and manoeuvre. But here, around Zhytomyr in December 1943, a fourth vital tactical approach was needed to actively defend the fragmented German lines and buy time by disrupting Red Army preparations to continue their breakthroughs to the west of Kiev. In German defensive doctrine, this was called the 'spoiling attack'. An article published in the 1950s (and republished in 2004) by the US Centre of Military History (CMH), based on interviews with unnamed captured German generals (almost certainly Hermann Balck, who was in America advising the US Army at this time), gives an in-depth explanation of the various and extensive defensive tactics used by the Wehrmacht between 1943 and 1945.[328]

In the Russian salient, Balck was aware that there were substantial Red Army forces, but exactly of what size he was not sure. In the lull between 30 November and 5 December, reconnaissance on the ground and in the air had failed to gather an accurate picture of just what was in front of LXVIII. Panzerkorps or facing the much weaker infantry of Hauffe's XIII. Armeekorps further north in front of Zhytomyr. Composed of 'tired infantry and security divisions', XIII. Armeekorps would not hold against any serious Russian offensive, and there were enough indicators that the Russians were pouring reinforcements into large assembly areas. This created a sense of urgency for the spoiling attack to come into play. The objective was to disrupt any imminent offensive against XIII. Armeekorps while pushing back the salient and creating a new stable front line manned by Hauffe's corps and backed up by LXVIII. Panzerkorps. In attack, Balck would look to his primary weapons of surprise and speed of manoeuvre to create panic and confuse the enemy into retreating while he rolled up the line and disrupted the Red Army preparations for a new offensive.

Von Mellenthin describes the extent to which Balck impressed upon his divisional commanders the vital nature of surprise, to the extent that there was to be no patrolling of the front lines by motorcycle or half-tracked infantry reconnaissance units, nor a long preparatory bombardment. Additionally, the CMH article reveals that:

> 'The XLVIII Panzer Corps, with the 1st and 7th, and 1st SS Panzer Divisions, was withdrawn from the front and assembled behind the center of the army sector.'[329]

To relocate an entire Panzer corps in an assembly area behind the lines was no small matter, and must have required immediate orders from Balck to be effectively and quickly transmitted to all units via von Mellenthin and his staff in order not to create total confusion. The success of the attack depended on the Russians having no indication that this build-up was happening; such was the nature of the spoiling attack.

Balck, von Mellenthin and the authors of the CMH article agreed that there was one major problem, in that to create a defensive position around their salient, the Russians had blown up all the bridges on the lines of advance. These all had to be repaired by engineers from all the divisions on the day prior to the attack, with the hope that the Russians would not investigate. Units were told not to approach any main roads, nor were they to be protected by any fighting units. All orders were given verbally and there were to be no major orders group meetings, as Russian spies were everywhere, looking for any evidence of a build-up for an attack. Once all was in place by 6 December, it would be a multi-division assault, with a newly refitted 7. Panzer-Division as the main weapon of attack to penetrate deeply into the Russian lines. In Hasso von Manteuffel, Balck had a talented divisional commander to lean upon.

One of the numerous aspects of this operation for which Balck deserves great credit is his movement orders just prior to the offensive. To move the entire corps at night would take two to three days, risking exposure or being trumped by the Russian offensive starting first. To solve this dilemma, Balck ordered all three divisions to march north-west on the main roads up to and through the recaptured streets of Zhytomyr, information which would undoubtedly be relayed quickly to the intelligence staff of the Russian Sixtieth Army by watching partisans. This would enable Balck to move the entire corps in one day to their forming-up points, and he hoped that the Russians would assume that XLVIII. Panzerkorps was actually moving north to join Heeresgruppe Mitte. Balck was proven correct, as that is exactly what the Soviet command assumed. However, on the evening of 4 December, all three divisions turned to face north-east and the Russian lines, fanning out into their prearranged start points as they did so.

In true Balck style – as he had done at Sedan in 1940, at Platamon Ridge in Greece in 1941 and often on the Chir River in 1942 – a feint attack began his assault by pivoting on Radomyshl. An infantry division was sent forward at the extreme end of the XIII. Armeekorps line, which further convinced the Russians that this was only a localized attack and that XLVIII. Panzerkorps had left the area. Timing is everything in life, and the same is true of the greatest military commanders. The Russians quickly moved forces from their assembly areas and sent them to concentrate on the feint attack, and when he felt the timing was right, Balck ordered all three of his Panzer divisions to arc around the Russian flank and attack at speed deep towards their main assembly area.[330]

A summer visit to this area today reveals flat horizons covered in tall grasses full of tics waiting to bite into their victims, deep marshes and swamps full of mosquitoes, dead trees and a wilderness on which to navigate. Thankfully, with a light covering of snow, fog and a frosty hard ground, the Panzer divisions were able to move quickly. Nevertheless, any rain would bring the whole manoeuvre to a halt in deep mud. As often seemed to happen, the attack caught the Russians completely by surprise, with the wide arc that the Panzers took meaning they were driving into the rear of the Soviet tank concentrations. Balck was in his usual place in the front lines, either in his small Kübelwagen or a command tank, popping up in the area of each division to chart progress and issue orders as he went, keeping in his head a map of the entire canvas of the battlefield.

With the withdrawal of Russian forces to the east, LIX. Armeekorps broke out of its encirclement at Korosten and its two infantry divisions headed for the swampy forests to support Balck's attack, but they were unable to shift the Russians. On the fourth day of the assault, Russian resistance stiffened and counter-attacks were launched at the main lines of Hauffe's XIII. Armeekorps and the XLVIII. Panzerkorps. Balck decided to join the jaws of his pincers rather than risk overextending his thrust, revealing the sixth sense of a great commander, knowing when the maximum extent of the attack has been reached. The 1. SS-Panzer-Division 'Leibstandarte' and 1. Panzer-Division thus joined together, with the intention of annihilating all Russian forces now caught on the west bank of the Teterev. As an aside, von Mellenthin is especially complimentary about the support received from Luftwaffe elements and rocket launchers – the Nebelwerfer units – in destroying Russian formations, with the close cooperation between Balck and his Luftwaffe counterpart, Generalmajor Hans Seidemann – commander of VIII. Fliegerkorps – being redolent of the early successful days of Blitzkrieg. All remaining Russian bridgeheads were destroyed and the bridges blown again to create a new German line along the Teteriv. Intelligence staff reported to Balck that an entire Russian army had been destroyed and another badly weakened, with over 200 Russian tanks destroyed and 800 artillery pieces captured.[331] For his part, Balck recorded:

> 'The Wehrmacht daily report of 14th December noted for our area: "From 6 through to 13 December the enemy lost 4,400 prisoners, about 11,000 killed, 927 guns and 254 tanks."'

Such was the power of exaggeration at the Nazi Ministry of Propaganda. Of greater interest is what Balck stated next:

> 'On 13 December I noted in my journal: "Ran into several columns of prisoners today. Fifty percent children, aged between 13 and 17; forty percent Asians; ten percent old people. No young or strong men at all. The Russians are scraping the bottom of the barrel."'[332]

Von Mellenthin recorded:

> '[T]he Panzers were withdrawn into reserve [for repairs and refuelling] and the infantry of 13th Corps took over the new front along the rivers Teteriv and Irsha. The Russians were certainly flabbergasted by these ghost-like thrusts, which seemed to come from nowhere, and their wireless traffic provided abundant evidence of their bewilderment and anxiety.'

The success at Radomyshl having straightened the line so that it now faced due east, XIII. Armeekorps resumed its defence of this part of the front. Korosten had been relieved and the spoiling attack had, at least for a time, totally disrupted Russian preparations for a new offensive south-east into XIII. Armeekorps. Both von Manstein and Hitler were pleased. According to the war diary of Generalleutnant Walter Warlimont of the OKW, Hitler's situation conferences could last hours and become mired in the minutest of details, even down to the morale of individual regiments. The Führer was therefore well aware of what Balck had just achieved.[333]

There was little time to rest on their laurels, however. Motorized reconnaissance from XLVIII. Panzerkorps had reported the location of a new Soviet build-up in a small pocket near Melini on the River Irsha, just to the east of Korosten. Initial suggestions were that there were two Russian infantry divisions in the area between the junction of LVII. Panzerkorps and XIII. Armeekorps. Balck immediately suggested to 4. Panzerarmee commander Raus that a quick enveloping attack, as a defensive measure, would eliminate this threat, and Raus agreed. On 12 December, 1. Panzer-Division and the 'Leibstandarte' were again ordered to start their engines, move south-west then north, and attack the Russian divisions, with assistance from the infantry of LVII. Panzerkorps.

Clearing the Irsha River of hostile forces would protect Korosten and help the linkage between LVII. Panzerkorps and XIII. Armeekorps, so there were added advantages to this defensive attack. The 7. Panzer-Division, along with 112. Infanterie-Division under Generalleutnant Theobald Leib, attacked from east of Melini as the two Panzer divisions arrived from the west. However, there were new indications of even more Red Army reinforcements arriving in the area and to the east at Melini, but von Mellenthin records how a complicated attack plan was perfectly executed by these four experienced divisions and a pocket formed around Melini before any Russian reinforcements could arrive to help them.

Between 14 and 19 December, the 'Leibstandarte' alone destroyed forty-three Russian tanks, and altogether some 150 T-34s were eliminated, with black burning hulks strewn across the open battlefields. However, on 20 and 21 December, 'their [Russian] forces in the pocket launched counter-attacks on a scale that took our breath away'.[334] From documents taken from a dead Soviet officer, the staff at XLVIII. Panzerkorps were able to report to Balck that no less than three entire armoured corps and four rifle corps were in fact crammed into the new pocket; clearly, a major offensive towards Zhytomyr had been brewing, and the German divisions had unwittingly been poking a hornets' nest with a stick. In a decision of breathtaking audacity and confidence, Balck ordered the 'Leibstandarte' and 7. Panzer to continue their advances and link up at Melini, but this was one step too far; by 21 December, both were forced to fight defensive withdrawals behind the new front line held by XIII. Armeekorps, 7. Panzer destroying another sixty-eight Russian tanks in the process.

The operations recapturing Zhytomyr, relieving LIX. Armeekorps in Korosten, protecting XIII. Armeekorps and re-establishing the new front line, and lastly creating the Melini Pocket, had been exhausting for officers, men and equipment alike. One can only wonder how emotionally and physically drained Hermann Balck was too. There was much to celebrate, and von Mellenthin sums up matters well:

'Thus ended the offensive battles of 48th Panzer Corps in the Kiev salient. From the tactical aspect the conduct of operations was the most brilliant in my experience. General Balck handled his corps with masterly skill; he showed a complete understanding of the classic principles of manoeuvre and surprise, and he displayed a resourcefulness, a flexibility, and an insight into tactical problems strongly reminiscent of the methods of the great captains of history.'³³⁵

Could such a thing be said of Rommel, von Kluge, von Kleist, von Rundstedt, Hoth or even Hoepner? Perhaps only von Manstein comes close to parity, but even then, he was a staff planner, a genius certainly, but Balck was a battlefield general – brittle, direct, not very popular with his peers, did not suffer fools and yet a master of *Auftragstaktik*.

The recapture of Kiev in late 1943 was beyond the strength of what was left of the German Army. Huge losses had been inflicted on the Russians on the southern front, and 4. Panzerarmee under Hoth and then Raus could boast of over 700 Soviet tanks destroyed and tens of thousands – if not over 100,000 – Russian soldiers killed or wounded. Miraculously, Balck only just survived himself. When, as usual for him, he was touring the front line of 1. Panzer-Division, he found himself only 100 metres from Russian T-34 tanks which had suddenly appeared in a village and were driving straight at him and his Kübelwagen. With shells and machine-gun bullets whizzing near him, his driver slammed down the accelerator. At the other end of the village, five tanks from Panzer-Regiment 1 were standing off to one side.³³⁶ Balck swung into them and, still commanding in his usual style, he ordered a young Leutnant to wait while the T-34s drove past, then swing out and destroy each one of them from the rear. Similar to his wounds received in the trenches of the First World War or the shell fragment that killed his adjutant, Major von Webski, standing next to him at Voronezh , it had been a close shave with death. Balck wore his Gold Wound badges with pride, as if they were a talisman.

Despite the German successes of November and December, a new Russian breakthrough had occurred in the front of XXIV. Panzerkorps near Brusyliv on 22 December. Balck and his staff were ordered to move immediately to Zhytomyr, where they would try to save 8. and 19. Panzer-Divisions and elements of 2. SS-Panzer-Division 'Das Reich' from being cut off. It was a desperate situation, but by Christmas Day, Balck and his corps staff were setting up in the now badly shelled, bleak and chaotic Zhytomyr, where many units had retreated in the absence of clear command structures in the face of the Russian advance.³³⁷ Balck sent 1. SS-Panzer to try to blunt the Russian advance and stiffen the resolve of retreating units, and waited to see what survived of 8. Panzer-Division as units flowed through, along with SS formations from 'Das Reich'. However, there was no sign of 19. Panzer-Division, which was surrounded. Tempted to reach out and find them, Balck records that it was the most difficult decision of his life not to send help, but his corps strength was still fragmented:

'I sat in my room in a dark mood as the hours passed. Then the door flew open and a beaming von Mellenthin stood there holding the most recent radio report from the 19th: "Currently conducting a somewhat orderly withdrawal toward the west."'[338]

Generalmajor Hans Kallner, who had only taken full command of 19. Panzer-Division on 1 November, was a calm and capable cavalry officer with a distinguished record. For his actions in destroying fifty Russian tanks and brining 19. Panzer back to safety, he would be awarded the Oak Leaves to his Knight's Cross on 3 February 1944. Kallner would also receive the Swords in August 1944 for actions north of Warsaw, but was killed in action visiting the front lines near Olomouc on 18 April 1945, aged 46.

Balck rallied his troops to mount defensive attacks throughout January 1944, but these had to stop in February with the onset of the thaw and the return of the mud of the *rasputitsa*. Once more it was a time for both sides to prepare for the offensive season in the spring. Balck reigned supreme with his troops, his divisional commands and with the OKH, which may not have warmed to his personality but trusted his competence and ability to hold the lines in front of 4. Panzerarmee against some of the strongest attacks in the East. Stalin was driving the Red Army to seal off the Caucasus and Crimea, while Hitler was desperate to hold on to them.

For Hermann Balck, there were five key elements to his maintenance of successful operations. Firstly, he was insistent on having the best staff officers around him, which sometimes meant requesting they be transferred in from other units, von Mellenthin of course being the best example. Secondly, Balck and von Mellenthin believed in simple staff work, eliminating unnecessary reports to 4. Panzerarmee and bypassing requests for operational manoeuvre. Thirdly, Balck maintained that he would never put his command centres, either at corps or divisional levels, in places where the enemy might strike. Unlike Rommel or von Kleist, Balck avoided prestigious locations, castles or grand houses and hotels in towns and cities. Instead, Balck preferred basic, anonymous villages in deep forests and rural areas, so that when a sudden Russian advance occurred, he was always able to maintain communications with his units rather than having to pack up and rush to a new location and lose control over the battlefield. Balck ordered his divisional commanders to do the same, and there was never any question of a rout or desperation when a communications failure occurred during a retreat. Fourthly, Balck placed the highest priority on his signals units, which had to maintain the highest quality of transmission and receiving at all times. It was Balck's signals units that often received the most praise and awards for their service. Finally, Balck was an offensive general; even in defence, he believed that the tank was an offensive weapon and he attacked as he withdrew.[339]

In the withdrawals between 25 December 1943 and 3 January 1944, Balck's forces destroyed 396 Russian tanks, a figure that rose to 530 after further retreats. Such staggeringly high tank losses could not have been achieved by tank and artillery actions alone. By the autumn of 1943 and into 1944, the Luftwaffe had its new weapon, the Ju 87G Stuka, with its twin mounted 3.7cm cannons, which became synonymous with ace pilot Hans-Ulrich Rudel in their ground-attack role, specifically to destroy Russian tanks (3,000 tank kills would be claimed by the war's end). Numerous other tank kills were recorded by the charismatic commander of Panzer-Regiment 1 of the 'Leibstandarte', SS-Obersturmbannführer Joachim Peiper, whom Balck also thought highly of as a skilled leader of armoured forces. Peiper was one of the very few SS officers whom Balck seemed to recognize as a soldier. Relations between Balck and the SS were usually sour, and his memoirs are peppered with accusations and criticisms of the amateurish leadership of SS units.

On 1 January 1944, Balck had lost a kindred spirit as the cavalier Hasso von Manteuffel was transferred from 7. Panzer-Division to command Panzergrenadier-Division 'Grossdeutschland' from 1 February.[340] In Generalmajor Adelbert Schulz, Balck had a more than adequate and highly decorated replacement divisional commander for 7. Panzer. Schulz had already been awarded the Knight's Cross with Oak Leaves and Swords before he was promoted to Oberst in August 1943, and he received the Diamonds on 14 December 1943.[341] Schulz's working relationship with Balck, however, was to be a short one, as he was wounded in action near Shepetivka in western Ukraine just nineteen days after taking up command, and died the same day. Such was the fickle hand of fate that spared Balck but not others.

A finger in the dyke – the Styr River, Tarnopol and poor relations with the SS, February–April 1944

With February largely quiet, it came as a shock for Balck and his command to receive another urgent message from Raus at 4. Panzerarmee to move the headquarters of XLVIII. Panzerkorps, with its ever-changing divisional composition, to Radekhiv in the far west of Ukraine, north-east of the major city of Lviv. Arriving on 16 February, the corps was now some 300 miles west of Kiev – which is a measure of the inexorable pressure that the Red Army was putting on the OKH to hold the Eastern Front together. Their mission was to plug the gap between Heeresgruppe Mitte and Süd, which remained an open wound the Russians kept picking at, hoping to force a breech. Beyond that,

XLVIII. Panzerkorps was to advance and push the enemy beyond the Styr River and, if possible, recapture the small city of Lutsk.

By 23 February, 7. Panzer-Division, now with its third commander in little over a month in the person of Generalmajor Dr Karl Mauss, had arrived and was ready for action. Again like Balck, Mauss had served in a Jäger unit in the First World War, but he then trained as a dentist, receiving his medical doctorate in 1929. Following on from von Manteuffel and Schulz was a hard task, but Mauss was an outstanding tank officer and knew how to handle the division.[342]

The lead elements of 8. Panzer under Generalmajor von Radowitz were also arriving and, together with a Waffen-SS Kampfgruppe commanded by zealous Nazi Obergruppenführer Erich von dem Bach-Zelewski, they quickly seized the bridges over the Styr and by 2 March the entire line was in German hands but bogged down in terrible mud, with the Russians once more threatening an encirclement. The plan to take Lutsk was shelved in the face of the disastrous problems that were looming on the banks of the Seret River in eastern Ukraine during March, and XLVIII. Panzerkorps' headquarters was again detached and moved 100 miles south to Tarnopol (modern Ternopil), where German forces were surrounded and 'things looked bleak'.[343]

In Führer Order No 11 on 8 March, Hitler had declared Tarnopol the first of his new *Festung* (fortress) locations designed to hold up the Russian advance and exploit the fealty of his soldiers to fight to the death. Hitler wanted them to allow themselves to be encircled and then tie up Soviet forces – holding up their advance – and await relief. In reality, the fortresses became quickly encircled and a relief operation would need to be mounted. Consequently, all such a strategy did was to use up valuable time, energy and equipment as other units struggled to relieve the surrounded formations. Balck was now faced with this challenge at Tarnopol (and would be again at the end of 1944 in the disaster of the *Festung* of Budapest).

In his excellent book *Sons of the Reich*, Michael Reynolds exposes the fractious relationship between Hermann Balck and members of the SS leadership.[344] Balck was not shy of openly criticizing officers whom he felt were not giving their all to a mission or were incompetent, and several careers came to an abrupt end under his command. In late 1944, Balck's criticisms of the Schutzstaffel would lead to a serious clash with SS chief Heinrich Himmler and a nosedive in his career, but the root seems to have begun here at Tarnopol. Balck spends time in his memoirs denouncing the performance at this time of the 9. SS-Panzer-Division 'Hohenstaufen' commanded by SS-Obergruppenführer Wilhelm ('Willi') Bittrich; this would not be the last time that Balck vented his unhappiness with the performance of the 9. SS-Panzer.

On 25 March, Balck ordered a relief operation in the form of a Kampfgruppe (KG) led by Oberst, later Generalmajor, Werner Friebe of 8. Panzer-Division. Friebe was a very experienced General Staff officer and had rejoined the Heer in 1924 after surviving the First World War. By 1942, he was so highly thought of as a staff officer that he became chief of staff of XLVIII. Panzerkorps under General der Panzertruppe Werner Kempf. With a growing shortage of good general officers, men like Friebe were given a chance in the field, and he received command of 8. Panzer-Division. His first combat command now came when he put together KG Friebe. This was what Balck would have praised as a fast-reaction force – a 'fire brigade', and a very substantial one at that, comprising a regiment of Panzergrenadiers plus twenty-four Panther tanks, nine Tiger Mk I tanks and more than 100 armoured carriers plus artillery. This powerful force was created with men and equipment from both 8. Panzer and the 'Hohenstaufen'.

The first assaults towards Brody from 20 March and Tarnopol from the 25th onwards went badly, and Balck and Friebe were recorded as having heated arguments about the way Friebe was using his forces, even to the point where there is a reference to Balck having had a mild heart attack given the level of his anger. But Balck was also critical of the tactics used by Bittrich and his 9. SS-Panzer-Division; it can perhaps be understood why in this comment from Russian General Vasily Arkhipov of the 53rd Guards Tank Brigade:

> 'On a front of 2 to 2.2 kilometres between the motorway and railroad about a hundred tanks and SP guns were advancing on us. They were moving forward in columns of 15–17 tanks each. Tigers were advancing in front of columns followed by Panthers with infantry moving at the tail of each column. Very rarely I could see such combat order in the assault. German infantry was usually walking behind tanks but here infantry was carried in SPW [armoured cars] not even scattered. Maybe it was to allow the infantry to break our defence along with tanks or maybe 9th SS-Panzer Division, which just arrived from France, did not understand the realities of the Eastern Front in 1944?
>
> 'When they approached us at a distance of 400–500 metres I ordered to open fire and combat began. We were covered by low-flying IL-2 aircraft, which started combing the German tank columns. Many panzers and SP [self-propelled] guns were in flames.'
>
> – Beshanov, Vladimir, *Stalin's Ten Blows* (Minsk, 2004)

By 10 April, the 'Hohenstaufen' Division was failing to make the ground that Balck expected and both divisions were recalled to their start lines. Tarnopol fell to the Russians on 16 April, with the commander of the garrison, Generalmajor Egon von Neindorff, killed in the final Soviet assault.

In the days after the fall of Tarnopol, Balck was critical of both Bittrich and Friebe to the OKH, doing all he could to absolve himself of blame for the failure to reach the city.[345] During the fighting, KG Friebe and the 'Hohenstaufen' between them destroyed seventy-four Russian tanks, 108 artillery pieces of various sizes and twenty-one anti-tank guns, killing an unknown number of Russian troops.

The OKH clearly did not share Balck's assessment of the ability of Oberst Friebe, promoting him to Generalmajor on 1 June, placing him in formal command of 8. Panzer-Division and recommending him for the Knight's Cross.[346] It is worth noting, given Balck's vehement criticism of the fighting quality of both 8. Panzer and the 'Hohenstaufen', that the commander of the latter division's SS-Panzer-Regiment 9, SS-Obersturmbannführer Otto Meyer, and the commander of Schwere Panzer-Abteilung 507 (the Tiger tank unit), Major Erich Schmidt, also received the Knight's Cross.

As for the popular commander of the 9. SS-Panzer-Division, Willi Bittrich, Balck also complained about his lack of competence on the battlefield and unimaginative use of his tanks in the assault witnessed by General Arkhipov. Apart from the loss of 1,200 dead and wounded from 'Hohenstaufen', eighteen tanks were also lost along with twenty-four half-tracks. It was Heeresgruppe Nord Ukraine commander Generalfeldmarschall Walter Model, who knew Bittrich from past commands, who seems to have shielded him from Balck's criticisms. The end result at Tarnopol was due perhaps to unimaginative command by Bittrich and Friebe but also the impossible mud and rain, which Balck seems to ignore in his own memories of the attack. Earl Ziemke echoes Balck in *Stalingrad to Berlin*:

> 'The 9th SS-Panzer division, as almost always the case with new SS divisions, was a splendidly outfitted aggregation of raw troops and inexperienced officers.'[347]

Perhaps sheltering within Balck's overt disdain for the competence of the Waffen-SS was a deep-rooted jealousy that he was the trained soldier fighting battles in an army with hardly any new equipment, having to repair and make do and sustaining heavy losses, while the patronage of the SS by Hitler and Himmler saw masses of new equipment wasted on divisions whose officers had little or no military background.

After the collapse of Tarnopol, Balck detached the 1. SS-Panzer-Division and 7. Panzer-Division northwards to try to hold the line west of Tarnopol against the rising tide of Russian attacks. Yet even after destroying over 100 Russian tanks between 3 and 7 May, this made little impact. On 12 May, 4. Panzerarmee sent three new infantry divisions forward to support Balck in holding the line: the 395. Infanterie-Division was sent to the north of the city, while the 68. and 359. were ordered to attack to push the Soviet 6th Guards Mechanized Corps and two Russian infantry divisions towards 7. Panzer coming up from the south-east. Balck knew he could rely on Generalmajor Paul Scheuerpflug of the 68. Infanterie, whom he had commended in the attacks on Zhytomyr, and aided by Generalmajor Karl Arndt of the 359., the operation was almost a complete success by 20 May – despite the mud.[348]

At 0500hrs on 21 May, the signals units of XLVIII. Panzerkorps were sitting quietly in their requisitioned huts and signals trucks with their ersatz coffee when they heard a huge rumble of guns in the distance. Signals traffic suddenly sparked into life. All along the lines, the Russians had broken through in great force. By 0700hrs, the 359. Infanterie- Division – even with more than forty new Tigers – suddenly found itself surrounded, a gap had been opened up between 1. SS-Panzer and 7. Panzer, where Russian tanks were pouring through, and 68. Infanterie-Division called for help to avoid being overrun. Balck knew he had to withdraw and that all hope of keeping the ground that had been gained was gone. He thus ordered a general fighting withdrawal back across the Styr River, while 4. Panzerarmee sent reinforcements to him and moved control of 1. SS-Panzer and 7. Panzer to XIII Armeekorps so that Balck could focus on saving the three infantry divisions. The arrival of the II SS-Panzerkorps was a saving grace, along with two more infantry divisions – the 349. and the 100. Jäger.[349]

Despite von Mellenthin's praise for how well all senior commanders faced this storm of attacks, all along the southern front, German formations had been forced to retreat and the Russian spring offensive was a great success:

> 'If Army Group South and Army Group A were not annihilated in the first months of 1944 the credit must go to the German commanders and troops, who refused to panic and fought their way out of the most critical situations. Nevertheless, the effects of the campaign were most serious. General Guderian says: "The severe casualties suffered during the heavy winter fighting had utterly confounded the OKH." He points out that these losses played havoc with the programme for building up forces in the West to meet the Anglo-American invasion, now certain to come in the first half of 1944.'[350]

It is all too easy to view the Normandy campaign through the narrow prism of Western eyes. But among the many reasons why the D-Day landings were a success, surely one of the most crucial must be the huge sacrifices made by the Red Army in denuding the Wehrmacht on the Eastern Front so seriously that there was insufficient left to defeat the Allied landings.

While von Manstein's wrists were tied by Hitler's 'no retreat' order, he had still worked miracles in stabilizing the line. Von Manstein was presented with the Swords to his Knight's Cross at the Berghof (Hitler's holiday home in the Bavarian Alps) on 30 March but was then promptly sacked. Von Manstein handed over control of the newly designated Heeresgruppe Nord Ukraine to Feldmarschall Model, never to command again; like Balck, he also left the body of his son behind Russian lines. Von Manstein turned his conscience away from the activities of the Einsatzgruppen in Russia. Amongst the numerous occasions when he was told what was going on and asked to do something to stop the murders, he responded by telling Hauptmann Ulrich Gunzert to forget what he had seen and to concentrate on fighting the Red Army. Whether this was because, deep down, von Manstein shared a hatred of the *Untermenschen* or because he knew he could do nothing to stop Nazi racial policy we can only theorizes, but the Wehrmacht was certainly not 'clean' of a share in helping the SS to eliminate millions of people.

Balck spent a couple of months behind the lines, where XLVIII. Panzerkorps had been withdrawn to rest, train new recruits and refit. The corps was stripped down to only the 1. and 8.h Panzer-Divisions.[351] Balck also dealt with partisan matters in the rear areas, and his memoirs clearly lament the lack of a positive policy in Nazi handling of Ukraine. Instead of trying to work with the people of Ukraine and turn them against their old enemy, Russia, Nazi policy was based on racial lines and failed to do anything other than drive the Ukrainians into the hands of the Soviets.

The vital nature of lines of command – the destruction of Friebe's 8. Panzer-Division, July 1943

Now part of 1. Panzerarmee, which Raus had been moved to command, there was time for Balck and his staff to meet with and evaluate the iconic Walter Model. According to von Mellenthin, phrases like 'well above average', 'jumpy', 'interfering' and 'a dapper fiery little man' characterized the new Heeresgruppe commander. In June, XLVIII. Panzerkorps moved back into the line in anticipation of the Russian summer offensives. Uniquely, however, it had no Panzers. The corps now consisted of eight infantry divisions and an artillery division, 1. and 8. Panzer having been made part of the reserve under the command of III. Panzerkorps.[352]

Early July saw an increase in both Russian radio traffic and reconnaissance patrolling. Although there was no concrete signs as yet, it was logical to expect the southern part of the Eastern Front to burst into life at any moment. The first blow fell in the north on 22 June, when Heeresgruppe Mitte was hit by a storm of four Russian army groups containing 146 infantry divisions and forty-three tank brigades. On the southern front, little unfolded until 14 July, when their turn finally came. Balck recorded how thousands of Russian aircraft now dominated the skies, which prevented the movement of forces and destroyed communication routes, adding that Soviet artillery bombardments of the infantry front lines were colossal.

When they began, the Russian tank attacks rolled over and through more than one of Balck's infantry divisions. Balck duly contacted Generalleutnant Hermann Breith at III. Panzerkorps asking that 1. and 8. Panzer-Divisions be released to him, which Breith agreed to do. What seems not to have been agreed were the terms on which the line of command was to be structured and this was to contribute to a disaster.

The fighting on the southern front during July was vicious. Balck and von Mellenthin were exhausted with command decisions, their formations in action both day and night. At Baranov and Koshenice, where two Russian bridgeheads had quickly formed, there was a danger that the whole front could collapse, the infantry regiments in the untested German divisions unable to hold. The arrival of 1. Panzer-Division quickly blocked the Russian advance, and the same should have been true of 8. Panzer-Division.

On 14 July, as soon as the division had been released into his command, Balck gave strict instructions to Friebe and 8. Panzer to move due east through a dense forest north of Zolochiv to attack Russian forces that were now over the Siret River. Standing procedures forbade the use of roads due to the danger now posed by the significant Russian air threat.[353] Balck does not directly name the commanding general of 8. Panzer-Division, but it was Generalmajor Werner Friebe – already a marked man in Balck's eyes for the disaster at Tarnopol and the numerous arguments there had been between them – who ignored these orders and, probably for the sake of speed, told 8. Panzer to use the main roads.

The background to these events is relevant. Balck had often complained that the selection policy at the OKH was faulty. Preferring a detailed selection process for divisional commanders, one that included psychological profiling, Balck could see well-qualified but poorly suited officers being given divisional commands. Friebe had always been given senior staff appointments, rather than combat commands. However, Friebe was also one of the few senior officers to have survived the almost total destruction of 8. Panzer-Division in its attempt to save the Kiev front and then again at Zhytomyr, losing eighty-two officers in the deadlock around that part of the front. Friebe had been in both battles as a regimental commander, and in May 1944, with the division little more than the size of a small combat force, Kampfgruppe Friebe was his first substantial command in the field before he took over the whole division. This experience did not alter the fact that, personality wise, Balck considered him unfit for the role.

When they found 8th Panzer out in the open and unable to manoeuvre, pilots of the Soviet air force could not believe their luck. They swarmed down onto the new tanks, trucks and well-equipped Panzergrenadiers and wrought devastation – nearly 40 per cent of the upgraded division was lost. Balck was furious, putting the disaster down to Friebe not being up to the job and and having probably also been taking his orders from Hermann Breith at III. Panzerkorps. Balck described a meeting with Friebe a few days later:

> 'On 17th July a wreck of a human being sat in front of me, the likes of which I have never seen before, nor since. The commander of the 8th Panzer Division had not slept or eaten for three days. He was smoking constantly. It was horrible …. He was an especially good, very smart, well educated, and highly qualified officer; a shrewd general staff officer; an accomplished Panzer leader. He had always received glowing evaluation reports from top Panzer commanders; but he nonetheless was a second-rate man.'[354]

Even the best of back-handed compliments does not hide the particularly venomous level of dissatisfaction with the Wehrmacht officer selection system which Balck uses in his memoirs to illustrate his point with Friebe. He called his anger with selection his 'festering wound':

> 'It has not been my intention to condemn and pile the guilt on a perfectly honourable officer who believed he was doing his best.'[355]

Having said all this in retrospect from the comfort of his 1970s apartment somewhere in either the US or Osnabrück, Balck perhaps should have reminded himself that, at the time Friebe was sitting in front of him – undoubtedly suffering from PTSD, tired and shaken – once Balck had finished with him, he sacked him.

Von Mellenthin recalled how, on 16 July, XLVIII. Panzerkorps had managed to stabilize the front, but this was little thanks to 8. Panzer-Division, which would take weeks to recover. Balck immediately placed von Mellenthin in command of what was left of the division and asked him to do what he could to facilitate the extraction of XIII. Armeekorps, which had been devastated though not destroyed in the area around Brody. As it turned out, the leadership of Generals

Lasch and Lange managed a Soviet-style mass breakout which saved thousands of men – but not their guns and heavy equipment. It was a disaster, but not a fatal one, and XLVIII. Panzerkorps could now look towards its infantry divisions and stabilize the line again. Balck ordered two infantry divisions forward over the Strypa River to the south to help evacuate the steadfast 1. Panzer-Division, destroying 150 Soviet tanks and 300 aircraft in the process.

The strategic situation was grim, and 4. Panzerarmee continued to be battered and pushed back over the Polish border towards Lublin and the Vistula River by the Russian 1st Ukrainian Front command by Marshal Ivan Konev. Konev's powerful 3rd Guards Army and 13th Army had seemingly endless reserves, their ability to constantly commit fresh forces a reflection of the attritional nature of Russian force. The creation of the Brody Pocket, which contained Hauffe's XIII. Armeekorps, was a prime example of German infantry divisions being unable to manoeuvre fast enough to handle the massive tank incursions now being achieved by the Red Army. The corps contained Generalmajor Johannes Nedtwig's 454. Sicherungs-Division (Security Division) on the left flank with Generalleutnant Otto Lasch's eroded 349. Infanterie-Division on the right and an amalgam of units in a formation called Korps Abteilung C, which was composed of the remnants of the 183., 217. and 361. Infanterie-Divisions commanded by Generalmajor Wolfgang Lange. Lastly, the newly activated Waffen-SS-Division 'Galizien' had just arrived, untested and composed of Ukrainian volunteers, which added to the sense of vulnerability that Balck and his staff officers must have felt.

Chapter XVI

Commanding 4. Panzerarmee in Poland, August–September 1944

We can conclude with some certainty that Hermann Balck had no part in the 20 July 1944 attempt to kill Adolf Hitler.

The Impact of the July Plot

Although the withdrawal of XIII. Armeekorps left a wide-open breech in the lines which Marshal Konev was keen to exploit with a drive towards Lemberg/Lviv, Balck managed to create some stability. On the morning of Thursday 20 July, he was writing up his diary entry from the night before – as he did every day – and Balck reveals that there was complete shock throughout the Wehrmacht and Panzerwaffe when news started to arrive during the day of the events at the *Wolfsschanze* in north-eastern Poland.

The armies that were fighting on the Eastern Front, we are told by Balck, were loyal. He believed it was disgruntled officers, those not able to cope with the 'unique stress' in the East and those transferred to the West who lead this revolt, by which we can assume that Balck is referring obliquely to Rommel. Balck creates a sense that officers and men in the East had no time to talk and plot like those sitting on their backsides in Paris, Rouen or Berlin. He underscores this by saying that when he visited formations in the front lines on 21 July, he was greeted by the *Deutscher Gruss* – the Nazi salute – more than he was by the standard German military salute, as a mark of loyalty.[356]

Of Oberst Claus von Stauffenberg, who carried out the bomb attack, Balck is most complimentary. He hails him as being one of the few whom he regarded as having what he often refers to as the 'harmonious union of strengths' so admired by Clausewitz; not just intelligence and military experience, but an officer's ability to display and maintain human virtues against the chaos of being in an environment of permanent danger and violence. Balck seems more inclined to provide a personal as well as professional view in this section of his memoirs, and we are guided through his position on both von Stauffenberg and the plot generally.

Commanding 4. Panzerarmee in Poland, August–September 1944

Apart from the admiration he clearly felt for von Stauffenberg, Balck tries to paint an ironic and apologetic inference: that Hitler and von Stauffenberg were similar in character and appearance, both had a dream and both were dedicated to the state and winning the war. The key difference between them, Balck asserts, was that von Stauffenberg believed in the 'culmination point' in a battle or a war – a point where victory became displaced by the certainty of defeat – whereas Hitler could not accept defeat. Balck also felt that von Stauffenberg was a different man after his wounds and experiences in North Africa. He even reveals that he had discussed a coup with von Stauffenberg, but Balck's logic was that an uprising would see the Eastern Front collapse and Bolshevism overwhelm Germany, and that the SS would merely replace Hitler.[357]

Von Stauffenberg did not look for allies alone. Balck tells us that he was also sounded out on his views more than once by Oberst Eberhard Finckh,[358]) who had been quartermaster of the 6. Armee and was later moved to work under Generalleutnant Günther Blumentritt, chief of staff of OB West, in Paris. Balck's responses ensured that he was never drawn into any aspect of the conspiracy – a typical experience, no doubt, for numerous officers of the Wehrmacht. Another example can be found in the memoirs of Alexander Stahlberg, who at the time of the plot was aide-de-camp to von Manstein. On a visit to Berchtesgaden – location of the Führer's Berghof holiday home – on 11 July, Stahlberg relates how General der Nachrichtentruppe Erich Fellgiebel, the Chief of Army Communications, was frantic to know if von Manstein had changed his mind regarding his refusal to be involved in the plot or a post-Hitler government. Numerous people seemed to know that von Stauffenberg was in the process of planting his bomb that month (there were two failed attempts before the third exploded), but knowledge of it was not widespread; even Stahlberg's brother knew nothing of the plot, and he worked as a staff officer in Berchtesgaden.[359] In general, apart from shock, Balck records that the armies in the East – the *Ostheer* – knew very little and quickly got back to the business of fighting and staying alive. They did not dwell on events and politics in Berlin – that was for the failed conspirators to deal with themselves as they were arrested, tortured and executed over the coming weeks.[360]

During the week from 22–28 July, Balck's diary recorded increasing Soviet pressure, forcing him to pull back and shorten his lines. Balck recalls that Hauffe's XIII. Armeekorps, which had withstood so much pressure throughout the year, was

> 'completely physically exhausted. Some were without boots and they moved along sluggishly. Some of them pulled dogs along on leashes. Interspersed with the column were Russian kitchen maids wearing steel helmets and carrying hand grenades, who fought courageously alongside the troops.

During the last storm assault, the Russians overran everything. All general staff officers had been in the forward lines at the time. General Arthur Hauffe, the corps commander, was killed along with his chief of staff. Altogether, between fifteen and twenty thousand men seemed to have made it through.'[361]

The unfortunate Hauffe had been captured visiting the front lines and was being transported to a POW camp when the vehicle ran over a land mine, killing all on board, on 23 July in the area of Skvarzav, near Lviv. There was a determined attack by the Russians on 31 July against positions held by the much-depleted 8. Panzer-Division and 357. Infanterie-Division. When reports came through that there was near total collapse in their lines near Dolna, Balck responded by ordering all headquarters staff of these units into the front lines with their men and that there should be no retreat. These were desperate times for the once superior and admirable units. Balck also ordered 100. Jäger-Division forward and, after very fierce fighting, they relieved the beleaguered divisions. The new Waffen-SS-Division 'Galizien', only recently transferred to XIII. Armeekorps, was cut to pieces, with only 3,000 of its 11,000 Ukrainian volunteers surviving.[362]

By 3 August, following German counter-attacks, another strong Russian assault was launched against the exhausted 1. and 371. Infanterie-Divisions, which were part of Balck's ever-changing XLVIII. Panzerkorps. Both held firm, although ammunition supplies were falling low and the logistical support units were struggling to locate their new positions after the retreats in recent days.

Around the Ukrainian city of Dolna (modern Dolyna), where the UPA (Ukrainian Insurgent Army) had murdered thousands of Poles in 1943 – one of many such events as they sought to take back lands from Poland and ethnically cleanse Ukraine – Balck once again turned around an apparently hopeless situation with an attack that resulted in the destruction of another Russian formation, the 271st Infantry Division. General der Panzertruppe Raus, still 4. Panzerarmee commander, sent a message of congratulations:

'I commend the leadership and troops of the XLVIII Panzer Corps for the action in the vicinity Dolina Skola, which turned into a significant victory by adhering to a decision.'

Promoted to Army commander, Poland, 1944

Around 0500hrs on 3 August, Hermann Balck was called to the field telephone for an urgent call from Raus, who told him to take a plane immediately for OKH in East Prussia. On the morning of 5 August, Balck, who was by now well practised in such things, said his goodbyes to the various staffs of XLVIII. Panzerkorps. Driving to 4. Panzerarmee headquarters, he was given a 'most touching farewell' by Raus, who had always supported Balck and 'covered his back' on more than one occasion. Balck then took off for the Wolf's Lair.[363]

At the OKH advanced headquarters, Balck was able to reunite with Guderian, who was now back in the fold as Chief of the General Staff. Also present was Generalleutnant Walther Wenck, whom Guderian had appointed as his Chief of Operations.[364] Balck's reputation now preceded him, and he was praised and saluted with enthusiasm wherever he went within the secure compounds. It was no surprise when he learned that he was to be promoted again, this time to General der Panzertruppe, and to take over command of 4. Panzerarmee. This was a significant promotion for Balck, who now stood on a level field with the great names of the Wehrmacht. After a briefing from Guderian, Balck set off again and arrived back at the front to find that his former commander, Raus, had already been posted to command 1. Panzerarmee. Balck actually took over from General der Panzertruppe Walther Nehring, who had been in temporary command. Like a tragic game of musical chairs accompanied by the music of Stalin's organs (nickname for the terrifying Soviet Katyusha rocket launchers), the OKH and Hitler had shuffled the pack yet again, trying to find the old magic that now eluded them on the battlefield.

Balck faced a situation where 4. Panzerarmee needed revitalizing. He recorded that one of his first jobs had been to to deal with the laxity with which staff work at Army headquarters was done.[365] Balck was saved the task of having his chief of staff reassigned, as another task he was given almost straight away was to order Oberst Georg Schulze-Büttger to return to Berlin, as the Gestapo wished to interview him for his involvement in the July Plot. Arrested at Tempelhof airport, Schulze-Buttger was put on trial and hanged in Berlin-Plötzensee on 13 October. Requesting von Mellenthin as a replacement was a natural step, and he joined Balck a few days later from XLVIII. Panzerkorps, which was now commanded by Generalleutnant Fritz-Hubert Gräser.

The main threats that currently faced 4. Panzerarmee were the bridgeheads established across the Vistula in the wake of the disaster at Brody. The largest area of concern was the Russian presence on the west bank of the Vistula at Baranov, to the south of 4. Panzerarmee's front, which von Mellenthin feared was the start of a Russian plan to 'roll up the front from south to north'.[366] Fortunately, all four of Balck's corps commanders were good men. On the left was LVI. Panzerkorps under Generalmajor Johannes Block, on the far bank of the Vistula, facing east. In the north, Balck had General der Infanterie Hermann Recknagel and his XLII. Armeekorps, whom he referred to as 'undaunted, courageous and prudent', but his line faced south. Both of these corps had only infantry divisions at their disposal. The III. Panzerkorps, assembling in the rear, would in time provide Balck with a reconstituted 8. Panzer-Division and 17. Panzer-Division. Finally, his trusty old XLVIII. Panzerkorps, now commanded by Fritz-Hubert Gräser, was still in the field with the 1., 16. and 23. Panzer-Divisions – all of whom, however, were understrength. It was still a very formidable army, despite the colossal losses of men and materiel over the previous nine months. It also remains a testament to the German genius for planning and administration that the supply routes were still operating, the factories and trains were still running full-time, and the supplies so badly needed in the East just kept coming, as Balck was emphatically able to point out:

'Our supply bases were full and positioned right behind the front lines, and reinforcements were coming in from all directions.'[367]

This is one of the few occasions that Hermann Balck refers to the adequacy, or otherwise, of his supply lines. In this respect, Balck was, as we know, very much in the mould of Napoleon Bonaparte, who, in a list of observations to assist his brother Joseph as King of Spain, reiterates what is really important:

'We will not discuss here if the line of the Ebro [River] is good …. All these questions are pointless. In war, three-quarters turns on personal character and relations; the balance of manpower and materials counts for only the remaining quarter.'[368]

Napoleon was writing well before the advent of the tank, which certainly would have affected his proportionality, but nevertheless, the assertion that good leadership can overcome bad supplies was certainly one that Balck held dear in his own thinking – hence his predisposition for removing weak officers from his commands.

Eliminating the bridgeheads over the Vistula

At Baranov, between 5 and 9 August, Recknagel and XLII. Armeekorps were fighting large Russian tank forces trying to emerge from their bridgehead. Unique units of 'tank destroyer commandos' were formed to assist with the destruction of swarms of T-34s; they were far more mobile than the Panzerjäger anti-tank companies and this enabled troops to get close in behind the Russian tanks when they were stationary. As XLII. Armeekorps fought their defensive action, Balck sought to relive the pressure on them with an attack on the rear of the Russians using III. Panzerkorps led by Generalmajor Hermann Breith. Von Mellenthin comments that this attack was a great success and the bridgehead was reduced to a small pocket – though crucially not eliminated altogether.[370] On the last day of August 1944, Balck received a telegram from the OKW informing him that he was to be awarded the Diamonds to his Knight's Cross, Oak Leaves and Swords. No doubt smiles and congratulatory applause rang around his various staff areas as a happy antidote to the fighting all around them.

New tactics against the Russians

Other bridgeheads existed on 4. Panzerarmee's front defending the west bank of the Vistula, and at Kozienice in south-east Poland and to the front of Generalmajor Block's LVI. Panzerkorps, Balck employed a new tactic – one of massing huge quantities of artillery. Kozienice was one of many towns near to Treblinka Concentration Camp that were totally cleansed of Polish Jews during the occupation.[370] The three Russian infantry divisions that were holding Kozienice were to experience the combined firepower of '120 assault guns, the artillery of XLIInd Corps and the entire artillery of three panzer divisions'. With the intensity of the short but overpowering bombardment, an entire Russian division dissolved under the weight of the explosions – with, according to Balck, only the division commander surviving by swimming back across the Vistula. On 9 September, Balck was yet again mentioned in the daily reports of the Wehrmachtbericht (the daily Wehrmacht High Command mass media communiqué):

> 'In the Vistula bridgehead west of Baranov, troops under the command in chief of General of Panzer Troops Balck, and commanded by the Generals of Panzer Troops Breith and Gräser as well as the General of the Infantry Recknagel prevented the breakout last month of the massed Soviet forces and narrowed the enemy bridgehead by counterattacking successfully.'[371]

In the third week of September, Balck flew from the Eastern Front back to the Führer's headquarters at Rastenburg, where, on 21 September, he once again had a personal meeting with Adolf Hitler to receive the Diamonds. Interestingly, the photograph taken of this event shows that the award was made outside; usually Hitler is pictured in a gloomy, poorly lit ante room at one of his various headquarters. Surrounding Hitler and Balck were a variety of well-known figures such as Generaloberst Josef Harpe, who was Oberbefehlshaber Nord Ukraine. The Chief Adjutant to the Führer, Oberstleutnant Erik von Amsberg, stood close to Hitler. Von Amsberg was the temporary replacement for Balck's close friend Rudolf Schmundt who had been wounded and subsequently died after the bomb explosion on 20 July. Generalfeldmarschall Willhelm Keitel, chief of the OKW, observed, as did Hitler's personal assistant, SS-Hauptsturmführer Otto Günsche. This decoration elevated Balck to membership of the elite of the Third Reich as he became only the nineteenth officer, of what would be a final total of twenty-seven, to receive the order.

During the two days that Balck was locked away in the rarified cloisters of the Führer's headquarters, the outside world was very much at war and the Third Reich was crumbling. On Friday 8 September, the first V2 rocket had been launched at London and landed in Chiswick. By the time Balck was packing his overnight bag on 19 September, Operation Market Garden had begun and fighting all around Arnhem was under way, the rising in Warsaw was coming to an end as the Russians watched and did nothing to assist, and on the 21st itself, as Balck and Hitler shook hands amongst the tall, sweet-smelling pine trees of northern Prussia, the British Eighth Army had liberated Rimini in Italy and a Polish parachute brigade was dropping around Arnhem.

In his private conversations with the Führer, we will never know if the matter of the attempt on Hitler's life was discussed. Interestingly, Balck does reveal that he was never challenged about meeting the Führer with his loaded pistol still on his belt. Hitler was supposed to be sealed off from all possible threats. In the conversations between the two men, we do know – because Balck tells us – that the overall strategic situation was discussed, including the matter of the Russian advances into Romania with the objective of taking Bucharest. While they may not have agreed on grand strategy, Balck was keen to emphasize how much Hitler admired his abilities; Hitler, in turn, knew he had the complete support of Balck as one of his most celebrated senior officers.

While Balck was at Berchtesgaden, he discussed future operations with Guderian. As the Balkans collapsed to the south, so the drive through France by the Allies was gathering pace and a brake needed to be applied. Indeed, brakes were needed everywhere by the autumn of 1944. Guderian saw Balck's role from September as no longer in the East but the West, but for now, Balck boarded a plane back to the Eastern Front, where a new battle was raging, this time around the Dorotka bridgehead in Poland.

Despite wearing his sparkling new decoration, the reality of the hardships of the Eastern Front soon resumed. The Russians had packed 'between four and six divisions' into the bridgehead, which was now about to be attacked in similar style to that at Kozienice. Balck would commit a small infantry force of six battalions for a frontal attack during a heavy bombardment by as many artillery pieces, mortars and aircraft that could be brought together to reduce the enemy position to a shambles.

Deftly and without being detected, the guns of the 1. Infanterie-Division, 2. Panzer-Division and corps artillery units were all moved into new positions, fired their salvoes at a prearranged time and immediately moved back to their parent units. This unique tactical style was entirely Balck's, but sadly he fails to mention the identity of the 'excellent senior artillery officer' who was responsible for the co-ordination of moving 'several hundred' heavy howitzers into and out of position from across the army. When the barrage had ended, tanks from two Panzer divisions struck into the flank of the bridgehead and cut it off from the rear, while the infantry attacked from the front, supported by 120 assault guns. Another group of Soviet divisions were annihilated and the German line was again stabilized, this time almost exactly where they had started from in June 1941 for the opening of Operation Barbarossa.

Shortly after the Dorotka assault, which Balck considered 'one of the most modern, if not the most modern of the war', he decided to take six days of leave with his family in Silesia. He rightly sensed that there would now be a short lull in the fighting, during which he could grab a chance to see his devoted wife and what wider family he could now that they were out of Berlin.

Chapter XVII

Commanding Heeresgruppe G – the Western Front, September–December 1944

'The battlefield is a scene of constant chaos. The winner will be the one who controls that chaos – both his own and the enemies.'

(Napoleon Bonaparte)

In the two weeks before Hermann Balck had met with the Führer under the pine trees in Rastenburg to receive the Diamonds to his Knight's Cross, Hitler and the OKW had been reacting to the impending advances of the American First and Third Armies towards Alsace, Lorraine and eventually the Westwall – the latter still far from complete.

The response was another restructuring of the senior command, and on 5 September, Generalfeldmarschall Gerd von Rundstedt was invited back out of the darkness of the Führerreserve to become Oberbefehlshaber (OB) West. After his successful but short period on the Russian front commanding Armeegruppe Mitte, Generalfeldmarschall Walter Model was brought to the West as OB Armeegruppe B, alongside Generaloberst Johannes Blaskowitz, who still commanded Heeresgruppe G. Other changes included recalibrating the army groups themselves. Balck's former commander in the East, General der Panzertruppe von Knobelsdorff, was also moved into Armeegruppe G as OB 1. Armee. Then on 11 September, Armeegruppe G was upgraded and retitled Heeresgruppe G.[372] For Balck, the award of the Diamonds was accompanied by another promotion, this time to the command of an army group, having only briefly commanded 4. Panzerarmee. On 21 September 1944, he became OB Heeresgruppe G. This was a role that Balck would hold for the next three months, until he was relieved on 23 December during a critical phase of fighting in the Vosges against General George Patton's US Third Army.

From his conversations with the Führer, Balck describes Hitler as 'completely normal and in full command of his mental faculties', despite all that was going on around him and the weakening German position on all fronts:

'He [Hitler] was always friendly and personable toward me and he assured me again and again that I had his full trust.'[373]

In Hitler's view, the Allied forces could not sustain their intense level of operations in the West for much longer. He believed they would start to slow and be at their weakest by November, at which point, he revealed to Balck, he planned a massive offensive in the Ardennes to break their lines and recapture Antwerp, which would badly disrupt their lines of supply. Balck's new task as OB Heeresgruppe G would be to hold the Americans back from the borders of the Reich to the south, where Patton was driving his men forward on a daily basis.[374] Furthermore, although Balck had total authority from Hitler, he should not expect or ask for any assistance from other units – there would be none, as everything was being held back for the Ardennes offensive. Hitler needed time: to complete his secret weapons, build the Westwall (which had been stripped for the Atlantic Wall) and prepare his war-winning offensive in the Ardennes. Hitler looked to Balck to buy him this time, and if at all possible, reconquer what had been lost.

While at Rastenburg, Balck met with the Minster of Armaments, Albert Speer, who divulged that it was time that he needed most too, to develop 'super weapons' that could win the war. Gaining Hitler's permission to once more have von Mellenthin as his chief of staff in Heeresgruppe G, Balck set off to his new headquarters as an army group commander.[375]

The situation of Heeresgruppe G, 15 September 1944

The Allies had landed in southern France on 15 August in Operation Dragoon, and it was Blaskowitz who had to try to contain their advance.[376] Blaskowitz and his 19. Armee had lost several units to the black hole of the Eastern Front, and despite a lack of equipment and mostly *Ostlegionen* (Eastern legion) replacements, he had commanded a masterly withdrawal northward to the Vosges Mountains. The 5. Panzerarmee, now under General der Panzertruppe Hasso von Manteuffel, arrived to join Heeresgruppe G alongside 1. Armee and 19. Armee. Many senior German commanders could not believe how many troops had actually been saved from the south, as Joachim Ludewig states in his outstanding book *Rückzug: The German Retreat from France, 1944*:

> 'The units of Army Group G reached the Dijon bridgehead by September 10th. Despite the losses suffered in the process, the retreat movement from southern France was a success because of Blaskowitz's leadership. The results surprised both Hitler and Model. One important reason for this success was the relatively free hand that Blaskowitz had in conducting the operation that had started with the most unfavourable prospects.'[377]

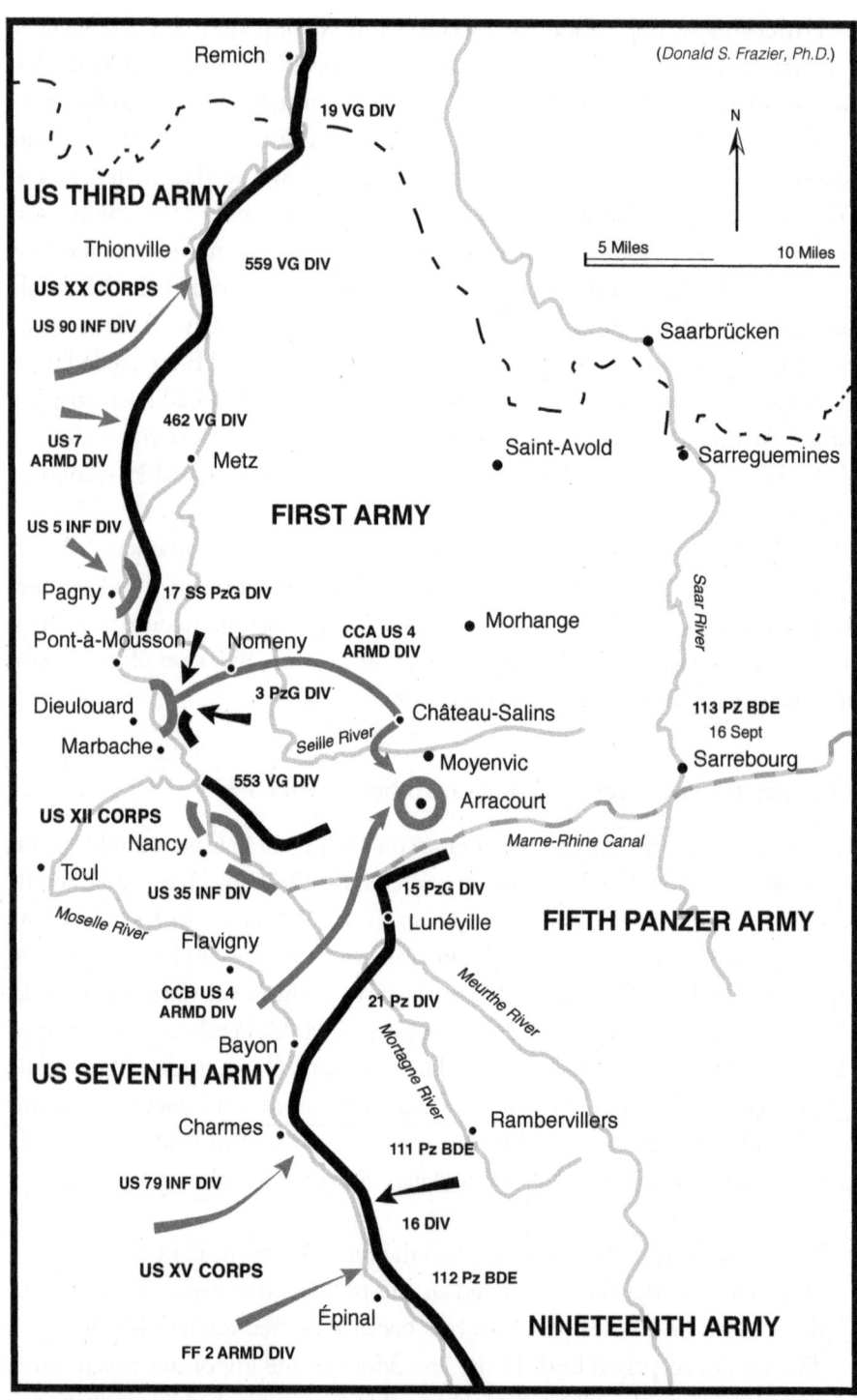

Map 7. Strategic situation of Heeresgruppe G on the Western Front, 15 September 1944. (© *2015 The University Press of Kentucky. Used by permission*)

As army group commander, Blaskowitz, received reports of American thrusts all along his front. In the north, the weakened regular and new Volksgrenadier (Reserve) infantry divisions of von Knobelsdorff's 1. Armee were holding against the US XII Corps under Major General Manton Eddy and US XX Corps (Major General Walton Walker) along the Moselle. In the centre, von Manteuffel's 5. Panzerarmee was under sustained pressure and its line had been broken in the centre; despite spirited resistance from 553. Volksgrenadier-Division and 3. Panzergrenadier-Division, the Americans were pushing through to Arracourt and the Saar River. In the south, the poor relation of the other two armies, 19. Armee, now commanded by the excellent General der Infanterie Friedrich Wiese, were holding around Épinal with a mixture of Kampfgruppe formations and elements of what was left of the once outstanding 21. Panzer-Division and 15. Panzergrenadier-Division. These were all hard fights, where American superiority in tanks, men, guns and aircraft meant that every day had to involve a superhuman effort by German forces to survive let alone hold.

During the first three weeks of September – while Balck had been flying back and forth from Russia dealing with the Dorotka bridgehead, then to Silesia for a brief reunion with his wife and back again to Rastenberg – Patton's Third Army had almost overcome its shortages of fuel and was ready to start moving again. Their opening attacks were determined and took them towards Metz. On 13 and 14 September, a very depleted and weakened 21. Panzer-Division had been ordered to try to blunt the advance of the American XV Corps around Épinal in the southern part of the Heeresgruppe G front. The war diary of 21. Panzer details events in this battle and serve to indicate just what forces were available in Alsace as Balck arrived.

Épinal and Arracourt, 13–29 September 1944

Given the new impetus of the American attacks in the south of the Heeresgruppe G front, the OKW was insistent that a more aggressive posture was needed, even though the units of 19. Armeewere worn out. Heeresgruppe G ordered Wiese, to deliver an attack on the US XV Corps using the XLVII. Panzerkorps, commanded by the highly decorated General der Panzertruppe Hans von Funck. Two units were ordered forward on 13 September – Kampfgruppe von Luck, which comprised the majority of what was left of 21. Panzer-Division, and 112. Panzer-Brigade, commanded by Oberst Horst von Usedom.[378] Had Balck already been in post, it is very likely that he would have resisted the pressure to attack in daylight, as his experiences on the Russian front with the destruction wrought on 8. Panzer-Division taught him the acute danger of enemy control of the skies. However, he was not there yet and Blaskowitz was still in command.

The result was a disaster. Caught by accurate ground-attack aircraft, more than sixty very valuable and mostly new tanks were destroyed. Without waiting for orders, the old school and popular von Funck ordered both units to retreat to the east bank of the Moselle River. He paid the price by being relieved of his command, being replaced by General der Panzertruppe Heinrich von Lüttwitz.[379] But the damage was done, and the French 2nd Armoured Division and US 79th Infantry Division prepared to cross the Moselle.

This failure did not go unnoticed, and underscored what the OKW saw as a lack of fighting spirit. Another attack was ordered, this time using 5. Panzerarmee, with the objective of recapturing Lunéville using what was left of 112. Panzer-Brigade and 21. Panzer-Division. On 17 September, just as Balck was getting ready to travel to Rastenberg, 21. Panzer reported the following order of battle:

Panzergrenadier Regiment 192	300 men
Panzergrenadier Regiment 125	200 men
2. Kompanie Pioneer Abt	160 men
Two batteries of light howitzers	4 guns
One battery of heavy howitzers	3 guns
Five 8.8cm Pak anti-tank guns	
Seven 2cm Flak	

To this could be added the following for 112. Panzer-Brigade:

Panzer Mk V Panther	2 (then 10 after repairs to those damaged at Épinal)
Panzer Mk IV	17 (then 25 after repairs)
Armoured cars	2
7.5mm Pak	2
7.5mm Pak self-propelled	2[380]

The combined strength of these two units created only a weak Kampfgruppe, which was now retitled Kampfgruppe Feuchtinger after the controversial and ultimately disgraced commanding officer of 21. Panzer-Division, Generalleutnant Edgar Feuchtinger. Up against the fully equipped American 4th Armoured Division complete with M4 Shermans with their new 75mm guns, M18 tank destroyers and 155mm artillery batteries, it was to be a very tough fight which started just as Balskowitz handed over to Balck on 20 September. On paper, his 5. Panzerarmee looked strong, with the following formations:

15. Panzergrenadier-Division	Generalleutnant Rodt
11. Panzer-Division (en route)	Generalleutnant Wend von Wietersheim
21. Panzer-Division	Generalleutnant Feuchtinger plus the newly formed 111., 112 and 113. Panzer-Brigades

In reality, 5. Panzerarmee was weak. The 21. Panzer-Division was really just a small Kampfgruppe, and the entire Panzer army contained only seventy-five Mk IV tanks, 107 Mark V Panthers and eighty assorted armoured vehicles including some assault guns, while the US 4th Armoured Division could field 270 tanks alone, plus thirty-six M18 tank destroyers, artillery and air support.

On 18 and 19 September, with the addition of 111. Panzer-Brigade, Kampfgruppe Feutinger assembled near the Rambervillers–Baccarat road and, despite early advances, the American ground-attack aircraft put nearly twenty tanks out of action. The town of Lunéville was briefly recaptured and Hasso von Manteuffel monitored events as they unfolded. Lunéville was held by the reconnaissance abteilung of 15.Panzergrenadier-Division, a tough and experienced unit equipped with a small number of deadly 88mm flak guns in anti-tank roles. As troops from the US 42nd Squadron approached the town with M18 tank destroyers, the German 88mm guns suddenly and accurately blew the first vehicles apart. American reinforcements soon overpowered the German defenders, who withdrew, but the OKW in Berlin sensed an opportunity to envelop the US 4th Armoured Division and ordered a larger-scale counter-attack.[381]

The accumulating losses in the battles at Épinal and Lunéville did not cost Blaskowitz his job – they merely added to Hitler's conviction that Balck would be more aggressive and successful, as he had been in Russia. When, on 21 September, Blaskowitz was relieved, so was his very experienced General Staff officer, chief of staff Generalleutnant Heinz von Gyldenfeldt.[382]

Change of command

Not everyone appreciated the arrival of the new OB Heeresgruppe G on 24 September. Away from the rarified atmosphere of complete subservience to the Führer with his overwhelming charismatic chemistry of power and control, it was back to the realities of war. Von Mellenthin reveals how von Rundstedt 'shook his head' because Balck had no experience in fighting the Western Allies.[383] In his 1952 book *The Struggle for Europe*, Chester Wilmot echoed this sentiment when he said:

> 'The command [of Army Group G] was given to General Hermann Balck, an experienced tank commander and a notorious optimist with a reputation for ruthless aggression. This appointment was not welcomed by von Rundstedt, for Balck had no experience of operations against the Western Powers. With Hitler, however, this was no doubt a point in his favour.'[384]

However, both von Rundstedt and Wilmot were wrong. Balck knew all about American tactics and equipment from his corps command in Italy, specifically fighting both the British and Americans at Salerno. But there were other issues with Balck's pedigree as far as von Rundstedt was concerned, in that he frowned at the speed with which Balck had been promoted. Within a year, Balck had gone from divisional commander through corps command and then army command, and was now commanding a Heeresgruppe. This was unheard of, except in the current unusual circumstances where Germany was facing destruction and a man like Hitler was able to patronize those officers whom he trusted. This was a career path that would normally have taken a lifetime, yet Balck had completed these jumps within a year.

It was also not easy replacing a war hero. Respected throughout the Heer as a fine leader, with a record of successes in Poland and France, Johannes Blaskowitz was nevertheless an outspoken critic of Himmler and the activities of the SS in France. Consequently, while Blaskowitz was admired by his staff, he had been on the receiving end of many a tirade for what Hitler saw as his 'Salvation Army attitude'.[385] The ability of Hitler to be petty and resentful to those who defied his will was well illustrated when, after the fall of France in 1940 and in the glow of the Führer's delight, Blaskowitz was the only Generaloberst not promoted to Generalfeldmarschall.[386] Whether what Cole described as Balck's ardent pro-Nazi sentiments was what drove his promotions is open to debate. There is little evidence of Balck openly voicing Nazi philosophy or principles, but this does not acquit him of these charges.

The predictably frosty start with von Rundstedt seems to have been smoothed out somewhat by the personal connections of von Mellenthin, who enjoyed a very good relationship with the highly thought of and experienced Generalleutnant Siegfried Westphal, Rundstedt's chief of staff. Interestingly, as the Blaskowitz chapter at Heeresgrupe G closed (although it would reopen in December), Balck makes absolutely no mention at all of his predecessor – not even in the index of his memoirs. This deliberate omission of this renowned name cries out for an explanation. Perhaps it was the case that their handover was less than cordial.

The order of battle for Heeresgruppe G, 21 September 1944

As both the new commander and chief of staff for Heeresgruppe G received their briefings from the headquarters' staff, Balck was aware that he had three army formations under his command, of differing strengths and composition but all with strong commanders.

To the north, 1. Armee was still commanded by General der Panzertruppe von Knobelsdorff, was spread across the Metz-Château-Salins region and was quickly rebuilding. This was time bought with the sacrifices being made in the siege at Metz, where troops under von Knobelsdorff's command were defending a ring of forts around the city from a very frustrated Patton's US Third Army. Metz would hold until December in a remarkable display of command and defiance by Generalleutnant Heinrich Kittel that provided endless positive news and relief for the hard-pressed Nazi propaganda agencies. Balck's 1. Armee comprised the following formations:

19. Volksgrenadier-Division	Generalmajor Britzelmayr
48. Infanterie-Division	Generalleutnant Casper
36. Volksgrenadier-Division	Generalmajor Wellm
462. Infanterie-Division	Generalleutnant Lübbe
17. SS-Panzergrenadier-Division 'Gotz von Berlichingen'	SS-Oberführer Klingenberg
3. Panzer-Division	Generalmajor Hecker
553. Volksgrenadier-Division	Generalmajor Bruhn
559. Volksgrenadier-Division	Generalmajor von Mühlen

In the centre was General der Panzertruppe von Manteuffel and the weakening 5. Panzerarmee (whose current structure has been described above), now heavily engaged in the fighting at Arracourt.

To the south of the line was the battered 19. Armee, commanded by General der Infanterie Wiese. The speed and ferocity of the American advance, together with the difficulties of retreating and defending the mountainous terrain, saw 19. Armee partly encircled, with many captured and 17,000 killed or wounded as it had retreated northwards during late August and early September. By the time Balck arrived, it was a formation with a fully equipped headquarters but was weak in equipment and had virtually no artillery. However, it had only been thanks to Blaskowitz, in a perfect example of *Auftragstaktik*, that Balck had this army to command at all. Neither was it 'broken and disorganised', as Eisenhower's Supreme Headquarters liked to report. It was now composed of:

16. Infanterie-Division	Generalleutnant Haeckel
198. Infanterie-Division	Generalmajor Richter
716. Infanterie-Division (en route)	Generalleutnant Richter
338. Infanterie-Division	Generalleutnant René de l'Homme de Courbière

Together with a variety of small Kampfgruppe made up of dissolved divisions, Heeresgruppe G thus looked, on paper, formidable. However, the reality was that many of these 'divisions' were in fact only fragments of regiments and not actual divisions at all.

Late September to October 1944 – stabilization and '*Attaquez donc toujours*'

In the last week of September, the most pressing area for Balck to deal with was the ongoing battle at Arracourt between 5. Panzerarmee and the US 4th Armoured Division, while Patton's Third Army was pressing hard further south. At Arracourt, sensing that they were chasing a scared wild boar into a corner, the Americans of XII Corps now saw that the boar had suddenly stopped, turned around and was baring its fangs as the new OB Heeresgruppe G, Hermann Balck, ordered Hasso von Manteuffel again to urge his tank forces forward. A large number of new Panther Mk V tanks, with their sloping armour, together with a range of Mk IVs and Panzergrenadiers, emerged from the hills and forests in the early morning mists. They drove at the American M4 tanks in and on the outskirts of the town, with their own 75mm guns plus M18 self-propelled tank destroyers and M7 105mm howitzers. The commander of the American 2nd Cavalry Group was Colonel Charles H. Reed. Described as 'one of the outstanding American senior officers of the war', Reed reacted quickly, as did Major James H. Pitman, in command of 42nd squadron. Despite being caught by surprise, both Reed and Pitman managed to divide the German forces into fights for the town and the woods that surrounded Lunéville, at the same time as bringing up massive 105mm howitzers firing at just 1,500 yards – as opposed to their maximum range of some 12,000 yards – and the German attack faltered. Better weather allowed more Allied air sorties against 5. Panzerarmee between 22 and 29 September. Balck could see von Manteuffel suffering serious losses in new tanks and equipment, with 200 vehicles destroyed in four days of fighting. However, the Americans had also stopped advancing. Ironically, the fighting at Arracourt convinced Balck and von Manteuffel that they had stopped Patton and his Third Army. However, the reality was that although Patton was chafing at the bit and wanted to crash onwards to the Rhine, he was held in check by Eisenhower, who ordered a general halt in the south on 22 September so that the effort in the north, in support of Montgomery's efforts to cross the Rhine at Arnhem, could be given priority in fuel and supplies. The battle at Arracourt has often been overlooked, but Balck and von Manteuffel threw themselves into the four-day effort which was the largest tank battle involving US forces to date since the invasion of Normandy almost four months earlier.

The delay in early October allowed Balck to reorganize Heeresgruppe G:

> 'Units that had no chance of surviving were disbanded, including the entire Volksgrenadier Divisions. [This was an initiative which only occurred in Army Group G. No other commander would have dared challenge Himmler in this way. In effect this was only a temporary measure, as Volksgrenadier divisions became commonplace in 1945.] Those members who were trained soldiers were sent to existing units. Untrained individuals were sent to special training units. Youths were sent home.'[387]

An incredulous Wiese was also ordered to gather what he could from the remnants of numerous units and throw them at the Americans, at least to give the impression of a stiffening defence as opposed to that of a collapsing army. 'Always attack' became the mantra for 19. Armee in the days ahead, and despite having lost all their valuable artillery, many died anonymous but heroic deaths in carrying out their orders.

Balck had also decided that the best he could do with the very mixed forces of Heeresgruppe G was to hold a thin front line and be prepared to rush reserve formations to any gap that appeared. This is why he issued his very unpopular order for each division to withdraw an infantry or grenadier regiment from the front line to be kept in reserve so that it could be committed to any American breakthrough. This was creating a number of small 'fire-brigade' units, as he had done so successfully in Russia:

> 'The leadership of Army Group G worked to influence the battle by avoiding the total destruction of our own units, while simultaneously shifting constantly from evasive action, to tenacious resistance, to intense counter-attacks, all with the purpose of confusing the enemy about our methods and our intentions.'[388]

After disciplining groups of officers who had lost the will to fight and improperly placed useless bridging over the upper Rhine – where the Heeresgruppe would need to withdraw at some point – Balck bumped into a new feature of war in the west: the disruptive and divisive influence of Heinrich Himmler. Having been appointed commander of the Reserve Army (Ersatzheer), Himmler, with no military training or background whatsoever, began to create yet another private army led by criminals, brigands and psychopaths, devoted not to the salvation of Germany, but to the creation of an SS state. Living in his fantasy world of unbridled power for so long, Himmler had no experience of combat command. Additionally, the Volksgrenadier Divisions 'were only staffed with officers of his choosing, many of whom had criminal pasts. There was no concern for capability'.[389]

Both the OKW and OKH had been hoping to intercept and stop the American advance well in front of the Westwall (called the Siegfried Line by the Allies), with the Main Line of Resistance (MLR) consisting of numerous obstacles and defensive positions constructed between the Westwall and the current front lines. In the area of 19. Armee, this defensive position was called the 'Vosges Forward Position' and was as much a psychological front line as a practical one to stop troops simply retreating to the safety of the Rhine. Balck made his position crystal clear to all his commanders with his order dated 1 October:

> 'In the event of enemy penetrations of the M.L.R. the original line of the M.L.R. is to be restored with counter-assaults or counter-attacks. I forbid any straightening of the front to the rear on local initiative.'[390]

By 10 October, Balck had decided that he needed to clarify matters even further, this time in writing to Hitler, and took a two-pronged route to ensure the Führer read his letter. The first went direct to Generaloberst Alfred Jodl at the OKW and included the following passages:

> 'I have never led such motley and poorly equipped troops ... In the jungle-fighting of the Vosges and the forests of Lorraine the quality of the man is decisive ... The condition of the First Army and of the Fifth Panzer Army are tolerable, that of the Nineteenth Army, lamentable. If we are able to pull it off here, and it is also finally possible to be able to send the 3rd Panzergrenadier division north [OKH had requested reinforcements be taken from Balck and sent to Model at Aachen] it will only be thanks to the miserable and laggardly American and French command and that the German troops, including the motley hordes, put up an exceptional fight. It is incredible what both generals and men are achieving here, both of which are, many times, fighting in the front lines against forces that have extreme superiority in manpower and materiel.'[391]

Sensing that Jodl would read but not relay his letter to Hitler, Balck sent a second copy direct to the Führer via his trusted National Socialist Leadership Officer, retired Dragoon officer Freiherr von Lersner. Balck was reassured a few days later that Hitler had actually seen both letters, yet he received no response and certainly no reinforcements.

Balck's often abrasive style did not endear him to many officers in the West, many of whom seemed to have made up their minds that the war was lost and that they would choose to fight or die in the way they felt best. Equally, deciding to command where Himmler was the senior authority was dangerous – interfering with the Volksgrenadier units that were under Himmler's control as well as the Wehrmacht's was bound to attract the wrong attention in Berlin.

Balck's fighting withdrawal, 8–16 November 1944

Hermann Balck describes how the Americans would attack a hill (a common objective in the Vosges), be beaten back, offer a flag of truce and then infiltrate the position to the point where the German defenders had no choice but to make an often fatal attack and lose the position. Consequently, Balck now forbade any officer to agree to a truce without his permission. One unnamed officer ignored this order and, with a failed counter-attack that had been very costly in German lives, Balck ordered a court-martial. Through a combination of a rigged court, changes in testimony and connections, the officer was acquitted and became a 'fanatical enemy' of Balck, who in turn saw him as a rather inadequate officer.[392] Having spent most of the war on the Eastern Front, where orders were followed without question and the general quality of the fighting men was high, Balck no doubt found it challenging to be commanding an army of such mixed abilities.

The tactical aspects of holding the Moselle line and as much of Alsace as he could was a challenge. In parts of Wiese's 19. Armee, units arrived straight from the parade ground with no experience at all, while next to them might be an experienced unit such as Balck's old 11. Panzer-Division. The front line was thin and the hugely inconsistent levels of combat effectiveness a constant concern, but Balck still ordered an offensive posture; every attack at least slowed the Allies' advance towards the frontiers of the homeland itself.

One of the best units that Balck could lean on was still 11. Panzer. The division had suffered terrible losses in breaking out of the Korsun-Cherkassy Pocket in Russia in February 1944, and was withdrawn from the Eastern Front and sent to western France near Bordeaux for refitting. When the Allies invaded southern France in July 1944, 11. Panzer had been in the Toulouse area as part of 19. Armee and was commanded by Generalleutnant Wend von Wietersheim, who led the division north up through the Rhône Valley as part of Wiese's attempts to delay the American 36th Infantry Division's drive northwards. By 26 August, while Balck was preparing to leave the Eastern Front to meet Hitler for the award ceremony for his Swords, 11. Panzer-Division was north of Lyon and being punished every day by air attacks, ultimately losing 70 per cent of its equipment and nearly 2,000 men, having to shelter under trees and cover in daylight hours.[393] One of the few lighter moments in Balck's terse and blunt narrative style is when he described how he finally disposed of the 1,500 Reichsmark bonus he had been awarded at the end of his command of 11. Panzer. Any man of any rank who was still alive and had served with Balck in Russia on the Chir River was invited to a five-day period of leave, with all expenses paid.

New equipment would and did arrive. The Mk V Panther tank appeared on the Alsace battlefield during September, with German factories and the logistical supply network still working miracles despite day and night bombing raids and rail disruption. Through a combination of intelligence, determination, skill but above all endurance, Balck ensured that Patton's forces were on the receiving end of numerous attacks, especially when they overextended their lines or inexplicably paused when the way to Germany was all but wide open. Nevertheless, the American offensive was ready to resume in early November, before Hitler could launch his own in the Ardennes. Balck noted:

> 'On 8 November the Americans attacked, as we had expected. There were no surprises. The imbalance in materiel was horrific. As a typical example, on 12 November in Lorraine thirty of our Panzers and assault guns were fighting against seven-hundred American tanks: we had zero German air sorties against approximately twelve hundred on the American side. That was a normal day; other days we faced even less favourable force ratios.'[394]

Regardless of casualties, Patton drove Eddy and XII Corps onwards with a determined offensive spirit. Having crossed the Moselle River in September, liberated Nancy and defended Lunéville, met the German Panzers at Arracourt and reached the Seille River by 9 October, Patton and Eddy now aimed for the Saar River. Getting through the so-called 'Luxembourg Gate' was their main objective. Consequently, it was against von Knobelsdorff's 1. Armee, south of Metz, that the Americans attacked the line held by 17. SS-Panzergrenadier-Division, 21. Panzer, 36. Volksgrenadier-Division and 361. Infanterie-Division. The main advance was courtesy of the US 35th Infantry Division and the battle-hardened 4th Armoured Division., between whom, in mid-November, they crippled the 48. Infanterie-Division and 559. Volksgrenadier-Division at Morhange, the latter formation commanded by Generalmajor Kurt von Mühlen.

Despite the poor quality of his troops, von Mühlen, who was a veteran of the Russian front and held the Knight's Cross from 1942, led the division well in the costly defence of Nied-Stellung on 11 November and Morhange on 15 November. Von Mühlen's weak division was badly shaken by the number of its casualties, as well as by the mud, frost, difficult tank terrain and tenacity of the American 4th Armoured. Balck would have been in close contact with von Mühlen and tried to help by committing what was probably still his best formation, 11. Panzer, to attack; not only did they retake Rodalben, they also destroyed the 3rd Battalion of the 104th Infantry Regiment of the 26th US Infantry Division.

While the ever-reliable von Wietersheim's 11. Panzer held onto the high ground around Morhange, staff at Heeresgruppe G headquarters looked at the casualty reports coming in and, on 15 November, Balck decided to join what was left of the 48. and 559. divisions into a small Kampfgruppe, which continued to fight on the Rhine.[395] For his leadership of the 559. Volksgrenadier-Division at Morhange, Balck saw to it that von Mühlen was awarded the Oak Leaves in December.[396]

Yet again, Hermann Balck's use of the Feuerwehr had come to the rescue of broken front lines and shattered units. Asked why 11. Panzer-Division was always able to perform so brilliantly, Balck answered Generalleutnant Adolf Heusinger by saying that it was a combination of Panzer-Regiment 15 being the best in the Panzerwaffe and constantly having the right commanders to

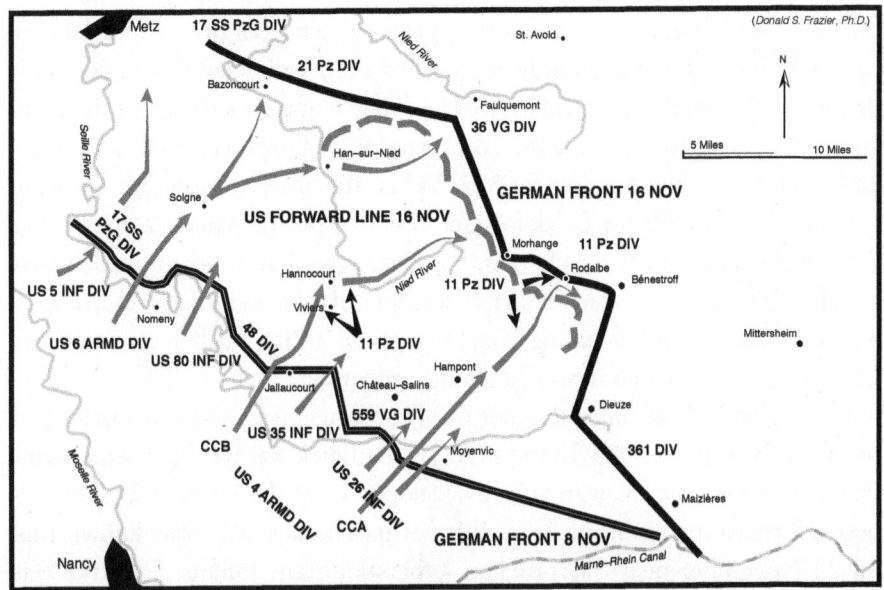

Map 8. US XII Corps' advance and the collapse of the German front south-east of Metz, 8–16 November 1944. (© *2015 The University Press of Kentucky. Used by permission*)

maintain the best standards. There were also 'forgotten' men like Oberfeldwebel Kurt Reuschel, who was part of II/15 Panzer and in charge of the maintenance section. Reuschel rescued broken down or partially destroyed tanks and worked 24/7 to repair them, plundering parts and making things happen to get a tank back into service.[397]

Sacrifices and sacrificial lambs, late November – 23 December 1944

Balck was not short of disciplinary issues as lines of communication became increasingly fragmented and unit cohesion broke down. Hitler had mentioned to Balck that the increasing incidence of failures in discipline needed to be dealt with.

Apart from his efforts to court-martial the officer who had conducted his own truce negotiations back in October, Balck had to face an even more serious problem with the leadership of 21. Panzer-Division. Balck again keeps the officer's name anonymous, but he is easily identified as Generalleutnant Edgar Feuchtinger. The fact that someone like Feuchtinger could have existed at all, yet alone command a Panzer division, is evidence that Hitler and his Nazi hierarchy had a soft spot for the brigand, the criminal and the chancer. Feuchtinger was all three, added to which he was a traitor in the post-war period, passing on secrets to Soviet military intelligence.

Balck had his reservations about Feuchtinger when, in mid-November, his division failed to move because of an apparent shortage of fuel. A fuel delivery for a full division had been ordered, but had been redirected to Feuchtinger's private castle. Feuchtinger had little or no interest in the sacrifices his men had and were making, and allowed local commanders like the excellent Oberst Hans von Luck to run the division for him. When the army group judge advocate general brought a file for Balck to sign off with a pre-prepared statement that there were no grounds for charges, Balck disagreed and recommended that Feuchtinger be investigated further. Balck did not dismiss him because, despite his shady dealings, commanding from the rear and having a half-Jewish mistress, Feuchtinger had proved himself a good commander.[398]

Dealing with unsavoury characters like Feuchtinger was not all that Balck had to face in November 1944. In the 1970s, when Balck was writing his memoirs, he would have been unaware of the development of the internet. Despite his best efforts to maintain the anonymity of individuals, it is now known that on 24 November near Saarbrücken, Oberstleutnant Johann Schottke was the commander of Artillerie-Regiment 347, the divisional artillery for 347. Infanterie-Division, commanded by Generalleutnant Wolf Trierenberg.[399]

The 347. Infanterie-Division was fighting to defend the approaches to the Westwall and the Saar Heights. Balck states in his memoirs that he received a telephone call from 1. Armee commander von Knobelsdorff informing him that 347. Division had been unable to complete an attack on the 24th due to a failure of the divisional artillery. Trierenberg had reported that Schottke had been found to be drunk at his post. With characteristic brevity, Balck explains that he was angry and it was within the military code to have this officer executed; if a court-martial were to be held, he would be found guilty and shot. Balck was right: the military code covered every aspect of this incident, so Balck circumvented the process and ordered Schottke to be shot by firing squad on the evening of 25 September. He expanded his reasoning by saying that he needed an example to be set across the army group and that he had the support of the command's judge advocate for coming to the conclusion he did. Finally, Balck openly stated that had he gone down the route of a full court-martial, this would have come under Himmler's new jurisdiction and the officer would in all likelihood have been acquitted as Schottke 'was the type of person that Himmler pulled into his personal orbit'. Balck would be put on trial for his actions here in Stuttgart in 1948; he had considered his actions as being a simple matter of expediency, it never crossing his mind that he may have acted in a peremptory fashion, but after the war the authorities did not see things in the same way.

Operation Waldfest and Gérardmer

Friction between the Waffen-SS and Wehrmacht were commonplace. Any respect for the courage of SS formations in the front lines was not matched by the activities of low-quality SS units operating in the rear, and it was here that most atrocities occurred.

Hitler had discussed with Balck the problems Heeresgruppe G was having with the French Resistance throughout the area. As the Americans, but especially the Free French, forces pushed ever closer to liberating the Vosges and Alsace, the bravado and confidence of the resistance was growing in intensity and intimidation. Balck had witnessed the same in Italy, but in France there were the especially troublesome Maquisards, local bands of resistance fighters. In rural areas, up in the Vosges Mountains and across Alsace, they were able to escape into the hills, along forest tracks and roads as they disrupted communications and ambushed German troop movements, causing delays and casualties.

With the activities of these groups in mind and the strategic goal of holding back the French and American forces of the US Third and Seventh Armies, it was Himmler who took a lead role in the design and implementation of Aktion

Waldfest ('Operation Forest Feast'). Regarding this matter, Balck once again becomes trapped between his desire to defend his legacy and the truth.

Stephen Robinson devotes only one paragraph in his biography of Hermann Balck to the events of September–November 1944, when, against the background of the intensive daily struggle to fight the Americans for every yard of ground, Balck was also responsible for the actions of his soldiers in Heeresgruppe G:

> 'In November 1944, while Balck opposed the American advance through Vosges, he ordered the civilian population of Gérardmer towards the Allied lines. In the subsequent fighting, his forces virtually destroyed the town. In 1950, a French military tribunal in Paris tried Balck in absentia with the war crime of destroying Gérardmer and sentenced him to twenty-years in prison, a verdict he condemned as hypocritical [Balck commented: "It was predictable that the French would show no understanding of the case, although they later did exactly the same sort of things in Indonesia and Algeria."].'

However, there was no fighting in Gérardmer, and a sentence of twenty years in prison would not have been given simply for the destruction of a town. The reality was quite different, but when Balck was recalling this affair in the 1970s, he must have convinced himself that this was all he did. Sadly for his legacy, the truth was very different.

When Himmler visited Gérardmer on 5 and 6 September 1944, Blaskowitz was still in command of Heeresgruppe G and Wiese commanded 19. Armee, which was located in the town. A meeting was arranged between Blaskowitz, Himmler and Carl Albrecht Oberg, who was the supreme SS and Police authority in France (Höherer SS-und Polizeiführer, or HSSPF), and this took place in Géradmer in the Villa Chevalier.[401] The result of the meeting was a plan to immediately support the construction of the High Vosges defence line, or Vosges Crest Position, 'to the west of the border of the Greater German Reich'. The labour for yet another defence line would come from the transfer of 30,000 members of the Hitler Youth from Baden and Alsace to build anti-tank defensive fortifications. Additionally, the meeting decided that the large number of members of the SD (Sicherheitsdienst, the Security Service) and Gestapo who had run from the American and French advance would be caught as they streamed over the Rhine bridges, turned around and sent back into the Vosges to ensure that the Maquis were either kept under control, rounded up and executed, or sent to concentration camps. These came under the command of Oberg's deputy, Obersturmbannführer Friederich Suhr, who was a notorious killer and had commanded Einstazkommando 6 in Russia. Balck would no doubt have been aware of his actions.

By the time Balck took over command on 21 September, the SS and SD programme was already well advanced and thousands had been deported and hundreds executed; he cannot be blamed for this. However, these deportations continued right through Balck's three-month command, becoming more extreme with a new phase that included the destruction of towns and villages; not as some punishment for attacks on German troops, such as happened at Oradour-sur-Glane earlier in the year at the hands of the 'Das Reich', but as part of a co-ordinated plan of scorched earth to deprive the Allies of any protection once the winter arrived. The town of Gérardmer was one of many that came into this category.

To support the fight against the Maquis, and while Balck was in command, on 24 September and from 5–6 October, Suhr ordered that the towns of the high Vosges be cleared of men:

> '[Y]oung people and men of entire villages aged between 16 and 50 were arrested in two waves and deported to concentration camps.'[402]

Balck fails to mention any of these actions in his memoirs; instead, he states that he went out of his way to prevent casualties. The reality was that he ordered his units in 19. Armee to support the SD and SS in the rounding up of civilians and seeing them sent to concentration camps. Perhaps he simply forgot this part of the operation, only recalling the positive, but the villages of Le Saulcy, Pexonne, Senones, Ventron, Rabodeau, La Bresse and Hurbache all saw all their men of all ages marched away, many to never be seen again. Some 3,762 men from the Vosges villages were deported to concentration camps, of whom two-thirds died – thus the sentence of twenty years *in absentia* for Hermann Balck begins to seem more appropriate. Another 4,746 men and women were also rounded up across the region of 19. Armee's front and sent to Germany as forced labour, while 376 people were shot across various towns and villages in the Vosges between September and November 1944 while Balck was still in command.

Most plausibly, Balck also describes how, in his language, he saved the remaining townspeople by passing them over to the advancing American forces:

> 'We decided to hand most of the citizenry over to the enemy. When our front line was still far to the west of Gérardmer, the population was conducted to an area right behind the front lines and was supplied with food and medical supplies.'[403]

At first sight, this passage reads well enough, Balck keen to emphasize how hard he tried to save the local people and look after them. However, this is not what happened. The SS expelled populations from the towns and villages across the Vosges defence line, which was in fact done to rid the Germans of the responsibility of feeding and sheltering them once they had plundered the towns and destroyed all their homes. Whole populations were simply marched off to the American lines in snow and sleet to give the Allies the problems of accommodation and food, despite Balck's efforts to paint a different picture:

> '[W]e managed to supply the civilians in the department of Montbéliard with food, baby milk and medicine from Switzerland to avoid unnecessary casualties.'[404]

As for Gérardmer itself, it was not American or German artillery that would be responsible for the destruction of the town. Balck's apparent concern that innocent lives would be lost by artillery exchanges with the Americans is only a thin veneer, easily penetrated by the facts:

> 'On November 19th, 1944 Gérardmer was liberated. Liberated but seriously bruised, the city was methodically destroyed for several days by the occupier. 85% of the city was wiped out. On November 8th, all men over the age of 16 were required to [go to] Xonrupt-Longemer for fortification work. The recalcitrant forcibly rounded up, on 9th November the rest of the population of Gérardmer was grouped together in the centre of the town. We asked the captain in charge of the operations for an explanation, and here is what he said:
>
> "'The population of the town will be severely tested and the town will be destroyed. Yes, your beautiful country, so romantic, will be nothing but ruins before long; it will be frightening, more terrible than aerial bombardment.'"[405]

Troops from 19. Armee were detailed to position Luftwaffe bombs at the base of factory walls, the walls of the church and all the houses in the town, while the mayor and the townspeople were concentrated in a small ghetto in the centre of the town.[406] They sheltered as huge explosions were set off by the army engineers, and all the factories and houses were destroyed except for some outlying properties at the edges. Even the farms overlooking the town were set on fire, and when the Americans arrived on the 19th, the walls were still hot, the people were in shock and everything they owned had been destroyed. These actions had nothing to do with protecting the people from the likely effects of shelling, as Balck protested and Robinson believed. Across the front, some 7,500 buildings were destroyed in the attempt by Himmler and his subordinates to deprive the Americans and French of anything habitable in the Vosges Crest Position.

Fire in the Houses was published in 1947, the diary of a Gérardmer resident named Nicole Chabert. After detailing how the town thronged with retreating Germans in August, Nicole also recalled the visit of Himmler in September, the looting of their homes in October and the destruction of the town in November. Referring to other events, the diaries noted the 'ferocious repression of the Vosges maquis by "German soldiers", the "Waffen-SS" and the "fratricidal militiamen"', but also the civilians who supported them – a final, vicious attempt to settle old scores before the Germans left the town, especially with any remaining Jews. Nicole added that 'as far as the eye can see, there are flames, flames that twist, lie down, intertwine'.

One final proof of Balck's enduring part and guilt in these events is that we also have an order that survives from this period, one that was signed by Balck, no doubt dictated to von Mellenthin and sent direct to Wiese at the headquarters of 19. Armee:

'Instruction from General der Panzertruppe Hermann Balck, OB Heeresgruppe G to Army High Command 19 [Armee] 2nd November, 1944

'It is intended to take AOK 19 [19. Armee] in the sector from Montigny [Meurthe-et-Moselle] to La Bresse [Vosges] back to the western position from 15 November 1944. To this end the following orders are given in detail:

'The total evacuation and destruction of the area west of the western position.

a) 'This area must be completely cleared of all living and dead inventory that can be of any use to the enemy by the 10th of this month. In particular, the entire livestock, all horses including harness and vehicles, the harvest including hay, all foodstuffs to be evacuated.
b) 'The population aged 15–60 who are fit for military service must be transported across the Rhine as a group, while the other population – in a village – must remain in the area to be vacated. These districts are to be chosen in such a way that they are covered by Art [artillery] fire.
c) 'All localities (except where the civilian population are [sheltering]) are to be destroyed. The opponent must not have a comfortable house available in the cold season … All bridges are to be destroyed …

'Signed Balck'[407]

In an otherwise glowing account of his superior, von Mellenthin singularly fails to mention the events surrounding the construction of the Vosges Crest Position.

Defending the Rhine

Every part of the front line was under pressure, and during November the Vosges Crest defences were punctured by heavily supported and armed Allied reconnaissance units. Heeresgruppe G faced the overwhelming superiority of US Third Army in the north, US Seventh Army in the centre and Free French First Army in the south. It was in the centre, and straight through the most challenging parts of the Vosges, that the largest gains were made by the Americans.

Just as in Russia, Balck had managed to get near enough to his individual units in 19. Armee to come under shellfire. Once again, he was more fortunate than other generals, such as Generalmajor Hans Oschmann, commander of 338. Infanterie-Division, who was ambushed and killed by the Maquis on 16 November while visiting his front lines.[408] The front was slowly collapsing, but the units that were being ordered to fight did so tenaciously when the easiest option was to turn and run behind the Rhine, like the tens of thousands of German civilians had been doing for weeks, along with masses of Nazi Party officials, members of the SD and SS, and local government officers fleeing from France.

Balck, still in his distinctive cloth forage cap, continued to inspire confidence. There were numerous acts of heroism among his forces, with individual units distinguishing themselves, once the breakthroughs to the Rhine began during November. Balck relates how, when Allied forces attacked near Saarburg, the entire 361. Volksgrenadier-Division, commanded by Generalmajor Alfred Philippi, was overrun, but the 553. Volksgrenadier-Division held fast. Under the orders of Generalmajor Johannes Bruhn, the 553. Division not only manoeuvred well in fighting in the Saverne Gap between 15 and 20 November, but also retreated in good order through difficult terrain. Returning with its heavy equipment, the 553. provided a buttress against the ongoing attacks from the American and French forces of the US XV Corps and French 2nd Armoured Division aiming for the Belfort Gap in the last week of November before crossing the Rhine.[409] The 11. and 21. Panzer-Divisions also continued in their fire-brigade actions, supporting small-scale counter-attacks or rescuing cut-off infantry forces. There was no time to rest; it was a daily battle to repair, recondition and rescue tanks as well as throw in replacements whose names were unknown to their comrades.

Often feeling 'just short of one more division', both Hitler and Balck had hoped that the arrival of the refitted Panzer-Lehr-Division would provide the edge that was needed, but even that elite formation could not stop the Allied thrust through Saverne-Strasbourg which necessitated another withdrawal by 19. Armee – but one that Hitler and the OKW refused to give. Balck's mission had been to hold the Americans and French back through to the New Year, but he was failing, despite what Hitler continued to see as adequate provision of new divisions. The French attack in late November through the Belfort Gap and on towards Mulhouse was alarming, as this brought them on a direct route towards Strasbourg and the Rhine, a situation Balck had been appointed to prevent. The disparity between what the OKW and OKH saw on their daily situation maps with what was actually happening on the ground is perhaps well demonstrated by this extract from Kortenhaus regarding the 21. Panzer-Division:

> 'The combat strength of 21. Panzer Division, which was still considered to be a Panzer division by the higher commands, had so diminished that it was now only a Kampfgruppe. The strengths of the three grenadier battalions that were being committed new in the Wallerfangen area amounted to no more than 120–150 men each. [This would make an infantry regiment on paper look like 1,800 men when in fact it had only 450.]'[410]

Balck received a debilitating 'no retreat' order to stand and hold Mulhouse, so he ordered his 'reliable' 198. Infanterie-Division to attack alongside a vastly reduced in size Panzer brigade. Commanded by Generalmajor Otto Schiel, Balck would have known the 198. Division well as it had once been part of Heeresgruppe Süd in the heady days of the advances into the Caucasus Mountains in 1943 when the world seemed to be at the Wehrmacht's feet. The 198. was considered one of the traditional Wehrmacht infantry divisions, had lost two divisional commanders killed in battle and had fought in Denmark, France, Greece, at Rostov and Kharkov in Russia, and in southern France against the Allied landings. It had been part of Blaskowitz's retreat to the Vosges and was now asked, one more time, to commit fully and defeat the French forces near Mulhouse. But it was an exhausted and 'fought out' unit of far less than divisional size, and the result was inevitable.

In past actions in Fance and especially Russia, Balck had been very critical of fellow commanders who committed their forces piecemeal as they arrived at train disembarkation points. This almost always led to disaster. Yet in the fight at Mulhouse, the American official history is very critical that Balck himself immediately ordered forward only partially formed units of the 198. Division as they arrived instead of 'concentrating a tank brigade for a rapid, powerful thrust'.⁴¹¹ Balck fails to mention this decision in his memoirs, but it was made due to the pressure the enemy was placing on his lines and the express need to shore up the lines. Both formations withdrew badly depleted and even less combat-effective, and a badly destroyed Mulhouse was liberated by the French forces of General Béthouart on 21 November. The failure at Mulhouse was not quite the last straw for Hitler; that was to come at a previously unknown bridge.

The bridge

At some point during Saturday 2 December 1944, an American reconnaissance plane was flying over the city of Saarlouis, situated on the east bank of the Saar River and the border of Germany and France, only 100 miles from the Rhine itself and in the front commanded by von Knobelsdorff's 1. Armee. The aircraft spotted that a bridge remained intact and was still being used for traffic. During the early morning of 3 December, a unit of the US 379th Infantry Regiment made a dash across the Saar River in rubber assault boats from Wallerfangen and captured the bridge intact. The bridge had been fitted with explosives, as per Balck's order of 2 November, but this little bridge in an obscure part of von Knobelsdorff's 1. Armee sector was still there. By the early evening, the same unit had captured the first bunker in the Westwall.

In Berlin, Hiter's fury knew no bounds. His orders to destroy everything had not been carried out. Not only that, but the Americans had now set foot on German soil and had possession of a bridge; new reports suggested they already had tanks across. The honourable and loyal von Knobelsdorff received a telephone call from the OKW in Berlin to inform him he had been relieved of command with immediate effect.⁴¹²

There were other notable dismissals, Balck witnessing the removal of his chief of staff, the trusty von Mellenthin. He was relieved on 30 November, a few days before the incident at the bridge, so he was not a casualty of that disaster. According to David Zabecki in his editorial notes on Balck's memoirs, von Mellenthin's removal was because he had 'ran afoul of Himmler'. Von Mellenthin was not only dismissed from his post, but removed from the General Staff – a humiliating punishment for a loyal and committed soldier. Von Mellenthin deals with this in his memoirs very pragmatically, writing that he went on leave with his family, pointing out that it was not Balck who wanted him removed but the OKW and Hitler, who had embarked on a witch hunt for scapegoats.⁴¹³ As a postscript to this outstanding officer's achievements, Guderian – no doubt after talking to Balck – quickly stepped in and, ignoring the views of the OKW, promoted von Mellenthin to Generalmajor almost straight away and then appointed him to command 9. Panzer-Division in the Ardennes operaton – the Battle of the Bulge – which began on 16 December.

Radical new measures came on 11 December when Heinrich Himmler – like Sepp Dietrich, a man with no military experience at all – was given direct command over 19. Armee.

Alongside his new chief of staff – the highly respected General Staff officer Generalmajor Helmut Städke – Balck continued to try to steadily withdraw and reconstruct his excessively exhausted forces while still frustrating the enemy advance. The Americans were determined to give Balck no time to regroup his forces, and on 7 December, the US XII Corps began its next push towards the Westwall at Saarbrücken and Zweibrücken. The official *American History of the Lorraine Campaign* describes the state of the German 1. Armee at this time:

> 'The German First Army was ill disposed to meet a further attack by XII Corps. Artillery ammunition was running short; on a number of days past the entire First Army had been able to fire no more than 7,000 rounds. [First Army was also critically short of artillery pieces, with the materiel lost in the summer retreat to the Vosges never being made up by new deliveries.] Armor was available only in small allotments of ten to twelve tanks. The infantry divisions were burned out, and the 5,700 replacements that had arrived during the first week of December were, to use one German general's expression, only drops of water on a hot stone.'[414]

Even in these dire circumstances, where 1. Armee faced an existential threat as a formation, OB-West von Rundstedt now ordered the transfer of three divisions north to support Heeresgruppe B. At 1. Armee, von Knobelsdorff complained bitterly that the order to release Panzer-Lehr, 11. Panzer-Division and the 401. and 404. Volksartillerie Korps was unreasonable, and that he could not then take responsibility for defending the Westwall, which resulted in the decision by the OKW to have him relieved of his command. OB West had good reason to need these reinforcements as he feared an American breakthrough at Aachen, which would open up the way into the Cologne Plain, but Balck was not going to yield to his adversary von Rundstedt. Instead, Balck lied and reported that he had only enough fuel to move one Panzer division. Thus he managed to keep his beloved 11. Panzer, and Panzer-Lehr began to move north on 5 December.

By 7 December, Balck was at his most pressurized when he realized that a renewed American attack could achieve a strategic penetration in the Saarbrücken area and through what remained of the old Maginot Line fortifications where German defenders waited for the American advance. Without waiting for authorization, Balck again resorted to the method of command that had proven so successful in the early years of the war. *Auftragstaktik* was not just a methodology for times of victorious advance, but also for tactical defence, and it was crucial to try to keep his commands combat efficient and whole.

Seeing the danger, Balck ordered Städke to create a special command named Gruppe Höhne. General der Infanterie Gustav Höhne was a respected veteran of the defence of the Demyansk Pocket on the Eastern Front. Recently appointed to command the battered LXXXIX. Armeekorps, Höhne was told by Städke to sweep up all homeless units in the area of the Saar River, including what was left of 11. Panzer, which was on the receiving end of the American attack that began on 8 December.

Worthy of note at this juncture is that on 11 December, Balck opened an investigation into the far higher than usual incidence of men reported missing in action. As chief of staff, Städke would have collated the daily reports from all units as an Order of Battle to identify the combat strength on any given day. The 1. Armee had just reported that between 29 Novcember and 10 December, nineteen officers, 215 non-commissioned officers and 2,128 men were 'missing'. In reality, some were still being blown to pieces by the very heavy and daily American shelling, but a growing phenomenon was that many were voluntarily surrendering to the Americans or leaving to rescue their homes and families in the East as the Russians closed in on Germany.

For the next week or so, some of the hardest and most brutal fighting of the entire war in Lorraine took place as the German defenders fought for every foot of what was now German soil. Höhne inspired his men – exhausted soldiers from units such as SS-Panzergrenadier-Regiment 37, Panzergrenadier-Regiment 110, 17. SS-Panzergrenadier-Division and 11. Panzer-Division – and they inflicted very heavy casualties on American units. Large numbers of US troops died or were wounded in towns or while caught on hillsides, advancing along forest tracks, crossing rivers and assaulting pillboxes in the Westwall. Nevertheless, the advance remained the same – forever eastwards.

On 15 December, Balck told OB West that the American attack had penetrated the 'bunker line' in three or more places around Saarlautern and the situation was becoming critical. His tactical appreciation suggested withdrawal and shortening the line. Any small reserve forces that had been created in earlier days had already been committed, and there was no hope of reinforcements. His request was refused.

The last dramatic operation that Balck executed as commander of Heeresgruppe G was the complicated withdrawal of LXXXIX Armeekorps, which was now all that was left of the Heeresgruppe alongside 1. Armee commanded by von Knobelsdorff's successor General Hans von Obstfelder. Positioned near Hagenau, LXXXIX. Armeekorps was already reeling backwards under the

American assault towards the Westwall at the same time as reserve units were arriving to reinforce it. Balck took the view that the two forces should meet at the Westwall, necessitating a further planned withdrawal by Höhne. They could then restructure to turn and face the American advance. Leaving LXXXIX. Armeekorps to stand and fight might leave these arriving fresh units with no formation to join.

Balck and Städke planned a three-stage withdrawal. At first, there was no comment from any superior authority about the move to the Westwall, but in the second phase, von Rundstedt ordered the corps to stand fast where it stood. With only 3–6km to go to join with their reinforcements, Balck considered this irrational and allowed the move to continue into the third and final phase. Von Rundstedt was furious. Calling Balck at 0330hrs on 16 December, Balck recalled that von Rundstedt ordered the corps back to its previous positions immediately. The whole concept of *Auftragstaktik* had, by this stage of the war, been lost, and too many generals were worried about being relieved of command, their pensions and their legacy, to disobey orders. Von Rundstedt was no different; he had also never welcomed Balck into his role in the first place. According to Balck, the OB West commented to him:

> 'I will report to the Führer that you have disobeyed an order three times in the face of the enemy. You can picture the consequence.'[415]

Balck chose to bypass a pointless argument with von Rundstedt and instead argue his decision with the chief of staff at OB West, General der Kavallerie Siegfried Westphal. Westphal had huge experience and connections, having been on the operational staff for Rommel in North Africa and then promoted to chief of staff for Kesselring. Balck was comparatively young to have reached his high level of rank by the age of 50, but Westphal was even younger – being promoted as Hitler's youngest ever general. Aged 42 compared to von Rundstedt's 70 would have allowed Westphal to see the war through different eyes – eyes that were not coloured by the total obligation of the Imperial Army or the First World War.

Any officer who was selected to act as chief of staff for von Rundstedt deserves the greatest respect; not just because of the challenge of working so closely with this icon of the Wehrmacht, but also because he must have been equipped with the most impressive of diplomatic as well as military skills. In his now largely forgotten 1952 book *The German Army in The West*, Westphal argues openly in his acceptance of some of the key problems faced by German generals under Nazi rule. One admission that emerges was that the officer corps was aware of the 'frightful crimes which have so befouled the German good name' while another was that the Wehrmacht's leaders were 'petrified in the attitude of obedience' to Hitler, and this applied to von Rundstedt at this moment.[416]

As a vastly experienced chief of staff who already held private views that senior officers such as Kesselring, Rommel and von Rundstedt were 'guilty of a moral resignation which is not to be glossed over', Westphal also saw this petrification in von Rundstedt – a 'nothing can be done so I will do nothing' approach. The men on the front lines paid with their lives for the obfuscation and deliberate calcification that did not allow for arguing with or ignoring orders from the OKW, Keitel, Jodl or of course the Führer. When Balck contacted him and explained how the men of Gruppe Höhne stood to be destroyed because of Rundstedt's arbitrary acceptance of the attitude of the OKW, Westphal saw the obvious logic of what Balck was trying to do and supported him. Quite how Westphal squared this circle with von Rundstedt will probably never be known, but both von Rundstedt and Westphal coming from Saxony probably helped, as did Westphal's relationship with von Mellenthin, even though he had now left Balck's side. A curt telegram direct to Balck from Hitler thanked him for his service but hoped that he would hold the current line. The brevity of the message spoke loudly of Hitler's warning to behave as he required him to do, but one senses that the 'intrigues' referred to by von Mellenthin had already done their damage and Balck's days were numbered.

As the Battle of Bulge was starting to turn against Hitler and Balck was sitting down to dinner in his usual way on 23 December, an urgent telephone call from the OKH informed him that he was to report immediately to Zossen, south of Berlin, from where he was to take command of a re-formed 6. Armee in Budapest within twenty-four hours. Balck too now felt the emotions of having been sacked.

Epilogue

After the war, Hermann Balck learnt that Guderian, as chief of staff at the OKH, had written in his memoirs that Balck had 'fallen victim to Himmler's intrigues'. Why Himmler should have been interested in bringing down Balck remains a matter of conjecture. Given the complexity of Himmler's political intrigues to undermine the Führer, take over Germany and make peace with the Allies in the West, it is a tough ask to see exactly where the downfall of Balck fits in. Possibly, Himmler saw control over Heeresgruppe G in its entirety as an objective – he was already commanding 19. Armee and was seen by Hitler as the defender of the Rhine. Perhaps it was as Balck himself pondered, that Himmler felt Balck was 'too tough' on his SS divisions; an odd conclusion, but as Balck commented, 'Himmler was no friend of mine', and that in itself may have been enough to place his head on Himmler's hit list. Balck liked to think, as his memoirs illustrate, that his latest move was because Hitler wanted someone loyal and reliable who would carry out his orders in Hungary. Comforting though that may have been to Balck's considerable ego, it does reveal a lot about him as a Wehrmacht general: by his own admission a loyal commander to the Führer, willing to carry out his orders, although often in his own unique way. Whatever the reason for Balck's removal, Hitler would have had to approve it, revealing that not even a holder of the Knight's Cross with Oak Leaves, Swords and Diamonds was immune from the whim of the Führer.

Most peculiar, however, was the reappointment of Blaskowitz to his former position as at the head of Heeresgruppe G. It was an odd decision on the surface, given Hitler's earlier disdain for his performance, but perhaps not when the relationship that Balck had with von Rundstedt since September 1944 is considered. There was clearly no love lost between them, and von Rundstedt had many occasions to argue with Balck, order Balck and even threaten Balck, only to see that he had been ignored. It is most likely that, out of all the 'intrigues' swirling around Hermann Balck in the autumn battles in Lorraine, it was a private telephone call to the OKW from von Rundstedt requesting the return of Blaskowitz that ended Balck's command.

Chapter XVIII

6. Armee, Hungary, December 1944–May 1945

'After an interview with General der Panzertruppe Balck appeared in 1977 in the *Welt am Sonntag* newspaper, in which he repeated his false, unjustified and shameful accusations against the Hungarian Szent László Infantry Division (and against the IV SS-Panzer Korps), a storm of protests was raised by former Hungarian participants in the war and commanding officers. The protests were supported in writing by the former German commanding generals, General der Kavallerie Harteneck and General der Gebirgstruppe Lanz.'

(Georg Maier, deputy chief of staff 6. SS-Panzerarmee)

It should probably not be a surprise, when considering that Balck had been relieved of his command for the first time in his life, that, without waiting for a formal handover of Heeresgruppe G back to Generaloberst Blaskowitz, Balck cleared his desk, packed his large black leather briefcase, took his knobbed walking stick and carried out his orders to get to Zossen as quickly as possible.[418]

Immediately upon arrival, at 0300hrs on Christmas Eve, the new commander of a reconstituted 6. Armee met with Guderian as Acting Chief of the General Staff of the OKH and was brought up to date with his mission in Hungary and the situation in and around Budapest. Balck would have felt somewhat bruised that he had been demoted by Hitler from command of an army group down to a single army, but given the atmosphere, he was probably grateful that Guderian had saved him from total obscurity prior to the war's end. An often-overlooked consequence of the failed July 1944 bomb plot was the fact that thousands of talented officers were removed from their posts and executed or jailed, leaving appalling holes in the chain of command all over the Wehrmacht. Having officers of Balck's ilk – with his Oak Leaves, Swords and Diamonds around his neck – was a talisman if nothing else.

Both Balck and Guderian had known all along that Hungary was a dubious ally of the Nazi state. From the very beginning, in March 1941, when Balck was an Oberstleutnant leading his Panzer-Regiment 3 through Hungary and Yugoslavia, Nazi foreign minister von Ribbentrop had been forced to exercise too much pressure on Hungary to bring the nation into the Axis fold to ever really be certain of its loyalty. There were constant rumours of treachery from the Hungarians, and by early 1944, with upwards of 200,000 of its men killed on the Russian fronts, Hungary vacillated in its commitment to fascism. Hitler felt forced to occupy Hungary on 19 March 1944 in Operation Margarethe.

With the arrival of Nazi fanatic General Döme Sztójay, the deportation of Hungarian Jews to the concentration camps sprang into life, with ghettos formed across the country. In less than two months, during April and May 1944, some 440,000 Jews were taken from Hungary, mostly to Auschwitz, in what was Adolf Eichmann's *pièce de résistance* as far as his train transportation system was concerned. By July 1944, the only Jewish community left in Hungary was in Budapest, the nation's capital.[419]

The rest of 1944 was spent by the Hungarians trying to defend their country from the invading Russians. While Balck was almost always dismissive of the fighting quality of Hungarian troops, during October 1944 they had managed to severely damage a number of Russian mobile forces of General Issa Pliyev. But despite some courageous Hungarian defence, the Soviet encirclement of Budapest had been on the cards for weeks. It was only further defensive sacrifices, such as that by the German 271. Volksgrenadier-Division under Generalmajor Martin Bieber, that gained time for Hitler to send reinforcements in the shape of an SS-Gebirgskorps into what he must have known would be certain defeat in Budapest. Further troops and equipment flooded into Budapest, largely remnants of German regiments and divisions.

While German and the even weaker Hungarian formations fought to defend the nation, the far-right Arrow Cross Party of Ferenc Szálasi brutally attacked, raped and murdered as many Jews as they could find in Budapest, stealing what they could and trying to purge the city of Jews before the Russians arrived. Szálasi even became prime minister in October 1944 based on this record. By Christmas Day 1944, Budapest was virtually surrounded. A mixture of German units were encircled in the city, which according to new 6. Armee chief Balck were

'remnants of the 13th Panzer Division and the 60th Panzergrenadier Division, two SS cavalry divisions, and Hungarian-Germans with little training and not much combat value. Overall, we had approximately thirty-thousand Germans and at best seventy thousand Hungarian soldiers.'[420]

The situation map for the last week of December was stark. It showed that Budapest was indeed encircled, with a smaller version of Tarnopol or Stalingrad developing as six fully mobile, well-equipped Soviet corps surrounded the city. They had only one objective in mind – to destroy all resistance within Budapest.

According to Balck, in totality these Russian units equalled 'fifty-four infantry divisions, five mechanised corps, three tank corps, four air defence divisions, seven antitank brigades and three rocket launcher brigades'.

Although Balck fails to elaborate on where he gained these staggering figures, he was probably on the right track. Furthermore, the Russians had pushed the new front lines well beyond the west of the city, and the new front was held by seven Soviet corps, with a the total of thirteen army and mechanized corps forming the Soviet Fourth Guards Army within the 2nd Ukrainian Front. Facing them in this sector was Balck's relatively weak 6. Armee, whose first mission was to try to relieve Budapest.

Command changes

This was the political and military backdrop to the arrival of the new German 6. Armee commander in Hungary; a country falling apart, half-occupied by Russian forces, held together by brutality and fear, with an army on the verge of extinction and a Führer in Berlin aware that he had lost the war but clinging to his desire never to withdraw.

Commanding 6. Armee as it stood in December 1944 was no enviable task for any field commander. An exhausted General der Artillerie Maximilian Fretter-Pico – a vastly experienced staff officer and general who had the distinction of once leading his own division, Armeeabteilung Fretter-Pico – was relieved of command on the night of 22 December after a telephone call from the Operations section of the OKH. He was told he had not been aggressive enough in his posture, and the hope was that Balck would do a better job. Leading 6. Armee during the second half of 1944 in south-eastern Europe had been incredibly demanding and draining, but Fretter-Pico was still sacked by Hitler and put into the ZBV (*zur besonderen Verwendung*), on standby for use in any special duties at the discretion of the OKH.

At Heeresgruppe level there were also changes, with Generaloberst Johannes Friessner removed from his post. Friessner had been commanding Heeresgruppe Süd (which had replaced Heeresgruppe Süd Ukraine once that region had been lost) for the past four months but had been unable to stop the tsunami of Soviet Marshal Fyodor Tolbukhin's forces. Operation Spätlese, which had been set in motion early in December, had been intended to utilize Friessner's carefully harboured Panzer forces – some 235 operational tanks in all – to stop and then break through Tolbukhin's Sixth Guards Army. The axis chosen was southeast between Lake Balaton and Lake Velencze, and included Generalleutnant Wilhelm Philipps' 3. Panzer-Division, 6. Panzer-Division and Generalmajor Gottfried Frölich's 8. Panzer-Division. Even the massive new Panzer Mk VI

Königstiger (King Tigers) were available in General der Panzertruppe Hermann Breith's III. Panzerkorps as part of 6. Armee, but the mud, challenges with command and control and the onset of new Russian offensives saw this operation splutter, stall and grind to a standstill by the third week of December.[420A]

Balck now reported to the new commander of Heeresgruppe Süd, the laconic General der Infanterie Otto Wöhler, another very experienced officer who had been chief of staff to von Manstein in the Crimea. Post-war, he was described by von Manstein as having been 'such an invaluable support in the difficult days of the winter and played a leading role in the preparation of "Bustard Hunt" [the Battle of the Kerch Peninsula in December 1941]'.[421]

Wöhler was a man of caution and obvious *sang-froid*, which had served him well in numerous challenges on the Eastern Front, and his character fitted well with that of his new 6. Armee commander Hermann Balck. Wöhler was also no stranger to standing up to the OKW and OKH, but he was not cut from the same cloth as Balck and had no personal grudge to repair or enmity with the SS – both of which afflicted Balck's judgement. For Balck, Hungary was another change of front line and very different in nature from the Western Front, but it was a chance to prove himself again – or at least to end the war from a position of comparative success. A significant change can be seen in the way Balck now went about business, and it is in this concluding episode of his career that the greatest criticism of his actions has been made, especially through the work of the Deputy Chief of Operations at 6. SS-Panzerarmee (which would also soon arrive in theatre), Oberst Georg Maier.

The situation of 6. Armee in Hungary, 25 December 1944

According to Douglas E. Nash in his excellent book on the fate of the Dirlewanger Brigade, Operation Spätlese had not been a complete failure, with Wöhler and Balck receiving reports that the Soviet Sixth Guards Tank Army had lost nearly 150 tanks and the Russian advances had been blunted, although at great cost.[421A]

By the last week of December 1944, Wöhler's Heeresgruppe Süd was composed of 2. Panzerarmee, 3. Armee, 6. Armee and the Hungarian 8th Army. All four armies suffered from severe shortages of everything except grim determination. The last products of the main efforts of the factories in Germany would soon arrive, including brand new tanks, but the quality of leadership among the armies was not so easily replaced. Unsurprisingly, there were problems everywhere, but the Führer had commanded that the defenders of Budapest be rescued as a priority, and Wöhler ordered Balck and 6. Armee to do exactly that.

On 25 December, Balck's new chief of staff, Generalmajor Heinrich Gaedcke, reported that 6. Armee comprised the IX. SS-Gebirgskorps, LVII. Panzerkorps, LXXII. Panzerkorps and III. Panzerkorps.

The IX. SS-Gebirgskorps was the substantial formation that was now trapped in Budapest. It contained a mix of different parts of 22. SS-Panzer-Division, 8. SS-Kavallerie-Division 'Florian Geyer', 22. SS-Kavallerie-Division, 13. Panzer-Division and Panzergrenadier-Division 'Feldherrnhalle'.[422] There were also the remnants of a small Kampfgruppe of the 271. Volksgrenadier-Division, a small unit of the 4. SS-Polizei-Division – the SS-Polizei-Regiment 1 – and a host of parts of Hungarian divisional units under the command of General Iván Hindy. The corps as a whole was commanded by 56-year-old SS-Obergruppenführer Karl Pfeffer-Wildenbruch, a senior SS-Police officer who had moved into military command under Himmler's auspices in 1943. The IX. SS-Gebirgskorps was therefore a large but diverse force defending *Festung* Budapest.

From the outset, Balck was critical of having Pfeffer-Wildenbruch as the military commander within Budapest. Quite apart from his SS affiliation, Balck saw Pfeffer-Wildenbruch as a policeman and 'politician' rather than a leader of fighting men. Balck's attitude towards communicating with and trying to save the IX. SS-Gebirgskorps would be shaped and coloured by his obvious contempt for the SS. Balck had lost his son in the fighting in Russia, but he was perhaps unaware that Pfeffer-Wildenbruch had also sacrificed two sons in the war and that they shared a similar bitterness towards the Soviets.

> 'Balck had also clashed with Himmler (as we know this probably played a part in his demotion to command Sixth Army), because of the general's [Balck's] open disdain for all SS divisions. Balck was, in fact, highly prejudiced against the Waffen-SS and all of its officers, and he did nothing to hide his contempt for them.'[423]

Although many members of the senior command had a sincere respect for Pfeffer-Wildenbruch, given his vast experience and committed nature, Balck did not.

By 27 December, the Soviet ring around Budapest had closed, trapping the entire force of some 35,000 mostly Waffen-SS troops and a further 40,000 Hungarian soldiers.[424]

The LVII. Panzerkorps was composed of 357. Infanterie-Division (sometimes referred to as the Rintelen Division from the name of its commander, Generalleutnant Josef Rintelen), 96. Infanterie-Division, commanded by the recently promoted Generalmajor Hermann Harrendorf, and the familiar 8. Panzer-Division. LXXII. Panzerkorps contained the 3. and 6. Panzer-Divisions plus two Hungarian formations, the Szt László Division and 2nd Tank Division;

III. Panzerkorps was very weak, containing the 271. Infanterie-Division and 1st Hungarian Cavalry Division.[425]

Hermann Balck also had command over the Third Hungarian Army and a mixed cavalry corps of battered units of the 1.Panzer-Division and 23. Panzer-Division. On paper, therefore, the reconstituted 6. Armee looked formidable, but most, if not all, of its formations were mere shadows of their former selves, denuded by months of heavy fighting against the Red Army, retreating and losing much their equipment, and with an exhausted leadership.

On 24 December, as Balck looked at the situation maps with Guderian in Zossen, he had been surprised to see that both 3. Panzer-Division and 6. Panzer-Division had their armoured units south of the Danube, aimed at Budapest, while their infantry and support units were all positioned the other side of the river in the north. As soon as he arrived on Christmas Day, and after sarcastically commenting that 'this must have been done by a real armour expert', Balck ordered Gaedcke, his chief of staff, to get the two divisions back together in single formations. According to his memoirs, Gaedcke spluttered out that the current dispositions were due to an explicit Führer order. Regardless of this, Balck told him to get moving and hoped that Guderian would support him once news of the new dispositions were reported to Hitler. This could have been the shortest posting in Balck's career, but again he heard nothing in response.

The predictably grim strategic background whereby the recent German offensive, Friessner's Operation Spätlese, had ground to a halt with serious losses in tanks and men, meant that it was only a matter of time before there was a renewed Soviet offensive throughout the southern front. Although Malinovsky and Tolbukhin, both proven army group commanders, had been winded by Spätlese, they soon regained their composure and launched a series of attacks north of the Danube which saw German and Hungarian divisions to the north and south of Lake Velence swept away under an avalanche of Russian artillery, tanks and infantry. Thus, by 24 December, the possibility of rescuing Budapest had become far harder; those troops who had fled there for safety now found themselves imprisoned by Soviet thrusts north and south of the city.

Getting rid of the worst of the SS

One of the first messy problems that Balck had to deal with, in a command that was to be fraught with disappointments and failures – not that Balck would agree with any such judgement – was the issue of the Dirlewanger Brigade, commanded by SS-Oberführer Oskar Dirlewanger. This infamous yet still misunderstood formation had been created as early as 1940 as the Sondereinheit Dirlewanger ('Special Unit Dirlewanger') and was composed of 'convicts, criminals and misfits' whose mission was seemingly to rape, pillage, murder and loot their way through Europe as part of any SS military operations in theatre.[425A] After brutally assisting in the suppression of the Warsaw Rising in August 1944, the enlarged 2. SS-Sturmbrigade Dirlewanger found itself part of Operation Spätlese and was expected to play a major role, through its violent fighting conduct, in stopping the onslaught of the Soviet Sixth Guards Army between 13 and 18 December. In the event, through a combination of disorganized deployment and a lack of any heavy weapons, the Sturmbrigade was destroyed in fighting around Ipolyság in modern-day Slovakia. Strangely, the unit became singled out for blame for the encirclement of Budapest, with critics citing its poor fighting quality. However, this should perhaps come as no surprise. With officers such as Hermann Balck already convinced that Waffen-SS units were not disciplined, well trained or as well led as those of the Heer, the very existence of something like the Dirlewanger Brigade was a complete anathema to the concept of a trained, honourable German Army – it ranked beyond even the repulsive activities of the Einsatzgruppen.

The eroded IV. SS-Panzerkorps, however, needed men and the Dirlewanger Brigade provided between two and three partial battalions of infantry, of varying quality, to various units within the corps. Oskar Dirlewanger positioned himself in the rear assembly area and seems to have had little control over his dispersed units, such as the 300–400 men fighting with the Horst Wessel Division in late December. Reports suggest that the Dirlewanger companies acquitted themselves well, but as so often happened, their discipline broke down on 23 December and fifty-six residents of a small village were locked into a house by a Dirlewanger unit, then shot and burned as retaliation for the plunder of a German baggage train.[425B]

Originally attached to the 2nd Hungarian Armoured Division, in the dislocation of battle and chaos of decimated units, some small groups of the Dirlewanger Brigade found themselves under the command of Kampfgruppe Hafner – itself part of 357. Infanterie-Division – and it took some days for Gaedcke to locate them. For Himmler in Berlin, it was vital that his shock brigade of murderers was kept intact, and he was firmly against its surviving battalions being dispersed to make up the numbers of other units. Balck seems to have been willing to devote quite a lot of time in these first frantic days of his command to getting the unit away from his theatre, as radio traffic between 6. Armee and subordinate units between 30 December 1944 and 3 January 1945 demonstrates (see Annex II):

'December 30th, 1944
SECRET: Long-Distance telegram to Army Group South
The remaining elements of the Dirlewanger Brigade have been removed from subordinate command and put in motion. In the E-Transport, the following have arrived:

SS Panzer Division Totenkopf: so far 33 trains
SS Panzer Division Wiking: so far 20 trains'[425C]

Thus, on 26 December, Heeresgruppe Süd instructed 6. Armee to withdraw all Dirlewanger troops to their assembly area near Nemce. Balck wasted no time and ordered that any member of the Dirlewanger Brigade be withdrawn from the line. The orders can be seen filtering through during 29 and 30 December from the new German-Russian digitization project, where many of the records of 6. Armee seem to have ended up. Clearly, Balck did not wish to have this unit – of all SS units – to be under his command; for once, Reichsführer-SS Himmler agreed with him.

Efforts to rescue Budapest – Konrad I, II and III, January–February 1945

For Hitler, still living in his goldfish bowl of sycophantic acolytes and refusing to recognize publicly that once the Ardennes offensive had failed he had lost the war, cities became symbols of resistance and targets for salvation. In a replay of the failures at Tarnopol and Stalingrad, the defenders of Budapest were refused permission to break out and Hermann Balck was tasked to mount a rescue for the *Festung*, as Hitler had declared it. At the same time, Balck was to keep his defensive front intact, as the Austrian border was now not far behind him and nor was Vienna, which the Führer wished to see defended at all costs.

Somehow, replacement vehicles and supplies were still reaching Heeresgruppe Süd. As can be seen in the second part of the radio message of 30 December detailed above, a major development was that Hitler had ordered IV. SS-Panzerkorps to move, as discreetly as was possible with four tank divisions, to support the drive to rescue the German and Hungarian forces trapped in Budapest. Hitler was less interested than ever in the tactics of just how that could be achieved. General der Artillerie Walter Warlimont at the OKW watched and noted as Hitler mused to Generalmajor Wolfgang Thomale on the night of 29 December:

'I started this war with the most wonderful army in Europe; today I've got a muck heap. I have no leaders any more, my generals are incompetent, the officers are no commanders, the troops are wretched.'[426]

Hitler's harsh, unfair and unfounded description was redolent of a man who had no emotional connection with his troops. They were there to be used and abused, just like everybody else, to do his bidding.

To the north and west of Budapest, Balck was planning how best to use his 'muck heap' of courageous men, still willing to lay down their lives for the Führer. Commanded in exemplary fashion by Balck's former superior General der Panzertruppe Friedrich Kirchener, LVII. Panzerkorps was able to withdraw in good order, and by 31 December the front line was at least stable. The Russians seemed to be taking a breath and awaiting developments.

Further south, Balck knew that IV. SS-Panzerkorps was being delivered by train into his sector, and he was soon shaking hands with the corps commander, the mercurial and iconic SS-Obergruppenführer Herbert Gille. 'Papa' Gille was highly experienced and had fought in France and Russia, escaping from the Cherkassy Pocket, and was a veteran member and commander of the formidable 5. SS-Panzer-Division 'Wiking'. Given Balck's well-known opinions on the fighting abilities of the Waffen-SS, it might have been a tense first briefing between them. Like Balck, Gille was a blunt personality, although Balck would have tried to make it abundantly clear who was in command here – and it was not Himmler in Berlin or Gille.

There was tension in the room. In February 1944, Balck's now chief of staff, Gaedcke, had been trapped in the Cherkassy Pocket along with Otto Wöhler, Hermann Breith and the remnants of Heeresgruppe Süd. In the disaster of the encirclement, Gille and his SS staff had decided to escape side-by-side with their men. One of the staff officers of their commanding corps was Gaedcke, and there had already been a serious falling out over a supply matter. After the breakout, Gille claimed that they had left Gaedcke with a rearguard unit, only to find that Gaedcke had abandoned his men and broken out independently to save his own neck. Whether or not this was true remains unclear, but this meeting with Balck was the first time that they had met since that time. Hence, Balck wrote in his memoirs:

> 'My chief of staff became pale when he found out that the IV SS-Panzer Corps was arriving. "That is Gille. I know him from the Cherkassy Pocket." Gaedcke then told [me] about Gille's troublemaking and his disinclination to follow orders. When Gille reported to me he struck me as a strong, egocentric type who had no understanding of operational context and possibilities. Probably he was quite courageous. He was the type of Waffen SS commander who as a matter of principle always resisted orders from any army officer.'[427]

6. Armee, Hungary, December 1944–May 1945

Clearly, Balck made up his mind about Gille's qualities as a commander very quickly; thirty years later, he had not changed his opinion. Apart from his ego and devotion to the Nazi cause, Gille brought with him the 3. SS-Panzer-Division 'Totenkopf', his own 5. SS-Panzer-Division 'Wiking' and the 1. and 3. Panzer-Divisions to fight west of Budapest – but only parts of them. Hitler's desire to get his forces shifted from Poland to save Budapest meant that the corps was only partially formed when the first attacks were ordered, as can be seen from Mitch Williamson's analysis:

> 'At that time [1 January 1945] only 32% of 5th SS Panzer (Wiking), 66% of 3rd SS Panzer (Totenkopf) and 43% of 96th Infantry Division was in place. Of the 711th Infantry Division there was no sign. [The divisions were not fully complete until 8 January and after Operation Konrad I had stopped.]'[428]

Time was of the essence, Operation Konrad I beginning the very next day with an attack by 96. Infanterie-Division on the night of 1 January 1945. The division crossed to the south of the icy Danube in assault boats and then, turning east, Harrendorf drove his men forward in their half-tracks and his artillery punched a hole in the Russian lines. On their way across the Danube in their rubber boats, they may have noticed the steady flow of bloated bodies floating down the mighty river; these were the Jewish men, women and children who were being executed daily on the banks of the river by ruthless gangs of Arrow Cross Fascists.[429]

As the Russians slowly reacted to this assault, further south, the whole of IV. SS-Panzerkorps exploded eastwards into the Soviet lines around Agostyán and Tarján, heading directly for Budapest. Their left flank linked up with the infantry of the 96. Division as they forged a passage along the southern bank of the Danube. Balck records that the Soviet Forty-Sixth Shock Army was taken by complete surprise by the advance of the SS-Panzer troops. The recently arrived but experienced 711. Infanterie-Division under Generalleutnant Josef Reichert joined in the attack and managed to regain the city of Esztergom.[430] Crucially, however, not only were Gille's SS divisions understrength, they also were up against superior numbers. For example, Mitch Williamson found that

> 'the Wiking Division, was confronted on 3 January by one heavy tank regiment, four assault-gun regiments, three rifle divisions, one mechanised brigade and six technical battalions [this was the Soviet 18th Tank Corps, against one single and only partially complete SS-Panzer division] – three times the Germans' strength.'

The 'Wiking', as it so often did, fought tenaciously to try to break through to Budapest, where many members of the division had friends and family. However, they were also be criticized for their tactical naivety by Balck, who was furious at their losses in men and materiel for so little gain.

To the south, in typical Balck style, another defensive attack was underway by III. Panzerkorps. This second phase of the operation was designed to confuse the Russians about the location of the main attack, and the assault on Székesfehérvár took them within 20km of the outskirts of Budapest. It managed to relieve numerous small units trapped along the way; even some desperately exposed field hospitals were recovered, together with thousands of grateful wounded German and Hungarian troops. But progress towards Budapest slowed as Russian anti-tank and aerial defences began to harden around the incursions, dramatically disrupting the advance of both the elite SS-Panzer divisions. Although, on balance, Balck favoured maintaining the momentum to create a corridor to the beleaguered city, Gille did not, and Hitler intervened to order a regrouping. Balck was greatly annoyed that Gille moved via Himmler to get the Führer's backing for Operation Konrad I to be declared at an end. In his memoirs, Guderian recalled flying to meet with Balck and Gille at this time:

> 'During the period January 5th–8th I visited General Wöhler ... General Balck and the SS-General Gille; I discussed with them the future prosecution of operations in Hungary and found out why the attack to relieve Budapest had failed. The principal reason seemed to be that the initial success won during the night attack of January 1st had not been exploited with sufficient boldness to constitute a breakthrough on the following night. We had neither the commanders nor troops of 1940 quality any more; otherwise, this attack might well have been successful and troops might then have been available for transfer elsewhere, and the Danube front might have been stabilised for a time.'[431]

This account by Guderian smacks of his having been pestered by Balck to accept his version of events – that the SS units were sub-standard. This was a continuous refrain that Balck seems to have used in every case where a reverse was suffered. He was partially correct; even the SS divisions no longer had the ferocious and skilled quality of past years, but they had also been committed piecemeal by both Hitler and Balck. Indeed, Balck could have delayed their commitment with an alleged radio 'malfunction' or diversion, had he wished to. Balck was probably right to tell Guderian that the 'Wiking' had not executed the advance well enough, but it was not the division of 1942 or 1943, its ranks having been depleted of the best and most experienced over three years of solid fighting. The influx of new tanks and heavy armoured reconnaissance vehicles from factories across Germany was no substitute for experienced and skilful leadership.

Within a few days, the Red Army had pushed its Sixth Guards Tank Army southwards into the left flank of LVII. Panzerkorps, and by 6 January had broken through, heading westwards again. Only the timely visit of Guderian to meet with Balck enabled a quick decision to call on 20. Panzer-Division to move south from Slovakia to shore up the front of LVII. Panzerkorps. The 20. Panzer, under heroic and legendary commander Oberst Hermann von Oppeln-Bronikowski, performed miracles, the single German division driving the entire Sixth Guards Tank Army back on its heels with heavy losses in tanks and equipment.[432] Further south, the Red Army also poured reinforcements in between IV. SS-Panzerkorps and Budapest; the reality was that once Konrad I had stopped, so too had any chance of creating a corridor of salvation to the city.

With Hitler's declaration of Budapest as a fortress, he repeatedly denied permission for the defenders to try to break out. Furthermore, he ordered a resumption of the relief attack in what now became codenamed Konrad II. This time, on a snow-covered and freezing 8 January, Kampfgruppe Breith was created by the 6. Armee staff with the objective of attacking, with III. Panzerkorps and I. Kavalleriekorps, 40 miles south-west of Budapest and moving beyond Székesfehérvár to puncture some of the mounting pressure on IV. SS-Panzerkorps. This in turn would enable Gille to restart his own assault towards Esztergom and then hopefully manage to break through into Budapest. The advance was initially positive, and Kampfgruppe Breith was quickly reporting upwards of seventy Russian tanks destroyed. In the north, Gille was making good progress, overrunning the 86th Guards Rifle Division and reporting they were just 14 miles from the city's suburbs. It was at this crucial moment that Hitler decided to issue another stop order. Even though the city skyline was in sight, with its plumes of black acrid smoke from burning Russian tanks, Konrad II also came to a shuddering halt. In Hitler's mind, new and grander strategic ideas were germinating, and he decided to end the attack prematurely without reference to the commanders on the ground. Nothing could be done to change his mind. Balck believed Hitler's order flew in the face of every concept of common sense and German military convention (*Auftragstaktik*), which traditionally held that tactical and operational decisions should be made by local commanders. Balck said that he, along with Herbert Gille, Karl Ullrich and many other senior officers, were convinced that they could have freed their comrades, had they been allowed to do so.

Whether Balck actually agreed with Hitler or just wanted to see Gille stopped from achieving the glory will never be known, but there does seem to be a dismissive tone in Balck's memoirs that suggest he had already decided that Budapest could not be saved and that, given that it was full of SS troops, he should let it be destroyed anyway. According to historian Samuel Mitcham:

> 'Hitler's fertile imagination had, in fact, produced another grandiose plan, one that went far beyond just a relief operation: he had decided to destroy the bulk of the 46th and 4th Guards Armies by launching a double envelopment west of Budapest. The IV SS-Panzer and III Panzer Corps would form the southern pincer while the 6th Panzer Division and 3rd Cavalry Brigade enveloped the Soviets from the north. Simultaneously, IV SS-Panzer would relieve Budapest.'[433]

This new master plan had possibly formed in Hitler's mind because he sensed the attack was going so well that, if they paused and reinforced, the whole front could in fact collapse and they could get back to the Danube. This would become Operation Konrad III and would begin as soon as the units of IV. SS-Panzerkorps had completed their move south. This would take until 17 January to be done, and despite complaints from many quarters, there was no way of changing Hitler's mind. The OKW also ordered IV. SS-Panzerkorps to move further south to the eastern end of the huge Lake Balaton in preparation for Konrad III. If there was one thing that the Russians thrived upon, it was taking advantage of any strategic pause by the Germans to completely reinforce and rejuvenate their defences, and this crucial error by Hitler was to cost many lives and seal the fate of the population and defenders of Budapest.

By now, Budapest had turned into a second Stalingrad, with all the horrors associated with a city population ravaged by war on all sides. There were severe food shortages, no medical services, privations for women and children, and wounded, dead and dying soldiers, disease, destruction and desperate civilians everywhere. Local priests and nuns did what they could – holding Mass in the sewers and cellars of the city, running hospitals in churches – but that was nothing compared to the actions of the appalling Arrow Cross extermination squads who searched the city for Jews, dragging them to the banks of the Danube and executing them before dumping their bodies in the river. Many of these death squads would pay the price and be executed after the war, but that, of course, gave no solace to the thousands they murdered and whose bodies were washed ashore along the Danube for hundreds of miles downstream.

As the Russians worked their way westwards, block by block, through the city, Balck and his staff worked to prepare IV. SS-Panzerkorps for Konrad III with the dual purpose of breaking through to Buda but also now eliminating the partially encircled Russian forces. The assault by the four experienced and

6. Armee, Hungary, December 1944–May 1945   253

combat-hardened Panzer divisions began on the night of 17 January and saw the Red Army initially overwhelmed. By the 19th, 3. and 5. SS-Panzer-Divisions had advanced nearly 50km in forty-eight hours, reaching the Danube south of Budapest and turning north to head along the freezing grey railway tracks into the city suburbs.

This success had been hard-won, but created a dilemma which once again brought Balck and Gille into confrontation: should they continue the momentum

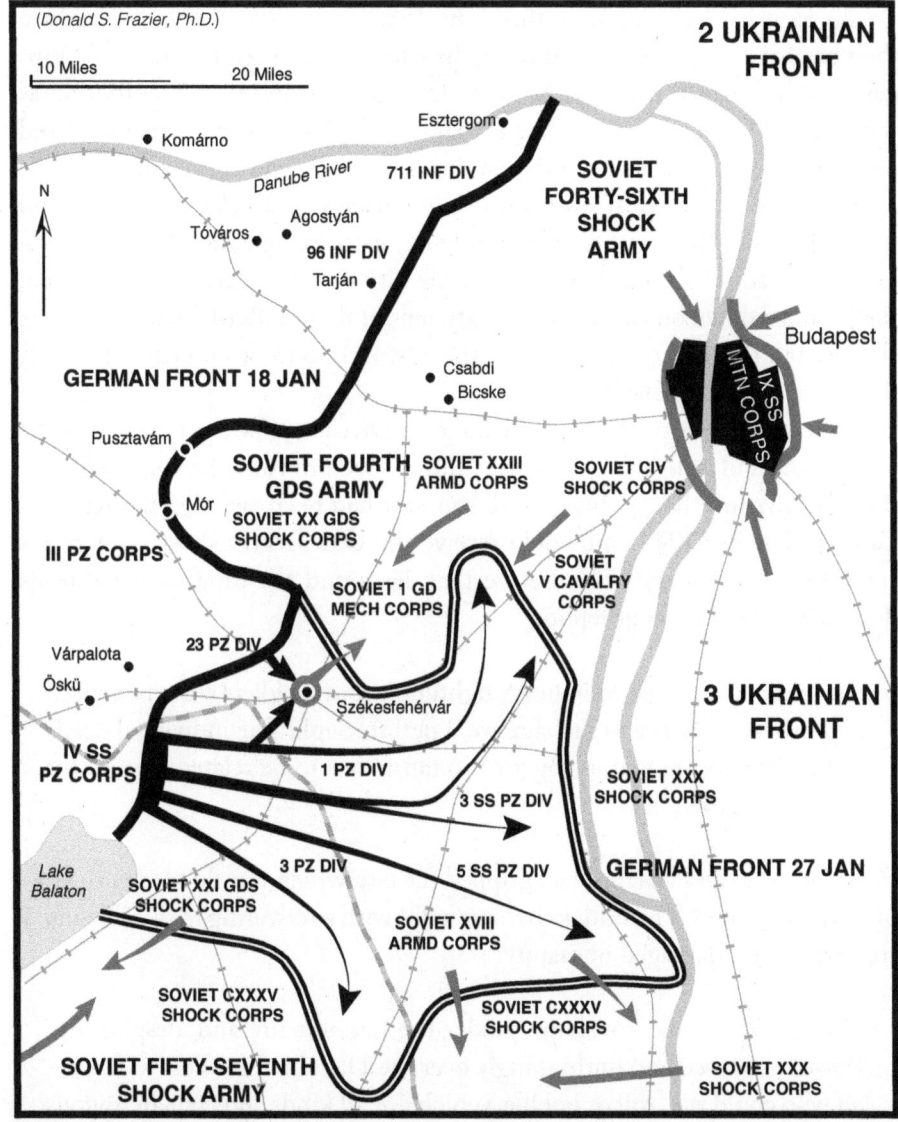

Map 9. Operation Konrad II and the rescue attempt for Budapest by IV. SS-Panzerkorps, 18–27 January 1945. (© 2015 The University Press of Kentucky. Used by permission)

and break through to Budapest, which was now clearly within reach, or pause to destroy the disconnected but still substantial Russian forces west of the city? For Balck, the big picture was what counted and he foresaw a worrying situation:

> 'If we moved on Budapest immediately, we would end up with two instead of one SS Corps in the city, but there would be no forces to prevent the surviving Russian units from coming back at us.'[434]

Balck's logic is hard to argue with, but in Pest, where Gille's SS units could see their brethren desperate for salvation, the Russians were gaining more suburbs daily in the eastern parts of the city – destroying, raping and murdering as they went. The post-war estimate is that over 50,000 women were raped and murdered by the Soviets in Budapest during January and February 1945. The bridges from east to west over the Danube were crammed with civilian and military traffic. Buda, on the western bank, with its defended hills was seen as the last redoubt, even though the entire city was now surrounded. Russian shells rained down on all parts of the city, tens of thousands of terrified civilians sheltered in the sewers and cellars of the city, and SS troops prepared for their deaths on the hills of Buda.

The commander of the 8. SS-Kavallerie-Division 'Florian Geyer' was the charismatic and well-liked SS-Brigadeführer Joachim Rumohr, who had taken over the division the previous April. Rumohr had been awarded the Knight's Cross in January 1944 and would receive the Oak Leaves shortly before his suicide on 1 February 1945. Before that, he found the time to write in his despatches the following report:

> '[W]e are again engaged in heavy fighting, but my soldiers are experienced and in good spirits and I'm sure we'll pull through. The individual deeds of heroism we are witnessing are too numerous to be related now, or for that matter, ever.'[435]

Panic, disorder and violence had gripped the city, which was flooded with news of Soviet atrocities. The bridges became solid with a retreating mass of haunted, frightened and damaged humanity:

> 'The Bridges stood constantly under the heaviest fire and, despite this, flowed confused and unthinkingly over the Danube from Pest to Buda – all who could run, roll or hobble, vehicles of all kinds and civilian wagons covered with canvas with shying horses, wretched mothers, crying wives and children and many, many wounded soldiers. When the mortar rounds

fell in the moving mass of humanity, men and materiel were thrown from both sides of the bridge into the Danube.'[436]

On 18 and 19 January, the commander of Buda, Pfeffer-Wildenbruch, ordered the five bridges between Buda and Pest to be blown up, leaving many thousands to their fates at the hands of the Russians, including wounded SS soldiers who could only expect to be shot on sight. The black stumps of the spans of the bridges stood like sentinels between the possibility of hope on one side of the Danube and Hades on the other. Terrible things were done in Buda during those days.

Time was critical, with the Russians regrouping and constantly asserting their numerical superiority. Between 20 and 25 January, Gille pushed IV. SS-Panzerkorps northwards along the viciously defended western bank of the Danube towards the southern suburbs of Budapest. The Soviet 5th Guards Cavalry Corps, with 100 tanks and 360 pieces of artillery, began to take a heavy toll on IV. SS-Panzerkorps' right flank as it left the safety of the Danube and headed into the city from the south-west. For 1. Panzer-Division and 3. SS-Panzer-Division, the losses were also severe. Even the 'Wiking' Division had run out of steam and in the process lost one of its great heroes in Obersturmbannführer Hans Dorr, commander of the famous SS-Panzergrenadier-Regiment 'Germania', who was seriously wounded. Dorr was a legend in both SS and Wehrmacht circles. At the beginning of the war, he was a private in a division during the Polish campaign, and had subsequently been promoted through the ranks. Wounded fifteen times, his list of decorations was breathtaking and included the Knight's Cross, which came in 1942 when he led an attack under fire across a river in rubber boats, creating his own 'Dorr Bridgehead', and held it for three days under continuous air, artillery and mortar fire. Dorr also held the Close Combat Clasp in Silver, all three grades of the German Wound Badge and the Iron Cross 1st and 2nd Class. For his most daring action of all, he was awarded the Oak Leaves in November 1943. His death in April 1945 from his wounds suffered a few months beforehand was acutely felt throughout the division, as though their talisman had been ripped away.

Balck ultimately had to make a decision. With a new offensive from the Russian Fifty-Seventh Shock Army beginning on 27 January near Lake Balaton, he decided that IV. SS-Panzerkorps must stop and be withdrawn or risk being cut off and destroyed. This was the last possible moment when a planned breakout could have been made. With German troops and tanks south of the city, it should have been possible for the two to meet, despite what would have been the heavy cost in casualties. Once again, Pfeffer-Wildenbruch had messaged both Hitler and Balck to ask for permission to try to break out towards German lines; he was probably not surprised when, once more, Hitler refused. Balck, unsurprisingly, also supported the order of the Führer. It is worth pondering whether, if it had been the 11. Panzer-Division trapped in Buda, Balck would have changed his mind. Was his animosity towards the SS such that he was comfortable seeing them destroyed?

An epilogue on the fall of Budapest

This is a book about Hermann Balck and not about individual battles or events. They are assessed to chart the story of his military career and to illustrate how Balck performed as a commander, how far he reflected the values of his profession, how he went about dealing with military challenges and his attitude towards fighting on behalf of the Nazi state. With these preconditions in mind, the fate of Budapest offers an interesting insight into the man himself.

Once he had made up his mind about a commander of a unit, or indeed the entire SS, Balck was never going to change it. From the beginning to the end of the campaign in Hungary, Balck was critical of the 'political' nature of the garrison commander, Pfeffer-Wildenbruch, and the attempts by SS formations to manage a breakthrough. Balck does not at any point show regret for what happened to Budapest, nor does he shed any tears over the suffering that went on in the city or the bravery of the troops who died there or tried to save it – both SS and Heer. Certainly, no SS officer credits a mention other than Gille, and he only seems to be there as a whipping boy.

Although, in his usual style, Balck was reluctant to be critical of a person by name, he was correct in so far as Pfeffer-Wildenbruch was not a soldier; but neither was he the 'politician' that he liked to claim as a form of insult. Wildenbruch was a policeman by trade and a fiercely loyal disciple of the SS, of Himmler and the Führer. Perversely, it was precisely his willingness to die for the Führer and his strong disciplinary instincts that managed to keep order within Budapest for as long as he did. Balck displays an elitist Prussian military arrogance, as indeed did most senior Wehrmacht officers, towards his Hungarian allies and the tactical ability of the SS. He gives no credit for the victories and heroic defence by his Hungarian subordinates, instead describing them with racial slurs and as having 'no combat value'. Yet if it were not for the courage of tens of thousands of Hungarian soldiers, fighting as best they could against an old and hated enemy, then Budapest would have fallen far earlier, as indeed would all of Hungary. The temple that Balck erects around the supremacy of the Wehrmacht was dated and built on flawed foundations. After all, the German Army was now on the verge of losing a second war, and was itself riddled with complex issues such as peer jealousy, back-biting between commanders for Hitler's favours and internal political rivalries. Balck's blindness towards appreciating any merits in the Slavic races – be they Hungarian, Romanian or Russian – was typical of its time and had a racist root that Balck seemed unable to recognize, even by the 1970s.

Balck admits that they considered attempting a breakout. This was, as the senior commander in theatre, not a decision to be made by committee. Pfeffer-Wildenbruch should have been allowed to break out well before the noose was so tight that all hope was lost. Balck had it within his power to persuade Hitler that he could pull off this miracle, but he did not even try when his forces were just 10 miles from the city. Surely this would have been better than waiting for the inevitable to happen. When Balck ordered Gille to stop his advance at the end of Konrad III, Balck could just as easily have given the defenders of Budapest a chance to reach their lines under the concerted covering fire of the artillery and tanks that the Germans had available. Balck seems as culpable as Hitler for the resultant disaster. The worst that could have happened was that Balck would have been relieved of his command, but was that not more honourable in the Prussian value system than the alternative? Perhaps the Prussian values that Balck had grown up with had by then been long forgotten. To add vinegar to the open wound, Balck does not even blame Hitler. Instead, in his memoirs, he blames Pfeffer-Wildenbruch and his senior officers, who in his opinion did not have the capacity to save their own lives:

> 'In the end we decided against it because we did not trust the leadership in Budapest with the conduct of such an attack.'

Condemnation of Pfeffer-Wildenbruch was one thing, but to equally claim that all the staff officers and divisional commanders of IX. SS-Gebirgskorps within Budapest were not up to the job of organizing a breakout was the height of arrogance. It was also a tragic blindness to his own failings, looking around to find ways of absolving himself of any blame for the slaughter taking place in a city that held out until the end – as they had been ordered to do. Balck wrote:

> 'For a successful breakout you need tanks, assault guns, self-propelled artillery, anti-tank guns, sufficient communications equipment, and at least some trucks with fuel. Why they destroyed all that before they started will remain forever a mystery to me.'[437]

So it was, in Balck's eyes in the 1970s, their own fault. But why should this have been a 'mystery' to him? They were obeying orders, standing fast and preparing for the end, destroying their means of escape as any loyal troops would do. Paulus gave the same orders in Stalingrad: they expected to be relieved, but if they were not then they would fight to the end. None of this heavy equipment, other than anti-tank guns for which they had run out of ammunition, was of any use in house-to-house combat anyway. Furthermore, they had run out of fuel long before the end came. Well before the end, on 15 January, IX. SS-Gebirgskorps had radioed Heeresgruppe Süd to report:

> 'Artillery munitions are all used up … fuel is at an end. The supply situation is critical. The position of the wounded is catastrophic.'[437]

If Balck spent the rest of his life plagued by the 'mystery' of why they destroyed their equipment, then he was deceiving himself and lying to protect his own culpability, unless of course he felt their guns and vehicles could fire and run on fresh air.

A final clue to the true loyalties of Balck and his inability to blame Hitler comes on page 423 of his memoirs, where he states:

> 'About a year later [1946] my old regimental commander Field Marshal Maximillian von Weichs and I were being held in an American prisoner of war camp at Allendorf. He had been with Hitler near the final days of the war. Hitler had complained to him that everyone in Hungary had failed him, and he named the names of the senior army and Waffen-SS leadership. The only man that he had been able to rely upon, he said, had been Balck. Hearing that left me with a bitter and empty feeling. I had never held back, and I was usually right in my assessments, but what good was that praise after the fact when no one listened to me at the time.'

A 'bitter and empty feeling' for all those officers and men who had performed so well and courageously, but been ignored by Hitler, would be understandable. A 'bitter and empty feeling' for the sacrifices made by so many with their lives, which Hitler blandly disregarded, is also comprehensible. But was there also a 'bitter and empty feeling' that, despite knowing of the massive number of victims of the Holocaust, Balck still wanted to be able to pursue the war more successfully and for it to continue, no matter the further human cost on the battlefield and in German towns and cities? If the latter is so, it is unforgiveable, revealing where Balck's true loyalties lay. Balck could have ordered the opening of the gates for the defenders of Budapest to try to escape to the lines of Gille's IV. SS-Panzerkorps while there was still time and some sort of covering fire was possible, but he was not willing to do so. Instead, he sacrificed the city and its defenders to the Russians rather than defy his Führer.

Chapter XIX

The Final Offensive, April 1945

'By late January, the number of wounded German and Hungarian soldiers outnumbered those who could still fight. To be left behind in Buda after the breakout meant certain death and many chose suicide in their hospital beds. The fighting for the city cemetery saw shells opening tombs which became ready-made trenches where the corpses of ancient princes became mixed with dead horses and the fresh blood of hand-to-hand fighting. From the skies, military decorations were parachuted into Buda and distributed in an effort to raise morale.'

(Survivor of the 60. Panzergrenadier-Division 'Feldherrnhalle')

With the collapse of Konrad III on 25 and 26 January, what was left of IX. SS-Gebirgskorps in Budapest prepared for the end. The main citadel of Gellért Hill, situated amongst the hills of the western part of the city in Buda, was a rabbit warren of destruction, dugouts and defensive houses, where Pfeffer-Wildenbruch had his headquarters and planned a desperate breakout for 11 February. Surrounding his position were the remnants of the 'Florian Geyer' SS-Regiments 15 and 16 making their last stand, as were Panzerjäger-Abteilung 8, SS-Flak-Abteilung 8 and the Hungarian Maria Theresa 52nd and 53rd Regiments. What was left of 13. Panzer-Division also withdrew to the citadel, along with the few troops left of the 4. SS-Polizei-Division commanded by the young, popular and cavalier SS-Oberführer Helmut Dörner.

Despite Hermann Balck's disparaging remarks about the unreliability and combat ineffectiveness of these units, their commanders had stayed with their men and together had fought off Soviet attacks for nearly two months, facing in excess of 250,000 troops and innumerable tanks and artillery pieces. Budapest has become known as the Stalingrad of the Waffen-SS, and their bravery and courageous fighting spirit deserves far more recognition than just being a sideshow in the Second World War Two. Nor do they deserve the disparaging remarks of a talented but retired general trying to defend his legacy.

Whilst execution was almost certain for any member of the SS captured by the Russians, the Wehrmacht survivors continued to display a level of humanity. One of the stories that emerged from the ghetto of Buda concerned the commanding officer of 13. Panzer-Division, the respected Generalmajor Gehard Schmidhuber. A veteran of the First World War, the expansion of the Wehrmacht during the 1930s and the campaigns in France and Russia, and holder of the Knight's Cross, Schmidhuber was an officer of the 'old school'. He was no doubt eminently capable of organizing a breakout had either Balck or Hitler given the order.[439] According to Pál Szalai, a Hungarian police officer and former member of the despicable Arrow Cross Party, it was Schmidhuber who refused to allow the murder of any more Jews in his sector of Buda. Apparently, Adolf Eichmann was implicated in this last-minute attempt to eradicate what Jews were left in the city. Despite his final displays of humanity, Schmidhuber was wounded in the stomach during the final breakout on the night of 11 February; rather than face execution by the Soviets, he is reported to have shot himself. Schmidhuber had recently received a telegram from Hitler informing him that he had been awarded the Oak Leaves to his Knight's Cross on 21 January. Whether he was cheered by this we will never know. In the same group on the night of 11 February was the commander of Panzer-Regiment 13 from 15. Panzer-Division, Oberstleutnant Fritz Kucklick, who was also badly wounded and chose suicide, according to reports from survivors.

Although Balck hoped posterity would support his view that the reason he did not order a breakout was because the officers left in Buda were incapable or undertaking such an operation – and they had run out of vehicles – he ignored Schmidhuber and another experienced divisional commander still able to function, SS-Brigadeführer Joachim Rumohr of the 8. SS-Kavallerie-Division 'Florian Geyer'. Rumohr was a totally committed and ruthless member of the SS, but also very capable. His combat record covered France and Russia and he was liked by his men. Rumohr spent the final evening of his life as follows:

> 'Not long before the breakout began, a dispatch runner from the 8th SS Cavalry entered the command post of SS-Brigadeführer Rumohr. There were several high-ranking officers seated round the conference table (the runner recognised General Schmidhuber, the commander of 13th Panzer, among others), but no serious discussions were going on. The mood was relaxed – very relaxed – and the table was piled high with Schnapps bottles. All thought of rank was forgotten. "Come on and drink up my boy!" General Rumohr greeted the runner. "Once we leave here, we'll be dodging the shit soon enough!" There was no fear, but there were no illusions left either; all of those present realised that most of them would soon be dead.'[440]

It was said that Rumohr was also badly wounded that night during the breakout on 11 February; rather than be carried through the Russian lines by his men, he too chose suicide.[441]

There were therefore a swathe of experienced Wehrmacht and Waffen-SS soldiers able to command respect and, if ordered, plan a breakout, had Hitler or Balck allowed it.

At around the same time that Ruhmor was hosting a farewell drink with his fellow officers, with the constant noise of shelling in the streets above, in dirty and filthy uniforms, unshaven for days and having haunted, bleak and starving faces, Pfeffer-Wildenbruch was sending his last messages direct to Balck at 6. Armee headquarters. He laid out the exact time, direction and places of assembly for his breakout operation, requesting the air and ground support that he needed in order at least to distract and occupy the Russians:

'IX. SS-hng.hdt RADIO TELEGRAM 5.50 pm

1. The supplies have been used up, the last bullet in the tube. The choice is between capitulation or the massacre of the defenders without a fight. Therefore, I will attack with the last German parts, soldiers and Arrow Cross troops capable of fighting.
2. On the 11th of II [February], I will break out. I would like to be admitted between Szomor and Máriaholm. In case radio is not possible there, I will advance to the Pilis Mountains. I would like to be admitted there in the NW area of Pilisszentkereszt.
3. Light signal: 2 times green own team. Hallmarks for our troops and planes: spreading of jackets and canvasses in the shape of swastikas and waving.

Password: Hindenburg – Hitler

4. I ask for food and care for the wounded.
5. By the 12th of II strong fighter defence and bomber deployment are needed for the elg. Reserves and elg. [*sic*] To combat movements in the specified area, as well as to protect our own movement in a southwesterly direction. I call for the engagement of enemy forces by all means on all fronts.

**Pfeffer-Wildenbruch / Balck Army Group,
1/A. Nr. 225/45 G. Kdos**'[442]

Although this telegram was discovered in the files of Heeresgruppe Süd after the war, Balck makes no reference to this or any other communication from Pfeffer-

Wildenbruch in his diary. Balck is also silent regarding what, if any, measures were taken in response to the requests for diversionary fire or supporting air cover (of which there would be none), and makes no reference at all to what support he ordered for the breakout on the night of 11 February. This is definitely an area for more historical research. The ability of 6. Armee and its artillery units close to Buda to disrupt Soviet positions was considerable, yet the currently available evidence seems to suggest that the three massive breakout groups did so completely alone and without any diversionary help, either from 6. Armee or its subordinate IV. SS-Panzerkorps.

SS-Obersturmbannführer Kurt Portugall had been the commander of a Flak battalion of 88mm guns in Russia, and his small Kampfgruppe fought to the end on Eagle Hill in Buda. Portugall was the holder of the Iron Cross 1st and 2nd Class as well as the German Cross in Gold for his leadership Russia, and had destroyed numerous tanks in the fighting on the streets of Budapest. He was to be one of the extremely lucky survivors of the fall of Budapest. Captured on Rose Hill, he expected immediate execution as his combat smock was torn open, revealing not just his SS runes but also his decorations for bravery. Able to speak some Russian, he was taken to a Russian major who (according to the 'Axis History Forum' in 2002) told him:

> 'I have a lot of respect for the combat soldiers of the Waffen-SS. You will shortly be transported behind our lines. In our rear area there are as many swine as in your rear area. I'm telling you leave your SS runes and decorations here; it will be better for your future health. I will not keep your decorations nor will any of my soldiers because we are Guards soldiers – the Russian Waffen-SS!'

Incredibly, Portugall would survive both being taken prisoner and a decade of Soviet captivity. He died in Stuttgart in 1992 at the age of 83.

The 35-year-old SS-Oberführer Helmut Dörner, who commanded SS-Polizie-Regiment 1, would not survive. Awarded the Iron Cross 1st and 2nd Class during the fighting in France in 1940, by the time he was trapped in Budapest, Dörner had gained the Infantry Assault Badge, German Cross in Gold, Wound Badge in Black and Knight's Cross with Oak Leaves and Swords, the latter of which were awarded by Hitler on 1 February 1945, although it is doubtful he ever managed to wear them. Most accounts agree that Dörner was killed in the breakout on the night of the 11th, but according to a member of the Dörner family, Captain Ferenc X. Kovács of the Hungarian Army saw him as a prisoner assembly point on 13 February.

"'They're going to shoot us all dead!" said Dörner lethargically to him. Dörner has not been seen since.'[444]

Another senior Waffen-SS officer trapped in the city was SS-Obersturmbannführer Anton Ameiser, a soldier since 1934 and veteran of the Polish, French and Russian campaigns, where he was awarded the Iron Cross 1st and 2nd Class in the SS-Kavallerie-Brigade. In 1944, Ameiser was posted to 22. SS-Kavallerie-Division 'Maria Theresa', which was composed of volunteer *Volkdeutsche* (those who were racially German). As an SS-Hauptsturmführer, Ameiser commanded SS-Kavallerie-Regiment 52 and already had experience of organizing breakouts when surrounded by the Russians. Three months earlier, in October 1944, two small Kampfgruppen were formed from within the division as they had become encircled at Debrecen, due east of Budapest, by the Soviet spearheads of Marshal Malinovsky's 2nd Ukrainian Front. Together with SS-Hauptsturmführer Anton Vandieken, they counter-attacked the Russian lines to their west, reaching a river and crossing it. Vandieken's group made it to German lines, but those with Ameiser were blocked. Determined to never surrender, Ameiser led his men on a three-week, 200-mile trek behind enemy lines, and on 30 October made it through to the town of Dunaföldvár, just south of Budapest, then into the city itself, where the remains of the division had congregated. For this, the commander of LVII. Panzerkorps, General der Panzertruppe Friedrich Kirchner, recommended Ameiser be awarded the Knight's Cross on 22 December. This was exactly the sort of man who could have planned and led a breakout from Budapest, contrary to Balck's opinion that there was 'little confidence in their ability to mount such an operation'.

Men like Ameiser may have played their parts in atrocities and so deserved what was coming to them, but this does not alter the fact that they were available to organize and lead any breakout attempt and were desperate and courageous enough to attempt it. In the event, Ameiser was wounded by a shell fragment in the head and was flown out of Budapest before the airfield was overrun.[445]

Balck's order to withdraw his forces changed everything for Budapest, with any slim chance of a breakout lost. The intervening period put greater distance each day between those fighting on in Budapest and survival, to the point where, in the second week of February, they could go on no more. Pfeffer-Wildenbruch, at last, decided to disobey his Führer and lead a breakout on the night of 11 February.

On that night, anyone who could and wanted to try to breakout, hobbled, crawled, ran, walked or was carried and moved out in three huge groups through the empty suburbs of outer Buda. The streets had become eerily quiet as the Russians already knew of the breakout attempt and had withdrawn their troops from what was to become the slaughterhouse districts of northern Buda. Unbeknownst to the tens of thousands of troops and civilians, anyone who tried to head north out of the citadel stood no chance at all. The Russians poured artillery, mortar and machine-gun fire into the streets and houses of the northern districts. No thought was given to the murder of innocent civilians alongside SS troops, and it was a slaughter every bit as murderous as anything the Dirlewanger Brigade had perpetrated in Warsaw five months earlier.

Over that night, Soviet forces wrought atrocities across Buda. Of the estimated 28,000 men, women and children who tried to escape, only 5,000 survived to run into the fields and woodlands to the north-west of Budapest and along the main highway that led to Slovenia. In the coming days, the Russians combed the city and surrounding countryside, executing anyone they found in just as brutal a way as the Einsatzgruppen of the SS. The words of the Russian major to Kurt Portugall now rang true: the Russians did indeed have their own version of the SS. The Hungarian defenders of the city were especially cruelly treated, being seen as traitors, particularly by many of their comrades who had defected to the Russians during the battle. A 'regiment' of Hungarian students had defended the university area and held out for nearly fifty days in the suburb of the city – longer even than the defenders of Stalingrad. None survived the breakout. Balck's own words about the fighting spirit of the Hungarians only serve to condemn him:

> 'I knew the Hungarians well and did not have a lot of confidence in their military abilities. They were effective only when fighting in their homeland, and as long as the common soldier understood the goals, then also only in the attack – and less so in the defence.'[446]

In total, only 785 German soldiers made it back to their own lines. Most were from the Panzergrenadier-Division 'Feldherrnhalle', and were led by their temporary divisional commander, Oberstleutnant Joachim-Helmut Wolff. Just 170 men from all the Waffen-SS units made it out of Buda – mostly from the 'Florian Geyer' Division – the rest either mown down by Russian machine-gun or artillery fire or executed after capture. The only recognizable effort made by Balck's 6. Armee to help and co-ordinate with the breakout seems to have been a small 5km corridor created by the always 'calm and confident' General der Kavallerie Gustav Harteneck of I. Kavalleriekorps in the Pilis Mountains. A few dozen civilian and military survivors were able to reach there. Landwehr remarks that otherwise, Balck ordered no support as all available forces were being reserved for the new offensive planned for early March.[447]

One fact that looms out of Balck's memoirs is his wish that the fall of Budapest, and his partial failure, should disappear from history and remain a mere footnote. Balck has often been criticized for his coldness, his inability to work well with fellow senior command officers and his overt critique of the Waffen-SS. However, even more acute was the fact that his contemporaries also disliked his overoptimistic appreciation of his ability to succeed, and when he failed, his inability to admit mistakes and willingness to apportion blame to others. Balck's memoirs extend to 454 pages, but only a page and a half refer to the battle for Budapest, perhaps his most significant and embarrassing defeat.

The capture of Pfeffer-Wildenbruch signalled the surrender of Budapest and the tragic siege was over, but the city never surrendered. Casualties were horrendous on both sides. In Budapest itself, in excess of 50,000 civilians and soldiers were dead, another 60,000 were wounded and 40,000 taken prisoner, most of whom would die of starvation while working in Siberian gulags. Two entire Waffen-SS divisions, one Panzer division and a whole host of other units had been destroyed. Estimates of Red Army casualties in taking the city hover around 80,000 killed and more than 250,000 wounded, which no doubt contributed to the orgy of looting, pillaging, mass murder, rapes and deportations that followed. Even as late as July 1945, survivors from Budapest were turning up; nearly 600 crippled and maimed men arrived at the Austrian border, the sole survivors of the 3,600 wounded left behind in Budapest who had been taken to a Russian POW camp and simply let go after the end of the war. They could not be transported to Siberia, given the terrible state of their injuries. Theirs was an epic two week walk through Hungary, many in bare feet, and many died along the way.[448]

The final offensives – Unternehmen Frühlingserwachen, March 1945

As General der Infanterie Otto Wöhler's Heeresgruppe Süd and Balck's 6. Armee were pushed further west and north towards Lakes Balaton and Velencze, surprising news arrived that they were going to be reinforced. Wöhler had just returned from a meeting with Hitler on 19 February, and Balck noted in his diary that the Heeresgruppe commander was buoyant with the news that the entire 6. SS-Panzerarmee was being transferred to Hungary to throw the Russians back into the Danube; Balck was to support this drive with his 6. Armee, and at the front would be Gille's IV. SS-Panzerkorps.[449]

The Ardennes offensive had not only failed but deeply eroded the fighting power of Sepp Dietrich's 6. SS-Panzerarmee, and a mass of partly reconstructed and mostly partial divisions were taken from the defence of Berlin to try to push the Russians away from Vienna. For the first time, Balck would have the dubious pleasure of working alongside Generaloberst der Waffen-SS Sepp Dietrich, another 'politician' general and former personal chauffeur for the Führer who had been elevated far beyond his capabilities. What Balck could not deny was that, similar to Herbert Gille, Dietrich abounded in charisma and an ability to elevate the morale of his troops to superhuman efforts.

Given Balck's outspoken views on the competency of SS units, it was ironic that IV. SS-Panzerkorps was now his main fighting force. Inevitably, there was an uneasy tension which also infected his relationship with 6. SS-Panzerarmee.

As Balck worked to keep his front lines linear and intact, February also saw the start of the gradual – and secret – movement of 6. SS-Panzerarmee south beyond Vienna and into the positions still held by Balck. The epicentre would be Stuhlweissenburg – Székesfehérvár in Hungarian – which lay south-west of Budapest and north-west of Lake Balaton.

Extraordinary lengths were undertaken to hide Hitler's last gamble to turn the war in the East. To confuse the thousands of informants and spies in the rear areas, divisional cuff titles were to be covered up and code names were given to the units on the move, such as the 9. SS-Panzer-Division 'Hohenstaufen' being called 'Training Group South' and the 2. SS-Panzer-Division 'Das Reich' labelled 'Training Group North'. Some tank-trains were deliberately routed in the wrong direction and through Berlin before heading south to Vienna and then on into Hungary, in order to try to conceal their true destinations. As the Russians liberated Auschwitz in late January and the battles raged around Budapest in February, 6. SS-Panzerarmee was forming up in the rear of Balck's 6. Armee, preparing for what would be Hitler's final offensive of the war.

Hitler's aims for Unternehmen Frühlingserwachen ('Operation Spring Awakening') were to overwhelm the Soviet forces to the south of Budapest and in the Lake Balaton and Lake Velence areas, for which Dietrich's 6. SS-Panzerarmee would be supported by Balck's three corps of 6. Armee – the III. Panzerkorps, I. Kavalleriekorps and IV. SS-Panzerkorps. Having encircled Russian forces, they were to then strike east through to the Danube, cross the river and threaten the entire Eastern Front from the south. Despite both Balck and Dietrich voicing their concerns that such a thrust eastwards would open the entire force up to a flank attack from the direction of Budapest – where a Soviet army of four corps was already identified – and Balck's insistence in a phone call to Generalleutnant Walther Wenck at the OKH that the wet ground at that time of year would make such an attack a disaster, Hitler ordered it to begin on 6 March 1945.

Operation Spring Awakening dominated the southern front during March, and was designed to do what Operation Spätlese had failed to do in December 1944 – to punch holes in Marshal Fyodor Tolbukhin's front lines. While Budapest was now well beyond reach to the north-east, the hope was to force the Russians back as far as the Danube while at the same time recovering and protecting the last German oilfields at Nagykanizsa in southern Hungary. In Generaloberst Alfred Jodl's Nuremburg interrogations, he summarized this decision in the form of a conversation and near-argument between Hitler and Guderian, the latter wanting 6. SS-Panzerarmee transferred east of Berlin to hold back the Russian advances there. Hitler's response was: 'You want to attack without oil – good, we'll see what happens when you attempt that.'[450]

Balck's own description of his role in the elements that composed Spring Awakening is vague at best. It is possible that, at the time he was writing his memoirs, Balck had become tired of the story of the downfall of the Third Reich and did not wish to dwell on defeat in the depth of detail that he had been happy to use for his victories in the earlier years of the war. The ebullient tones of earlier chapters were replaced by rushed and general matter-of-fact accounts of events, Balck also losing objectivity and becoming more embittered as he continued to blame others. But these were written from the vantage point of the 1970s and he had no doubt forgotten the dozens of letters that he exchanged with his wife, Marianne, over the course of the war. Two examples of these letters retrieved from the German archives display a family man, as if he was able to live in two parallel worlds at the same time – one surrounded by death, suffering, blood and in-fighting with fellow officers, and the other a rural idyll with his wife and children in a world that no longer really existed.

Balck was careful not to reveal anything of importance, but he did write the following phrase in a letter home to Marianne dated 7 March 1945, the day after the launch of the final German offensive of the war:

> 'Today was a strange day. We heard about the great changes that are supposed to come soon. That brings hope but also fear, because no one knows what will happen next. People have become weary and it is difficult to believe in a better future.' (see Annex I)

Quite what the 'great changes' were is a matter of conjecture – possibly a final speech from Hitler over the radio hinting at the imminent use of his 'super weapons' – but the 'strange day' could have referred to the start of this last offensive, which was now underway all around him.

The change of gear in Balck's 1970s memoirs may also reflect his awareness that the great final offensive had failed. Nevertheless, there is a clear desire to skirt over what were to be failings on his part in what would be known as the creation of the Jeno Pocket, which developed as the offensive started to fail. Balck himself was not immune to criticism, both at the time and by posterity, yet this hardly forms part of the only currently available (myopic) biography by Stephen Robinson. Without reference to the excellently expressed and intricately detailed *Drama Between Budapest and Vienna: The Final Battles of the 6. SS-Panzer-Armee in the East – 1945* by Georg Maier, Chief of Operations at 6. SS-Panzerarmee, any biography of Hermann Balck is obsolete. Oberst Maier offers us an alternative insight of the actions of Balck in the closing weeks of the war; no longer a forgotten genius of the battlefield but a sly, uncomfortable commanding general, flattered by Hitler with his awards but unpopular with his peers and even untrustworthy.

Balck no doubt had his own sense of what could be achieved with the troops that were left in Hungary and the interplay between the weather, the return of the mud of the *rasputitsa* and the immensity of the Russian forces ranged in front of him. Balck, it seems, had to make the best of what he could in a deteriorating disaster. But Hitler was always looking at the political and strategic implications of keeping the war economy going. The OKW's Warlimont again provides an invaluable insight into Hitler's reasoning:

> 'Hitler considered the protection of Vienna and Austria as of vital importance and that he would rather see Berlin fall than lose the Hungarian oil area and Austria.'[451]

Balck's role in Operation Spring Awakening, March 1945

The 6. Armee played a largely supporting role in this major offensive, which had taken weeks to plan and prepare. It was essentially a flanking action in the north or on the left flank, with Dietrich's 6. SS-Panzerarmee heading for glory on the banks of the Danube, while in the south, 2. Panzerarmee would draw off Russian forces. It was not Balck who was dictating events but the new and powerful Soviet forces heading for Vienna, and their movements would throw him into considerable confusion about how to react and how to keep his forces intact.

Balck's 6. Armee had contracted considerably in terms of size since his arrival on Christmas Eve 1944, with all its units well below full strength. By March 1945, it contained the following formations (details taken from Maier, p.443):

Unit	Commander
III. Panzerkorps	General der Panzertruppe Breith
1. Panzer-Division	Generalleutnant Thunert
3. Panzer-Division	Generalmajor Söth

6. Panzer-Division	Generalleutnant Freiherr von Waldenfels
IV. SS-Panzerkorps	General der Waffen-SS Gille
3. SS-Panzer-Division 'Totenkopf'	SS-Brigadeführer Becker
5. SS-Panzer-Division 'Wiking'	SS-Oberführer Ullrich
Hungarian 2nd Armoured Division	Colonel Vitéz Zador
Hungarian 3rd Army	Lieutenant General Vitéz Heszlényi
356. Infanterie-Division	Oberst Kühl
I. Kavalleriekorps (to become attached)	General der Kavallerie Harteneck
3. Kavallerie-Division	Oberst von der Groeben
4. Kavallerie- Division	Oberst von Nordenskhold
711. Infanterie-Division	Generalleutnant Reichert
25th Hungarian Division	Colonel Kalko

The remnants of 23. Panzer-Division would later become attached to the remnants of II. SS-Panzerkorps.

As in Russia during 1943 and 1944, the difference between these forces on paper and their numbers, condition and combat effectiveness must always be borne in mind.

Disastrously for Heeresgruppe Süd, the attempt at concealing the arrival of 6. SS-Panzerarmee failed. Russian reconnaissance and intelligence had detected the arrival of major SS units in the south, on what they still called the 3rd Ukrainian Front, and noted that they were here rather than defending Berlin; that could only be for the reason of a new offensive action. In response, Front commander Marshal Georgy Zhukov had quickly moved Marshal Fyodor Tolbukhin into place with three massive armies totalling 400,000 men, 7,000 artillery pieces, over 400 tanks and, crucially, 1,000 aircraft – mostly ground-support tank killers. Their strategy was to absorb the coming German attack and then launch their own counter-offensive during March.

The omens were not good for the Germans. Before the offensive began, Dietrich's chief operations officer reported what Balck had already predicted to the OKW:

> 'In the constricted area between Lakes Balaton and Velence the mud became alarming. The closer one came to the ... assembly areas, the more widespread the land was under water – impassable for all kinds of vehicles. It looked the same ... in the enemy area ... a Panzer attack in open terrain under these conditions is out of the question.'[452]

The terrain was rolling hills covered in a light dusting of snow, with gullies and ridges cutting through at hidden angles. This was perfect country in summer for tanks to move at speed, but equally marvellous country for anti-tank defences, echeloned in depth, to destroy Panzers stuck in muddy ravines. Russian defences were certainly in depth – up to 30km in places. Recent research has exposed the extent to which the Russians had been reinforcing their front lines in anticipation of such an attack:

'[B]etween February 18th and March 3rd the 233rd Rifle division had dug 27 kilometres of trenches, 130 gun and mortar positions, 113 dugouts, 70 command posts, laid 4,249 antitank mines and 5,000 antipersonnel mines all this on a frontage of 5 kilometres … there was an average of 17 antitank guns per kilometre forming 23 tank killing grounds.'[453]

For Balck, Gille and now SS-Obergruppenführer Wilhelm Bittrich – commander of the II. SS. Panzerkorps, which was part of Dietrich's 6. SS. Panzerarmee – Hitler's stubborn refusal to work with his commanders and instead to issue a stream of nonsensical demands was not only fatal but also incomprehensible.

By the time Heeresgruppe Süd fired their opening artillery barrages on 5 March, Gille and his IV. SS-Panzerkorps still did not have their forces either in the right place or at full strength. The lack of ground cover had exposed their movements to constant dive-bomber attacks, the motorised infantry had been camouflaged up to 20km behind the front lines and were stuck in the mud, and the only two hard-surface roads in the area had collapsed under the weight of vehicles. Nevertheless, Gille advanced in echelon with what was available. On the second day of Spring Awakening, SS-Brigadeführer Sylvester Stadler, commanding 9. SS-Panzer-Division 'Hohenstaufen', reported two tanks had already disappeared into mud up to their turrets, and their attack bogged down well short of their initial objectives, with Russian artillery causing chaos. Stadler had already experienced criticism from his 6. Armee commander, Hermann Balck, and more was to come.

Right along the line it was a similar story, with all divisions making limited progress. Even the elite 1. SS-Panzer-Division 'Leibstandarte' was struggling to gain real momentum, and it took a monumental effort and heavy casualties for the 12. SS-Panzer-Division 'Hitlerjugend' of 6. SS-Panzerarmee to move nearly 10km on their front by 9 March. As if finally to doom the offensive, snow started to fall heavily on 9 March and Russian counter-attacks also began. From 10 March onwards, Balck watched as Bittrich's II. SS-Panzerkorps fought six new Soviet infantry divisions and worried how he could best hold his own fragile lines.

As with Gille, Balck also clashed badly on numerous occasions with SS commander Bittrich, who in Balck's eyes did not deserve his post-war fame as a successful and self-assured Panzer leader. It was possibly his portrayal by Maximilian Schell in the movie *A Bridge Too Far* that cemented in the public psyche the image of Bittrich as a confident and capable SS divisional commander. However, in the attempted relief of Tarnopol, Bittrich received such a dressing down from Balck over his apparent poor leadership of his division that Bittrich suffered a mild heart attack and was taken to hospital. Indeed, Balck requested Bittrich be relieved of his command and replaced with Generalleutnant Karl Arndt of the 359. Infanterie-Division, who had on more than one occasion demonstrated perfect command and control both in defence and attack. Naturally, Himmler refused the request. Balck was well known and supported by the OKH for relieving whom he saw as incompetent officers: both Generalmajor Johannes Schrepffer and Generalmajor Heinrich Kittel were sacked by Balck for what he considered their inept defence of Tarnopol, and there were no doubt many more whose names have been lost to history.

Balck's gravest error – his demand for a '*Rochade*' and creation of the Jeno Pocket, March 1945

It was towards the last week of March that Balck had perhaps the worst period of his military career. Up to that point, it was only localized resistance and poor surface conditions that were stifling the German advances. From 20 March, however, things changed dramatically as at least twenty-four Soviet rifle divisions and supporting tank corps emerged from the direction of Budapest and attempted to overwhelm the German forces in front of them. Balck and his exhausted men of the 6. Armee felt the full impact.

In the days before this new onslaught began, Balck had recognized the pivotal need to hold the area around Székesfehérvár (in German, Stuhlweissenburg) as 6. SS-Panzerarmee pulled back to save itself from encirclement and oppose the predictable huge Soviet counter-offensive approaching from the north. Balck also seems to have felt that 6. SS-Panzerarmee was better equipped than his own 6. Armee to blunt what was coming, so in the days before the Russian offensive began on 20 March, Balck discussed with Heeresgruppe Süd commander Otto Wöhler his strange and complex plan to interchange the two armies.

In chess, the German expression for the 'castling' move is known as a '*Rochade*', and right in the centre of the Heeresgruppe's front line, Balck asked to be allowed to do exactly this. In requesting permission for this complex manoeuvre, historian Douglas Nash is convinced that Wöhler succumbed to Balck's stronger personality and determination – a Type A commander dominating a Type B personality. This is very plausible, but Balck's motivations for wishing to execute such a huge manoeuvre at such a critical moment seem more sinister. It may well have been that in fighting spirit and equipment, Dietrich's 6. SS-Panzerarmee was more likely to be able to stop what German intelligence sources had reported was emerging. It takes time for information to filter through and evaluate the strength of enemy attacks, but Balck sensed that this was a potentially pivotal moment – one that could overwhelm his weakening army. It is possible that Balck's low opinion of the SS forces was such that he would rather see them defeated than his own Heer divisions, and so wished to push Dietrich and his more fanatically committed troops into facing the onslaught. Given his close relationship with Hitler, if such a disaster did unfold, Dietrich would probably survive in his role, whereas Balck's career may well have suffered a terminal blow. Balck's certain sacking from command, like so many before him, would leave in tatters his reputation for being undefeated. Whatever the deeper reasons for his controversial decision, Balck refused to discuss them in his memoirs – but we can.

Balck remained highly critical of the SS units and especially the IV. SS-Panzerkorps under Gille, with whom Balck had been having vehement disagreements since the battle for Budapest. In reference to the early phases of Spring Awakening, Balck wrote:

> 'I frequently was forward with the [IV. SS-Panzer] corps and I had requested the removal of the command group, to include the commanding general [Gille]. They were not up to the operational task. I could not do anything about them through performance evaluations because I could not get around Himmler's irrationality. I tried to get them removed for health reasons ... but we would have been worse off with his replacement.'[453A]

Sadly for history, we have no idea who this replacement for Herbert Gille might have been, but this attitude of mind towards the SS formations could suggest that Balck was preparing the ground to shift blame onto Gille and the SS. We already know that Gille had been unprepared at the start and that his units faced terrible conditions; March was almost the worst month of all to fight on the Eastern Front. However, in contrast to Balck's statements in his memoirs, we also have Georg Maier's detailed accounts of the fighting of 6. SS-Panzerarmee. More specifically, we can see that Gille and his two SS divisions were actually not only fighting well in their area, but also compensating for the disintegrating Hungarian 2nd Armoured Division on his flank 'west of Zámoly'. This collapse of Hungarian units was a disaster for the 6. SS-Panzerarmee and for Gille's IV. SS-Panzerkorps.[453B]

Between 14 and 19 March, there were a mass of telex communications between the various Heeresgruppe Süd headquarters and Wöhler himself over the two choices that could be taken. Wöhler could either try to reinvigorate the earlier attacks of Spring Awakening which had ground to a halt all along the line, or withdraw and reposition in the face of what was now looking like the main Russian counter-offensive. On top of this, Balck wanted Wöhler to interchange the field positions of two large army-sized formations. Naturally, Hitler and the OKH were adamant that there should be a resumption of the attack, while on the ground the fear was that the weight of Russian pressure could see their whole position collapse. According to the war diary of 6. SS-Panzerarmee, Balck continued to exude his usual overconfidence about what could be achieved, but at the front the situation seemed increasingly precarious.

Balck's normal positivism about his chances of success was no longer convincing to many of his fellow commanders, who were on the point of ridiculing this as now being actually dangerous to them all. Wöhler was so unconvinced of Balck's reports that his units were holding and winning that he decided to see for himself. He was concerned that Balck may have been underestimating the degree of Russian pressure on his lines, especially as the collapsing Hungarian units caused problems for the whole of Heeresgruppe Süd. After meeting Balck, Wöhler left for posterity a series of handwritten notes titled 'For the War Diary of Army Group South', including:

'15 March 1945: Commander-in-Chief went to Armeegruppe Balck and to the 6. Panzer Armee to discuss the situation and other details as well. Consistent clarity. General der Panzertruppen Balck displayed his well-known optimism in his estimate of the situation, even where it was out of place.'[453C]

Even more vehemently, Georg Maier comments:

'This can only mean that Balck had erroneously evaluated the situation. To include such a remark in the war diary for posterity, for the "history of the war", concerning the commander in chief of a field army, a man who had even commanded a field-army group, was a sharp and bitter criticism. It not only expressed General der Infantrie Wöhler's annoyance at General der Panzertruppe Balck's carefree highhandedness towards Heeresgruppe Süd, but it also characterised Balck's situation estimates as "self-serving estimates".'[453D]

In the end, whether succumbing to pressure from Balck or seeing a major problem unfolding, Wöhler pressed the OKH for the *Rochade* order for Balck's 6. Armee and 6. SS-Panzerarmee, which was agreed, despite the precarious state of the front lines. Both headquarters would have issued streams of movement orders to their various subordinate units to get moving and relocated on the nights of 16–18 March. Dietrich and Balck theoretically took over their new theatres, as this order from the War Diary of Army Group South (as quoted in Maier, p.458) shows. It was sent at 0430hrs on 19 March:

> 'MA: RH 19 V/63
> **Exchange of Sector Command and Control Responsibilities Between 6. Armee and the 6. Panzer-Armee.**
> 1. As of 19 March
> a) The 6. Armee is to assume the front sector between its former right boundary and the southwest point of Lake Velence.
> b) The 6. Panzer-Armee is to assume the front between the southwest point of Lake Velencei and the Danube.
> Assumption of sector command 14.00 hours.
> Signed Wöhler
> OB Army Group South
> 1a 996/45'

If Balck's intention was to make sure that his own 6. Armee did not bear the full brunt of the coming attack, and instead leave that to the SS, he was for the first time totally in 'Chaos' and not 'Order' – and his memoirs are elusively vague.

As the movement orders were being carried out, so the Soviet attacks increased in intensity. With the interchange only partly complete, whole divisions became embroiled in moving and fighting while Russian forces simply cut through entire chunks of the front lines. In his memoirs, Balck ignores this entire episode, merely clinging to his cracked record of blame:

> '[T]hey [the SS] should have been able to stop the Russian threat without difficulty. But they were falling apart rapidly. Their large numbers of incompetent leaders wrought havoc.'[453E]

The use of the 'us' and 'them' descriptions is very revealing. There is little doubt that Balck had long given up on any professional rapprochement with the leadership of the SS formations, because he had no respect for them. Although Balck was willing to praise the actions of more junior levels of the SS for their steadfast heroism, his professional disdain for the SS in general was such that it seems they were almost fighting a separate war to the one he and his troops fought. Balck's view in 1981 that the SS formations should have been able to deal with the Russian advances 'without difficulty' was still firmly held nearly forty years after the event. Even at the time, his views were ridiculed; he refused to accept any other explanation. Oberst Maier's monumental war diary of 6. SS-Panzerarmee contained various references to Hermann Balck which carry a weighty disdain for their once-admired Panzer commander. Maier was a significant officer and, as Chief of Operations for Sepp Dietrich, pivotally placed to view the conversations that were taking place. In addition to Balck's 'self-serving' estimates of enemy actions, Maier is critical of Balck's reputation for making sweeping statements about what could and could not be achieved. Gille was sending in reports of heavy fighting and that his men were holding, but only Balck thought that the situation was anything other than precarious:

> 'Still, at the headquarters of the 6. Panzer-Armee, one had calming news from General der Waffen-SS Gille. His corps was in well-constructed positions and capable of defending against even a major enemy attack of long duration. At no time in the field-army headquarters [however] did one share General der Panzertruppe Balck's facile optimism.'[453E]

Days earlier, during Spring Awakening, Maier had recorded another swipe at Balck when, in reference to the ninth day of fighting on 14 March, he wrote:

> 'General der Panzertruppe Balck seemed to sense the coming debacle on his field army's left wing, which had quite irresponsibly been shorn of forces (most recently the 6. Panzer Division). However, he would very cleverly extract himself from the affair ... while pushing the "black spot" off on someone else. [This would be his criticism of Gille.]'

Ultimately, it was the soldiers who suffered from this lack of mutual co-operation. In the area south-east of Lake Balaton and south-west of Lake Velencze, the Soviet assaults increased in ferocity, and units of both 6. Armee and 6. SS-Panzerarmee were caught trying to re-establish their positions. According to personal discussions with author Douglas E. Nash:

> 'Two corps, one (the 4th SS) with two SS divisions (the 5th and 9th SS-Panzer), the III Panzer Corps with the 1st and 3rd Panzer Divisions and 44th Infantry Division were trapped inside the [Jeno] Pocket (some 50,000 men) and all five divisions were severely mauled during the breakout. As a result, the front line of Sixth Army collapsed, forcing its troops to retreat about 80km along the northern shore of Lake Balaton.'

Across Balck's 6. Armee, German combat units were caught between relocating to their new positions and fighting Russian tanks and infantry pouring across the front lines.

Balck makes time in his memoirs to continue to criticize the command of 9. SS-Panzer-Division 'Hohenstaufen'. He had ordered SS-Brigadeführer Stadler and the 'Hohenstaufen' to remain in position covering the retreat units out of the Jeno Pocket, including the 44. Infanterie-Division. But according to Balck, Stadler simply decided that he had had enough and moved his division without proper consideration for the 44. Infanterie, which was left exposed.[454]

Like so many other German units, 44. Infanterie-Division had a rich pedigree, having been raised in the Wehrmacht expansion of the late 1930s and then fought across Poland and France, as well as in Barbarossa and at Kiev. The division ceased to exist when it fell as part of the Stalingrad disaster as part of the original 6. Armee.[455] The division was reconstituted around a small cadre of specialists who had been flown out of Stalingrad before it fell, and fought at Monte Cassino in Italy before being sent to the Eastern Front for a second time, fight for its survival in the Russian offensives of November and December 1944 during which it lost much of its establishment.

In Spring Awakening, what was left of the 44. Infanterie-Division was commanded by Generalleutnant Hans-Günther von Rost and was part of LXVIII Armeekorps in the attacks south of Lake Balaton, where it became entangled with elements of the 9. SS-Panzer-Division 'Hohenstaufen', 5. SS-Panzer-Division 'Wiking' and 1. Panzer-Division. Once the 'Hohenstaufen' had gone, trying to escape the developing Jeno Pocket, the 44. Infanterie was alone, without many vehicles and exhausted. According to Erickson, a narrow corridor still existed through which the three divisions could escape. It was during this breakout on 23 March that Rost was killed when a shell hit the half-track in which he was travelling.[456] Balck stated the 44. Division was 'badly mauled', and he was right; in two days, it lost more than 2,000 men and sixty-five officers. What was left as a fighting unit fell back towards Radkersburg on the Austrian border.[457] Balck tried to find out why the 44. Division had been overwhelmed by Russian forces and wiped out, putting the blame squarely on Stadler and the 'Hohenstaufen'.

Balck regretted that the 44. Infanterie-Division was the only major formation under his command that was destroyed during the entire war, but ignored the fact that his attempted *Rochade* manoeuvre left far more dead and wounded on the battlefield than just the men of Rost's division. In retrospect, it is almost inconceivable that Balck, a tactical genius, could have recommended such a large-scale movement of forces in the knowledge that a substantial Russian counter-offensive could come at any moment. The figures speak for themselves.

A review of the war diary of Heeresgruppe Süd between 17 and 23 March 1945 shows just how brutal the fighting was in these largely forgotten few desperate days. The following unit reports show the unnecessary losses inflicted on them by Balck's *Rochade* manoeuvre ('tanks' referring to operational tanks, heavy anti-tank guns, mobile assault guns and mobile tank destroyers):

'III Panzer Corps		
Lieutenant General Breith	**17 March**	**23 March**
1st Panzer Div.	15 Tanks	5 tanks
	16 Heavy AT guns	4 Heavy AT guns
3rd Panzer Div.	23 Tanks	8 Tanks
	7 Heavy AT guns	11 Heavy AT guns
I Cavalry Corps		
Lieutenant General Harteneck		
23rd Panzer Div.	25 Tanks	3 Tanks
	12 Heavy AT guns	15 Heavy AT guns
IV SS-Panzer Corps		
SS-Obergruppenführer und General der Waffen-SS Gille		
5th SS-Panzer Division 'Wiking'	20 Tanks	2 Tanks
	9 Heavy AT guns	5 Heavy AT guns
9th SS Panzer Division 'Hohenstaufen'	58 Tanks	36 Tanks
	15 Heavy AT guns	15 Heavy AT guns

From these reports on combat losses and heavy armour capability can be seen that the only division that survived almost intact was 9. SS-Panzer-Division 'Hohenstaufen'. Its commander, Stadler, could clearly see what was coming and moved his division quickly westwards firstly to defend the only escape route open for the rest of 6. Armee – as Balck himself had ordered – and then moved quickly away before it was too late. Although Stadler received the approbation of Balck at the time and later in his memoirs, and it also meant the end of 44. Infanterie-Division, Stadler clearly made the right decision for his men. Balck, on the other hand, did not.

This was not the dashing and 'leading from the front' Balck of Poland, France or Greece, nor was it the Balck of the Chir River, where overconfidence was a requirement for success. Instead, this was a Balck recognizing that defeat was inevitable, and in his search for scapegoats other than himself he blamed the SS. This was a man, in the convincing testimony of Oberst Maier, who was willing to deceive his superiors in order to get his own way. At a time when the German Army was almost on its knees and where he needed to find a new métier, it was a new method of leading from the front where his reputation could be maintained in the eyes of the Führer – not onto victory but into defeat, a defeat that he did not wish to accept was anything to do with him. It was no longer the glorious 'Panzer Commander' of Richardson's biography, his neck replete with all that Nazi Germany could bestow. The diamonds of his Knight's Cross were tarnished with the dust and sweat of battle, and so too was his reputation as the respect of his fellow officers evaporated. The shifting of the 'black spot' onto the SS secured him an infamous reputation as the war drew to a close.

With Spring Awakening an abject failure, the last week of March saw Balck witness a paradoxical mixture of sacrifice and cowardice on a significant scale. On 23 March, the war diary of 6. Armee recorded a message from Balck to Guderian:

> 'At 09.35 the commanding general of Sixth Army called. He reported that the units were no longer fighting as they should. Some are saying that the war is over anyway and they do not want to get killed before the end of the war.'[458]

According to Balck, the majority of troops disobeying orders and trudging towards Austria were from SS units. Guderian reported the same to Hitler and Himmler, whereupon, in early April, Hitler lost control and fumed that all SS units should remove their cuff titles from their uniforms as a mark of punishment. This ill-advised order merely exacerbated the problems. Sepp Dietrich was so enraged he is reputed to have sent his 'Das Reich' cuff band back to Hitler in a piss pot! It is now that Maier reserves his most vehement criticisms of Generaloberst Hermann Balck during the concluding phase of the war in Hungary.

29 March 1945 – a momentous day

In Berlin on 26 March, Heinrich Himmler had a meeting with the Führer – it would be the last time they saw each other. Himmler arrived in Hungary two days later, determined to take control and stop the Russian advance on Austria and Germany, and met with Wöhler at the headquarters of Heeresgruppe Süd. During part of that meeting, Himmler specifically rejected the criticisms of Balck regarding Stadler and the performance of 9. SS-Panzer-Division. If there was ever any doubt as to why Balck was never promoted to Generalfeldmarschall, then his ongoing rancour with Himmler – something that had been going on for years – is the answer. According to Wöhler, in what is a masterly use of understatement, Himmler 'energetically' defended the performance of the SS, especially the 'Hohenstaufen', in the face of criticism from Balck of the SS, 'whose leadership abilities the field army did not find satisfactory'.[458A]

The priority for the whole Heeresgruppe now was to simply hold the line and buy time for Hitler, but events were no longer under their control. On 29 March, from within 6. SS-Panzerarmee, Georg Maier describes how Soviet probes by 18th Tank Corps and 5th Guards Cavalry Corps had broken through at Zalaegerszeg, which was in the centre of Balck's 6. Armee, causing 2. Panzerarmee to have to withdraw in order to avoid encirclement. The Russians had learnt from the German tank tactics of 1941 and 1942 and were playing the outmanoeuvred Germans at their own game. Balck was now on the receiving end of tactics that he and Guderian had played key roles in devising. According to Maier, 6. Armee was on the verge of collapse. Balck mentions none of this in his memoirs.[458B]

Soviet breakthroughs on the 6. Armee front also threatened the position of I. SS-Panzerkorps. The once-proud and over-equipped divisions within that esteemed corps – 1. SS-Panzer-Division 'Leibstandarte-SS Adolf Hitler', 3. SS-Panzer-Division 'Totenkopf', 12. SS-Panzer-Division 'Hitlerjugend' and 232. Panzer-Division (the former Panzer-Division-Tatra) – were already ravaged and down to the size of Kampfgruppen. In the early hours of 29 March, further Soviet breakthroughs at Steinamanger and Güns, both in Balck's 6. Armee front, had also been critical. Amongst Wöhler's army commanders, however, it was only Balck who continued to hold out for a 'no withdrawal' position, still maintaining his now almost ridiculed positivity, that he was being successful and holding his front. Balck would later blame the failure and treachery of the Hungarian Szt László Division for allowing the Soviet advance, but this was not true. Nevertheless, the end was near. At 1145hrs on 29 March, Wöhler beseeched Berlin for permission to withdraw and regroup, telling Guderian that 'this step was unavoidable and it should be done immediately'. This was no longer about oil, but saving Vienna. At 1250hrs, Wöhler further briefed Guderian that the Soviets had reorientated north and were now heading directly for Vienna. Although Volkssturm (militia) divisions, plus the 356. Infanterie-Division, were trying to block this move, he said they would not hold. Balck's 6. Armee seemed to be collapsing.

It was now that one of the strangest events of Balck's story occurs. As further news arrived at Heeresgruppe Süd that Balck's 6. Armee was in a state of chaos, all communications were lost with Balck's headquarters at 1520hrs. Balck was known to now be 'drifting to the west' and had moved his headquarters, but the usual flow of radio reports stopped. The war diary of Heeresgruppe Süd contains no reports from 6. Armee at this juncture, a fact confirmed by Maier in his book. There was a desperate need to detach I. Kavalleriekorps and the 9. SS 'Hohenstaufen' from 6. Armee, and without any reference to the elusive Balck, Wöhler now ordered this to happen. An entire corps and a division were removed without the army commander's involvement; Balck does not even mention this in his memoirs. Furthermore, Balck never mentions that a whole artillery command was also transferred from 6. Armee to 6. SS-Panzerarmee at 1755hrs. According to Maier, 'Later on, Balck was not able to remember any of this either.'⁴⁵⁸ᶜ It was not until 1945hrs on 29 March that a transmission was once more received from 6. Armee; Maier reports the contents:

> 'The enemy made the breakthrough he had been striving for in the area of operations of 6. Armee after 14 days of bitter struggle. He succeeded in pushing into Steinamanger in attacks from the southeast, east and north.'⁴⁵⁸ᴰ

Maier calls this a 'mild description', but in fact it reads almost like a press release or even an obituary: curt, but containing enough self-praise hopefully to protect his job. According to Maier, for Balck it was just a matter of 'who was selected this time to act as a scapegoat'.⁴⁵⁸ᴱ The disdain and repugnance that Maier held towards Hermann Balck would not have been restricted to himself alone. Indeed, it seems likely that Balck was disliked throughout the SS command as much as he loathed them. Maier goes on to say, 'It soon became clear when Balck further signalled that IV SS-Panzer Corps would be better attached to 2 Panzer Army', suggesting that communications between Gille and Balck had finally broken down altogether and that Balck had blamed Gille for the collapse of his 6. Armee. After the war, there would be years of hatred from former members of the SS towards Balck, whom they considered arrogant and a snake in the grass. Maier is clear – Balck's actions against the SS 'lay deeper and somewhere else', as he carefully and subtly directed his army closer to the Americans in order to ensure that he was in a position to surrender to them rather than be captured by the Russians. This drift to the west and south-west is what caused the collapse of the front lines, as if Balck was fighting his own final campaign irrespective of the SS units on his flanks, whom he despised, and who were then left exposed.

But what were these 'deeper' reasons that Maier refers to? Balck had his own agenda. We are not privy to what this was, and now never will be. However, the fact that he had been relegated from commanding a larger formation – probably due to whispers from Himmler into Hitler's ears – left Balck with the inflated ego of a former army group commander and angry enough at the SS for him to act as he did, securing the survival of himself and his men in a war that had long since been lost.

The Hungarian Szt László Infantry Division

There was one other event concerning Hermann Balck that needs discussion before his military service ends, and that concerned the Hungarian Szt László Infantry Division. Maier is keen to point out the following excerpt from Balck's memoir:

'At the centre of the front the newly reconstituted Hungarian Szt László Division, which had fought well earlier, turned its weapons on us after deserting to the enemy and attacked us together with the Russians.'[458F]

Balck, it seems, had driven out to where the Hungarian division was meant to be, and as he could not find it, assumed that it had defected en masse to the Russians. There were plenty of examples where this had happened, and Hungarian troops were indeed now attacking German positions. But according to Maier at 6. SS-Panzerarmee headquarters, this accusation – about what was an elite infantry division – was totally false. Maier was vehemently backed up in his claim by SS-Obersturmbannführer Manfred Schönfelder, Gille's chief of staff at IV. SS-Panzerkorps, who wrote after the war:

'The Szent László Division never deserted and never attacked us along with the Russians. The advance of the Russian tank corps towards Graz was not the result, but the cause of the corps' movement.'[458G]

These decisions and actions by an experienced commander like Balck might be judged more generously when we consider the context of events, emotional pressures, inaccuracy of maps at this time, exhaustion and weight of command in the face of a Russian onslaught which had been going on since 1943. However, even thirty-plus years later, Balck had not reconsidered or even softened his stance. In 1977, he would give an interview to *Welt am Sonntag*, a German Sunday newspaper, in which he again, according to Maier, 'repeated his false, unjustified and shameful accusation' against the remaining officers and men of the Szt László Division. Following this interview, word spread across Europe and a 'storm' of protests flooded the airwaves, newspaper articles and letters columns as former officers scolded and berated Balck for his opinions. It turns out that those opinions were actually based on misinformation from Russian *agents provocateurs*. There were also other generals, former comrades of Balck, who now spoke out against him. General der Kavallerie Gustav Harteneck, the former commander of I. Kavalleriekorps in Balck's 6. Armee, and General der Gebirgstruppe Hubert Lanz, who had commanded the XXII. Gebirgskorps in

2. Panzerarmee, both wrote to *Welt am Sonntag* stating that Balck was incorrect. Yet even this did not stop Balck from reiterating his views when his memoirs were published in the 1980s.

Before the war ended, Balck and his 6. Armee staff had one last opportunity to position themselves in luxurious surroundings, requisitioning the castle of a Hungarian count. As the Wehrmacht retreated in the East, so the old world closed down, but not before the local and national aristocracy had one final party. Balck relates how the ballrooms and terraces were thronged with ladies in beautiful silk dresses, covered in jewels, while uniformed retainers and servants took silver platters of the best foods that could be found to guests who danced until the early hours. This was a ritual played out in the coming weeks in numerous feudal estates and palatial homes across old Europe in Hungary, but also in Romania, where, once the noble families had escaped, the Russian occupiers arrived and were going to stay:

> '[A] spectacular ball was held … by then there were Communist party spies everywhere, but, nevertheless, the ball was held and everyone who was still there attended and, not only that, but they delved into their strong boxes and produced with a flourish every last tiara and diamond necklace, every pearl, brooch and earring that they could muster.'[459]

Defending Styria and the Semmering Pass, 16–27 April 1945

In the final section of the Balck memoirs is an account of another series of dramatic events that is sadly not reflective of the gravity they deserved.

Across the southern front, Russian forces were closing in on the borders of Austria. As 6. Armee withdrew north-west towards the Austrian region of Styria, Balck at last tried to tie his forces to the right (or west) with 2. Panzerarmee, commanded by General der Artillerie Maximilian de Angelis, and to the left (east) with 6. SS-Panzerarmee and Sepp Detrich, the latter now in almost full retreat.

Balck's aim seems to have now been in line with the OKH and Wöhler: to delay Russian forces as much as possible, thereby buying time for Wehrmacht forces and the hundreds of thousands of displaced Hungarian and Romanian civilians trying to surrender to the Americans approaching from the west. At the same time, Balck wanted to ensure that the Soviets did not occupy Austria. He decided that the large, mountainous and scenic Austrian state of Styria must be defended until a ceasefire came into force. When that would be he did not know, but the end in Berlin was not far away.

The Russians moving through Hungary saw Vienna as their main objective, which gave Balck a small amount of time to put some order into the chaos of 6. Armee that surrounded him. He sent off streams of orders regarding keeping the passes and roads into Austria in good order, maintaining some semblance of flow. Balck states that Gille and IV. SS-Panzerkorps – still reluctantly under his command – was instructed to stand in the centre of his line, defending the main routes towards Graz, capital of Styria.

Driving out to inspect where he thought the Szt László Division and 5. SS-Panzer-Division 'Wiking' should be, he found neither. According to Balck, IV. SS-Panzerkorps had ignored his orders and headed north to get over the Rába River, clearly now in full flight from certain death if captured by Russian forces. It was becoming every man for himself. Worse still, the IV. SS-Panzerkorps had merged with the retreating III. Panzerkorps, meaning that 'everything now was mixed into an insoluble mass of humans and vehicles'.[460]

Through the gap where the SS units should have been, five Russian infantry divisions now headed towards Graz, using the Semmering Pass. If the Soviets reached Graz, then the entire 6. Armee and all those in the chaos of the retreat would be cut off.

Meanwhile, a terrible reality was unfolding throughout Styria, which was still controlled by the Germans. The SS and its SD intelligence agency there were trying to complete their 'holy' mission of exterminating the remaining Jews. Styria was packed with prisoners of war, concentration camp detainees and Jews from all over Europe. Over the past two years, the rapid extermination of Jews from Austria and Hungary (around 650,000) – mostly at Auschwitz, Mauthausen and Bergen-Belsen – had created a huge labour shortage in factories, mines, secret SS fortifications and defensive works on the Austrian border. These jobs had been filled by Jews from Yugoslavia and the Ukraine in late 1944; originally destined for Auschwitz, but rerouted into slave labour across Styria. The requests for workers by the RSHA and Nazi Gauleiters was insatiable, Adolf Eichmann – one of the architects of the Holocaust – responding by sending over 50,000 children and old and infirm deportees back to Vienna and Styria. However, as Balck defended the borders of Austria, so the SS and SD needed to evacuate this labour force in case it was needed to build further fortifications on the German border. Forced marches thus began.

In late March and early April, Balck frantically organized the once glorious but now broken 1. Panzer-Division, with its total of five operational tanks and a handful of rocket launchers, to attack Russian forces threatening Styria. Meanwhile, trains, lorries and roads became packed with starving, disabled, sick and infirm Jews and prisoners as the Volkssturm, SS and even Hitler Youth were put in charge of moving this sickly mass of humanity.

As they moved north, there was no food, water or cover at night. Snow was falling and thousands perished on these starvation marches through the countryside of Styria. Horror stories emerged after the war of those too sick to travel being brutally shot or stabbed in full view of the masses. The SS and SD would do anything rather than allow Jews to survive. Indeed, the only gas chamber in Hungary was opened at the Koeszeg Camp on 22 March 1945 to liquidate hundreds of Jews and political prisoners who were in danger of being liberated by the Russians.[461] Even straggling members of the 5. SS-Panzer-Division 'Wiking' turned up, guarding some of these marching columns. They were not where they were ordered to be by Balck, but then so many had lost their way and internal unit organization and cohesion had gone.

> 'This evacuation column had been heavily decimated even before departing on March 28th 1945, since eighty Jews, even though fit for the journey, had been shot by three members of the Waffen-SS "Wiking" Division.'[462]

Members of the Hitler Youth performed their own atrocities, shooting some 300 disabled Jews and those incapable of walking; they had sat down in a field, expecting to be collected by trucks.[463]

Such was the horror occurring in the rear lines as Balck defended Styria. He had a minor success with an attack by Generalleutnant Eberhard Thunert's remaining 1. Panzer-Division. Balck also gave a desperate order to Oberstleutnant Wolff, a member of his staff, to 'Take a Kübel[wagen] with two or three men, fill it with Panzerfausts (single-shot anti-tank weapon) and drive towards the Russian tanks corps and stop them'. Wolff did this, and took a number of walking wounded from a local field hospital to help him. They were never seen again.

On Hermann Balck's orders, drumhead courts-martial reappeared in 6. Armee, and a number of men appear to have been executed for desertion, although these did not make it into the post-war court system as war crimes. By 11 April, new units were still arriving for the defence of Austria, and Balck was able to rely on the heroic deeds of General der Gebirgstruppe Julius Ringel. With his cavalier-style beard, Ringel was tasked with defending the Semmering Pass with a hotchpotch of units which he welded into Kampfgruppe Semmering, or more officially the 9. Gebirgs-Division. Composed of training school NCOs, reserve battalions, airmen from a local airfield and Volkssturm volunteers, Ringel moved speedily around the various combat zones, reporting back to Balck that they were holding. Balck later commented: 'Once again "attaque toujours" [always attack] had resolved the crisis.'[464]

By this stage of the war, victory was assessed by the Germans by how far they had successfully withdrawn on any particular day. Balck, his headquarters staff and what remained of the three corps of 6. Armee fell back to Graz. Again, Maier devotes a lot of time to his condemnation of Balck's actions both at the time and in his later memoirs:

'In contrast to General der Panzertruppe Balck's memoirs, the enemy intelligence estimates of Heeresgruppe Süd confirmed that the renewed "chaos" in the sector of 6. Armee was the main problem along the entire front of the field army group south of the Danube ... Although every field army south of the Danube had been issued orders "to close both gaps by attacking", there were not enough forces left to make a real success of it ... Too many opportunities had slipped by. Heeresgruppe Süd had allowed the Commander-in-Chief of the 6. Armee to get away with his high-handedness for too long, and it had to be paid for in the end. He [Balck] did not maintain boundary lines between his field army and the others as ordered ... He repeatedly allowed his field army to withdraw to the west instead of the north-west as ordered ... the general's war memoir is silent on this point. But there is, however, a sentence in his memoirs that perhaps permits us to identify the real reason for his behaviour.'[464A]

The relevant passage in Balck's memoirs was:

'The Alpine passes behind us were covered with snow and mostly impassable. We had the impression that the enemy was directing his main attack on Vienna; as a result, we were moving out of the hot-spot of events. For the first time in weeks, we could breathe easily.'[464B]

From Maier's perspective, Balck had had enough and was keeping what was left of his army out of the path of the main Soviet advance. He may not have been running, but neither was he fighting. The war was lost anyway, so why waste more lives? Interestingly, the only units that seemed to be left behind in the path of the Russians were those of the 'Wiking' and 'Totenkopf' – both of whom continued to fight for their lives but were operating in dispersed and uncoordinated units, none of which could be accurately described as an intact Kampfgruppe. Such a charge, had it been made at the time and had Hitler not been preparing for his demise and focussed on saving Berlin, would certainly have seen Balck suffer dismissal, and very likely worse. Even the Diamonds on his Knight's Cross would not have saved him. This part of Balck's legacy may have contributed to why he became 'Hitler's Forgotten General'. These events would also explain why Balck was so reluctant to write his memoirs until the very last years of his life, and indeed why they are so superficial when it came to the final months of the war in Hungary. There was much that could tarnish his great reputation.

Throughout the rest of April, 6. SS-Panzerarmee continued to fight desperately against the Russian advance, with reports still streaming in of numbers of Russian tanks destroyed. The I. and II. SS-Panzerkorps were now managing what was left of their divisions on a Kampfgruppe basis – the 'Wiking', 'Totenkopf' and 'Das Reich' were each now units of only around a thousand men. Morning reports to Wöhler contained limited accounts from Balck and 6. Armee, but just enough to suggest that he was defending well, whilst moving steadily westwards in what might be described as a masterfully managed withdrawal. On 30 April, news reached all remaining units in Hungary that Hitler was dead. The front line fell silent for a few days, then the Russians resumed their attack towards Vienna. Would Austria survive intact into the post-war world? Balck tried to keep cohesion amongst his forces which could still resist, but he needed clarity amongst the confusion. Confusion and fear of capture by the Russians seemed to paralyze local attempts at negotiations with the American forces which had pushed deep into Austria and ended up close by. There were rumours that the Americans were refusing to accept the surrender of SS units. In all this uncertainty, on 6 May, Balck despatched his chief of staff, Generalmajor Heinrich Gaedcke, to approach American forces to discuss negotiations for surrender and to arrange a meeting between Balck and their commanding officer. All around, local commanders were now taking matters into their own hands and surrendering to American units, with teletype messages being sent to Heeresgruppe Süd revealing that they had put down their arms. Eventually, even Generalleutnant Heinz von Gyldenfeldt, chief of staff at the headquarters of Heeresgruppe Süd, sent out a final teletype to say 'Good-Bye and Good Luck' as they were collected by a young American lieutenant and driven away in a truck. With typical German efficiency, messages continued to stream around until, one by one, the radios and teletype machines finally fell silent, just like the guns had in 1918.

On 8 May, Balck was formally ordered by the OKH to pull back all his forces to the west and surrender immediately to the Americans. There was no time to spare, and Balck ensured all his forces were moving westwards before he and his staff headed, upriver by boat, to Kirchdorf near Linz, to the west of Vienna. Helpfully, the Russians had stopped attacking as Stalin worked out what he could take and what he could not. Balck was taken to meet with Major General Horace McBride, who was in command of the US 80th Infantry Division and would later command US XX Corps.

The US 80th Infantry Division had been in some hard fighting. Only a month earlier, the division had suffered terrible casualties in the Battle of Kessel, and it was by no means certain that McBride would accept the surrender of Balck and his large number of units in the area. However, detailed notes of this meeting survive, and the pair clearly developed something of a rapport. McBride informed Balck that the clock was ticking fast and that he had until 0100hrs on 9 May to get his men across the River Enns. The US general said that he would halt all remaining movement across the Lizen Bridge, due east of Hitler's mountain retreat at Berchtesgaden, at 0800hrs on the 9th. Balck was completely open with McBride. He did not know how far away the Russians were and neither did he know how many men he had under his command, as so many other units had fled into their ranks. Some of Balck's formations were too far away to make the crossing before the deadline, including much of the 5. SS-Panzer-Division 'Wiking', which had only three days' worth of rations per man remaining (see Annex III). McBride confirmed to Balck that he had already received the surrender of Generalmajor Wilhelm Söth and his 3. Panzer-Division – nicknamed the 'Berliner Bären Division' ('Bear Division from Berlin').

Now, in a rerun of what had happened to the poor souls of Pest during the fall of the Hungarian capital, officers, soldiers and families streamed from every direction towards the Lizen Bridge, knowing that their fate would be in Russian hands if they did not get over the river in time. Staff officers drove along all routes, pushing people forward, equipment was abandoned everywhere and reports regularly came in of local Nazi Party officials committing suicide. Hundreds of German troops dropped their equipment and swam across the river as Russian tanks suddenly appeared on roads from the south-east. Just before 0800hrs on 9 May, Balck travelled over the bridge in his Kübelwagen, complete with its army commander's pennant, and together with his newly acquired dog, his driver and his staff adjutant, they pushed through the crowds. That evening, after checking where his units were going to bivouac, Balck met with American officers. Looking worn out, thin and haggard, pictured in a hip-length leather coat and green paratrooper's trousers, carrying a walking stick and large leather briefcase – and with his Irish Setter at his side – this is how the Second World War came to an end for Hermann Balck.

Chapter XX

Surrender and the Post-war Period, 1945–1982

'He went on winning battles, just as Picasso went on painting pictures.'
(Freeman Dyson, theoretical physicist and mathematician, on
Hermann Balck)[470]

The mood music of a relatively respectful level of communication between Hermann Balck and Major General McBride continued for the few days, but suddenly changed on 21 May. Up to that point, Balck still commanded 6. Armee and spent each day sorting out the locations of his units, overseeing the disarming of his men and ensuring that discipline was maintained; the Americans were in no mood to forgive what they had seen and heard about German atrocities in the concentration camps since the Russian liberation of Auschwitz on 27 January. The music stopped on 21 May when Balck was ordered to meet with McBride, whereupon he was suddenly removed from command and arrested.

Such a change of gear was fostered from the very top, where signs of increasing cordiality between occupation forces and the Nazi state were frowned upon as the search for the most villainous perpetrators of Nazi atrocities began in earnest. Himmler had been captured on 20 May, which seemed to trigger a widescale removal of German commanders throughout the Allied occupation areas. Some senior generals came willingly, while others chose suicide, haunted by their crimes, the humiliation of defeat and what they felt was coming. Nonetheless, it was far better than being in Russian hands. Hermann Balck went into American captivity, and there his memoirs – after numerous pages trying to assess what had happened to Germany – finally end, leaving posterity to piece together his post-war life.

Like all German officers, Balck quickly found himself in an internment camp, the location of which is unknown. As soon as he was able, Balck would have written to his wife and children, who now lived in Stuttgart, telling them he was safe and in American custody. As the Allies caught their breath and took in the new geopolitical considerations of rapidly cooling relations with Russia, there were understandable demands for justice and retribution. Balck was not named at Nuremburg, but in the autumn of 1947 he was charged with manslaughter for the execution without trial of Oberstleutnant Schottke, the artillery officer found drunk at his post who was shot on Balck's direct order on the evening of 27 November 1944, while Balck was OB Heeresgruppe G.[465]

Upon reading the record of the trial, which was held during May 1948, it is possible to deduce that Balck was moved from his internment camp to prison in Stuttgart, where he could at least then have visits from his wife and see his three children.[466] The trial was also held in Stuttgart, and the proceedings provide a great deal more than his memoirs reveal about how Balck saw the incident and the basis on which he reacted. They reveal that on 24 November, after the division had gone into battle:

> '[Schottke] had learned from the orderly officer, Lieutenant Borges, that the division had called in the morning and reproached the [artillery] regiment for lack of support for the infantry in the preceding battle [the battle was the day before on the 24th]. Schottke had objected to this and had the commander of the infantry regiment in question confirm that the accusations were unfounded. He was very angry and also drank a few glasses of Mirabelle Plum schnapps. In the early evening, the officers of the regimental staff organised a joint dinner on the occasion of the retirement [of an officer] from the regimental staff at which Schottke – like the other officers – again drank a few, about 3–4 glasses, of Mirabelle Plum schnapps. The orders for the deployment and use of the artillery that night and the following day had been given beforehand. Between about 7 and 8pm, the Div. commander, Lieutenant General T[rierenberg] called the regimental command post to get a report on the situation. He did not understand Schottke whom he usually judged to be a decent person … and had the impression … that Schottke was drunk.'[467]

Whether Schottke had also been drinking on the 24th is not stated, but he certainly had been on the following day when his commanding general had called; Schottke was ordered to the divisional command post, where he could hardly stand up nor tell the general where his artillery was positioned on a map. Generalleutnant Wolf-Günther Tierenberg of the 347. Infanterie-Division contacted his corps command – XIII. SS-Armeekorps – and requested a new artillery officer to command the regiment. Schottke was ordered to report to corps headquarters the next morning. The corps commander then informed the Army commander, Generalleutnant Otto von Knobelsdorff – Balck's old XLVIII. Panzerkorps boss – and that is when Balck received his call. The court heard that it was not certain at the time that Schottke had also been drunk on the 24th – the day of the failure of the 347. Division to fulfil its mission – and that other factors may have been involved; Schottke himself had been understandably angry at the accusation that he had underperformed. However, he was certainly drunk the next day, and the causality between the two events seem to have struck von Knobelsdorff and Balck as a fair assumption.

Despite repeated requests from both von Knobelsdorff and the corps commander, and even Schottke's divisional commander, that it should be a matter for due process and a formal court-martial, Balck ordered that Schottke be shot immediately. This was carried out on the evening of 27 November. Schottke had even asked for a personal meeting with Balck, but this was refused.[468]

On 25 May 1948, the decision of the Stuttgart court was that Balck had overreached his authority. He received the relatively light sentence of three years imprisonment for manslaughter, with six months taken off for time already served in custody. Balck immediately appealed, and this was heard three months later on 15 September. The basis of the appeal was that Balck was merely following orders; specifically the authorization that he had received from Hitler to get control over the front, where discipline was failing. However, the court decided that it was still Balck's decision to have Schottke executed and that this had not been a mandatory instruction from Hitler. For an intelligent man and visionary general who spent much of his time pondering on how men reacted to battle and survived severe stress over long periods, it seems ironic that Balck had acted in the way that he did. If he really thought that his Heeresgruppe needed tightening up, then surely his reputation would have been enough to do that. To have resorted to execution by firing squad smacks of a desire to ensure that he could not be criticized for leniency.

While Balck no doubt sat and thought about the death of Schottke as he languished in Stuttgart prison, his compatriot and former chief of staff, Friedrich von Mellenthin, also spent over two years in an internment camp, being released in 1947. At some point thereafter, von Mellenthin left Europe and emigrated to South Africa, where he founded Trek Airways in 1953. This large and successful company, which must have been funded by a substantial initial investment, operated until 1994. Von Mellenthin passed away in Johannesburg on 28 June 1997. In that period, von Mellenthin also represented the German airline Lufthansa in Africa from 1961 until 1969 and spent a great deal of time in the USA, forging new business contacts and indeed becoming a very successful businessman.

In the early years after his release, von Mellenthin found time to follow the trend of former Wehrmacht officers and composed his memoirs. His seminal *Panzer Battles* was published in 1956. In line with the exculpatory theme of almost all of these many books, von Mellenthin avoided any controversy or focus on aspects where he or his commander, Hermann Balck, could be accused of any wrongdoing. Those who prefer a romanticized view of the Panzer war on the Eastern Front did and do still enjoy his book, but critics list von Mellenthin amongst those who produced unapologetic and biased interpretations of events, trying to paint a picture where the Wehrmacht was never really defeated – just overcome by the Russian dominance in men and materiel. Like his boss, von Mellenthin painted an image of the Russian as a 'primitive being' with little or no moral balancing mechanism – a brutal and often sadistic enemy. The historian Robert Citino spoke of von Mellenthin's memoirs as 'at best unreliable and at worst deliberately misleading', but nevertheless, they do open a window from the perspective of a staff officer rather than a general and thus provide insights into relationships from a fresh perspective.[469]

It is clear that Balck and von Mellenthin maintained a close personal contact after the war. While von Mellenthin worked on growing his airline business, Hermann Balck initially seems to have worked as a storeman in a warehouse, similarly to many former general officers of all sides. Balck was now a man in his early 60s with no home or pension, so any job would have to be accepted. There are references to von Mellenthin offering consultancy work to Balck, but evidence to support this is lacking. It would, however, seem a distinct possibility.

Undoubtedly through von Mellenthin's business contacts, during the latter part of the 1970s and spilling over into 1980, Hermann Balck and his ever-loyal companion were invited to participate in a series of conferences organized by a research company named BDM. Based in Virginia, USA, BDM was given a contract by the Defense Nuclear Enterprise and the Department of Defense in Washington to prepare observations on NATO tactics for the defence of Northern Europe in the event of a land war with Russia. Such discussions were especially pertinent at that stage of the Cold War, and ironically seemed even more so at the time of writing this study with Russia's war against Ukraine. Perhaps, too, it was a way of creating a swansong for his former commanding officer, while also providing income with a good consultancy fee.

In May 1980, both Balck and von Mellenthin were invited to a four-day conference in the Virginia town of McLean, with a concluding sand-table exercise on the US V Corps in a land battle against forces of the Soviet Union. A 165-page report was published in December of the same year. What became clear from the outset was that the American military had done little to try to understand the nature of warfare with the Russians.

Balck and von Mellenthin were able to startle their audience with insights into how the Russians thought, fought and commanded, and then showed how they could be defeated using many of the tactics and techniques of command that they had so successfully tested from 1943–1945. These included *Auftragstaktik*, the use of mobile artillery moving around the battlefield, the effect of Kampfgruppen as smaller, hard-hitting forces, and the skills of well-trained tank commanders. Throughout the report, Balck maintained his critique of the Russians as unable to cope when missions failed, being dependant on higher orders and unable to act independently on the ground, willing to engage in static tactics of attrition and prepared to sacrifice large numbers of men – much as seen in President Vladimir Putin's invasion of Ukraine.

Unlike von Mellenthin, Balck refused to contemplate writing his own memoirs, *Order in Chaos*, until the late 1970s, shortly before his death. It may have been due to the series of successful conferences in the USA that Balck decided to write them at all. Perhaps he felt that his views were still of value and that it was time to exculpate his own legacy for his three children of a second marriage (his eldest son, we may recall, having been killed on the Eastern Front in 1942).

Who was Hermann Balck and why was he forgotten?

Perhaps the easiest answer to this question can be found in a quotation from Freeman Dyson's outstanding book *Weapons and Hope*, which is also quoted in the foreword to the translation of Balck's memoirs by Carlo D'Este:

> 'He [Balck] went on winning battles, just as Picasso went on painting pictures, without pretensions or pious talk. He won battles because his skill came to him naturally. He never said that battle-winning was a particularly noble or virtuous activity; it was simply his trade.'[471]

For Balck, soldiering was what he had learnt from his father as a young Jäger and in his experiences of the First World War. Analysts of this period must always remind themselves that the men who rose to become the senior commanders in the Wehrmacht of Nazi Germany had been forged psychologically, philosophically and emotionally in the trenches and slaughter of the Great War. None of them ever forgot what they had seen, and it made them hard and pragmatic men with little compassion and a sense of duty that had been fashioned like cold steel in the Imperial period. They were not political men, and here Hitler had a distinct advantage in being able to outmanoeuvre and outthink the solidly loyal Prussian officer corps. Neither did any of them ever think that their abilities would be used, tested and played out in a new world war with a commander-in-chief who would be the leader of a cult dedicated to the racial slaughter of millions of innocents. How could any officer make the emotional and mental leap required to see such events rationally? It was safer to hide within the shadows and declare loyalty to the state.

Balck and those around him applied what they knew to the task regardless of Hitler, as they would have done for any other dictator. But for Balck especially, it was precisely because he was just a soldier that he did not engage in idolatry and self-promotion. His rise to Generalfeldmarschall would have been assured had the war not turned out the way it did. Balck's lack of tact in political public relations showed itself clearly in the diplomatic blunders he showed in respect of Himmler and his SS officers. In time, and with greater diplomacy or subservience, he certainly would have been awarded his field marshal's baton.

The fact that Balck decided against contributing to the US Army debriefing programme and against writing his memoirs until much later would ensure that his name did not become synonymous with the great rush of published works in the 1950s. Had he done so, and put his name alongside von Manstein, Guderian, Warlimont, Henrici, Kesselring and all the others trying to tidy up their image for posterity, then he would not have drifted into the shadows of history. Perhaps this was his aim all along, to become an anonymous past participant in the most savage war in history and to hope that his own military blunders would not be exposed by future historians and writers.

Hermann Balck was the most gifted Panzer commander of the Third Reich. Unlike nearly every other divisional, corps or army commander, Balck proved that he was able to manipulate the enemy with minimal forces and, moreover, display his abilities in all the main theatres of the war – the Eastern, Southern and Western Fronts. He was able to successfully defend as well as attack, fighting almost constantly without physical or emotional collapse. He could work through the most complex of strategic situations, be they in a Berlin building or fighting in France, Greece, Italy, Hungary or along the Chir River. Balck proved himself over and again to be completely versatile, to be not only the equal of Rommel in popularity with his men, but also superior to Hoth, Henrici, Hoepner and von Manteuffel in the Panzerwaffen. He was as gifted an administrator as Blumentritt and – as his Knight's Cross with Oak Leaves, Swords and Diamonds testifies – the Führer saw him as one of his most outstanding generals.

Balck was also, however, something of an anti-hero to his own side. He was an island amongst men, and only von Mellenthin seems to have been allowed to be close to him. When the British press were searching for propaganda reasons as to why they were losing in North Africa, they stumbled across the strategy of creating the myth of 'The Desert Fox' – the dashing, photogenic, adored Erwin Rommel – and the German press followed their lead. A smokescreen was drawn over the British lack of weapons, lacklustre leadership and – notwithstanding Auchinleck's best efforts – constant withdrawals. But despite Berlin's efforts to idolize Rommel, he ultimately failed. He failed to beat Montgomery, failed to hold Africa, failed to retain the confidence of the Führer and was set a task of building works supervisor on the Atlantic Wall – the defence of which also failed. Of course, Rommel could not conquer his devotion to the Führer – very few could, including Balck. And while Rommel was an inspirational leader, in terms of results he failed. When Hitler needed advice on how to deal with the Allied landings in Normandy, it was no longer Rommel whom he trusted. Hitler did turn to Balck on more than one occasion, but he was overawed by the questions and the confidence being shown in him. Rommel knew how to take a compliment and work the system; Balck did not – he was a worker bee rather than a queen bee.

Balck shared more in common with Patton than he did with Rommel, being unpopular but effective. The three men shared similar characteristics in terms of leading from the front, driving their men forward and dishing up victories, but it was Patton and Balck who delivered success on the battlefield. All three shared a love of identifiable marks: Patton had his pearl-handled pistols, Rommel his tartan scarves and Balck his cloth forage cap (von Manstein-style). However, Balck did not share either Patton or Rommel's love of the limelight. As Patton and Rommel gave speeches, courted the press and fed propaganda machines, so Balck was fighting, getting on with the job of winning battles with increasingly under-resourced and exhausted forces, making silk purses out of the sow's ears of destroyed and leaderless units, whether in defending or attacking. And he was always there for Hitler, who was the only person who seemed to matter to Balck other than his family; the hundreds of letters in his archive bear testament to that.

In Balck's memoirs, there is always a sense that he wished Hitler would have listened to him, rid himself of agenda-driven and incompetent advisors, kept his eye on the prize and trusted in Balck's friendship. Balck's naivety, however, exposed him to the blunt truth that narcissistic sociopaths have no friends and cannot be treated as normal human beings. Every decoration that Hitler presented to Balck was a further sign of their mutual respect and, Balck hoped, their closeness of understanding. Yet this did not make Balck an ardent Nazi. For Balck, Hitler was the Messiah who promised everything but was badly advised – with a racist core that so many Germans shared and sympathized with. Perhaps we have to accept that, as Balck did himself.

When we look at Balck's complicity in atrocities, we have to see these against the backdrop of events, the context in which they occurred. The fact that Balck tries hard to avoid blame for the massacres in Italy, the deportations of people and destruction of towns in the Vosges, the summary execution of his officers or the murders of Jews behind the lines in every command position that he held, merely confirms his complicity and shared guilt. Balck's brevity and at times silence on these issues shouts loudly at us from the pages of his memoirs.

Whether he had a choice or not remains a question, but Balck certainly was not the 'ardent Nazi' that Cole liked to portray. He was not a party member and is unlikely to have read *Mein Kampf*. He was, however, a supporter of Hitler, in as much as Hitler wished to restore the greatness of Germany. This makes Balck a nationalist, not a Nazi. Balck wanted to see Germany, and Hitler's policies for a Greater Germany, succeed against the systemic violence and corruption of the Soviet state. The perfidy of Kerensky was forever in Balck's psyche.

The post-war criticism of Balck, especially from former members of the SS, seems to have been justified. His memoirs, because they skirted over or totally ignored the less flattering aspects of his career, only inflamed a certain hatred of this lonely island of seeming ice-cold brittleness. Balck never lost his sense of duty and training from his days as a young officer in the Prussian Imperial Army, where devotion, honour and self-sacrifice mattered more than logic, truth or emotion.

The Communist threat of the Cold War era gave Balck a purpose; he was still fighting the Russians until the day he died. The early 1980s gave him a chance to continue to fight vicariously through the Americans, to prepare for a war which he saw as inevitable – and perhaps still is.

A visit to the grave of one of history's greatest generals is a humbling experience, just as Balck was humble. There is no pomp, no show, no flowers; only dead leaves decorate the tombstone of a man dedicated to soldiering, one who should be seen as not only one of Germany's most decorated soldiers but also one of its most talented. In peace or in war, Hermann Balck acted with the same rigid guiding principles. And because of his steadfast nature, his adherence to his trade rather than to the popularism that characterizes our times, he became forgotten – until now.

Appendix I

Balck's Letters to His Wife as Russian Troops Swarmed into Austria

Transcription

7 March 1945

Meine liebe Marianne,
   Von dir lange nichts gehört. Unsere Post wird seltener und bleibt wohl oft liegen, weil wir es kaum zu fassen vermögen, dass wir einen neuen Sinn für das Leben finden müssen. Ich hoffe, du und die Kinder seid gesund. Hier bleibt alles wie zuvor, doch die Hoffnung auf bessere Zeiten lebt.
   Heute war ein seltsamer Tag. Wir haben von den großen Veränderungen gehört, die bald
   kommen sollen. Das gibt Hoffnung und auch Angst, denn niemand weiß, wie es weitergeht. Die Menschen sind müd geworden, und es fällt schwer, an eine bessere Zukunft zu glauben. Doch wir müssen durchhalten.
   Es gibt nicht viele Neuigkeiten. Arbeit gibt es genug, aber sie macht keinen Sinn mehr. Alles, was wir bauen, wird wieder zerstört. Die Kinder spielen im Garten und versuchen, die Welt zu vergessen. Ihre Unschuld ist ein Trost.
   Ich hoffe, bald wieder von dir zu hören. Deine Briefe sind immer ein Lichtblick. Bleibe gesund, meine liebe Marianne.
   In Gedanken bei dir,
   B.

Translation

7 March 1945

My dear Marianne,

I haven't heard from you in a long time. Our mail is becoming rarer and often gets delayed, because we can hardly comprehend that we must find a new meaning in life. I hope you and the children are healthy. Here, everything remains the same, but the hope for better times lives on.

Today was a strange day. We heard about the great changes that are supposed to come soon.

That brings hope but also fear, because no one knows what will happen next. People have become weary, and it is difficult to believe in a better future. But we must persevere.

There is not much news. There is plenty of work, but it no longer makes sense. Everything we build is destroyed again. The children play in the garden and try to forget the world. Their innocence is a comfort.

I hope to hear from you again soon. Your letters are always a ray of light. Stay healthy, my dear Marianne.

Thinking of you,
B.

Transcription

23 March 1945

Meine liebe Marianne,

Soeben bekomme ich Deine Karte und den Widerhall. Wie schön, dass Ihr alle dort seid. Wir haben jetzt die schönsten Tage mit Regen und Sonnenschein. Aber niemals im Leben habe ich mich von den Eindrücken so tief ergriffen gefühlt, wie es jetzt der Fall ist.

Dein Brief ist angekommen, und ich habe mich so gefreut, ihn zu lesen. Es scheint, dass es allen gut geht, obwohl die Zeiten schwer sind. Mit den Kindern wirst Du viel Arbeit, aber auch viel Freude haben.

Und wie geht es Dir? Ich denke immer an unsere schönen Spaziergänge, die wir früher gemacht haben, und hoffe, dass wir sie bald wiederholen können.

Es sind solche Momente, die Kraft und Hoffnung geben. Hier ist alles wie üblich. Die Arbeit nimmt viel Zeit in Anspruch, aber ich finde immer Augenblicke, um an Dich zu denken.

Es gibt nicht viel Neues, aber es ist wichtig zu wissen, dass wir aneinander denken. Ich hoffe, diese Zeilen finden Dich gesund und glücklich.

Bitte grüße alle von mir und schreibe mir bald wieder.
Mit viel Liebe,
B.

Translation

23 March 1945

My dear Marianne,

   I have just received your card and response. How wonderful that you are all there. We are having the most beautiful days now, with rain and sunshine. But never in my life have I felt so deeply affected by impressions of how things are.

   Your letter has arrived, and I was so happy to read it. It seems that everyone is doing well, even though the times are difficult. With the children, you must have a lot of work, but also a lot of joy.

   And how are you? I always think of our lovely walks, which we used to take, and I hope we can repeat them soon.

   It is moments like these that give strength and hope. Here, everything is as usual. Work takes up a lot of time, but I always find moments to think of you.

   There is not much news, but it is important to know that we think of each other. I hope these lines find you healthy and happy.

   Please send my regards to everyone and write to me again soon.

   Much love,

   B.

Appendix II

Teletype Reports from Army Group Balck and Balck's 1st Staff Officer (1a) Colonel Marcks

Dated 30 December 1944, this is the original order reporting on the movements of SS-Totenkopf and SS-Regiment 'Eicke', the movement of the Dirlewanger Brigade out of Balck's theatre of command and the arrival of other SS units by train.

```
A-Gr.Balck / Ia        KR  Geheim                    30.12.44

        KR-Fernschreiben
            An
                    Heeresgruppe Süd

        Betr.:  Ia-Tagesmeldung.
        Zu Ziff.3:  SS.Rgt."Totenkopf"    Korpsgr.Breith unterstellt.
                    S.He.Pz.Jg.Abt.13 und SS.Rgt.Eicke
                                        Gruppe Pape unterstellt.
                    Restteile der Stu.Brig.Dirlewanger aus Unterstel-
                    lungsverhältnis ausgeschieden und in Marsch gesetzt.
        Zu Ziff.4:  Im E-Transport eingetroffen:
                    Von SS.Pz.Div.Totenkopf  bisher insgesamt 33 Züge
                    Von SS Pz.Div.Wiking     bisher insgesamt 20 Züge
                    Gneisenau-Einheiten:     16/XVII:            1 Zug
                                              7/XVIII:           2 Züge
                                              2/XVIII:           2 Züge.
                    A.Gr.Balck Ia Nr.6746/44 geh.
                                I.A.
                                        (Marcks) Oberstlt.i.G.
```

Appendix III

Original Surrender Transcript between McBride and Balck

SURRENDER OF SIXTH GERMAN ARMY............................

The following, submitted by FRED R. BODKIN (D-702 Tank Bn) is the conversation between Maj Gen HORACE L. McBRIDE, CG 80th Inf Div, and General der Panzer Truppe (US Lt Gen) BALCK, CG Sixth German Army at 1945 hours in KIRCHDORF, Austria.

G. Balck – I wish to introduce myself, I am Gen der Pz Truppe BALCK, Commander of the Sixth German Army.

G. McBride – Does the General wish to communicate with me and if so what are his questions?

Balck – I wish to pay you a visit as well as ask you several questions?

McBride – Go ahead.

Balck – I wish to surrender the troops under my command to the American General but I am afraid the Russians will interfere.

McBride – All German troops which are North and West of the ENNS River will be considered American PWs, however, the agreement made between the Allied and German Governments prohibit troops from moving after 090001 May 1945.

Balck – It is my understanding that I may move troops across the ENNS River, since I want to make sure that they will become American PWs.

McBride – Yes, but all movement will have to cease at mid-night tonight.

Balck – But my troops will not be in American lines when they are at LIEZEN?

McBride – As long as your troops are across the ENNS River, they will be in American lines; moreover, you may move your troops along the LIEZEN-SPITAL Road as far North as the Pyhrner Pass, otherwise as far North and West of the ENNS River as shown on map (McBRide outlines boundary on map).

Balck – How shall I behave towards the Russians who will arrive tomorrow?

McBride – All I know is that Russian troops will not cross the ENNS River.

Balck – Thank you very much; please understand that this was the main reason for my visit as General SOETH'S instructions were not entirely clear to me.

McBride – I have accepted General SOETH'S surrender and all German troops North of the ENNS River will be considered as American PWs.

Balck – I have taken over command of this sector and will follow all your orders, and I shall place somebody else in command of German troops South of the ENNS.

McBride – I shall have a small detachment of troops South of the PASS.

Balck – I can then use all road space South of the PASS?

McBride – Certainly; moreover you are free to move as well as to come and go as you witsh. How many rations do you have?

Balck – I have four days rations on hand for all troops under my command.

McBRide – Go slowly on them as food presents a very difficult problem.

- 1 -

Balck — Certainly, the entire Army has had orders to have eight days rations in their possession of a man. The reason I estimated only four days is, that so many additional troops have straggled into my lines. By the way, my men wonder what will happen to them, when they will be diecharged, and when they can go home.

McBride — I do not know but I assume that they will be demobilized and returned to their homes, but that is not official.

Balck — Please understand that I am out of communications with my rtoops coming in from the East (1st & 9th Mtn Divisions) and, moreover, I have no control over the troops further North which come under the Sixgh SS Panzer Army. (Points out on map boundary between Sixth Germand and Sixth Panzer Armies). My main reason for my visit was to get as many of my troops as possible into the the American lines before the deadline. My troops might do anything if they were threatened to become Russian PWs.

McBride — Do you have any Air Corps personnel under your command?

Balck — Yes, quite a lot, however they are all FLACK or Air Corps ground personnel. One of my Panzer Grenadier Regiments consists completely of Air Corps Pers.

McBride — No flying personnel, then?

Balck — No flying personnel except a few cub planes. Those, however, have been grounded because of lack of fuel.

McBride — How far are the Russians?

Balck — I am not sure. My front lines were approx. there (pointing to the map). Moreover, the Russians showd no intentions to attack, and the bulk of my troops was racing West.

McBride — How many troops are under your command?

Balck — I cannot give you an exact figure since there are a great many small units such as brigades and CTs. I have seven Divisions under my command.

McBride — Which divisions?

Balck — 1st and 3rd Panzer Divs, 1st and 9th Mtn Divs, 5th SS PZ Div, "VIKING", and the UKRAINIAN Div.

McBride — Are all these divisions going to cross the ENNS before midnight?

Balck — I don't believe so, the UKRAINIAN Div is in KAVRNTEN. I couldn't use those men against the Russians; also only a few elements of the VIKING division may be able to cross as they are still pretty far South.

McBride — By the way, did you ever command Army Group "G".
Balck — Yes, I did, last winter.

McBride — Then I guess we met Before at the SEILLE River and at ST AVOLD. Do you have any other questions?

Balck — No, thank you, but could I call General SOETH over the 'phone?
McBride — Certainly.

- 2 -

Telephone conversation between General BALCK and General SOETH.

Balck — Hello, General SOETH, this is General BALCK. I have just surrendered the Sixth Army to the American General. Now get this please.....Contact immediately General BRETT; you know where his Hq is, don't you?

SOETH — Yes Sir, I know.

Balck — Tell General BRETT to immediately start moving all our troops across the ENNS River. Hurry please. All troops must be across the River by midnight, tonight. Everybody who is North and West of the ENNS River by midnight will be American PWs. The American General says the Russians will not cross the ENNS River. Better tell that also to your troops in LIEZEN. But get in contact with General BRETT first. Any questions?

Soeth — No Sir.

Balck — O.K. I am leaving here at once.

* *

By Command of Major General McBRIDE

S.P. WALKER
Col, Cavalry
Chief of Staff.

OFFICIAL:
RICHARD R. FLEISHER
Lt Col, GSC

The original transcript of the conversation between Major General Horace McBride, Commanding General US 80th Infantry Division, and General of Panzertroops Herman Balck, Commander German Sixth Army, relating to the surrender of all German forces to the Americans before the deadline of the agreed cessation of hostilities. Note that McBride comments that they had met before in the battles the previous year at the Seille River and Saint-Avold.

Appendix IV

Hermann Balck's Decorations

Award	Date awarded
Iron Cross 2nd Class	15 October 1914
Bavarian Order of Military Merit	15 November 1914[1]
Iron Cross 1st Class	26 November 1914
Austrian Military Order of Merit	28 February 1916[2]
Knight's Cross with Swords	3 December 1917[3]
Wound Badge in Gold	10 May 1918
Iron Cross 2nd Class (Clasp)	12 May 1940
Iron Cross 1st Class (Clasp)	13 May 1940
Knight's Cross of the Iron Cross	3 June 1940
Panzer Assault Badge in Silver	14 October 1940[4]
Bulgarian Medal of Courage	2 December 1941[5]
Oak Leaves to the Knight's Cross of the Iron Cross	20 December 1942
Swords to the Knight's Cross of the Iron Cross	4 March 1943
Diamonds to the Knight's Cross of the Iron Cross	31 August 1944

Notes
1. 4th Class with Swords.
2. 3rd Class.
3. Hohenzollern House Order.
4. The silver *Panzerkampfabzeichen* (Panzer Assault Badge) was founded by Generaloberst Walter von Brauchitsch on 20 December 1939, and was for members of tank crews only in a Panzer division who had had participated in three engagements with the enemy on three consecutive days. Later, on 1 June 1940, the order was expanded to include the crews of other vehicles and other personnel, and was issued in bronze; it is this that Balck wore on his black Panzer tunic. The original design came from Ernst Peekhaus in Berlin. Later in the war, the number of engagements could be listed in a small feature at the bottom of the badge – up to 100 engagements. Interestingly, the award in silver is mentioned in Balck's memoirs, but his personnel office files state that the award was in bronze.
5. 3rd Class with Swords.

Notes

Chapter I
1. In his memoir, *Order in Chaos*, Hermann Balck displays genuine enthusiasm for his British military pedigree, no doubt underpinning his admiration for the British military *esprit de corps*.
2. The relationship of the Balck family with Osnabrück in Lower Saxony is further demonstrated by the fact the Hermann Balck is buried, with his wife Marianne and other members of his family, on the Hasefriedhof in Osnabrück, where he lived for the remaining years of his life.
3. Balck's father, Wilhelm, was becoming well known in military circles across Europe and in the USA for his detailed books on the use of cavalry in warfare and was certainly an early influence on the notion of *Auftragstaktik*.
4. Robinson, S. *Panzer Commander*, p.257.
5. Newland, S.J., US Army War College (2005), p.58.
6. On his father's death, Walter Krueger had emigrated to the United States when he was 8 years old. Fluent in German, Krueger enlisted for service in the Spanish-American War as a private and would be commissioned as a 2nd Lieutenant in 1901 at the age of 20.
7. *Order in Chaos*, pp.4–5.
8. Balck, Lt General Walter, Vol. II, p.35.
9. Robinson, *Panzer Commander*, p.80.
10. *Order in Chaos*, pp.96–97.
11. The battles of Tarnopol and Budapest are two key illustrations later in this book of how tactical use of tanks changed in the mind of Adolf Hitler from swift mobile units into siege engines.
12. This 2014 article reveals the nationwide concern over suicide rates across Germany in the 1920s and the extreme measures that the German High Command went to in order to cover up the high number of such deaths amongst German officers who felt unable to reach the standards expected.
13. Bonnell, Andrew G., 'Explaining Suicide in the Imperial German Army', *German Studies Review*, Vol. 37 No. 2 (May 2014).

Chapter II
14. *Order in Chaos*, p.5.
15. It was well known that Guderian, Rommel and indeed Hermann Balck were able to have frank and at times brusque conversations with Hitler, and although Guderian finally yelled at Hitler as he was sacked for a second time, they were able to get his attention.
16. See Kinna & Moss, 1977, for a detailed appreciation of the various Jäger uniforms at the start of the First World War.
17. *Order in Chaos*, p.6.
18. *Ibid.*, p.7.
19. See Chapter XVII, where Balck had to deal with large-scale resistance outbreaks from the Maquis as well as form the Vosges Defensive Line.
20. *Order in Chaos*, p.17.
21. See *Order in Chaos*, pp.384–85.
22. As the war turned against Germany, and with increasing losses of general officers through exhaustion and failure, Balck was often furious that he had to watch divisional commanders fail in the most basic of tasks, such as the destruction of the 8. Panzer-Division on 14

July 1944 at Zolochiv, which was entirely avoidable had it been commanded as ordered by Balck. See *Order in Chaos*, pp.354–55.
23. The only officer who seems to have adored Balck was General Friedrich von Mellenthin, his chief of staff in numerous commands.
24. *Order in Chaos*, p.220.
25. *Ibid.*, p.221.
26. *Ibid.*, p.34.
27. Fedor von Bock kept a war diary, which was first published in 1996. A complex yet capable man, his diary covers many aspects of his secret work during the 1920s to expand the Reichswehr under the noses of the inspectors.
28. *Order in Chaos*, p.53.
29. The Nazis merely altered the shape of the standard German Stahlhelm and added the swastika.
30. *Order in Chaos*, p.63.
31. Harding, David P., 'Heinz Guderian As the Agent of Change', p.26.
32. Often created on an ad hoc basis and for a specific task or situation, the only Allied equivalent was the American 'task force'.
33. *Order in Chaos*, p.75.
34. *Ibid.*, p.77.
35. Anton Drexler (1884–1942) was the founder of the DAP and set the core principles into which Hitler threw himself from 1919.
36. Hitler, Adolf, *Mein Kampf*, Ch. 7.
37. *Order in Chaos*, p. 99.

Chapter III
38. Józef Piłsudski (1867–1935) was the true father of the Polish state and one of the most important figures in Polish history.
39. For further information, see Gorka, p.55.
40. *Order in Chaos*, p.125.
41. *Ibid.*, p.127.
42. Walter Model (1891–1945) would rise to the rank of Generalfeldmarschall and fight in almost every European land theatre of the Second World War. His tenacious style was matched by his loyalty to the Nazi regime, and he is perhaps the closest in character to Hermann Balck of all Wehrmacht officers.
43. The Heerespersonalamt – or Heeres Personnel Unit – was formed in 1920 and was tasked with officer selection and then developed into the Wehrmacht Personnel Office.
44. Von Bock appointed Bruno Ernst Buchrucker to oversee around 20,000 additional men in these units.
45. *Order in Chaos*, p.141.
46. *Ibid.*
47. *Ibid.*, p.148.
48. General der Panzertruppe Oswald Lutz (1876–1944) is an often overlooked but pivotal early instigator of the creation of the Wehrmacht's Panzer Troop Command, the Panzerwaffe.
49. Harding, p.31.
50. Baynes, H.H., 'Germany Possessed'.
51. *Order in Chaos*, p.149.

Chapter IV
52. Generaloberst Kurt Haase (1881–1943) would later command III. Armeekorps in Poland and France as well as 15. Armee between 1941 and 1942. He died from heart disease in 1943.
53. *Order in Chaos*, p.157.
54. Not every Reichswehr officer thought as Guderian. In 1933, Reichswehr commander-in-chief General Kurt von Hammerstein-Equord described the Nazis as a gang of criminals and perverts.
55. US Department of Defense, Technical Information Centre audio discussion. Text of the Hermann Balck Interview, 12 January 1979, p.18.

56. *Ibid.*, pp.17–18.
57. General Ludwig August Theodor Beck (1880–1944) was chief of staff of the German Army High Command between 1935 and 1938 and was instrumental in the creation of the German Army Operations Manual, which is still in use today in the Bundeswehr.
58. May, Ernst, *Strange Victory*, p.33.
59. See Cooper, Matthew, 'The German Army 1933–45'.
60. Fritz, Stephen, *The First Soldier: Hitler as Military Leader*, p.54.
61. Hart, Russell, *Guderian: Panzer Leader or Myth Maker*, p.30.
62. *Order in Chaos*, p.164.
63. Balck interview (1979), p.17.
64. See Chamberlain, Peter & Doyle, Hilary, *Encyclopaedia of German Tanks* (1993).
65. *Order in Chaos*, p.163.
66. Weapons.Com, 'German Arms Production' (5 September 2020).
67. General Friedrich Wilhelm Fromm (1888–1945) was another career Reichswehr officer who initially fully supported the growth of the Wehrmacht and Nazi state. He was implicated in the July Plot and executed on Hitler's orders in 1945.
68. *Order in Chaos*, p.169.

Chapter V

69. Manstein, Erich von, *Lost Victories*, p.92.
70. Generalfeldmarschall Erich von Manstein (1887–1973) was a leading Wehrmacht officer who held commands at all levels and was ultimately responsible for guiding the war on the Eastern Front until he was sacked by Hitler in April 1944.
71. Manstein, *Lost Victories*, p.94.
72. *Ibid.*, p.94.
73. *Ibid.*, p.109.
74. Warlimont, Walter, *Inside Hitlers Headquarters*, pp.96–97.
75. May, R.E., *Strange Victory*, p.268.
76. The concept of these rolling raids in front of the advancing tanks had been devised through consultations between Guderian and General der Flieger Hugo Sperrle. If the artillery could not keep up, and were delayed in setting up and moving their guns, then the speed of the advance would be patchy at best, whereas a constant supply of aircraft hovering over the tanks called down by a Luftwaffe liaison officer enabled the tanks to keep moving through the devastation inflicted in front of their advance.
77. *Order in Chaos*, pp.176–77.
78. Robinson, p.31.
79. Mellenthin, F.W. von, *Panzer Battles*, p.22.
80. Netwig had arrived at this exact same point in his life along the same route as Balck – a young officer in the Prussian Pomorskie Artillery during the First World War, then serving in the Reichswehr, promoted to Hauptmann and then he met Guderian at Tank Troops School before leading Panzer-Regiment 1 in the invasion of Poland.
81. Balck interview (1979), pp.22–23.
82. Warner, Philip, *The Battle for France*, p.28.

Chapter VI

83. Fritz, *First Soldier*, p.86.
84. *Ibid.*, p.87.
85. *Order in Chaos*, pp.196–97.
86. *Ibid.*, p.197.
87. *Ibid.*, Footnotes to Ch. 11, 24.
88. Mellenthin, F.W. von, p.28.
89. Horst Ramsch (1914–2003) was a highly decorated Panzer officer, twice wounded and decorated with the Iron Cross 1st and 2nd Class, and the Knight's Cross on 24 December 1944.
90. The famous Field Marshals Ceremony took place at the Kroll Opera House in Berlin on 19 July 1940. Flushed by success, Hitler saw this as a huge propaganda exercise and twelve generals were chosen for promotion.

91. Tragically, once the fighting was over, a number of transport ships were torpedoed and sunk on their return from Greece, mostly from 2. Panzer-Division.
92. Butler, D., *Field Marshal: The Life & Death of Erwin Rommel*, pp.187–90.
93. Warlimont, pp.128–29.
94. *Ibid.*, p.129.
95. General der Gebirgstruppe Franz Friedrich Böhme (1885–1947) was a highly experienced officer of Mountain troops. Charged with war crimes after the war, he committed suicide in prison.
96. *Order in Chaos*, p.203.
97. *Ibid.*, p.204.
98. *Ibid.*, p.204.
99. Homer, *The Iliad*, Scroll 22, line 232.
100. *Ibid.*
101. Robinson, p.96.
102. *Ibid.*, p.100.
103. Oberstleutnant Karl von Decker was also from the north and Pomerania, so shared a cultural heritage with Balck. He was a courageous Panzer leader and became commander of 5. Panzer-Division, receiving the Knight's Cross with Oak Leaves. He committed suicide on 21 April 1945 rather than surrender.
104. McClymont, W.G., *The Official History of NZ in the 2nd WW 1939–1945* (Historical Publications Brance, 1959), p.248.
105. *Order in Chaos*, p.209.
106. McClymont, p.249.
107. *Ibid.*, p.251.
108. *Ibid.*, p.251.
109. See Robinson, pp.114–69.
110. *Order in Chaos*, p.210.
111. Garber, Megan, 'Pilot's Salt', *The Atlantic* (May 2013).
112. Ulrich, Andreas, 'The Nazi Death Machine: Hitler's Drugged Soldiers', *Der Spiegel* (May 2005).
113. *Ibid.*
114. Ohler, N., *Blitzed: Drugs in Nazi Germany* (Penguin, 2016).
115. The wreck of the *Marburg* was recently discovered by Greek diver Gerasimos Sotiropoulos laying in 300m of water. Underwater sonar images show it full of German tanks.
116. *Order in Chaos*, p.459.
117. *Ibid.*, p.217.

Chapter VII
118. *Order in Chaos*, pp.217–18.
119. Klee, Ernst, *Das Personenlexikon zum Dritten Reich* (Frankfurt, 2007), p.529.
120. Guderian, H., *Erinnerungen eines Soldaten* (13th edition, 1994).
121. General Walther Buhle (1894–1959) was a former Reichswehr officer who eventually became Chief of the Organisation Section of the OKH. He was loyal to Hitler and was seriously wounded in the July Plot of 1944.
122. General Fromm (1888–1945), Head of the Reserve Army, was executed on Hitler's order in March 1945 for his association with the July Plot.
123. Excerpt from the Hossbach Memorandum, 5 November 1937.
124. Fritz, p.155.
125. *Ibid.*, 121.
126. Fritz, pp.160–61.
127. *Order in Chaos*, p.242.
128. *Ibid.*, p.244.

Chapter VIII
129. Grossjohan, p.55.
130. See Parrish, Michael, *The Orel Massacres, the Killings of Senior Military Officers* (Praeger, Westport CT, 1996).

131. *Order in Chaos*, p.225.
132. General der Panzertruppe Leo Geyr von Schweppenburg (1886–1974) was one of the pioneers of the new Panzerwaffe. From an aristocratic background, with experience in the First World War and Reichswehr, von Schweppenburg rose to command at both Corps and Army levels.
133. *Order in Chaos*, p.225.
134. Glantz, David, M., *When Titans Clashed: How the Red Army Stopped Hitler*, p.80.
135. Flaherty, T.H., *The Third Reich*, p.168.
136. Balck interview (1979), p.24.
137. *Ibid*.
138. *Order in Chaos*, p.226.
139. Vasily Kuznetsov (1894–1964) was an ideologically committed member of the Red Army, and by 1941 he was commanding Third Army. Loyal and tough, Kuznetsov was one of the few officers who enjoyed Stalin's trust.
140. Erich Hoepner (1886–1944) was a ruthless and talented Panzer commander who openly supported the activities of Einsatzgruppen A within his theatres. He shared Balck's dislike of the Waffen-SS and became a central figure in the July Plot, for which he was executed in 1944.
141. Jones, M., *Leningrad: State of Siege*, p.35.
142. *Order in Chaos*, p.230.
143. Warlimont, p.149.
144. *Order in Chaos*, p.231.
145. *Ibid.*, p.228.
146. Hitler's fury at being openly disobeyed knew no bounds. Hoepner was sacked from the Army in disgrace, his pension removed and he was forbidden to wear his uniform or medals ever again.
147. *Order in Chaos*, p.237.
148. *Ibid.*, p.234.
149. *Ibid.*, p.230.
150. *Ibid.*, p.235.
151. *Ibid.*, p.239.
152. *Ibid.*, p.242.
153. *Ibid.*, p.243.
154. Forczyk, Robert, *Where the Iron Crosses Grow: The Crimea, 1941–44*, pp.131–33.
155. *Order in Chaos*, p.247.

Chapter IX
156. Fritz, p.229.
157. *Ibid*.
158. General Ludwig Crüwell (1892–1958) was another First World War and Reichswehr veteran, and by the time of Balck's arrival had already received the Knight's Cross with Oak Leaves. Crüwell was posted to command the Afrikakorps under Rommel in July 1941. He was taken prisoner in 1942 and became part of the pro-Nazi group of officers at Trent Park near Cockfosters in North London.
159. Riebel was killed soon after, on 23 August 1942, by shellfire south of Stalingrad.
160. Schaufler, pp. 46–51.
161. Grossjohan, p.65.
162. Wray, p.135.
163. Generalstab des Heers/General der Infanterie, Richtlinien für die Ausbildung der Unteroffiziere bei der Feld-Unteroffiziers-Schule, 24.3.42, BA-MA RH 53-7/v.234b.
164. Berger, pp.168–75.
165. *Order in Chaos*, p.246.
166. Fellgiebel, W-P., *Elite of The Third Reich*, p.305.
167. Niehorster, Dr Leo, 'World War Two Orders of Battle and Organisations', www.niehorster.org (2020).
168. Fellgiebel, p.307.

169. Piontek had been a Zugführer or Leutnant when Balck arrived in May 1942. In the August battles, Piontek distinguished himself; he was awarded the Knight's Cross on 9 October 1942 and was promoted to Hauptmann on 1 December 1942 by Hermann Balck to command III. Abteilung.
170. Hensel would be KIA on 26 January 1943 in the battle for Rostov.
171. Von Hauser would eventually be awarded the Knight's Cross with Oak Leaves in January 1943. His final command would be as Oberst leading Panzer-Lehr-Regiment 901. He died in April 1999.
172. *Order in Chaos*, pp.247–48.
173. Mellenthin, F.W. von, p.109.
174. Rutherford, J. & Wettstein, A., *The German Army on the Eastern Front*, pp.87–117.
175. Mellenthin, F.W. von, p.33.
176. Rutherford & Wettstein, pp.92–93.
177. *Ibid.*, p.92.
178. *Ibid.*, p.96.
179. *Ibid.*, pp.97–98.
180. Fritz, p.240.
181. *Ibid.*, pp.238–39.
182. *Order in Chaos*, p.249.
183. *Ibid.*, pp.250–51.
184. Forczyk, p.42.
185. Robinson, p.194.
186. Langermann was another commander who liked to lead from the front. He was killed 'in a foray to the front line' in October 1942.
187. Fritz, p.256.
188. *Ibid.*, p.255.
189. www.tracesofwar.com, 'Panzer Abteilung 61'.
190. Assman died in Loxstedt, Germany, on 26 October 1987.
191. *Order in Chaos*, p.257.
192. *Ibid.*, p.259.
193. Robinson, p.203.
194. Schmidt was found by the Soviets after the war and taken to Vladimir Central Prison in Moscow, where he was sentenced to twenty-five years in jail. He was released in 1955 but died in 1957.
195. *Order in Chaos*, p.259.
196. *Ibid.*, p.263.
197. *Ibid.*, p.261.
198. Wray, T.M., *Standing Fast*, p.140.
199. Armee-Oberkommando 2 1a Nr.1098/42 An Oberkommando Heeresgruppe B' dated October 1st 1942. NAM T-312/1660/000761 – 0007655.

Chapter X
200. Beevor, A., *Stalingrad*, pp.226–27, 231, 239–40.
201. Mellenthin, F.W. von, p.117.
202. Heim was made a scapegoat for the collapse of the front, even though he had perfect record as a Panzer commander of 14. Panzer-Division. Hitler did not wish to have to blame the Romanians, so Heim was selected. Hitler ordered him dismissed from the Army, similar to Erich Hoepner, and placed in solitary confinement, where he stayed until April 1943, when he was released to the 'retired' list. In August 1944, he was ordered to command the garrison at Boulogne. He survived the war and died in 1977.
203. Mellenthin, F.W. von, pp.120–22.
204. Wray, p.147.
205. See Records of Headquarters, German Army High Command, National Archives No. T-313, Roll 355. American Historical Association Committee for the Study of War Documents, 1960.
206. Hildebrand, K.F., *Die Generale der deutschen Luftwaffe, 1935–1945 Part II*, Vol. I (Abernetty-v. Gyldenfeldt, Osnabrück, 1990).

207. Mellenthin, F.W. von, p.120.
208. MS T-15 Historical Division, US Army Europe, 1947, pp.252–53.
209. Manstein, *Lost Victories*, pp.372–73.
210. Fellgiebel, p.97.
211. Robinson, pp.201–11.
212. Manstein, *Lost Victories*, p.120.
213. *Order in Chaos*, p.265.
214. Mellenthin, F.W. von, pp.120–21.
215. For more information on this epithet and the units that were considered Fire Brigade formations, see Nevenkin, Kamen, *Fire Brigades: The Panzer Divisions, 1943–1945* (Fedorowicz, 2008).
216. *Order in Chaos*, p.265.
217. *Ibid.*, p.267.
218. See article by Catherine Merridale, 'Culture, Ideology & Combat in the Red Army, 1939-45', *Journal of Contemporary History* (April 2006)
219. *Ibid.*, p.307.
220. *Order in Chaos*, p.267.
221. Merridale, p.307.
222. Glantz, *Companion to Endgame at Stalingrad*, p.294.
223. Wray, p.148.
224. *Order in Chaos*, p.271.
225. House of Commons Debate, 16 April 1946, Vol. 421 cc. 2513-9.
226. Karl Lestmann, commander of II. Panzer-Abteilung, was killed in action on 26 February 1943.
227. In his definitive pictorial history of 11. Panzer-Division, Gustav W. Schrodek provides some unique photographs of the coffin of Captain Piontek lying in state in a Russian Orthodox Church prior to burial, p.411.
228. Mellenthin, F.W. von, p.123.
229. *Order in Chaos*, p.269.
230. Wray, p.206.
231. *Ibid.*, p.207.
232. Fellgiebel, p.56.
233. Wette, W., *The Wehrmacht: History, Myth, Reality*, pp.204–06.
234. Mellenthin, F.W. von, p.178.
235. *Order in Chaos*, p.272.

Chapter XI
236. Axell, Albert, *Marshal Zhukov The Man Who Beat Hitler* (Longman, 2003), p.111.
237. Seaton, Albert, *The Russo-German War, 1941–45*, (Arthur Barker Ltd, 1971), pp.322–33.
238. Robinson, p.236.
239. *Ibid.*, p.237.
240. Glantz, *When Titans Clashed*, p.182.
241. *The Voice of Russia* (2009).
242. Tarnstrom, Ronald L., *Balkan Battles* (Trogen Books, 1998), p.395.
243. 'Real History On Line' (December 2021).
244. Mellenthin, F.W. von, p.134.
245. Paget, R.T., *Manstein: His campaigns and his Trial* (Collins, 1951).
246. *Order in Chaos*, p.274.
247. *Ibid.*, pp.274–75.
248. Fellgiebel, p.57.
249. Robinson, p.239.
250. *Order in Chaos*, p.276.
251. Mellenthin, F.W. von, p.135.
252. Seaton, *Russo-German War*, p.337.
253. *Order in Chaos*, p.278.
254. *Ibid.*
255. *Ibid.*, pp.277–79.

256. Fellgiebel, p.271.
257. Robinson, p.243.
258. Major Günter Hans Kaldrack (1911–1945) became Adjutant of 11. Panzer-Division, having already been company commander of Motorcycle Rifle Battalion 22 and on the General Staff of XLVI. Panzerkorps. Another Pomeranian with three sons and a daughter, Kaldrack was killed near Zützer on 28 January 1945.
259. Robinson, p.243.
260. KIA 26 March 1945 and buried in Montbaur (see 'Axis History Forum', October 2006).
261. Ganz, A., *Ghost Division: The 11th Panzer Division*, p.36.
262. *Ibid.*, p.19.
263. Schrodek, p.415.
264. Fellgiebel, p.237.
265. Schrodek, p.402.
266. Mellenthin, F.W. von, p.136.
267. *Order in Chaos*, p.283.
268. *Ibid.*, p.282.

Chapter XII
269. *Order in Chaos*, p.290.
270. Fritz, pp.282–83.
271. *Order in Chaos*, p.291.
272. *Ibid.*, p.295.
273. Warlimont, pp.294–96.
274. Gudmundsson, B.I., 'Slimming Down Grossdeutschland', *The Tactical Notebook* (March 2023).
275. *Order in Chaos*, p.297.
276. The full text of the Balck report can be found at US National Archives, Captured German Records, Microfilm Series T-78, Roll 620.

Chapter XIII
277. Fellgiebel, p.195.
278. *Order in Chaos*, p.301.
279. *Ibid.*, p.304.
280. Von Bonin was a cultured and intelligent former Reichswehr officer. He disobeyed a 'no retreat' order from Hitler, was arrested in January 1945 and set to be transferred to Dachau concentration camp, but was saved by a combination of luck and minor miracles. He survived the war.
281. *Order in Chaos*, p.302.
282. US Army Center of Military History, Salerno American Beaches 9 September–6 October 1943, Washington DC, 1990 CMH Pub. 100-7.
283. One of the best places in Italy to further understand the Salerno landings is the Museo dello Sbarco e Salerno Capitale, which can be found in Salerno itself, but you do need to make a personal appointment to visit. A second place of interest is the Salerno War Cemetery, where nearly 2,000 Commonwealth graves can be seen. This is open seven days a week.
284. *Order in Chaos*, pp.302–03.
285. Warlimont, p.337.
286. *Ibid.*, p.382.
287. *Order in Chaos*, p.306.
288. An excellent biography of McCreery is that by Richard Mead, *The Last Great Cavalryman*, published by Pen & Sword in 2024.
289. Ref. RH10/153 at BAMA Freiburg im Breisgau.
290. Atkinson, R., *The Day of Battle* (Holt & Co, New York, 2007), p.205.
291. *Ibid.*, p.207.
292. Not to be confused with his cousin, Heinrich Freiherr von Lüttwitz.
293. Molony, Brigadier C.J.C., with Flynn, Captain F.C. (RN), Davies, Major General H.L., & Gleave, Group Captain T.P., *The Mediterranean and Middle East, Vol. V: The Campaign*

        in Sicily 1943 and The Campaign in Italy 3rd September 1943 to 31st March 1944, History of the Second World War, UK Military Series (Uckfield, Naval & Military Press, HMSO, 1973), pp.299–300.
294. *Order in Chaos*, pp.309–10.
295. *Ibid.*, p.306.
296. *Ibid.*, p.306.
297. Hansard: Debates in Parliament, 22 March 2000.
298. *Order in Chaos*, p.304.
299. *Ibid.*, p.307.

Chapter XIV
300. Robinson, p.251.
301. Mead, R., *The Last Great Cavalryman* (Pen & Sword, 2012), p.130.
302. *Ibid.*, p.131.
303. Siekenhuis would lay down his life defending the Third Reich when he shot himself, having received a severe abdominal wound on 29 April 1945 whilst single-handedly attacking a Russian tank with a Panzerfaust.
304. *Order in Chaos*, p.306.
305. The events surrounding the massacre of the Acqui Division are complex and best read through the prism of Charles T. O'Reilly's 2012 book *Forgotten Battles: Italy's War of Liberation, 1943–1945*.
306. Atlante delle Stragi Naziste e Fasciste in Italia. This research project was funded by the German Foreign Ministry and published its findings in 2016. It offers a complete picture of the violence perpetrated against civilians by the German Army and its allied Fascists in Italy between 1943 and 1945. Over ninety researchers brought together the many individual studies and compared these with the Archives of the Historical Office of the German Army and the Historical Archives of the Carabinieri in Rome. The study also found that many files regarding Nazi and Fascist crimes, collected in 1960, had been concealed from the Prosecutor's Office in Rome.
307. *Ibid.*, ANNEX Of Names for the Bellona Quarry Massacre.
308. Mauke died in Hamburg in 1963 and Sandrock died in Cologne in 1995.
309. Atlante delle Stragi Naziste e Fasciste, 2016, and the Military Prosecutor's Office of Naples, 2013.
310. See German Historical Institute London Bulletin No. 25 2003 – Searle, Alaric, 'Revising the "Myth" of a "Clean Wehrmacht", Generals' Trials, Public Opinion, and The dynamics of Vergangenheitsbewältigung in West Germany, 1946–60'.

Chapter XV
311. *Order in Chaos*, p.312.
312. *Ibid.*
313. Mellenthin, F.W. von, p.161.
314. *Order in Chaos*, p.312.
315. Croce, Juliette, 'Brotherhood in Tension: The Militarised Appropriation of Homosocialism and Homoeroticism', *Flux International Relations Review* (November 2021), p.11.
316. Forczyk, p.75.
317. Mellenthin, F.W. von, p.161.
318. *Ibid.*, p.162.
319. 68. Infanterie-Division had been involved in terrible fighting in the defence of Kiev during September and October and was now effectively just a large Kampfgruppe rather than a division, whilst 7. Panzer was also well below strength.
320. Fellgiebel, p.181.
321. Kroener, Bernhard R., *'Menschenbewirtschaftlung' Bevolkerungsverteilung und personale Rustung in der zweiten Kriegshalfte 1942–1944* (Stuttgart, 1999).
322. *Order in Chaos*, p.322.
323. Mellenthin, F.W. von, p.163.
324. *Order in Chaos*, p.316.
325. Manstein, *Lost Victories*, p.386.

326. *Order in Chaos*, p.319.
327. LIX. Armeekorps was commanded by the highly decorated Generalleutnant Kurt von der Chevallerie.
328. *German Defence Tactics against Russian Breakthroughs* (Centre of Military History, US Army, Washington DC, 2004).
329. Ibid., p.16.
330. Ibid., p.17.
331. Ibid., p.26.
332. *Order in Chaos*, p.321.
333. Warlimont, p.552.
334. Mellenthin, F.W. von, p.166.
335. Ibid., p.167.
336. *Order in Chaos*, pp.324–25.
337. Balck records that his staff counted as many as 327 different units present in the city.
338. *Order in Chaos*, p.329.
339. Ibid., pp.331–32.
340. Von Manteuffel would command until August, whereupon he would become commander of 5. Panzerarmee.
341. Fellgiebel, p.33.
342. Mauss lost his leg in April 1945 but received the Knight's Cross with Oak Leaves, Swords and Diamonds, and carried on his dental practice until his death in 1959.
343. *Order in Chaos*, p.339.
344. Reynolds, *Sons of the Reich*, p.12.
345. In the event, only fifty or so troops escaped out of the 5,000 originally trapped there.
346. Fellgiebel, p.156.
347. Ziemke, E., *Stalingrad to Berlin*, p.288.
348. In fact Balck had asked the OKH if he could replace Werner Friebe with Karl Arndt to command 8. Panzer, but this request was refused.
349. *Order in Chaos*, p.341.
350. Mellenthin, F.W. von, p.173.
351. Ibid., p.174.
352. Ibid., p.175.
353. *Order in Chaos*, p.355.
354. Ibid., p.357.
355. Ibid.

Chapter XVI
356. From 24 July, the Nazi salute became mandatory throughout the armed forces.
357. *Order in Chaos*, p.360.
358. Ibid., p.361.
359. Stahlberg, p.357.
360. Fellgiebel was immediately arrested and tortured for three weeks, but gave up no names of co-conspirators. He was put on trial and hanged at Plötzensee Prison on 4 September 1944.
361. *Order in Chaos*, p.363.
362. Lysiak, O., *Brody: Zbirnyk* (Munich, 1951).
363. *Order in Chaos*, p.366.
364. Guderian, *Panzer Leader*, p.343.
365. *Order in Chaos*, p.367.
366. Mellenthin, F.W. von, p.178.
367. *Order in Chaos*, p.366.
368. Correspondence de Napoleon Ier publieé par ordre de 1-Emperor Napoleon III, Vol. 7 (Paris, 1868), pp.471–72.
369. Mellenthin, F.W. von, p.179.
370. Prior to 1939, an estimated 8,000 Jews lived in Kozienice, but by 1944 only seventy remained, who had been in hiding since 1940.
371. Military History Fandom/Wiki 2014.

Chapter XVII

372. Kortenhaus, W., *The Combat History of the 21st Panzer Division*, p.306.
373. *Order in Chaos*, p.376.
374. *Ibid.*
375. Oberbefehlshaber was the title given to a commander-in-chief at Army rank in the Wehrmacht, unlike in the Allied armies, where the title of commander-in-chief was reserved for perhaps one or two people at most. When Balck arrived in the West, there were eight OB commands in existence for various areas of the Western Front.
376. Originally, Operation Anvil was the codename for the invasion of Southern France and Operation Sledgehammer that for Normandy. Both saw the codenames change during the planning phases, to Dragoon and Overlord, respectively.
377. Ludwig, J., *Rückzug: The German Retreat from France, 1944*.
378. Kortenhaus, p.308.
379. Von Funck also suffered the ignominy of being dismissed from the Army in January 1945.
380. Kortenhaus, pp.309–10.
381. *Ibid.*, p.312.
382. Gyldenfeldt would be captured by the Americans and go on to write several works for the Historical Division.
383. Mellenthin, F.W. von, p.210.
384. Wilmot, Chester, *The Struggle For Europe*.
385. Kitchen, Martin, p.247.
386. Blaskowitz was captured by the Americans and was Case No 12 at the Nuremberg War Crimes Trials. He was accused of the execution order of two German deserters after the war had ended. Despite all his efforts to protect and protest the victims of the Nazi regime, he threw himself off a balcony in the courtyard of the court building and died of a broken neck on 5 February 1948.
387. *Order in Chaos*, p.383.
388. *Ibid.*, p.391.
389. *Ibid.*, p.381.
390. Kortenhaus, p.316.
391. *Ibid.*
392. *Order in Chaos*, p.385.
393. Axis History Forum, 29 September 2004.
394. *Order in Chaos*, p.389.
395. Yeide, H., *Fighting Patton*, p.289.
396. Fellgiebel, p.79.
397. Balck had to use the influence of Guderian to get the Knight's Cross awarded to Reuschel, who went missing from his homeland in May 1945.
398. After Balck had moved to his final command, Feuchtinger was arrested and found guilty, lost his rank – going down to private – and was sentenced to be executed. Hitler protected him and commuted his sentence. He evaded prison and the military police until 1945, then gave himself up to the Americans in a borrowed general's uniform. Feuchtinger ended up in Trent Park, North London, where his presence was a great affront to the legitimate generals present. After the war, he became a Soviet spy before his death in 1960.
399. The 347. Infanterie-Division had fought throughout Normandy and lost a lot of men in the savage Battle of the Hürtgen Forest on the border between Germany and Belgium, and was in the process of rebuilding.
400. Robinson, p.259.
401. Axis History Forum April 2015.
402. 'Gedenkorte Europa 1939–1945', report from research.
403. *Order in Chaos*, p.394.
404. *Ibid.*
405. Taken from 'Gérardmer Cité Martyre, 1940–1944', by Gilbert Martin.
406. *Ibid.*
407. Gedenkorte Europa.
408. *Order in Chaos*, pp.396–97.
409. Bruhn tape recordings at Trent Park.

410. Kortenhaus, p.330.
411. Clarke, Jeffery J. & Smith, Robert Ross, *Riviera to the Rhine*, p.427.
412. Von Knobelsdorff was replaced as OB 1. Armee by General der Infanterie Kurt von Tippleskirch for just over ten days, and then General der Infanterie Hans von Obstfelder.
413. Mellenthin, F.W. von, p.222.
414. Cole, Hugh, *The Lorraine Campaign*, p.534.
415. *Order in Chaos*, p.403.
416. *The Spectator*, 7 March 1952, The Spectator Archive.
417. *Order in Chaos*, p.405.

Chapter XVIII
418. Although Zossen is the usual name given for the official underground headquarters of the OKW and OKH, it was in fact housed in the suburb of Wünsdorf, 30km south east of Berlin.
419. *The Holocaust Encyclopaedia*, United States Holocaust Museum.
420. *Order in Chaos*, p.408.
420A Nash, Douglas E., *The Defeat of The Damned*, p.240.
421. Manstein, p.236.
421A Nash, p.245.
422. The 'Feldherrnhalle' Division was a reincarnation of the 60. Infanterie- Division which had been destroyed at Stalingrad and held the name of the Field Marshals' Hall in central Munich, where the Beer Hall Putsch had taken place in 1923. The division was commanded by Generalmajor Günther Pape, although he was very fortunately posted away from Budapest before the encirclement in order to create a new division. The 'Feldherrnhalle' was then commanded by Oberst Joachim-Helmut Wolff.
423. Mitcham, S.W., pp.236–37.
424. Glantz, *When Titans Clashed: How the Red Army Stopped Hitler*, p.224.
425. 'December OOB for German Sixth Army', taken from United States Army Combined Arms Centre Publications (2002).
425A Nash., p.242.
425B *Ibid.*, p.248.
425C This signal and five others in the thread were recovered from the German-Russian Project on the Digitization of German Documents in the Russian Federation, wwii.germandocsinrussia.org.
426. Warlimont, p.495.
427. *Order in Chaos*, p.408.
428. Williamson, M., 'Budapest Relief Attempts, Part I', *Weapons and Warfare* (May 2016).
429. Csosz, L., and Csonka, L., 'Murdered on the Verge of Survival: Massacres in the Last Days of the Siege of Budapest, 1945', *European Holocaust Research Infrastructure Project (EHRI)* (8 February 2017).
430. The 711. Infanterie-Division had fought in Normandy on D-Day, at Falaise and in Holland against British and Polish forces.
431. Guderian, *Panzer Leader*, p.386.
432. Oppeln-Bronikowski had been a tank commander in Poland and France, and in Russia commanded the 22. Panzer-Division in their desperate attempt to break through to Stalingrad. A heavy smoker and equally hard drinker, he managed to get his tanks to the D-Day coastline before being ordered to withdraw. He was awarded the Knight's Cross with Oak Leaves and Swords.
433. Mitcham, p.246.
434. *Order in Chaos*, p.413.
435. Landwehr, Richard, *Budapest: The Stalingrad of the Waffen-SS* (CreateSpace Publishing, 2012).
436. Howard, E., 'The Siege of Budapest', *History Net* (2006).
437. *Order in Chaos*, p.417.
438. '100 Days – The Waffen-SS and the Siege of Budapest', World War Two Axis Forum (2010).

Chapter XIX
439. Fellgiebel, p.309.
440. Mitcham, p.252.

441. Pierik, Perry, *Hungary 1944–45: The Forgotten Tragedy* (Aspect, 1998).
442. Translation from the War Diary of Sixth Army, OJ Microfilm Library 898/7213483-7213484, from www.arcanum.com and online digitalization database in Budapest.
443. Howard, 'The Siege of Budapest'.
444. Forum of the Wehrmacht, 17 May 2009.
445. Ameiser survived the war and died of complications from his head wound in Munich, where he had begun his SS career in 1933, on 29 February 1976.
446. *Order in Chaos*, p.417.
447. Landwehr, p.131.
448. *Ibid.*, pp.130–31.
449. *Order in Chaos*, pp.419–20.
450. Maier, G., *Drama Between Budapest and Vienna*, p.120.
451. Warlimont, p.499.
452. Reynolds, Major General Michael, 'Operation Spring Awakening: Adolf Hitler's Last WWII Offensive', *Warfare History Network* (May 2012).
453. *Ibid*.
453A *Order in Chaos*, p.420.
453B Maier, G., *Drama Between Budapest and Vienna*, p.223.
453C *Ibid.*, p.223.
453D *Ibid.*, p.223.
453E *Ibid.*, p.422.
453F *Ibid.*, p.207.
454. *Order in Chaos*, p.421.
455. The commander of the 44. Infanterie-Divison at the time was Generalleutnant Heinrich-Anton Deboi, who was offered a chance to get out but preferred 'to be with the infantry' when Paulus surrendered and died in Soviet captivity in 1955.
456. Erikson, *The Road to Berlin*, p.510.
457. Until the end of the war in May, the division was commanded by Oberst Hoffman.
458. *Order in Chaos*, p.422.
458A Maier, p.318.
458B *Ibid.*, p.319.
458C *Ibid.*, p.323.
458D *Ibid.*, p.323.
458E *Ibid.*, p.323.
458F *Order in Chaos*, p.425.
458G Schonfelder, Manfred, *IV SS-Panzer Korps*.
459. Kay, Geoffrey G.S., 'Letter to Skye & Cameron' (2020).
460. *Order in Chaos*, p.425.
461. Lappin, Eleonore, *The Death Marches of Hungarian Jews Through Austria in the Spring of 1945*, Yad Vashem World Holocaust Centre Archives.
462. *Ibid*.
463. *Ibid*.
464. *Order in Chaos*, p.429.
464A Maier, pp.327–28.
464B *Order in Chaos*.

Chapter XX
465. See Chapter XVIII.
466. Ruter, Dr C.F., & de Mildt, Dr D.W., *The East & West German Court Decisions for National Socialist Homicide Crimes since 1945* (Amsterdam, 2020), Case 060, pp.537–58.
467. *Ibid.*, p.541.
468. *Ibid.*, p.543.
469. Citino, Robert M., *The Wehrmacht Retreats: Fighting a Lost War, 1943* (University Press of Kansas, 2012), pp.204–05.
470. Dyson, Freeman, *Weapons and Hope* (Harper & Row, 1984).

Bibliography

Books
Atkinson, Rick, *The Day of Battle*, Vol II (New York: Henry Holt & Co, 2007)
Axell, Albert, *Marshal Zhukov – The Man Who Beat Hitler* (Pearson Longman, 2003)
Balck, Hermann. *Order in Chaos* (University Press of Kentucky, 2017)
Baynes, H.G., *Germany Possessed* (Routledge, 2018)
Beever, Antony, *Stalingrad. The Fateful Siege: 1942–1943* (London: Penguin, 1998)
Berger, Florian, *The Face of Courage: The 98 Men who Received the Knight's Cross and the Close-Combat Clasp in Gold* (Mechanicsburg, PA: Stackpole Books, 2011)
Blumentritt, Gunther, *Von Rundstedt: The Soldier and the Man* (Odhams Press, 1952)
Butler, Daniel A., *Field Marshal: The Life and Death of Erwin Rommel* (Havertown, PA/Oxford: Casemate, 2015)
Carver, Michael, *The Warlords* (Barnsley: Pen & Sword, 2005)
Chamberlain, P. & Doyle, H.L., *Encyclopaedia of German Tanks of World War Two* (London: Arms & Armour, 1999)
Clarke, Jeffrey J. & Smith, Robert R., *Riviera to the Rhine: United States Army in World War II* (Washington DC: Centre of Military History, 1993)
Cole, Hugh M., *The Lorraine Campaign* (Centre of Military History, 1950; reprinted 1993)
Cooper, Matthew, *The German Army 1933–1945* (Macdonald and Jane's, 1978)
Croce, Juliette, 'Brotherhood in Tension: The Militarised Appropriation of Homeosocialism and Homoeroticism', *Flux International Relations Review* (November 2021)
Dyson, Freeman, *Weapons and Hope* (Harper & Row, USA, 1984)
Fellgiebel, Walther-P., *Elite of The Third Reich – The Recipients of the Knight's Cross of the Iron Cross, 1939–45* (Helion & Co, 2003)
Flaherty, T.H., *The Third Reich: The SS* (Time Life Books, 2004)
Forczyk, Robert, *The Dnepr 1943: Hitler's Eastern Rampart Crumbles* (Oxford: Osprey Publishing, 2016)
Forczyk, Robert, *Where the Iron Crosses Grow: The Crimea, 1941–44* (Oxford: Osprey Publishing, 2014)
Fritz, Stephen, G., *The First Soldier – Hitler as Military Leader* (Yale University Press, 2018)
Ganz, A. Harding, *Ghost Division: The 11th 'Gespenster' Panzer Division and the German Armoured Force in World War II* (Mechanicsburg, PA: Stackpole Books, 2016)
Glantz, David M., *When Titans Clashed: How the Red Army Stopped Hitler* (Lawrence: University Press of Kansas, 1995)
Glantz, David M. & House, Jonathan M., *Endgame at Stalingrad, Book Two: December 1942–February 1943*, Volume 3 (Lawrence: University Press of Kansas, 2014)
Grossjohan, G., *Five Years, Four Fronts* (Presidio Press, 2005)
Guderian, Heinz, *Achtung Panzer* (London: Wellington House, 1999 reissue edn)
Hahn, Fritz, *Waffen und Geheimwaffen des deutschen Heeres 1933–1945* (Koblenz: Bernard & Graefe, 1987)
Hart, Russell A., *Guderian: Panzer Pioneer or Myth Maker?* (Potomac Books, 2006)
Hitler, Adolf, *Mein Kampf*
Holland, James, *Italy's Sorrow: A Year of War, 1944–1945* (Harper Press, 2009)
Jones, Michael, *Leningrad: State of Siege* (Basic Books, 2008)
Kinna, H. & Moss, D.A., *Jäger & Schützen: Dress and Distinctions, 1910–1914* (Argus Books, 1977)

Bibliography   319

Kortenhaus, Werner, *The Combat History of the 21st Panzer Division* (Helion & Company, 2014)
Landwehr, Richard, *Budapest: The Stalingrad of the Waffen-SS* (Bennington, VT: Merriam Press, 2012)
Ludewig, Joachim, *Rückzug: The German Retreat from France, 1944* (University Press of Kentucky, 2012)
Maier, Georg, *Drama Between Budapest and Vienna: The Final Battles of The 6. Panzer-Armee in the East – 1945* (Winnipeg: Fedorowicz Publishing Inc, 2004)
Manstein, F.E.G.E. von, *Lost Victories* (Greenhill Books, 1987)
May, Ernest R., *Strange Victory* (New York: Hill & Wang, 2000)
Mead, Richard, *The Last Great Cavalryman – The Life of General Sir Richard McCreery GCB* (Barnsley: Pen & Sword Books, 2012)
Mellenthin, F.W. von, *German Generals of World War Two* (University of Oklahoma Press, 1977)
Mellenthin, F.W. von, *Panzer Battles* (Gloucestershire: Spellmount, 1955)
McClymont, W.G., *The Official History of New Zealand in the Second World War 1939–1945* (Wellington: Historical Publications Brance, 1959)
Mitcham, S.W., *The German Defeat in the East, 1944–1945* (Mechanicsburg, PA: Stackpole Books, 2001)
Molony, Brigadier C.J.C., with Flynn, Captain F.C. (RN), Davies, Major General H.L. & Gleave, Group Captain T.P., *The Mediterranean and Middle East, Vol. V: The Campaign in Sicily 1943 and The Campaign in Italy 3rd September 1943 to 31st March 1944*, History of the Second World War, UK Military Series (Uckfield: Naval & Military Press, HMSO, 1973).
Nash, Douglas E., *The Defeat Of The Damned: The Destruction Of The Dirlewanger Brigade At The Battle of Ipolysag, December 1944* (Oxford: Casemate, 2023)
Ohler, N., *Der Totale Rausch: Drogen im Dritten Reich* (Kiepenheuer & Witsch, 2015)
Paget, R.T., *Manstein: His Campaigns and His Trial* (Collins, 1951)
Pierik, Perry, *Hungary 1944–45: The Forgotten Tragedy* (Aspect, 1998)
Raus, Ehard, *Panzer Operations – The Eastern Front Memoir of General Rause, 1941–1945* (De Capo Press, 2003)
Reynolds, Michael, F., *Sons of the Reich: II SS Panzer Corps, Normandy, Arnhem, Ardennes, Eastern Front* (Barnsley: Pen & Sword Military, 2009)
Ripley, Timothy, *The Wehrmacht: The German Army in World War Two, 1939–1945* (Routledge, 2014).
Robinson, S., *Panzer Commander Hermann Balck – Germany's Master Tactician* (Exile Publishing, 2019)
Rutherford, J. & Wettstein, A.E., *The German Army on the Eastern Front* (Barnsley: Pen & Sword Books, 2018)
Schaufler, Hans, *Panzer Warfare on the Eastern Front* (Barnsley: Pen & Sword, 2012)
Schrodek, G.W., *Die ii. Panzer-Division – Gespenster-Division 1940–1945* (Dorlfer, ?)
Seaton, Albert, *The Russo-German War, 1941–45* (Arthur Barer Limited, 1971)
Shepherd, Ben, *Hitler's Soldiers: The German Army in the Third Reich* (Yale University Press, 2016)
Warner, Philip, *The Battle for France* (Barnsley: Pen & Sword Books, 2010)
Warlimont, Walter, *Inside Hitler's Headquarters* (Weidenfeld & Nicolson, 1964)
Westphal, Siegfried, *The German Army in the West* (Cassell & Co, 1951)
Wette, Wolfram, *The Wehrmacht: History, Myth, Reality* (Cambridge, MA: Harvard University Press, 2006)
Wilmot, Chester, *The Struggle for Europe* (Collins, 1952)
Wray, Maj T.A., *Standing Fast: German Defensive Doctrine on the Russian Front During World War Two – Prewar to March 1943*, (Combat Studies Institute, Research Survey N5, 1949)
Yeide, Harry, *Fighting Patton: George S. Patton Jr Through The Eyes of His Enemies* (Zenith Press, 2014)

Articles
Bainton, Roy, 'The Salerno Mutiny of 1943', *BBC History Magazine* (4 September 2006)
Bonnell, Andrew G., 'Explaining Suicide in the Imperial German Army', *German Studies Review* (May 2014)

Center for Military History, 'German Defence Tactics Against Russian Breakthroughs', *CMS* (Washington, 2004)
Csosz, L. & Csonka, L., 'Murdered on the Verge of Survival: Massacres in the Last Days of the Siege of Budapest, 1945', *European Holocaust Research Infrastructure Project (EHRI)* (8 February 2017)
Dickerson, Bryan, J., 'The Battles of Lunéville: September 1944', *Military History Online* (2024)
Harding, David P., 'Heinz Guderian As the Agent of Change: His Significant Impact on the Development of German Armoured Forces Between the World Wars', *Army History*, No 31 (Summer 1994)
Howard, E., 'The Siege of Budapest', *History Net* (December 2006)
McTaggart, Patrick, 'The Battle of Kiev: How it Brought About an End to Nazi Terror', *Warfare History Network* (June 2014)
Natale, Fabiana, 'Pervitin: How Drugs Transformed Warfare in 1939–1945', *Security Distillery* (May 2020)
Newland, Samuel T., 'The Education of an Officer Corps', *Strategic Institute, US Army War College* (December 2005)
Reynolds, Major General Michael, 'Operation Spring Awakening: Adolf Hitler's Last WW2 Offensive', *Warfare History Network* (May 2012)
Searle, Alaric, 'Revising the "Myth" of a "Clean Wehrmacht", Generals' Trials, Public Opinion and the Dynamics of Vergangenheitsbewältigung in West Germany, 1946–60', *German Historical Institute Bulletin*, No 25 (London, 2003)

Documentary Sources

Atlas of Nazi and Fascist Massacres in Italy – Atlanta delle Stragi Naziste e Fasciste in Italia, German Foreign Ministry under the German-Italian Fund for the Future (2016)
Ruter, Dr C.F. & de Mildt, Dr D.W., *The East & West German Court Decisions for National Socialist Homicide Crimes since 1945* (Amsterdam: 2020), Case 060
Salerno. American Operations from the Beaches to the Volturno 9 September – 6 October, 1943, Historical Division, War Department for the American Forces in Action Series (Washinton DC: 1990), CMH 100-7
Schultz, Friedrich, *Reverses on the Southern Wing (1942–1943). Annex 5: The XLVIII Panzer Corps in Action between the Don and Mius River Sectors, 5 December to February 1943*, Foreign Military Studies N. MS T-15 (Historical Division, US Army Europe, 1947), pp.252–53

Index

Adam, Oberst Wilhelm, 120–1
Ameiser, SS-Obersturmbannführer Anton, 263
Arndt, Generalmajor Karl, 199, 271
Arracourt, Battle of, 214–15, 219–21, 224
Assmann, Obergefreiter Alois, 99, 109–11
Avalanche, Operation, 164–5, 169, 171

Bach-Zelewski, SS-Obergruppenführer Erich, 196
Badanov, Major General Vasily Mikhailovich, 136–8, 141, 148
Bakopoulos, General, 61
Balaton, Lake, 242, 252–3, 255, 265–6, 269, 275–6
Balck, Konrad F.A. Wilhelm, 3
Beck, General Ludwig, 21, 30, 35
Biedermann, Generalmajor Wolf von, 119
Bittrich, SS-Obergruppenführer Wilhelm, 196–8, 270–1
Blaskowitz, Generaloberst Johannes, 212–13, 215, 217–19, 228, 233, 239–40
Blumentritt, Generalleutnant Günther, 205, 293
Bock, Generalfeldmarschall Fedor von, 16, 28, 81, 86–7, 104, 107–108
Böhme, Generalleutnant Franz, 60, 63, 65
Boll, Heinrich, 68
Bonin, Oberst Bogislaw Oskar von, 163–4
Bosse, Oberstleutnant Alexander von, 123, 127, 129, 132, 136, 153
Brauchitsch, Generalfeldmarschall Walther von, 46–7, 76, 86–7, 132, 153
Braune-Krickau, Leutnant Andreas, 50
Breith, Generalleutnant Hermann, 201–202, 208–209, 243, 248, 251, 268, 277
Brody, Pocket, 197, 202–203, 207
Bryansk, Battle of, 82, 103, 106, 108, 111–12
Buhle, Generalleutnant Walther, 72–4
Busse, Oberst Theodor, 119
Butkov, Major General Vasilevich, 121–2

Case Blue, 96–9, 103–12, 149
Case Yellow, 41
Chir River, Battles of, 19, 115–36, 143–4, 149, 151, 175, 188, 190, 224, 277, 293
Choltitz, Generalleutnant Dietrich von, 153
Citadel, Operation, 157, 161–2, 259

Clark, General Mark Wayne, 164–5, 169–70, 176
Conrath, Generalmajor Paul, 167, 169, 178
Corps – German
  I Cavalry, 277
  II SS-Panzer, 199, 269–70, 286
  III Panzer, 201–202, 208, 243–5, 250–2, 266, 268, 275, 277, 283
  IV SS-Panzer, 240, 246–58, 262, 265–70, 272, 277, 280–3
  V Army Corps, 102
  IX SS Mountain, 244, 253, 257–9, 261
  XVII Corps, 136
  LVII Corps, 150, 191–2, 244, 248, 251, 263
  XIV Panzer, 161–79, 181
  XIX Panzer Corps Guderian, 47–9, 177
  XXIV Panzer, 84, 93, 97, 104, 107–108, 120, 187, 193
  XLVIII Corps, 93, 117–32, 137, 140, 144, 181, 189–90
Corps – Allied
  1st Russian Tank, 121
  3rd Russian Guards Tank, 145, 148–9, 150
  4th Russian Guards Tank, 145–6
  5th Russian Guards Cavalry, 255, 279
  6th United States, 165
  7th Russian Tank, 108, 127
  8th Russian Guards Armoured, 186
  10th British, 165
  11th Russian Tank, 109
  16th Russian Tank, 106
  18th Russian Tank, 249, 279
  24th Russian Tank, 136–41, 148
  157th Russian Tank Brigade, 126
  159th Russian Tank Brigade, 126
Crüwell, Generalmajor Ludwig, 93, 96

De Angelis, General der Artillerie Maximilian, 282
Decker, Oberstleutnant Karl von, 64, 66–7, 70
Dietrich, SS-Oberstgruppenführer Josef 'Sepp', 26, 61, 66, 153, 183, 235, 266, 272, 274–5, 278
Dirlewanger Brigade, 243, 245–7, 264
Divisions – German
  1. Panzer, 38, 41, 46, 49, 52, 138, 183–5, 190, 192–3, 201–203, 245, 255, 268, 276, 283–4

1. SS-Panzer 'Leibstandarte', 61, 183, 185–6, 190, 192, 195, 270, 279
2. Panzer, 38, 51, 55–6, 57–67, 70–2, 77, 81–3, 91, 105, 210
3. SS-Panzer 'Totenkopf', 247, 249, 269, 279, 285–6
4. SS-Polizei, 244, 259
5. Panzer, 93
5. SS-Panzer 'Wiking', 247–50, 255, 269, 276–7, 283–7
7. Luftwaffe Field, 119–22, 128, 131, 133, 137
7. Panzer, 45, 144, 185–6, 189, 192, 195–9
8. Panzer, 45, 193, 196–202, 206, 208, 215, 242–4
8. SS-Cavalry 'Florian Geyer', 244, 254, 260
9. Panzer, 61, 109, 235
9. SS-Panzer 'Hohenstaufen' 196–8, 266, 270, 276–9
11. Panzer, 7, 10–11, 87, 93–114, 117, 119–32, 134–56, 162, 172, 188, 217, 223–5, 235–6, 256
12. SS-'Hitlerjugend', 66, 270, 279
13. Panzer, 118–19, 244, 259–60
15. Panzergrenadier, 163, 168–9, 178, 215, 217
16. Panzer, 168–73, 175–6, 179
19. Panzer, 186, 193–4
23. Panzer, 91, 101, 208, 245, 269
24. Panzer, 96, 118
26. Panzer, 169
29. Panzergrenadier, 169–70, 173
44. Infantry, 276–7
48. Infantry, 219, 224
50. Infantry, 136
60. Panzergrenadier, 259
68. Infantry, 183–5, 199
72. Infantry, 63
130. Panzer 'Lehr', 233, 235
271. Volksgrenadier, 241, 244
302. Infantry, 144
311. Infantry, 93
336. Infantry, 119–33, 136–7
338. Infantry, 220
359. Infantry, 271, 199
371. Infantry, 206
553. Volksgrenadier, 215, 219, 232
559. Volksgrenadier, 219, 224–5
711. Infantry, 249, 269
Panzer Hermann Göring, 39, 163, 167, 169–70, 178
SS-Grossdeustchland, 84, 152–7, 161, 195
Divisions – Allied
2nd New Zealand Infantry, 60, 63
2nd Hungarian Armoured, 246
4th American Armoured, 216–17, 220, 224–5
6th Australian Infantry, 60
26th American Infantry, 225
33rd Russian Guards Rifle, 142
33rd Italian 'Acqui', 177
36th American Infantry, 165, 224
45th United States Infantry, 165, 170
46th British Infantry, 165, 169
50th British (Northumbrian), 172
51st British (Highland), 172
56th British Infantry, 165, 169
86th Russian Guards, 251
248th Russian Infantry, 150
Hungarian Szt László, 240, 281
Dörner, SS-Oberführer Helmut, 259, 262–3
Dorotka, Bridgehead, 210–11, 215
Dorr, SS-Obersturmbannführer Hans, 255
Drexler, Anton, 21, 26
Dumitrescu, Lieutenant General, 138

Eberbach, General Heinrich, 35–6
Ebert, Chancellor Friedrich, 25
Erzberger, Matthias, 20–1

Fangohr, Major General Friedrich, 187
Fiebig, Generalmajor Martin, 138–9, 141
Finckh, Oberst Eberhard, 205
Feuchtinger, Generalleutnant Edgar, 216–17, 226
Forest Feast, Operation, 228
Fretter-Pico, General der Artillerie Maximilian, 242
Freyberg, Major General Bernard C., 63–4
Friebe, Generalmajor Werner, 196–8, 201–202
Fritsch, Generaloberst Werner von, 27, 34
Fromm, Generaloberst Fredrich, 21, 36–7, 40, 72–4, 76
Funck, General der Panzertruppe Hans von, 215–16

Gaedcke, Generalmajor Heinrich, 244–6, 248, 286
Gariboldi, General Italo, 113
Gérardmer, 227–31
Gille, SS-Obergruppenführer Herbert 'Papa', 153, 248–51, 253, 255–7, 266, 269–72, 275–7, 280, 283
Golikov, Lieutenant General Filipp, 103
Goslar barracks, 14, 24–5
Groener, General Wilhelm, 6, 25
Guderian, Colonel General Heinz, 8, 10–19, 21, 25–30, 32–46, 48–52, 57, 71–2, 77, 81–6, 99, 112, 117, 156–7, 199, 207, 210, 234, 238–40, 245, 250–1, 267, 278–9, 293
Gyldenfeldt, Generalleutnant Heinz von, 217, 286

Harpe, Generaloberst Josef, 209
Harteneck, General der Kavallerie Gustav, 240, 264, 269, 277, 281

Index 323

Hauffe, Generalleutnant Arthur, 206
Hauser, Hauptmann Paul Freiherr von, 100–11, 127, 144, 153
Heim, General Ferdinand, 118
Heimann, SS-Hauptsturmführer Heinrich, 185
Henrici, General Sigfrid, 36, 74, 293
Hensel, Zugführer Gerhard, 99–100
Henze, Oberstleutnant Albert, 97, 123, 127–8, 132, 136, 153
Himmler, SS-Reichsführer Heinrich, 90, 117, 196, 198, 218, 221–3, 227–8, 231, 234–5, 238, 244–50, 271, 278, 280, 288, 293
Hindenburg, Feldmarschall Paul von, 21, 28
Hindenburg, Password, 261
Höhne, General der Infanterie Gustav, 236–8
Hollidt, Generalmajor Karl-Adolf, 135–8
Hörnlein, Generalleutnant Walter, 157
Hoth, Generaloberst Hermann, 74, 81, 103, 119, 150–1, 183–7, 193, 293
Hube, General der Panzertruppe Hans-Valentin, 35, 153, 161–2, 172, 178–9, 181

Kaldrack, Major Günter Otto, 146, 152–3
Kallner, Generalmajor Hans, 194
Kapp, Wolfgang, 21, 25, 28–9
Kempf, General der Panzertruppe Werner, 197
Kesselring, Generalfeldmarschall Albert, 163, 166–7, 170, 237–8, 305
Kleist, Generalfeldmarschall Paul Ewald von, 21, 26, 47–8, 193–4
Kluge, Generalfeldmarschall Günther von, 21, 27, 74, 81, 86–9, 193
Knobelsdorff, Generalleutnant Otto von, 120–2, 131, 136–7, 212, 215, 219, 224, 227, 234–6, 289–90
Konstytchev Forest, Battle of, 186
Kreysing, Leutnant Hans, 11
Krueger, Colonel Walter, 7

Lammerding, SS-Brigadeführer Heinz, 183
Lange, Generalmajor Wolfgang, 202–203
Langermann und Erlencamp, Generalleutnant Willibald von, 93, 97, 104, 107
Lasch, Generalleutnant Otto, 202
Leib, Generalleutnant Theobald, 192
Lemelsen, General Joachim, 36
Lestmann, Hauptman Karl Kurt, 99, 129–30, 149–50
Liss, Oberstleutnant Ulrich, 48–9
Lizyukov, Major General Alexander, 106, 108–109
Lucht, Generalmajor Walther, 119, 121–4, 127, 130, 136
Luck, Oberst Hans von, 56, 215, 226

Ludendorff, Field Marshal Erich, 17, 21
Lunéville, Battle of, 216–17, 220, 224
Luftwaffe,
  Luftflotte (Air Fleet) 3, 49
  II Fliegerkorps, 49
  VIII Fliegerkorps, 128, 138, 141, 190
Lüttwitz, General der Panzertruppe Heinrich von, 170, 216
Lutz, General Oswald, 30, 36–8

Mackensen, Generalleutnant Eberhard von, 146, 148, 150–1
Maier, Oberst Georg, 240, 243, 268, 272–5, 277–81, 285
Manstein, Generalfeldmarschall Erich von, 21, 26, 45–8, 91, 117, 120, 131, 137, 143–4, 153, 155, 181, 183, 187, 191–3, 200, 205, 243, 293–4
Manteuffel, Generalmajor Hasso von, 185, 189, 196, 213, 215, 217, 219–21, 293
Manychskaya, Bridgehead and Battle of, 148–9
Massow, Colonel von, 15
Mauke, Oberst Wolfgang, 179
Maus, Generalmajor Dr Karl, 196
McBride, Major General Horace, 286–8
McCreery, Lieutenant General Sir Richard, 165, 167, 171, 173, 176
Medvedev Forest, Massacre of, 83
Mellenthin, Generalmajor F.W. von, 5, 51, 55, 100, 117–20, 127–31, 140, 143, 150, 181–6, 189–94, 200–202, 207, 209, 213, 217–18, 231–4, 238, 290–4
Metaxas, Ioannis, 57, 60–1
Model, Generalfeldmarschall Walter, 26–7, 35, 198–200, 212–13, 222
Morhange, Battle of, 214, 224–5
Morozovsk airfield and railway, 128, 135–7
Mühlen, Generalmajor Kurt von, 224–5
Mulhouse, Battle of, 233–4

Netwig, Oberst Johannes, 51, 71

Oberg, SS-Obergruppenführer Carl Albrecht, 228
Oppeln-Bronikowski, Oberst Hermann von, 251
Oschmann, Generalmajor Hans, 232

Pannwitz, Oberstleutnant Helmuth von, 90, 145
Patton, General George, 213, 220, 224, 294
Paulus, Field Marshal Friedrich, 26, 38, 110, 118, 120–1, 135–6, 138, 142, 257
Pavelkin, Major General Mikhail, 106
Pervitin, 67–9, 83
Pfeffer-Wildenbruch, SS-Obergruppenführer Karl, 244, 255–7, 259, 261, 263, 265
Philippi, Generalmajor Alfred, 232

Pinios River crossing, 65, 67
Piontek, Hauptmann Klaus, 99, 130, 143
Popov, Lieutenant General Markian, 109, 125–7, 144–5
Portugall, SS-Obersturmbannführer Kurt, 262, 264
Pukhov, Major General Nikolai, 104

Radtke, Hauptmann, 13
Ramsch, Leutnant, 56
Raus, General der Panzertruppe Erhard, 141, 187, 191–3, 195, 200, 206–207
Recknagel, General der Infanterie Hermann, 207–209
Reichenau, Generalfeldmarschall Walter von, 104
Reichert, Generalleutnant Josef, 249, 269
Riebel, Oberstleutnant Gustav-Adolf, 94, 99
Rodt, Generalmajor Eberhard, 168–70, 178, 217
Romanenko, Major General Prokofy, 121–2, 124, 128
Rommel, Generalfeldmarschall Erwin, 21, 26–7, 35, 37, 47–9, 58–60, 75, 112, 117, 153, 165–6, 175, 182, 193–4, 204, 237–8, 293–4
Rost, Generalleutnant Hans-Günther von, 276
Ruhmor, SS-Brigadeführer Joachim, 261
Rundstedt, Generalfeldmarschall Gerd von, 41, 46–7, 193, 212, 217–18, 235–9
Rzhev, Battles of, 110, 115

Salerno, Battle of, 163–75, 177, 218
Scheffer-Boyadel, General Reinhard von, 15
Schell, Generalmajor Adolf von, 37, 40, 71–4, 85, 184
Schell, Maximilian, 271
Scheller, Generalmajor Walter, 96
Scheuerpflug, Generalmajor Paul, 183, 199
Schimmelmann, Oberstleutnant Theodor Graf von, 99, 123–4, 129–30, 137, 144, 146–50, 153
Schobert, Generaloberst Eugen Ritter von, 91
Schmidhuber, Generalmajor Gehard, 260
Schmidt, Generaloberst Rudolf, 112, 120, 122, 138, 141, 149, 153
Schmundt, General of Infantry Rudolf, 90, 157, 162, 181, 209
Schörner, General Ferdinand, 66
Schottke, Oberstleutnant Johann, 226–7, 289–90
Schulz, Generalmajor Adelbert, 153, 185, 195–6
Schweppenburg, General der Panzertruppe Leo Geyr von, 35, 84

Sedan, Battle of, 47–8, 50–1, 190
Seeckt, General Johannes 'Hans' Friedrich Leopold von, 27, 29, 33
Sele River, Battles of, 47–51, 165, 169–71, 173, 176, 190, 196
Sieckenius, Generalmajor Rudolf, 168–70, 175–6, 179
Sovchos 79, Battle of, 121–2
Speer, Albert, 37, 40, 85, 213
Stadler, SS-Brigadeführer Sylvester, 270, 276–8
Stalingrad, Battle of, 19, 38, 93, 97, 107, 109–21, 125–8, 132, 135–8, 140–3, 152, 156, 161–2, 198, 241, 247, 252, 257, 259, 264, 276
Stauffenberg, Oberst Claus von, 90, 204–205
Stollbrock, Oberstleutnant Karl, 64
Stumpfeld, Generalmajor Hans Joachim von, 120
Styr River, Battles of, 195–6, 199
Sutherland Highlanders, 3
Szálasi, Ferenc, 241
Sztójay, General Döme., 241

Tarnopol, Battle of, 195–8, 201, 241, 247, 271
Tatsinskaya, airfield, 128, 135–41
Tempe Gorge, Battle of, 62, 66–7
Timoshenko, Marshal Semen, 103
Tolbukhin, Marshal Fyodor, 242, 245, 266, 269

Vatutin, General Nikolai, 109, 115–16, 128, 141, 184
Veiel, Generalleutnant Rudolf, 57, 60–1, 64–5
Vietinghoff, Generaloberst Heinrich von, 163, 166–70, 175–6
Vorozneh, Battles of, 108

Warlimont, Generalleutnant Walter, 48, 59, 88, 154, 166, 191, 247, 268, 293
Weichs, Generalfeldmarschall Maximilian von, 61, 113, 144, 258
Wenck, Oberst Walther, 138, 207, 266
Westphal, Generalleutnant Siegfried, 218, 237–8
Wisch, SS-Brigadeführer Theodor, 183
Wohler, General der Infanterie Otto, 243, 248, 250, 265, 271, 273–4, 278–9, 282, 286

Zeitzler, General der Infanterie Kurt, 113, 118, 152, 154
Zhukov, Marshal Georgy, 82–3, 110, 114–15, 121, 125, 135, 141, 269
Zhytomyr, Battles of, 183–9, 192–3, 199, 201